Advanced Group Leadership

Advanced Group Leadership

Jeffrey A. Kottler

University of Nevada, Las Vegas

Brooks/Cole Publishing Company
Pacific Grove, CA

I(T)P ™ The trademark ITP is used under license.

 A CLAIREMONT BOOK

Brooks/Cole Publishing Company
A Division of Wadsworth, Inc.
© 1994 by Wadsworth, Inc., Belmont, California 94002.

Printed in the United States of America
10 9 8 7 6 5 4 3 2 1

Library of Congress Cataloging-in-Publication Data
Kottler, Jeffrey A.
   Advanced group leadership / Jeffrey A. Kottler.
      p. cm.
   Rev. ed. of: Pragmatic group leadership.
   Includes bibliographical references and index.
   ISBN 0-534-21150-X
   1. Group counseling. 2. Group psychotherapy.   I. Kottler,
Jeffrey A. Pragmatic group leadership.   II. Title.
BF637.C6K68 1993
158'.3—dc20   93-15942
                                                     CIP

Sponsoring Editor: *Claire Verduin*
Editorial Associate: *Gay C. Bond*
Production Editor: *Marjorie Z. Sanders*
Manuscript Editor: *Barbara Kimmel*
Permissions Editor: *Karen Wootten*
Interior and Cover Design: *Laurie Albrecht*
Art Coordinator and Interior Illustration: *Lisa Torri*
Indexer: *James Minkin*
Typesetting: *Bookends Typesetting*
Cover Printing: *Phoenix Color Corporation*
Printing and Binding: *Arcata Graphics/Fairfield*

To my colleagues at the University of Nevada, Las Vegas,
whose support and encouragement provide such a fertile group environment
for creativity and growth

About the Author

Jeffrey A. Kottler is an associate professor of counseling and educational psychology at the University of Nevada, Las Vegas. He has studied at Oakland University, Harvard University, Wayne State University, University of Stockholm, and he received his Ph.D. from the University of Virginia. He has worked as a group leader and educator in a variety of settings, including hospitals, mental health centers, preschools, high schools, clinics, universities, corporations, and private practice.

Jeffrey Kottler is the author or co-author of the books *Pragmatic Group Leadership* (1983), *Ethical and Legal Issues in Counseling and Psychotherapy* (2nd edition, 1985), *The Imperfect Therapist: Learning from Failure in Therapeutic Practice* (1989), *Private Moments, Secret Selves: Enriching Our Time Alone* (1990), *The Compleat Therapist* (1991), *Introduction to Therapeutic Counseling* (2nd edition, 1992), *Compassionate Therapy: Working with Difficult Clients* (1992), *On Being a Therapist* (2nd edition, 1993), *On Being a Teacher* (1993), and *Teacher as Counselor* (1993).

Contents

Preface

Group methods of treatment have exploded in popularity in the last few decades, spawning the publication of a dozen journals, hundreds of books, and thousands of articles devoted exclusively to the subject. Whereas once upon a time, taking one graduate level course in group work was considered sufficient preparation to employ the group modality (especially considering that the first few generations of counselors and therapists had no formal training whatsoever), practitioners now are expected to have two, three, or sometimes even four times as much exposure to theory, research, methods, and supervision.

In the decade since I first wrote *Pragmatic Group Leadership*, the first edition of this volume, changes in the field of group counseling have been legion. Whereas once the philosophy of pragmatism emphasized throughout that book was considered somewhat innovative, the norm now is for group practitioners to integrate theory, research, and clinical methods into a unified model of practice. Although *Advanced Group Leadership* reflects an even more pragmatic approach than its predecessor—an approach that combines the best contributions from myriad leadership approaches—the emphasis is now on those *advanced* skills, concepts, paradigms, and research methods that are most useful for students, interns, and practitioners who have had some experience in leading groups.

Advanced Group Leadership is thus designed for those who are already familiar with the theory and research of group work, who understand the basic mechanisms by which change occurs in a group setting, and who have some leadership experience. It is for those who wish to integrate interdisciplinary knowledge, a wide range of useful skills, and a plethora of accepted theories into a universal model of helping people change in groups. This philosophy permits advanced students and practitioners to imprint their own personal styles and therapeutic preferences onto a synthesized model of helping people in groups.

There are dozens of excellent texts and resource manuals available for those who are first learning the basic methodologies of group leadership, but the advanced student of the field is interested in a number of issues that are beyond the comprehension of the beginner. Already aware of group dynamics, stages, and processes and already skilled in the basic helping strategies, advanced group leaders are hungry for more sophisticated conceptual models and a greater variety of interventions that they might use in diverse clinical settings. This book offers advanced students of the field opportunities to add to their knowledge base, to integrate personally what they understand, and to increase the therapeutic options available to them.

Anatomy of This Book

What to include in this book became an exciting decision process. Chapter outlines were repeatedly revised. Everything, it seemed to me, in the fields of sociology, psychology, political science, linguistics, philosophy, history, and even physiology had some bearing on what I wanted to include.

I knew that I would first have to deal with theory and all that philosophy means for advanced group leaders in their search for truth. The first section of the book includes some of the philosophical threads that help bind our profession together. In spite of the differences between practitioners, there is common agreement on certain assumptions that we believe to be true. Chapter 1 summarizes this "glue" that holds our nucleus of truth together.

Chapter 2 discusses the role of the advanced group leader as a philosopher/scientist. This includes mastering the conceptual and empirical basis for the field as well as having a working knowledge of pragmatism as a means to unify and apply what is known.

If the desired outcome of counseling or therapy groups is positive behavioral change for each member, it seems imperative that group leaders have a thorough understanding of why, when, and how people change. Chapter 3 addresses the question of how people change. What are the processes, the intervention strategies in groups, that result in new learnings in individuals or in new decisions that permit or cause new feelings and actions? Chapter 3 also includes an interdisciplinary outlook, wherein theoretical propositions are formulated from which operational directions and intervention strategies can be drawn. When a leader does anything or permits anything in a group to begin or continue, what theoretical behavior-change rationale will support such action?

The second part of the book includes the most significant dimensions of group leadership. Chapters 4 through 8 discuss the most appropriate rules, attributes, and reasoning processes of the pragmatic group leader.

Traditionally, the concept of modeling has been centered largely in the language of the social learning theorist, or the psychodynamic concept of identification. It is my premise that the way group leaders act, the personal characteristics they demonstrate, and the force of their personalities significantly influence successful group member performance. Regardless of actual approach or leadership style, those who exhibit dimensions of personal mastery in their own lives tend to be more effective group leaders. Chapter 4 includes specific suggestions for expanding the roles of therapeutic modeling in groups, examining such factors as appropriate self-disclosure, semantic modeling, role reversals, and "groupside manner."

Because spoken language is the chief medium through which group work occurs, a leader's expertise depends in large measure on how language is employed. It behooves the group worker to become a psycholinguist, a semanticist, a student of what is linguistically current as well as of what idioms are peculiar to various ethnic and age groups. Chapter 5 makes a strong case for avoiding certain words, phrases, concepts, and structures that are confusing, obstructive, or not suited to the outcome goals of the individuals in a group. These include technical terms that constitute the special jargon of the therapy and group field; sexist or class-discriminating terms; terms that reinforce erroneous concepts about the nature of thought and emotional processes; and terms that reinforce directions, attitudes, values, or goals that are inimical to positive behavioral change on the part of individual members. Replacement terms and concepts are offered and discussed, and suggestions are made for determining how messages are received.

Chapter 6 takes up the crucial area of diagnostics: understanding the make-up of individuals and diagnosing what is going on in the group as a whole, including the formation of subgroup coalitions. The process of productive labeling and how it is therapeutically beneficial is also discussed here. The goal is to provide the advanced group leader with a comprehensive framework for understanding what is happening in the group and within the members at any given time. As part of the process involved in macro- and microdiagnosis, certain predictable problems and critical incidents will occur in most groups. Chapter 7 focuses on the most typical and presents case examples and suggestions for handling them. Chapter 8 deals more specifically with those difficult group members who challenge even the advanced leader's ability to keep things under control.

As marriage, family, and sex therapists have known for years, there are numerous advantages for members and leaders alike when partners lead a group in tandem. Leaders can depend on one another to provide support, demonstrations, or to monitor more effectively the reactions of group members. Teamwork is an essential part of effectively breaking in a less experienced leader. There are considerations involved in the pairing of leaders that may militate against or promote smoother operation—issues such as ideological differences; training variances; division of labor; differences in skill levels, personality types, and experiential backgrounds. Then, too, some group techniques and structures are more suitable for use when leader-pairs conduct the group sessions. Chapter 9 focuses on the important issues and nuances of co-leadership.

The third section of the book focuses on specific techniques and strategies for the pragmatic group leader who wishes to augment a base of traditional skills. These chapters may be seen as merely examples of the types of creative advancement that are possible.

Whether one is initiating or ending a relationship, making a career or lifestyle change, practicing novel behavior, confronting a significant person, or disclosing personal history, there are always risks accompanying pursuance of the unknown, the untried. Chapter 10 considers risk taking in depth and discusses how group leaders can invite more constructive risk taking among participants.

Group leaders have no technological hardware to aid in helping people. They have only their minds and their skills of communicating what is in their minds. The more refined and expert group leaders become in their use of language, the better they will become at making telling interventions. Chapter 11 focuses on the use of metaphors and images that can both facilitate insight and motivate growth. Although the clinical application of verbal images in groups is emphasized, much of the material here is borrowed from all the communication disciplines, including literature, philosophy, the sciences and humanities, and even children's stories.

Participation in a therapeutic group can be intensely serious, laden with conflict and tension. Frequently the only laughter heard is the nervous giggling that is the telltale sign of anxiety. Yet the important tasks of a therapeutic group need not be compromised by the leader's effort to bring humor into the setting. With all the hard work involved in the process of changing, comic relief promotes a more relaxed, natural, desirable atmosphere. Humorous anecdotes are used throughout Chapter 12 to describe how group leaders can make their sessions more enjoyable. Although virtually everything worth learning in life tends to be painful or difficult, no one has ever said that a spirit of fun cannot accompany it.

Chapter 13 provides an impetus for advanced group leaders to increase their range of possible intervention choices. Described are creative group structures such as subgrouping, spatial interventions, thinking on one's seat, and other therapeutic strategies that only the experienced practitioner could make work.

Chapter 14 moves into adjunct structures. It is not what clients say and do in group sessions that makes a definitive difference; it is how they act in the outside world. Limitless resources are available to the creative group leader who wishes to supplement scheduled sessions with opportunities for further client growth. Many practical adjunct strategies that allow the group leader to stimulate progress toward client change between sessions are described. Among other structures, this chapter discusses environmental programming, people monitoring, journal keeping, and psychological homework.

Chapter 15 draws together the separate strands of the book and touches on a number of areas under the topic of ethics. It looks to the future of group work, where the field seems to be headed, and to the future of group leaders.

This overview of the book's contents makes certain themes evident. The principal emphasis is on integrating existing knowledge in the field, bringing together diverse approaches into a format that is useful for the practitioner.

I am most grateful for the expertise and vast experience held by the esteemed reviewers of this manuscript. If ever there were "advanced" group leaders who have helped to shape the direction of the field, they are Gerald Corey, California State University, Fullerton; George M. Gazda, University of Georgia; Samuel T. Gladding, Wake Forest University; David Zimpher, Kent State University; and David Zinger, University of Manitoba.

Jeffrey A. Kottler

The Threads That Bind Group Helping Systems

Among the skirmishes and conflicts between group leaders and the dialogues between theoreticians and researchers, there is an emerging consensus as to the most effective means to promote change. There is general agreement in the field about certain underlying assumptions of leader behavior; about explaining how group members learn, and hence change; and about the philosophic orientation that ought to be part of a therapist's or counselor's diagnostic and treatment process. Pragmatism permits the practitioner to function as a philosopher/scientist, inductively and deductively weaving the most stable threads of all helping systems into a comprehensive model of group treatment.

CHAPTER 1

Assumptions of Advanced Group Leaders

What Makes a Group Leader Advanced?

Nathan and Hillary are preparing to co-lead a group together. Nathan is participating in this project as part of a requirement for a group course in which he is expected to gain some experience working under the supervision of a more veteran partner. Hillary is a doctoral student who has been running groups in various clinical settings for a number of years.

Both group leaders feel apprehensive as their clients begin to file in for their first session, although the nature of their concerns is quite different. Whereas Nathan's internal dialogue is focused on his doubts regarding his suitability for the profession and whether he will have what it takes to be a polished professional, Hillary is concerned much more with the overwhelming practical issues related to launching a group successfully. Perhaps the best way to distinguish the differences between a beginning and advanced group leader is to note the ways that leaders such as Nathan and Hillary process what is occurring in their group by examining the internal dialogues that take place inside their heads.

> **Nathan** (a beginning group leader): I'm so excited to be here. I can't believe it! I am finally a group leader, or I should say *acting* like one. Will I recognize the various group dynamics and process stages when I see them? How will I know when I should do something? Maybe I'll just let Hillary do the work for awhile and I'll just sit back and watch.
>
> No, I can't do that. She will think I don't know what I'm doing, and so will all the group members. But maybe I *don't* know what I am doing. I know the theory, and I have seen some groups in action—even led some structured sessions—but this is the real thing. This is my big opportunity to prove myself, to show that I have what it takes to be a great group leader.

What if I don't have anything to say or I don't know what to do? What if a situation comes up that I can't handle and Hillary won't bail me out? That's another thing; I wonder what she thinks about me so far?

Hillary (*an advanced group leader*): I don't know who is most nervous: the group members or my co-leader over there. Poor Nathan, he looks sick with worry. He sure expects a lot from me; he almost puts me on a pedestal, as if I can do no wrong. That makes it even harder for me to consult with him, since he believes I already know everything. How am I going to get some honest feedback on my behavior if he needs me to be so perfect?

It is going to be really hard to remain patient and not try to take over the group. I have a problem with that anyway. I have witnessed these group processes unfold enough times that sometimes I try to push things along too quickly. What if I anticipate so much that I don't actually see what is happening?

I have also got to be careful to avoid acting out my control issues. I sense that Nathan wants me to take over for him, and I know that it would not be a good thing for me to do—for him or for me. I see a number of group members here who have authority problems to begin with, so I will be an obvious target. I sure hope I have the strength to resist taking the bait.

Nathan and Hillary are co-leaders of the same group and yet are at vastly different stages of their careers. As developing group leaders, they each require training and supervision that reflects their current levels of confidence, experience, and expertise.

As is typical of beginning counselors and therapists, Nathan needs help in several areas, such as in boosting his self-confidence and in minimizing both technical errors and countertransference issues related to his need to prove himself (Robertiello & Schoenwolf, 1987). Beginners also tend to make mistakes in areas related to the timing and execution of their interventions, and they tend to become hypervigilant as a result of their fears of failure (Kottler & Blau, 1989). Such is certainly the case with Nathan.

More advanced practitioners also struggle with issues related to fears of failure, but the questions are not so much "What if I don't know what to do?" or "What if I make a mistake?" as they are variations of the theme "What if others find out that I am a fraud and that I don't know what I am doing?"

Evolving Characteristics of Experienced Leaders

It is clear that advanced group leaders, compared to their less experienced colleagues, have a number of unique concerns and characteristics. Several studies on the qualities of experts in such fields as medicine (Lesgold et al., 1988), education and urban planning (Schon, 1983), chess and geology

(Soloway, Adelson, & Ehrlich, 1988), and psychotherapy (Glaser & Chi, 1989; Kopta, Newman, McGovern, & Angle, 1989) have led to a consensus on how experts function alike.

Because advanced practitioners of any profession are more procedurally efficient and faster than are their less experienced colleagues, they tend to function automatically. Comments such as "Oh, here is another one of those," or "Time to do my pep talk number 2" might commonly be made internally by a veteran.

Experts process information quickly and tend to think more abstractly than do novices. Experts have more habitual responses, take more shortcuts, and focus more on narrowly restricted sectors for their diagnostic scanning. Novices, on the other hand, are more data-based, theory-driven, probing, cautious, exploratory, sequential, and thorough in their reasoning (Dumont, 1991). The differences between the novice and the expert are illustrated in the following example of a particular group event—a period of collective silence in which no member has spoken for a while. Although each leader reached the same conclusion, the differing reasoning processes demonstrate the more efficient, intuitive, and complex style of the advanced clinician as contrasted with the more deliberate, analytic method of the beginner.

Response to Collective Silence

The Novice

"Silence. Is this silence?"

"What kind of silence is this? Time to reflect? Confusion needing direction? Collective anger toward my control? A pregnant pause?"

"I'll wait them out a while."

"Four members seem restless. The others won't make eye contact. Do they share the same motive for their withdrawal?"

"They seem to be communicating with one another. I see them waiting for me to do something."

"Should I rescue them? How long should I wait?"

"I see no evidence for confusion. Just before the pause they seemed to be tracking. They must be waiting for me."

"Maybe I should confront this unwillingness to assume responsibility."

"I'll give it another minute first."

The Expert

"This is the typical 'lull before the storm' silent treatment."

"Time to confront their denial of responsibility for progress."

It is apparent that when advanced group leaders become more automatic and less reflective in their style, their experience can contribute as many liabilities as strengths. Advanced knowledge and skills are most useful when we couple them with the thoroughness of the beginner.

One other point, mentioned by Zimpfer (1992), also deserves attention. There is not a true dichotomy between a practitioner who is a beginner and one who is advanced. Some of us are still neophytes in some areas, less skilled and knowledgeable than we would prefer to be, and yet advanced in other aspects of group leadership. For example, I consider myself quite expert at leading groups of adolescents and adults as well as minority groups of Hispanics, African Americans, and some Native American tribes. Yet, in spite of similarities among client populations and in spite of my having logged over two decades of group leadership practice, I still consider myself a novice in working with senior adults, younger children, and groups of Asian Americans or Arab Americans. I am certain that this specialized expertise is true for most of us: each group leader is both a beginner and a veteran.

The Perils of Being Experienced

Beginning group leaders know that they do not know very much, so they are understandably cautious and tentative in their approach. Advanced practitioners, on the other hand, can fall victim to what Starak (1988) calls a "guru mentality," in which they believe that they know both what is best for people and what people need to do to improve their lives. As "glandular optimists," they cheer people on with the unfailing belief that if only they work hard, they will get whatever they want.

Although advanced practitioners enjoy a number of benefits not generally afforded beginners, this experience does not necessarily ensure greater success. There is, for example, no compelling evidence to indicate that expert judges, economic forecasters, or psychologists perform significantly better than do their novice colleagues (Johnson, 1988).

Dumont (1991) speculates that, although experience does give advanced practitioners a base of *canonical knowledge*, there is a very small consensually sanctioned domain of information in our field on which to rely. With so many competing models of change and theories of group intervention, advanced practitioners remain almost as confused as beginners regarding what works best. In fact, Dumont contends, advanced therapists are even at a distinct disadvantage because of their tendencies to assume that expertise naturally evolves with seasoning in the profession. Experienced practitioners struggle not so much with the problem of not knowing enough as assuming they know things that they really do not (Kottler, 1992). These overgeneralizations and invalid assumptions about client behavior and group processes can lead to the following pitfalls.

Misdiagnosing Client Issues. The advanced group leader immediately assumes, for example, that a client's passivity and withdrawal stems from feeling rejected by other members in the group. In fact, the client has a biologically based depression that has thus far gone unnoticed. The leader's experience leads him to automatically assume certain cause/effect relationships based on prior group dynamics; a beginner may not make this same error in judgment, since he or she would assume very little without first considering all the clinical possibilities.

Misreading Group Dynamics. Invalid assumptions affect not only individual client issues but also the group process as a whole. Because the leader had been warned to expect that a group of adolescents would give her a hard time, she naturally assumed this was the case when, the first time she set limits, there was a rebellion against her proposal to establish certain rules. What she failed to consider was that the teenagers did not mind the rules so much as they resisted the arrogant style in which she communicated: ''I know what is best for you and you will do this because I say so.''

Engaging in Backward Reasoning. The beginning group leader starts with the phenomenon that is occurring and then tries to make sense of it by applying a number of models that can provide explanations and suggest interventions. By contrast, the expert begins with his or her preferred theory and then tries to find data to support it (Snyder & Thomsen, 1988). Needless to say, this kind of confirmatory reasoning leads to greater distortion and bias than does the more cautious and analytic approach favored by neophytes (Pain & Sharpley, 1989).

Moving Toward Greater Diversity. As recent graduates, beginners are more homogeneous in their clinical approach than are those who have been in the field for a while. They follow longer, more methodological, and more uniform procedures than do veterans who have discovered shortcuts. Therefore, there is greater variation among experts in the ways that they operate.

When presented with a critical incident—say a member who refuses to speak—beginning group leaders will do exactly what they were told to do in such situations. This rigidity, of course, can lead to a number of clinical errors, mostly in terms of skill competency. In a collection of advanced leaders, however, individuals may move in diametrically opposed directions in handling a given situation. Advanced leaders are more likely to be creative, innovative, intrusive, intuitive, spontaneous, and thus they may be more likely to make bigger mistakes than are more cautious trainees.

Failing to Allow Sufficient Cohesion and Alliance. Whereas the beginning group leader will be cautious and err in the direction of waiting too long before intervening to cut off rambling digression or a diffused focus, the more advanced group leader may jump in too quickly. Before cohesion, trust, and bonding have had a chance to set, the experienced clinician may work to counteract "inertial drag," which is one of the biggest culprits leading to dropouts (Colson, Lewis, & Horwitz, 1985).

In her investigations of failures in family therapy, Coleman (1985) found that a weak alliance with family members was cited most often as the reason for unsuccessful treatment. In group situations as well, creating an environment of trust, cohesion, and intimacy is crucial to any work that will take place. This is a principle that beginners rarely forget, since it recently has been drummed into their heads in graduate school.

Once group leaders get in the field and accumulate experience, however, they tend to move away from basics and on toward more sophisticated, complex, and challenging therapeutic strategies. I notice that the whole atmosphere of my groups and individual sessions change when I am teaching a basic counseling skills class. I relearn the simple value of reflective listening and more subtle relationship-building skills by teaching them to others. Often these are leader behaviors that I have neglected in favor of more advanced and dramatic interventions.

Over the years, the more groups I have led, the more active I have become in trying to make things happen that I just *know* would be good for people. It takes a beginner, a co-leader I am working with, to point out that I may be trying a little too hard to push things too quickly, and that I am taking too much responsibility for therapeutic outcomes. I am thus reminded that somewhere along the way I have lost what Zukav (1979) lauded as the innocent spirit of the beginner's mind who can "see the world as it is, and not as it appears according to what we know about it" (pp. 117–118).

The training needs of an advanced group leader, therefore, involve not only supplementing knowledge and skills with additional information and therapeutic options but also retaining the fresh spirit of the beginner, who does not have enough experience to assume much of anything without carefully observing what is transpiring and then responding with the minimum force necessary to move things along. Despite the perils of being an expert that have just been mentioned, advanced group leaders are able to see, hear, and sense many things going on in a group that beginners might miss. Following is only a partial list of what experienced practitioners look for and what they can do that beginners cannot.

What Advanced Leaders Look For

- potential dropouts and casualties
- patterns of systemic dysfunctioning
- hidden agendas of group members
- coercive pressures stifling individuality
- potential ethical conflicts before they occur
- "pulse" of group functioning
- beginnings of destructive coalitions

- challenges to group leader authority
- signs of stagnation
- members who are *quietly* struggling
- cries for help
- forms of "corruptive" resistance

What Advanced Group Leaders Can Do

- process information more quickly and act decisively
- screen out poor risks
- change leadership style, depending on what is needed
- diffuse conflicts before they begin
- let go of strategies that are not working
- confront members nondefensively
- reflect deeper-level empathic resonance
- model higher levels of personal effectiveness
- handle crisis situations without disturbing group balance
- balance work with fun
- introduce complex therapeutic structures
- confront their own personal issues as they arise
- forgive themselves for mistakes and misjudgments

What makes a group leader advanced is much more than completing an introductory group course and accumulating some basic leadership experience. The truly advanced practitioner is one who is making a concerted effort to integrate what she has learned thus far and who is interested in so much more than learning new group techniques and structures. Such a group leader is working hard to construct a model for understanding how people grow and change in group settings—an individually constructed paradigm that reflects the clinician's unique personality, professional values, clinical skills, thinking processes, and treatment situation. This model of group leadership, regardless of its theoretical origins, is likely to include a number of universal assumptions with which most group leaders would agree.

A Model of Group Leadership

In fewer than 40 years (if one does not take into account the pioneering research of sociologists who made earlier discoveries in group dynamics), the technology of helping people in small groups has become a formidable discipline. Following World War II, the group work field enjoyed a growth period that came into full flower in the 1960s and early 1970s, similar to what the field of family therapy is undergoing today. Small groups were being tried in every social arena. The encounter group became familiar to the aware layperson. Brainstorming groups, rap groups, consciousness-raising groups, and peer-counseling groups became familiar designations, especially to mental health and allied professionals. Psychotherapy and counseling-group literature swelled with new discoveries, learnings that poured forth from experimenters in dissimilar contexts—from marathon group enthusiasts; from Esalen; from Synanon; from the family counseling movement; from psychodrama; from schools, hospitals, churches, and community agencies. This growth has now leveled off to a plateau where what is known is being consolidated through the publication of numerous books that are repetitive in their offerings.

This means that group work has become institutionalized, validated. More mental health workers, through training, professional organizations, and licensing procedures, are being required to know about therapeutic group procedures in order to effectively lead groups to achieve positive treatment outcomes for their clients or patients. Professional organizations have developed training standards and guidelines as well as ethical codes concerning group work. The Association for Specialists in Group Work and the American Group Psychotherapy Association are two of the most viable organizations seeking to promote the profession through respected journals and sponsored training workshops, among their other activities. They typify the visibility and respectability that group workers, small group structures, and the group process are accorded in mental health and educational circles and by society at large.

The diversity of professionals who identify themselves as group leaders makes it understandably difficult to create a singular image of the field. Disciplines as wide-ranging as management science, sociology, social work, medicine, education, nursing, psychology, and counseling have spawned theoreticians, researchers, and practitioners who have made significant contributions to the body of knowledge about group work. It is increasingly evident that the systematic and effective practice of group leadership will require professionals with an education that bypasses and bridges the arbitrary divisions of academic curricula. Yet such a generalist must also have some fairly specialized training in the techniques unique to group practice.

In addition to the range of professional labels that group leaders use to describe themselves—psychiatrists, psychologists, social workers, nurses, educators, counselors, human relations specialists, management consultants, therapists, facilitators—further differences are manifested through theoretical affiliations. Thus, a Gestalt leader is of quite a different breed from a behaviorist; similarly, a psychoanalytic practitioner appears to have little in common with a colleague who practices out of a rational-emotive orientation. Then there are the varied settings in which group leaders deliver their services: schools, prisons, hospitals, industry, community agencies, universities, mental health centers, and private practice.

The interaction among disciplines, training programs, theoretical orientations, and settings would not appear to be conducive to agreement among this group of professionals. Notwithstanding that we tend to work in circles, use a high frequency of "you seem to be saying" statements, and are impassioned about the subtle complexities of human interaction, what concepts are most group leaders likely to agree with, regardless of implicit individual differences? What consensus can we reach about the nature of group leadership based on current research, theory, and practice?

As a means of synthesizing and summarizing the current state of the art, assumptions are presented here that represent a foundation on which to build more advanced group work knowledge. They provide us with a sense of continuity and cohesion for the field and collectively serve as an integrative statement for most practitioners.

Unifying Assumptions about Groups

There Are Different Kinds of Groups for Different Purposes.   Although the generic term *group work* describes the therapeutic process of helping people learn about themselves for the purpose of making constructive behavioral and life changes, there are specific varieties of group treatment that are uniquely geared for special goals, situations, and client populations. There is, however, enough confusion in the field as a result of trying to distinguish *counseling* from *psychotherapy* without adding the complexities contained in the taxonomy of various group strategies.

Betz, Wilbur, and Roberts-Wilbur (1981) attempted to clear up the confusion surrounding the various group processes by creating a structural blueprint of group modalities. The Task Group Cluster (composed of committees, meetings, and conferences), the Socio-Process Cluster (guidance and discussion groups), and the Psycho-Process Cluster (therapy and counseling groups), which compose the principal focus of this book, are distinguished by several variables. Depending on group size, stated objectives, leader behaviors, member expectations, duration of sessions, length of treatment, participant composition, and techniques employed, the various forms of group work may be delineated into fairly discrete categories.

Guidance groups, counseling groups, T-groups, task groups, rap groups, discussion groups, sensitivity groups, human potential groups—all bring to mind a particular image of group work in action. If group members act somewhat unorthodoxly and are wearing pajamas, we are probably watching a therapy group with hospitalized patients. If members are wearing business suits and taking notes on clipboards, we may be witnessing a discussion group. In fact, the varieties of group work can themselves be grouped on a continuum according to their status on certain variables. Essentially, the more severe the client's difficulties and the longer the treatment, the more likely the group will follow a medical model; an educational model more appropriately fits groups that are structured and task oriented.

This continuum of group work styles is no longer as valid as it once was. The field has matured in the past few decades to the point at which

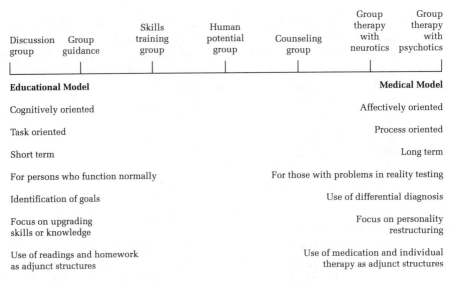

Figure 1-1

pragmatism has become much more an operating principle than the maintenance of theoretical or structural purity. In the classic model that is presented in Figure 1-1, educational groups traditionally have been portrayed as primarily cognitive, whereas therapeutic groups are considered affectively oriented. Yet Zimpfer (1992) notes that this perspective is seriously flawed: "Would a cognitive therapist agree that group therapy is affective? Would a structured interventionist agree that treatment must be long term? Would a supportive therapist agree that the focus of treatment must be on personality restructuring?" Nevertheless, this chart, however flawed, does summarize some of the major traditional views of group leadership.

Group Work Is Similar to Individual and Family Treatment Modalities and Yet Is Quite Different.   Some authors (Hill, 1990; Pilkonis, Imber, Lewis, & Rubinsky, 1984) question whether there are any real differences between individual and group modalities in terms of their underlying processes; however, it does seem clear that there are at least some *apparent* differences. It is obvious, for example, that additional competencies are required of group leaders in general, and of advanced practitioners in particular, in much the same way that there are differences between tutoring and classroom instruction.

Group work has its own identity, even though it does share a number of similarities with individual treatment—especially with family therapy (Trotzer, 1989). And although group work has a number of contextual and process similarities to family therapy, there are also some notable differences. For instance, whereas a family is a kind of group, it is also made up of people who have a long history together and will be going home together after the session ends. There are also differences between the modalities in requirements for inclusion, degree of enmeshment, structural hierarchies, norm establishment, and ways in which therapists and counselors relate to members (Hines, 1988). Nevertheless, systemic thinking and family theory have had a tremendous impact on group work, just as the notions of group dynamics and coalitions have influenced the work of family practitioners.

Counselors and therapists—whether they are conducting individual, family, or group sessions—rely on a set of generic therapeutic principles and clinical skills. In their comparative analysis of individual and group process variables, Fuhriman and Burlingame (1990) identified several common dimensions, such as the bond between therapist and client; the development of a trusting atmosphere; the clinician's demonstrations of empathy, responsiveness, attentiveness, and engagement; and process variables such as catharsis, reality testing, and identification. A number of other factors, such as placebo effects, vicarious learning, role induction, consciousness raising, risk taking, rehearsal, and task facilitation, are also operative in all three therapeutic modalities (Kottler, 1991).

A number of group leadership skills have also been identified by Dyer and Vriend (1975), Nolan (1978), and Corey (1990). Yet such behaviors as self-disclosure, giving feedback, goal setting, initiating, and linking are hardly unique to group settings.

Group Work Has Certain Advantages and Disadvantages in Comparison with Individual Treatment.   Group work has several distinct advantages over individual treatment. Practitioners can reach many persons in a group setting within a specific block of time. The built-in support system is conducive to more serious commitment on the part of clients, and the nurturing environment makes group members more willing to explore and try out new ways of thinking, feeling, and behaving. Further, a group setting more closely parallels the social milieu of the client's real world. It allows participants to improve their interpersonal skills at the same time that they are working in specific problem areas. Then there is the vicarious learning and identification process that inevitably occurs as a result of observing individuals receiving specific help.

The collective experience of so many assistant helpers available in a group and the high-intensity interaction also make the learning process more potent. Therapeutic groups act as safe laboratories in which to experiment and rehearse new behaviors for the outside world; they enable participants to learn success skills for surviving in a world of groups. Participants gain an unusual and cherished opportunity to receive honest and constructive feedback: a more accurate mirroring of their attitudes, beliefs, biases, feelings, and behaviors, which is perhaps the most valuable aspect of group work.

Even with the zeal that typifies those of us who are committed to group work as the preferred mode of helping, however, these advantages are counterbalanced by some disadvantages that are difficult to ignore. Potential problems seem directly proportional to the number of persons we attempt to help simultaneously. In a group, the leader has less situational control than is possible in individual counseling or therapy; more things can go awry. Difficulties are more likely to develop if the group leader cannot effectively balance the need for freedom versus the need for structure (Lieberman, Yalom, & Miles, 1973).

Each client receives less attention in a group because there always seems to be a shortage of available time. Confidentiality is more difficult to mandate and virtually impossible to enforce because group members are not bound to ethical codes or to the leader's promises (Davis & Meara, 1982). The coercion and peer pressure toward conformity that are part of every group process operate at intense levels in a therapeutic group, subtly shaping individuals toward accepted norms and dangerously curbing individual initiative. This factor must be explored more closely.

Therapeutic Groups Can Act as Coercive Influences to Stifle Individual Autonomy.   Case examples abound of the power that groups wield in corrupting individuals far beyond a point where they ever believed their value systems would allow them to go. The news media predictably reveal their continuing astonishment when apprehended assassins disclose that they were raised in ordinary middle-class families. The fact remains, however, that after a few months in a terrorist training camp, or of radical religious indoctrination, a great many ordinary people are turned into murderers. Jim Jones and the People's Temple are examples of mutant group forces at work. In this instance, hundreds of people were induced to renounce first their possessions and then their lives at the whim of a powerful group leader. Although their goals may be dissimilar, the Moonies, Ku Klux Klan, and youth gangs are also highly proficient in group brainwashing techniques that maximize cohesion, solidarity, and peer pressure.

According to Bar-Tal (1990), there are three types of beliefs that group members hold. *Personal beliefs* are the unique, private perceptions that define a person's individuality. *Common beliefs* are those values shared by others as part of an organization, family, religion, or profession. *Group beliefs* are a kind of common belief system that group members are aware they share and that defines them as a group identity. These shared beliefs are the basis of a group member's sense of belongingness and ultimately regulate behavior related to the collective.

Often group beliefs are explicitly stated, such as the raison d'être of many organizations. The Amalgamated Flying Saucer Clubs of America, for example, define their group belief as the affirmation that vehicles visiting from other planets are real and their existence is being covered up by our government. More often, however, especially in therapeutic settings, individual beliefs are much more open and clear than are the underlying group beliefs. Sometimes these group beliefs can become so strong in their sense of "we-ness" that individuality and uniqueness are lost in the process.

In some cultures, this loss of individual autonomy is an explicit goal rather than an abuse of rights. In India, China, Korea, Japan, and other Asian societies, members do not generally believe that promoting individual goals over those of the community is necessarily desirable. Group treatments thus become a powerful vehicle to promote compliance to sanctioned cultural values.

In a group guidance class in Singapore, students learning group leadership skills were asked to generate, in their own small groups, a list of rules that should be established and enforced. Similar to participants in North American settings, the students identified some familiar norms, such as shared responsibility, but there were also some fairly unique suggestions, characteristic of Singaporean culture. Rules such as the following were mentioned: "Bring a smile every day"; "Always do what the leader says"; "Give support no matter what"; "Be polite and courteous." Since enforcement of rules is such an integral part of this society, the participants were equally as definite about what should happen if group members did not do what was expected: if a member came late to group, he or she should be fined; if a member was not courteous, he or she should be made to wear a "discourteous badge."

People tend to conform to group norms, however inappropriate, illogical, or distorted they may be. The shared reality of persons in a group may take precedence over individual perceptions. In his classic experiment illustrating the effects of group behavior on the conformity of an individual, Asch (1951) discovered that a person will actually "see" distortions in perceptual reality if others in the group claim such common experience. In judging the length of a line or the passage of time, people will ignore their own judgments in favor of the majority opinion.

Milgram (1965) placed a subject with two confederates in a group situation and found that peer pressure induced the subject to inflict more pain on an innocent victim than was otherwise likely. Festinger's concept of *deindividuation* is also noteworthy in this context (Festinger, Pepitone, & Newcomb, 1952). A person attempts to reduce internal cognitive dissonance by submerging the self in the group, thereby (1) reducing inner restraints, (2) liberating deviant norms, (3) diffusing responsibility, (4) facilitating anonymous participation, and (5) reducing the likelihood of negative consequences for any individual. This lynch mob mentality can make intelligent, responsible, moral people temporarily capable of suspending their personal standards against committing atrocities (Shaw, 1981).

In group situations, people attempt to enhance their status by appearing more as risk takers (Brown, 1965, 1974). Also, because responsibility is diffused and multiple authorship of a decision is shared among members, people in groups tend to make collectively riskier decisions than they would make alone (Runyan, 1974; Spector, Cohen, & Penner, 1976; Stoner, 1968).

More "spectatoring," self-judgment, and self-evaluation occur in the presence of others. People tend to make more comparisons about how they stand up to their peers. This "pacing behavior" ranges from comparing neighborhood lawns to comparing infant development ("my baby has three teeth and is crawling, and *he* is only six months old"). The mere presence of others enhances well-memorized performances, such as reciting standard social lines like "what I do for a living," but hinders performances that involve trying out new behaviors (Baron, Moore, & Sanders, 1978; Markus, 1978).

Groupthink (Janis, 1972) occurs when group members experience such cohesion, loyalty, and uniformity that they deteriorate in their individual capacities for reality testing, logical analysis, and moral judgment. Shaw (1981) lists several other consequences of the groupthink phenomenon:

1. Group members rationalize their loss of personal identity.
2. Moral consequences of actions are more often ignored.
3. Stereotypic views of others are perpetuated.
4. There is an unwillingness to say or do anything to destroy the perceived happy balance.
5. There is an emergence of gestapo-type "mindguards" to ensure that complete stability is maintained.

Jeffries (1973) views counseling groups as vehicles for deradicalizing minority and creative children. Kids who demonstrate mannerisms not approved by "the System" are yanked out of class—for backtalking, for being funny or disruptive, or merely for being different from the rest—and are sent to the school counselor for appropriate disciplinary tactics to stamp out the subversive elements. In spite of the fact that the greatest thinkers of our time have been troublemakers in school, we continue to treat such delinquents as threats to the status quo.

In their classic study of eminent thinkers, Goertzel, and Goertzel (1962) discovered that, after feeding the biographical information of our 100 greatest thinkers into a computer to sort out commonalities, the majority of these great scientists, politicians, artists, and writers had had serious school problems. Bertrand Russell, Albert Einstein, and Sigmund Freud would all have ended up in their counselor's office as precocious, unruly discipline problems, pressured to give up their disruptive behaviors in favor of preserving the peace of conventional students and teachers.

> Thus, group counseling serves as a potent vehicle for the counselor to use a knowledge of peer group pressure to help large numbers of children conform and maintain the status quo.
>
> It is important to deradicalize people while they are in the developmental stages of childhood and incarcerated in the schools.
>
> If they escape the process, they may grow up to push toward real change in the established institutions of society. (Jeffries, 1973, p. 115)

Although the negative effects of the Many on the One have less to do with therapeutic groups than with those that are task oriented, the contamination is still active in diluted forms. A silent group member or dissenting participant is prodded to conform to the norm. In fact, the following episode is predictable in the course of every group.

> **Member**: I don't know about the rest of you, but I'm tired of spilling my guts in here and having Sandra stare at me as if I'm some animal in a cage.
>
> (After having been directed to speak directly to Sandra.)
>
> **Member**: It's true. You always sit there with that smile on your face, as if you're better than the rest of us. Why don't you ever say anything? How come you never participate? I don't think you belong with us unless you start acting right.

Such confrontations do produce results. Sandra will burst into tears, mumble apologies, and promise to do better. And, in fact, she will *appear* to *perform* better. She will memorize her lines, recite her speeches, say the correct things at the appropriate times. Everyone will feel better, including the leader, now that Sandra is *cooperating*.

It is only after reading the process journals of the participants that we will learn that Sandra had been growing the most of all members in the group. Although behaving shyly in the group, her life outside the group had turned around. She had been searching desperately for an identity, a self apart from her parents and husband who constantly pressured her to conform. In the group she had experimented with deliberately stifling approval-seeking comments. She had decided that until she could truly speak her own mind, reasonably certain that she was not playing her usual games, she would keep quiet. Now her journal entries reflected the recent surrender to her peers' preferences. After all, she had had lots of practice at mimicry; she could be the superstar of the group in delivering what was expected. Similarly, some of the most well-behaved, talkative, cooperative members of the group were among those who changed the least. Their journal entries tended to take the form of lecture notes, memorized phrases, shallow comments, and stereotyped jargon.

The advanced group leader intuitively understands the deceptions of appearance, the implicit booby traps in groups that make them such powerful places to change, for better or for worse.

Group Work Is the Treatment of Choice in Some Therapeutic Situations and Is Contraindicated in Others.   Group work is not for everyone. Because of the reflexive interaction that occurs among clients, one person in a group may strangely affect the experiential outcomes of the others. If a particular client is aggressively domineering, irresponsibly abusive, extraordinarily passive, hostile, or devoid of reality-based orientation, such characteristics may block growth for others. People prone to manipulating, monopolizing, rambling, intellectualizing, approval seeking, dependency, and game playing, or who tend toward vulnerability, present varying degrees of handling difficulty for group leaders. However, they are not necessarily candidates for exclusion from a group experience, since they may in fact make dramatic progress in mitigating or eliminating their self-defeating behaviors as a result of the confrontive feedback (Kivlighan, 1985).

On the basis of available research, Yalom (1985) also concludes that group work should not be used with persons who are paranoid, brain damaged, suicidal, acutely psychotic, sociopathic, hypochondriacal, or narcissistic. On the other hand, those who have moderate intelligence, a cooperative attitude, the ability to communicate fluently, high expectations for positive change, and a degree of extraversion are considered to be prime candidates for group work (Giedt, 1961; Heslin, 1964; Yalom, 1985). Group membership implies the right both to influence and to accept the influence of others in that group. If prospective clients are appropriately screened to ensure that only reasonably suitable individuals are admitted, many of the disadvantages can be minimized.

Many Public Fears and Myths Are Associated with the Practice of Group Work.   A number of myths about group work have been perpetuated over the years (Anderson, 1985; Geis, 1973; Kottler, 1983; Yalom, 1985). It is a professional obligation of advanced group leaders not only to know about these misconceptions and erroneous beliefs but also to be able to correct them for the benefit of the public and clients (Childers & Couch, 1989).

All human beings seem to harbor a deep desire for belonging. Gregarious creatures by nature, we have a long evolutionary history of group membership that goes back to our Neanderthal cave-group days. In our literature, Robinson Crusoe–type stories are rare. When, on 25 January 1972, a press release from Guam reported that Sergeant Shoichi Yokoi of the 38th Infantry Regiment of the World War II Japanese Imperial Army had finally surrendered to American soldiers after living alone in the jungle for 28 years, the world was flabbergasted. The awe and admiration of people worldwide was focused not so much on his survival techniques as on how he could have made it without the company of others. Short of death, the severest forms of punishment are solitary confinement, banishment, exile, being marooned, or becoming a shipwrecked castaway, cut off from all company and communication with other people.

Myth 1: Groups are enclaves for brainwashing. Belonging is so potent a drive that most humans are perpetually ready to trade personal freedom for group membership. Knowing this, both benevolent and malevolent group leaders use a variety of methods to lock followers into place. Many groups consist of homes or family circles that dispense love and protection, provide a spiritual meaning for being alive, enlist the lonely wanderer into service for a just cause, and help the recruit to feel enlarged, transcended, important beyond the boundaries of self. Members acquire worth and status as a result of belonging.

Preparing athletes to function at maximum limits depends on team spirit, or esprit de corps, and coaches work overtime to build loyalty to the team into each player. Military organizations use group methods of indoctrination to shape recruits into warriors willing to kill or be killed, to see other humans in the black-and-white categories of friend or foe. Street gangs, the Ku Klux Klan, the Black Panthers, fraternities, the Mafia—all build a "one for all and all for one" spirit into each initiate through the promise of the communal sharing of wealth, power, and gains of the group. Dissenters are weeded out. Once an initiate is sworn into full status, the penalty for unorthodoxy, nonconformity, or disobedience ("a chain is only as strong as its weakest link") is ostracism, excommunication, disbarment, and, not infrequently, death.

In therapeutic groups, confidentiality is a mild form of bonding through secrecy; only the privileged know what goes on in the inner sanctum. The leader states it at the beginning:

> **Leader:** What goes on in this group belongs only to us. It's our business and no one else's. If someone in here relates personal material and someone else in here reveals such information to someone outside of this group, harmful consequences can occur. If anyone of us believes that what is revealed here will leave this room, none of us will feel safe enough to talk about personal concerns. Does everyone understand this? Is there anyone in the group who cannot subscribe to this, who feels she or he won't be able to respect this code and live by it?

It would be difficult to convince any adult today that his or her fears over the potential dangers a psychologically sophisticated villain might cause are not justifiable. Adolf Hitler, after all, was a brilliant tactician of group dynamic factors, using peer pressure, authority, cohesion, dress coding, rituals, ingroup identification, even group goals that promised world dominance for the chosen ones. Charles Manson knew instinctively how to get his "family" of crazy killers to do his bidding by using principles of group norms, social reinforcement, transference, sexual bonding, modeling, and programming. The public has also seen religious leaders manipulate disciples to donate all their worldly possessions, as well as their rational minds, to an elusive cause.

It is not difficult to translate the actions of a few irresponsible zealots, who have used groups of confused searching minds for their personal playgrounds, to the practice of group therapy by trained professionals. This connection is the more apparent when supposed experts in our field, famous psychiatrists or psychologists, disclose their personal approaches to group leadership as if they were representative of what all practitioners do. Martin Shepard, for instance, has produced several widely read books in which he describes his rather erotic style of group therapy.

> "I have an encounter game I'd like to play, if you're all willing. It's called the Truth Game. What we do is go around the room and say truthfully what is on our minds. . . ."

> After everybody had their tediously profound say concerning man's fate, the French girl's turn came.
> "I can't really think of anything," she said, looking bored and uninterested.
> Just as I was considering going home, her husband hit the nail squarely on the head.
> "I'm thinking that if the orgy doesn't start in five minutes, I'm leaving. . . ."
> "Well," I said, "if an orgy's going to start, we might as well take our clothes off," and with that I began to undress. (Shepard, 1972, pp. 94–95)

In a significant contribution to our field, Rowe and Winborn (1973) identified 50 articles critical of group work that appeared in professional journals and popular publications. Through careful content analysis, they were able to identify 37 different specific fears.

Most professional group practitioners are aware of, and sensitive to, a negative press that has alarmed the public to potential dangers and spend a good part of their therapeutic energies ensuring that members are not coerced into doing anything that they believe would not be in their best interests. While it is true that many subtle forms of psychological pressure arise in groups, these factors contribute significantly to the safe, accepting, and trusting climate that clients find so invigorating. In most therapeutic groups, participants are not forced to do anything against their wills except, perhaps, to confront self-deceit.

Myth 2: Groups are for sickies. Why is it that we must open our initial group sessions with an impassioned speech similar to the following?

> **Leader**: I applaud your decision to join this group. Many people don't have the courage to admit that they are less than perfect, that they could substantially profit from a group experience in which honest self-analysis is the order of the day. Although most of you don't necessarily have serious problems, you do recognize that there are ways that you can improve the quality of your life. You need not exhibit pathology, mental illness, psychotic or even neurotic symptoms to get help from a group such as this. The very fact that you're here says that you are far ahead of most people who are content with a mediocre, lackluster existence. This group is a place where, regardless of your current level of behavioral functioning, you can become more masterful in your life.

Most clients seem defensive about their membership in a therapeutic group, as if preferring to get help with their concerns means that they are not in charge of their worlds, that they are psychologically or socially dysfunctional in some pathological ways. Although we know that such an assumption is invalid, the general public image of group work nevertheless inaccurately portrays participants as being inadequate, just as, and in about the same measure, subjects who go for individual psychotherapy are generally seen to be.

Myth 3: Groups are toilets in which you spill your guts. Both Yalom (1985) and Corey and Corey (1992) are concerned with the public perception, reminiscent of the 1960s encounter movement, that groups are places where people confess their awful secrets, are ripped apart by attacks on their character, and then lose their identities by becoming part of the collective mass. Following are some typical misguided perceptions.

- "It sounds downright communistic, if you ask me."
- "I hear they use Wesson oil and roll around on rubber sheets."
- "I know one guy who told me that sometimes they become so violent they hit one another with baseball bats. I mean encounter bats. Same thing."
- "It's just a bunch of wimps who get together and cry on each other's shoulders."
- "I would never go to one of those because they make you hug each other and stuff."
- "It's like mass hypnosis or something. You know, like how David Koresh and Jim Jones made those people kill themselves."

Experienced group leaders could help to dispel these and other myths associated with our profession by becoming more literate in the field's current research. What distinguishes advanced from beginning practitioners is their ability (and inclination) to read the most up-to-date literature, interpret and analyze the data critically, and extrapolate implications for clinical practice.

In a complaint against group practitioners who remain ignorant of changes in our rapidly evolving specialty, Dies (1983) summarized the implications that could be drawn from research up to that point in time. He was especially concerned about advanced group leaders who failed to understand how to use group dynamics and process to produce individual member changes and who insisted on using individual session interventions that did not translate well to group settings.

We can take this request for better research literacy among advanced practitioners one step further and warn that we may even pose dangers to our clients if we do not attempt to conduct our own evaluation research to measure the effects of what we are doing (Bednar et al., 1987; Conyne, 1983; Rose, 1989; Stockton & Morran, 1982). In a call for more systematic efforts on the part of group leaders to evaluate the impact of selected interventions, Robison, Morran, and Hulse-Killacky (1989) offer a number of practitioner-oriented designs (ABAB, single-subject, multiple baseline) that lend themselves particularly well to the realities of group work practice. Clearly, it is up to advanced group leaders to help bridge the gap between research and practice that keeps clinicians feeling so cynical about what empirical studies can offer them.

Geis (1973) believes that the one thing missing most in purported experts in the field is the conceptual maturity to be more critical of what they read and were taught by so-called authorities. Myths can be confronted only by healthy skepticism, not "by reading others' articles on groups, writing one's own articles and then reading others' writings based partly on one's own previous writings" (Geis, 1973, p. 356). Geis continues by advising those advanced group leaders who truly wish to live up to the ideals of what it means to be an expert to consider the following:

- continuously refine and develop your own theory of action that guides behavior
- stay in supervision with someone wiser than you are
- be self-reflective in confronting your own feelings and thoughts as they impact your life and work
- be an activist in working toward advancement of knowledge

And finally, Geis admonishes that we should doubt *everything*—including what he just proffered.

These myths and fears, among scores of others, are part of the legacy with which all group leaders, regardless of their theoretical orientation, must contend.

Associated with Therapeutic Group Work Is a Specialized Technology of Intervention Strategies That Lead to Real-Life Problem Resolution. Among such strategies, to list a mere half-dozen, are:

1. Receiving feedback from members
2. Acting out conflicts in psychodramatic structures
3. Receiving support in an atmosphere of mutual trust
4. Committing oneself publicly to attain self-declared goals
5. Expressing one's feelings and thoughts more fluently and honestly
6. Producing growth through information processing, which predictably occurs as the result of interaction among diverse people in their exchange of ideas

If a Group Is Considered to Be a Collectivity, There Are Successive and Predictable Stages in Its Development. If one wishes to abstract sequential-process components that occur in every group—although the number, titles, and order are open to debate—one can easily find support in most group-work literature. Rogers (1970) talks about stages like "milling around" and the "cracking of facades." Hansen, Warner, and Smith (1980) use such terms as "conflict stage" and "cohesiveness," whereas Tuckman and Jensen (1977) and Lichtenberg and Knox (1991) prefer such expressions as "forming," "storming," "norming," and "performing." Whatever the names used, it is confusing to figure out when one process component ends and another begins: "Each stage of the group is like a wave that has momentary identity as it crests but whose beginning and demise are swallowed up in the constant movement of the sea" (Trotzer, 1977, p. 52).

Most group-work theoreticians would concede that every therapeutic group has a beginning wherein participants persist, adjust, and explore; a middle during which they develop insight into their concerns and interact intensely; and an end when they attempt to incorporate their learnings into some form of action beyond the tenure of the experience.

Participation in a Therapeutic Group Involves Personal Risks Related to Potential Life Changes.   Insofar as the overall goal for most participants in therapeutic groups is to help themselves formulate and make constructive changes in their lives, there are always risk factors involved. All clients hear echoing in their brains throughout the duration of every session: "Is this *really* a safe place? Will these people keep to themselves what I reveal to them? Can I *really* trust them? Should I tell them how I feel right now? Maybe I should just leave well enough alone; my life isn't *that* bad." Most often they tell themselves "this hurts" or "I'm scared."

Professional group leaders would agree that developing a productive therapeutic atmosphere is crucial to making the inherent risk taking in groups more safe. In large part, the intensity and depth of client disclosures, risk-taking gestures, and stated concerns are determined by the cohesion levels that have been created. More eye contact, disclosed concerns, and client improvement occur in sessions where a cohesive atmosphere is prevalent (Flowers, Booraem, & Hartman, 1981). Thus, pains are taken to enforce confidentiality and promote intimacy, trust, openness, and cohesiveness. It is only after such conditions exist that people develop a sense of safety, acceptance, and the confidence that enables them to take risks they would not ordinarily take in individual therapy.

Group Work Is Filled with Paradox.   The advanced student of group leadership is presented with a paradox. On the one hand, the culture of group work emphasizes values of cooperativeness, congeniality, authenticity, acceptance, equality, and warmth; yet on the other hand, the culture of academia in which group leadership is learned is largely competitive, evaluative, hierarchical, critical, and contrived. Our system of training negates the basic principles we are trying to teach (Goodman, 1992).

Benne (1968) and Berg and Smith (1990) mention several other paradoxes inherent in group work that highlight both its greatest strengths and its greatest weaknesses:

- Groups are among the safest and the most dangerous environments.
- Does the group exist for individuals (autonomy) or do the members exist for the group (cohesion)?

- Diversity among members allows for breadth of input and yet makes things more prone to conflict.
- If the group leader supports both members in a conflict, the fighting escalates.
- Mutual dependency is necessary before individual independence can develop.
- Boundaries within the group both encourage and limit member actions.
- Members are encouraged to become worse before they get better.

These paradoxes make it quite evident that group leadership requires more skills and training than does individual counseling. There are greater pressures on maintaining the boundaries of each member's sense of self and identity; power and authority issues are multiplied; individual needs may be in conflict with group needs; and there is a greater potential for loss of control (Gillette, 1990).

Therapeutic Groups Are Effective Means for Helping People to Change.   It goes without saying that we believe in our therapeutic service delivery in groups, even if positive results cannot clearly be supported by research findings. Outcome studies on group treatments, while by no means demonstrating overwhelming evidence that every type of group setting and leader style produces positive results, still indicate that we are not wasting our time.

There has always been some disharmony between skeptical scientists and zealous practitioners. Scientists maintain that until empirical evidence can substantiate hypotheses adherent to formal research methodology about group work, it is no more precise or valid than the practice of witch doctors. Pragmatic clinicians counter with claims that they *know* they are making a difference in their clients' lives. They see emotionally wounded and desperate people walk into their groups and, a few months later, watch them leave apparently cured of their suffering. "What other proof is necessary?" they cry.

Considering that about 85% of all research investigations on group counseling deal exclusively with outcome variables, there seems to be a consistent trend toward demonstrating effectiveness empirically (Gazda, 1989). While the debate continues as to whether group treatment—or, for that matter, *any* form of therapeutic help—is really of any lasting value, group leaders go about their work doing the best they can. An impressive body of evidence indicates that certain aspects of a group setting are much more likely to produce desired outcomes than are other settings. For instance, groups that are structured to allow for constructive, supportive feedback focusing on specific member behaviors tend to be more profitable than those that do not (Jacobs, 1974; Jacobs, Jacobs, Feldman, & Cavior, 1973; Kivlighan, 1985; Ohlsen, 1977; Stockton & Morran, 1982).

Many additional assumptions could have been added to those presented in this section. Although a majority of group leaders might agree in principle with any additional selections, some would take exception—perhaps vehemently—to any listing. Take, for example, the assumption that the leader's role is mainly that of a counseling expert and chief behavioral model but *not* that of a group member. Although I strongly support this notion of professional responsibility, there are those operating from a "group facilitator" orientation who see themselves as "player/coaches," and they would feel handicapped by the restrictions placed on their options for spontaneous involvement. And if it were more specifically mandated that, in their roles as experts, group leaders should have a defensible rationale for every instance in which they intervene, the opportunity for gut-level, spontaneous leader behavior would be further curtailed.

One of the purposes of including a list of underlying assumptions that almost every group leader could support is to concentrate on what our field has established as a foundation. The preceding statements provide just such a skeleton on which to hang the viscera that are the core of our profession, the nervous system that facilitates intercommunication between varied colleagues, and the muscular system that mobilizes synergistic progress in a group movement that is becoming more identifiable as a behavioral science field and as a discipline that is becoming more integrated and professionally accepted.

CHAPTER **2**

The Advanced Group Leader as Philosopher/Scientist

Imagine a room with a group of people seated in a circle, looking like a wagon train about to be attacked by a band of hostiles. From nowhere a deafening silence emerges, leaving only the sound of shuffling feet. You wait patiently, knowing from theory and experience that people need some quiet time in which to ponder and process previous happenings. After a few minutes you begin to notice squirming movements and other nonverbal cues that lead you to conclude, on the basis of a particular theory, that people are anxious and uncomfortable.

You decide to wait them out, let them squirm a little. After all, isn't there a theory somewhere that says group members must take responsibility for their progress? In the flash of the next few seconds you survey a list of other explanations for the collective behavior. They're resisting; they're relaxing; they're confused. Finally, in desperation, you throw theory to the wind and ask someone what is going on.

"Regina, I notice that everyone seems a bit quiet. Do you have an explanation?"

"Well," Regina replies, "I can't speak for anyone else," (you feel proud— she remembers the importance of speaking only for herself) "but I don't have anything to say right now."

There's the explanation. They're waiting for some direction.

No one can say you, as this group's leader, did not operate from a fairly organized set of propositions about the nature of the world. Indeed, within this brief span of time, theories of metaphysics, logical relationships, ethics, human behavior, motivation, learning, and development all came into play.

In the words of Argyris and Schon (1974, p. 29), a theory of action was applied, wherein "In situation S, if you intend consequence C, do A, given assumptions $a_1 \ldots a_n$." In creating the major premises and minor concepts that guide the choice of interventions, the practitioner functioned as a philosopher. By making observations, drawing inferences, formulating hypotheses, predicting outcomes, testing assumptions, and evaluating results, the practitioner functioned as a scientist. In fact, all effective group leaders, transcending their self-categorizations, tend to operate as pragmatists. Whatever we do that produces desirable results, we will tend to do again in similar circumstances. If a procedure doesn't work, even though a theory says that it is supposed to, we abandon it or (more likely) make it work in the future by adapting it to our unique situation.

Philosophy, Theory, and Action

A group leader never operates in a vacuum. Somewhere deep within the smoky recesses of the brain, motives are formulated, underlying attitudes and values are constructed, interpretations of the world are made, and a philosophy is articulated in the hope of answering life's ultimate questions. The philosopher/scientist critically explores puzzling questions to make sense of confusion and to guide professional behavior (Russell, 1961). ''Philosophers desire ultimately to have an overall view of the world so that every event can be explained in terms of general principles and the occurrence of other events'' (Glossop, 1974, p. 5). The philosophy guiding therapeutic practitioners is thus responsible for their unique set of beliefs about the world, about clients, and about how clients can change in a world of groups.

The theoretical preferences of group leaders are chosen or created on the basis of consistency between personal philosophy and primary postulates of a theory of action. If a group leader believes in the intrinsic healing powers of the human system, prefers to view the environment as an extension of each individual, and sees client concerns as manifestations of a sick soul, it is likely that a theory will be adopted that is compatible with these personal convictions.

Similarly, specific therapeutic interventions will sprout from one's theoretical orientation, just as theory will arise from one's underlying philosophies regarding the mechanisms of the universe. The group leader's actions, including *any* intervention, from a complex psychodramatic scenario to a simple nod, are direct extensions of a systematic philosophy known as the *scientific method*, wherein: (1) observations are made of situation-specific behaviors, (2) operating assumptions are formulated regarding actions taken, (3) problems are clearly identified and related hypotheses stated, (4) possible solutions that are likely to alleviate the problems that are generated, (5) probable consequences are deduced and desired outcomes predicted, (6) some action is taken, and (7) results are evaluated in the light of preferred outcomes. There is, of course, an obvious similarity between this systematic application of philosophy/science to the method that all group

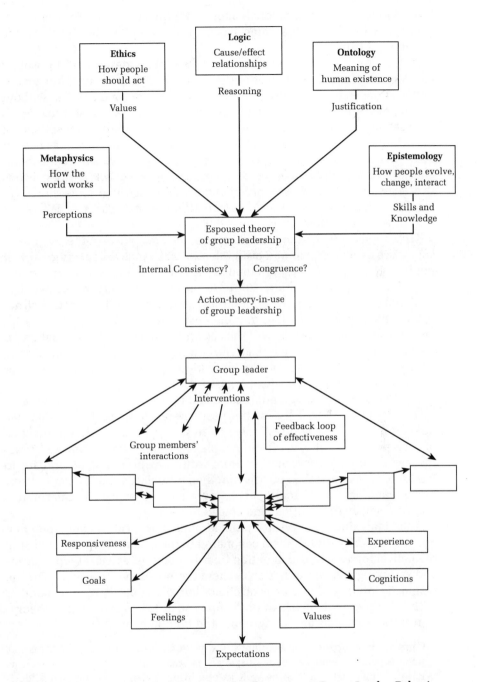

Figure 2-1 Theoretical and Philosophical Influences on Group Leader Behavior

leaders follow. Reichian, rational-emotive, Rolfing, reality, or Rogerian practitioners will all use the same basic format even if their philosophic preferences differ radically.

In 1911, Ambrose Bierce (1940, p. 99) facetiously described philosophy as "A route of many roads leading from nowhere to nothing," but practitioners, from architects to group leaders, would be rendered helpless without it. We practitioners are more than applied engineers; we must think. More than gather data, we must integrate it. More than note observations, we must make inductive generalizations. We must contemplate the meanings behind what we do, reflect on our actions in retrospect, and from such conceptual analyses a philosophy is born, an internally consistent set of propositions that leads to an *espoused theory of action*. This theory of professional intervention includes both a body of scientific postulates as well as a series of philosophic criticisms (Bolan, 1980).

The espoused theory, to be distinguished from an *action-theory-in-use*, comprises the knowledge and overt intentions to which the practitioner will publicly claim allegiance, even though the latter will more accurately guide behavior (Argyris & Schon, 1974). A profession's body of knowledge, methods of practice, and code of ethics, as well as such normative structures as the law, accreditation, training, institutional policies, colleague approval, and situational cues, will thus be arranged by each individual group leader into a fairly well-organized philosophy, which in turn leads first to an espoused theory and later to an action-theory-in-use that will steer specific professional episodes (Argyris, 1976; Bolan, 1980).

The fields of psychology, education, and medicine have been dominated by empirical epistemology for the past several decades. Before that, we pondered metaphysical questions. Just in the past century, in the practice of therapy, widely divergent philosophical trends have influenced practitioner action. We have moved from intuitionism and structuralism to functionalism and logical positivism, then to subjectivism, existentialism, phenomenology, and finally to cognitivism, behaviorism, interpretive dialecticism, hermeneutics, and integrationism.

After analyzing these philosophical trends, Royce (1975) concluded that only *constructive dialecticism* can maintain the tension between opposing theoretical forces while elaborating their limitations, assets, and paradoxes and resolving the contradictions. There are no simple solutions. For the pragmatic group leader there is no choice but to become thoroughly familiar with the different branches of philosophy so as to create an action-theory-in-use that is consistent, congruent, and comprehensive.

> Once we have opened the Pandora's box of "total man," that is, seeing man as unconscious as well as conscious, man as irrational and emotive as well as rational, man as cognitive as well as conditionable, man as motivated, curious, creative, and contemplative, and man's "being" as well as his "doing"—once we go beyond simplistic conceptions of "behaving" to the complexities of

"mind"—it seems ridiculously obvious that we will be forced into more sophisticated philosophic-conceptual analyses of what we are doing and why. (Royce, 1975, p. 2)

Metaphysics

What constitutes science and what is more legitimately a part of philosophy is a muddled distinction that was never even considered until the mid-19th century. Plato, Archimedes, Newton, and Harvey were grouped as philosophers. America's first psychologist, William James, taught in a department of philosophy. Even laboratory implements like Bunsen burners were called "philosophical instruments." With the publication of Kant's *Critique of Pure Reason* (1781), however, the stage was set for a parting of philosophy and science, a separation that has only become reconciled through the disciplinary collaborations so necessary to our field. The therapist today must garner knowledge from any conceivable source—from textbooks and from the streets—to create a working model of how the world works, a model that can be readily explained to clients in their search for metaphysical answers.

To clients who ask "Why?" the group leader must respond as a philosopher, helping the seeker find an approximation of personal truth. Whereas science tests hypotheses that can be confirmed on the basis of experimentation, philosophy works with untestable hypotheses, those that cannot be verified even though they have universal interest. The group leader is a composite of both worlds. The group therapist attempts to instruct through challenge, discourse, philosophic inquiry, and scientific hypothesis testing. That scientific training is necessary for the effective functioning of group leaders is no great surprise. Medical, psychological, and social work programs are top-heavy with course work of a scientific nature—physiology, statistics, research, social and physical science. Yet the therapist also applies every distinct branch of philosophy to the practice of group work.

Metaphysics attempts to describe the universal features of reality. In the process of change, such as the dissolution of a marriage, do the same laws apply as in the physical change of a liquid to a gas? Are people's lives predetermined with the same inevitability that causes the earth to rotate in regular cycles? Is the process by which a person becomes depressed the same process that elicits anger? In such speculations, the group leader attempts to construct a comprehensive view of the world that will allow for application in explaining any single phenomenon. Further, group members are helped to develop personal schemata of metaphysics when they are challenged to define reality, fabricate a meaning for their actions, or discern the essence of their lives.

One branch of metaphysics, *ontology*, is particularly useful for group members struggling to understand themselves. To understand our Being, our essence, and to give meaning to our existence is the legitimate scope of ontology. Whereas Descartes found his thoughts to be proof of his existence, contemporary philosophers such as Gabriel Marcel, Jean-Paul Sartre, Karl Jaspers, and Martin Heidegger have looked deeper into the mysteries of what it means to Be, to exist. "Ontology seeks to discover the basic structures of existence—the structures which are given to everyone at every moment" (May, 1969, p. 112). Naturally, much of what constitutes psychotherapy is ontological in nature—helping clients find underlying meaning in their sometimes empty lives.

Ethics

One of the most enduring branches of philosophy, ethics has become a phenomenal preoccupation of group leaders in deciding how we ought to act. Ethical issues in group work are more complex than they are in individual therapy. In group work, for example, confidentiality is virtually unenforceable. Verbal abuse of others is more likely to occur since the therapist has less control over proceedings. With little legislative regulation, ambiguous laws, watered-down ethical codes, and greater risks, group leaders have no choice but to become ethical philosophers.

What should we do when we discover a colleague having sex with his or her clients? How should we handle coercion from a supervisor demanding to know the content of group sessions? What should we do if our negligent actions result in substantial damage to group members? These are the larger ethical issues, but there are also small voices nagging:

> "Was my last self-disclosure really necessary, or was I just trying to impress them with my experience?"
> "Was it fair for me to try out this new technique in the group before I tested it in a safer situation?"
> "Is it allright for me to lie a little, exaggerating the services I can provide but knowing that I'm being helpful by setting up favorable expectations?"
> "Am I being negligent by not following up on my group members' reentry problems?"
> "Am I seeing these clients longer than is absolutely necessary because I need the income?"

Group leaders pondering such issues are in good company. To whom we are ultimately responsible for our actions has preoccupied philosophers from Plato and Epictetus to Hobbes, Hegel, and Mill. Do we answer primarily to our clients, to the parents of the young, to our supervisor, to the Constitution, to the Ten Commandments, to God, or to ourselves? Questions of moral obligation, values, responsibility, duty, conscience, rights, good and bad, and right and wrong plague the group leader at every turn. The methodology of ethical inquiry requires the use of both philosophical and scientific principles to produce explicit imperatives for action.

For example, in making ethical decisions, group leaders must apply both philosophical inquiry and scientific methodology by addressing questions such as the following.

What Ought I to Do?

Philosophical Inquiry	Scientific Inquiry
What values do I wish my clients to learn?	What verifiable hypotheses are plausible?
What moral propositions do I know to be true?	How may they be tested experimentally?
What obligations do I have for the welfare of my clients?	What predicted outcomes are likely given certain actions?

Logic

In the systematic process of problem solving, in the diagnosis of client symptoms, in making ethical decisions, or in effectively coordinating group behavior, the branch of philosophy known as *logic* comes into play. Since most psychopathologies and self-defeating behaviors involve disorders in reasoning, much of what group leaders do constitutes the application of deductive and inductive logic—the former conclusions based on valid arguments, the latter conclusions established by degrees of probability.

Logical analysis is less concerned with matter than with the form it takes. It makes not the slightest difference whether a group member wishes to work on controlling temper tantrums or losing weight; similar logical processes of change are involved in developing impulse control. The logical flaws in the client's reasoning are identical: "Because I have acted this way before, I must continue to act that way in the future."

The Aristotelian syllogism becomes the cornerstone for rebuilding shaky logical foundations. Although there is little that can actually be proved within the ambiguous nature of group work, therapists nevertheless wish to formulate operating assumptions that can withstand critical scrutiny. Arguments must be not only convincing in their delivery but also sound in their underlying propositions and concepts. The group leader must often systematically refute invalid client premises, such as "If I open up in this group, I will only get hurt as I have every other time before" and counter with inductive explanations that have a greater probability of being true.

"First, you confuse terms and definitions. You have never actually opened up before, since engaging in small talk about how much money you make doesn't exactly involve being open. From observing your behavior in this group, I believe that you misinterpret 'openness' to mean spilling all your darkest secrets at once. Also, the people you have previously chosen to be open with, such as strange people in bars, do not qualify as being potentially responsive candidates.

"Second, you imply that there is a causal relationship between self-disclosure and vulnerability, which is only true in circumstances of obvious inequality. In this group situation, where everyone is open, there is actually a clearer relationship between disclosure and intimacy. The more open you become, the more likely others will gravitate toward you.

"Third, you assume that you can be hurt by other group members. Aside from any physical interaction, which is not permitted, it is impossible for anyone to wound you psychologically unless you allow it. In fact, you can't 'get hurt,' although you may certainly decide to 'hurt yourself' after you're done hearing my little speech.

"Finally, you make a value judgment that being open, vulnerable, hurt, and intimate are signs of weakness, which they are in your cutthroat business world of high finance. But those assumptions are not necessarily generalizable to this situation, in which the rules and goals are quite different."

Epistemology

The nature and limits of knowledge and belief are part of *epistemology*, the branch of philosophy concerned with inferring truth. Given the often radical discrepancies between clients' experience and reality, the epistemological group leader has much work to do in the role of passionate truth seeker.

In an autobiographical anecdote, Bertrand Russell describes how he first became infatuated with philosophy at age 11. Tired of tenuous truths, tentative discussions, and inconsistent knowledge, young Russell discovered geometry because someone told him it could prove things. Pure mathematics is perhaps the only discipline in which an epistemologist may feel comfortable. Russell therefore begged his brother to teach him geometry so that he might experience the joys of true knowledge.

> My brother began at the beginning with the definitions. These I accepted readily enough. But he came next to the axioms. "These," he said, "can't be proved, but they have to be assumed before the rest can be proved." At these words my hopes crumbled. I had thought it would be wonderful to find something that one could *prove*, and then it turned out that this could only be done by means of assumptions of which there was no proof. I looked at my brother with a sort of indignation and said: "But why should I admit these things if they can't be proved?" He replied: "Well, if you won't, we can't go on." (Russell, 1961, pp. 56–57)

Each branch of philosophy, each component of the critical thinking process, acts as a catalyst for group leader behavior. If the world is believed to be essentially a safe place, clients will be encouraged to venture forth and experimentally test new behaviors that may be risky. If guilt is seen as a useless, destructive emotion, efforts will be made to wipe it out. If the principal purpose in life is to live each moment to its fullest potential, group members will be taught to appreciate the fragrance of a thorny bush. If it is believed that human emotional suffering is the result of unresolved, unconscious conflicts of the past, interventions will be designed to facilitate awareness of these disguised maladies. In each case, a specific philosophic assumption guides the practitioner's actions.

Unfortunately, philosophy and theory are as often mutated to limit effective behavior as they are used to enhance productivity. When philosophy becomes rigid, stagnant, and dogmatic, it ceases to function as an aid to critical thinking and acts as a blocking force toward further development.

Tenuous Truths

Philosophy is intended to help group leaders make sense of the world. It should be a guide for producing change and a structural basis for measuring progress (Hansen, Warner, & Smith, 1980). It aids in prediction by providing a schematic representation of relevant information (Shertzer & Stone, 1980). Group work philosophy and theory should be a blueprint (without all the lines penciled in) for any action the leader takes. Notions about how the world works, what is good for clients, and how best to help clients find what is good for them are all part of this proposed theory (Geis, 1973). A conception of how people learn, how their personalities are constructed, how they develop, what obstructs growth, and how groups work are also part of any useful theory.

Yet, in the face of the human need to wipe out ambiguity and uncertainty, to replace the unknown with delusional security, we buzz around like worker bees with a single motive in life: to make sense of the things around us. The 3-year-old child has a burning curiosity to know why the moon is following her. We only wish to understand why people do what they do.

We still know very little about why people act the way they do in therapeutic groups, and what we do know and understand is quite tenuous. In their comprehensive review of studies on the subject, Kaul and Bednar (1986, p. 62) conclude "The accumulated evidence suggests that group treatments have been shown to be effective, at least to some degree under some conditions which are, unfortunately, basically unknown." They further lament that whereas there have been hundreds, if not thousands, of studies demonstrating that group work is helpful, we still know very little about which specific process elements or conditions of group composition, leadership, theoretical orientation, or client characteristics are most associated with constructive client changes.

The logical question, then, is "What truths do we accept today as part of group counseling theory when in just a few years we will look back and laugh at our primitive efforts?" It wasn't so long ago, after all, that our ancestors in group therapy conducted stake-burnings and bloodlettings as the treatments of choice for the mentally afflicted. One popular group treatment of its time, trial by water, involved throwing "clients" into a deep lake with their hands and feet bound. The theory suggested that persons who sank and drowned must have been innocent of any emotional problems, while those who floated were to be burned at the stake as witches. A hundred years from now, what will they say about "active listening?"

The Wholey Wars

For beginning group leaders, the concepts of *philosophy* and *theory* had a fairly narrow personal meaning. Some time after the practicum started but before it was over, students were expected to fully articulate their theory of choice. The most intelligent decision under the circumstances was to select an existing theory, *any* theory, although it was advantageous to select the one the instructor followed. This shotgun wedding between therapist and theory continues to be a monogamous relationship long after the practicum ends; and it really *does* feel as if one is cheating by sampling delicious fruits of another point of view.

At a more advanced level, flexibility is the order of the day. Rigidly following the tenets of a particular theory can eventually become as much a handicap as an aid. The theory becomes a closed system that forces conformity and compliance. As is characteristic of perceptual input systems in human beings (group leaders included), we look for things that confirm what we already know, ignore things that contradict our beliefs, selectively interpret the world to fit our expectations, and vehemently refute those things that jeopardize the stability of our theory.

Freud set the precedent. Whenever his disciples became too feisty, independent, or critical (as did Jung, Adler, and Rank), he would throw them out of his group. He also set up a brilliant organizational defense mechanism in claiming that, to criticize psychoanalysis legitimately, one had first to undergo the experience. If on completing the analysis the critic persisted in his attacks, the psychoanalysis obviously had been unsuccessful.

It has often been observed that Sigmund Freud, Carl Rogers, Albert Ellis, Fritz Perls, Eric Berne, and the rest of the field's leaders were all effective clinicians. Each theory that its respective high priest represents has an impressive body of evidence demonstrating that it is the true heir to the throne of Truth. In fact, however, *all* theories seem to work in some situations, depending on who is practicing them. Each has a proven utility in helping people, even though radical divergencies in philosophy, therapist role, techniques, and other factors attest to their differences. Thus, that Jungian patients dream in Jungian symbols, that Freudian patients all seem to have transference/oedipal/defense mechanism problems, and that Gestalt patients all have fragmented souls speaks more for the effective indoctrination of the jargon systems than as actual proofs that these concepts are universally true.

The vast majority of clinicians, approaching 75% of mental health professionals across four different disciplines, describe themselves as eclectic in their orientation (Jensen, Bergin, & Greaves, 1990). This integrative movement will continue to grow, especially in group modalities, for a number of reasons. First, research investigations are demonstrating the superiority of situation-specific client treatments that are individually designed over those that are universally and invariably applied.

Second, the evolving maturity of our profession is moving away from provincial bickering and more toward a direction of reconciliation and integration of theory. Group work is, by its very nature, an interdisciplinary effort. The movement was influenced, in part, by contributions in psychiatry, psychology, and social work; by J. L. Moreno and psychodrama; by the child guidance movement originating with Adler and Dreikurs; by the National Training Laboratory; and by the self-help and Human Potential Movements (Gazda, 1989).

Almost all group leaders now employ the techniques of cognitive, behavioral, gestalt, and other theories. The boundaries between these approaches are becoming blurred. Dies (1992) predicts that the future of group work will be characterized by treatments that are more focused toward specific populations, and they will be differentially structured to include specific ingredients for particular client issues. Further, there will be even greater integration of diverse treatment models (psychodynamics and psychopharmacology or process and goal-oriented approaches) into combined methodologies.

Advanced group leaders may be distinguished from their less experienced colleagues by what they know, the therapeutic options available to them, and the related skill with which they implement interventions; however, experienced leaders are almost as confused as beginners when it comes to defining their theoretical allegiances.

In celebrating the 50th anniversary of the American Group Psychotherapy Association, Dies (1992) classified the principal models of leadership currently in practice by surveying senior members of the profession. Of the 111 prominent practitioners who responded to the questionnaire, the majority described themselves as eclectic or stated that they employed multiple treatment models. This is consistent with similar studies that have been completed over the years with regard to individual treatments. Of those affiliated with a single orientation, respondents were divided primarily between psychoanalytic, systemic, and gestalt approaches. In the second tier of popularity, interactional and cognitive/behavioral models were used. Last, and to a lesser extent, existential/humanistic and psychodrama were mentioned.

These theoretical models are hardly discrete; there was even considerable confusion among these veterans as to the purity of each model. For example, whereas there was a fairly consistent belief that Irwin Yalom is a major player in the group work scene (he was mentioned most often by the experienced group leaders as influential), he was described as being a member of the existential school by some, of the interpersonal model by others, and even of the psychodynamic or "group as a whole" approach by others.

The primary value of Dies's study is not in providing definitive categories of how advanced group leaders practice but rather in highlighting issues that most clinicians agree are important. Almost every one of these senior practitioners, for example, identified countertransference and transference issues, as well as here-and-now interactions, as significant factors to be considered. Many of these consensual variables will be discussed in greater detail in the next chapter.

A third factor contributing to integration is pressure from the legislature, public, media, and prospective clientele demanding that we practitioners get our acts together and agree on a set of consistent therapeutic principles that operate universally. It is unseemly—not to mention embarrassing—for us to be arguing in public about whether groups should be cognitively or affectively oriented, insight or action driven, client or leader directed; it has been perfectly obvious for quite some time that these are more parts of a continuum than mutually exclusive polarities. In his comparative investigation of the six major systems of group leadership, Long (1988) concentrated on a number of ways in which group leaders differ in their approaches, focusing on such things as problem solving or personality change, manifest or latent meaning in client communication, and the past versus the present. Nevertheless, it *is* possible to combine elements of many approaches, depending on client needs, leader preferences, and agency policies.

Clearly, the field is evolving toward being more pluralistic, integrative, and pragmatic in its approaches (Omer & London, 1988). Although there is some disagreement among the ranks as to the most appropriate label for these efforts—whether preference is given to eclecticism (Lazarus, 1986), (Millon, 1988; Norcross & Napolitano, 1986) or pragmatism (Kottler, 1983)—the intention is abundantly clear: let's find out what we can all agree on in terms of what effective practitioners should know, should sense, should think, and can do; what they understand, and what they are like as people; and then let's work toward teaching one another to do this better.

Pragmatism

The philosophy of pragmatism is a distinctively American invention credited to physicist, logician, and historian Charles Peirce (1839–1914). Stressing the importance of logical inference in dealing with contemporary problems, Peirce created the Metaphysical Club, a diverse group of Harvard thinkers, to examine critically such significant unresolved issues as Darwin's (then novel) theories of evolution. Chauncey Wright, William James, John Fiske, Oliver Wendell Holmes, and John Dewey, among the greatest minds of their era, coordinated their efforts to build a new practical philosophy.

In this new philosophy, all courses of action were to be examined in terms of their likely consequences. According to James, the pragmatist "turns away from abstraction and insufficiency, from verbal solutions, from bad a priori reasons, from fixed principles, closed systems, and pretended absolutes and origins. He turns toward concreteness and adequacy, toward facts, toward action and toward power" (James, 1907). Pragmatism, then, is an active rather than a contemplative philosophy. It deals with facts and their outcomes. It is concerned with observable consequences of human action. The sum of all possible consequences constitutes the action's meaning.

I. S. Cooper, in his personal account of life as an experimental neurosurgeon, graphically demonstrates the pragmatic spirit as applied to medicine. While demonstrating his new technique of chemopallidectomy for treating the symptoms of Parkinson's Disease, he was queried by an eminent colleague about exactly where in the brain he inserted his surgical probe. X rays were taken to observe the results. Cooper, a brash youth who was revolutionizing the field of neurosurgery with his flexible disregard for the accepted theories of his day, responded with the basic guiding principle of his distinguished career.

> It doesn't really make any difference, . . . his tremor is gone. The rigidity too. He can move his arm and leg. The patient can speak and is unharmed. The X ray was a means—not an end. If we don't find out for a hundred years where the tip of the probe is, what difference will it make? Eventually we will know. (Cooper, 1981, p. 91)

As it happened, Cooper was off by a few centimeters in his theory, even though the execution of his technique was stunningly effective.

> We are not operating to produce an X ray, but to produce a clinically rewarding result. When I interpreted the X ray erroneously, it was a stupid mistake. Fortunately, I learned a great deal from this and no one was harmed. Happily, that day in December of 1953 was really the birthday of thalamic surgery for movement disorders. (Cooper, 1981, pp. 95–96)

Similarly, group leaders are not operating to produce an X ray or an elegant theory "but to produce a clinically rewarding result." It would seem that all great discoveries were made by pragmatic scientists who were bound by neither their existing theories nor their limited visions but who struggled to combine compatible elements into novel procedures. The basic tenets of a pragmatic philosophy are already a part of the methodology of most group leaders. The logical reasoning that allows a practitioner to consider several possible courses of action, systematically projecting likely outcomes, rejecting unsuitable alternatives, and finally electing the intervention most likely to produce desirable consequences is one such example.

Pragmatism, however, is *not* synonymous with eclecticism, which focuses on choosing the best technique from diverse sources and systems (Dimond, Havens, & Jones, 1978). An underlying philosophy becomes a hindrance to such a style because the emphasis is solely on collecting problem-solving techniques without regard to their origins. The eclectic approach has sometimes been criticized as being evasive, wishy-washy, and as operating from a philosophic desert with little theoretical grounding.

Indeed, there are problems in any field for a professional who has memorized a lot of gimmicks and techniques to solve problems but who doesn't understand how conflicts arise or the theory behind making systematic change efforts. And so every counselor and therapist, regardless of what theoretical label is used for purposes of simple classification, has a uniquely personal idea of how people develop emotional/behavioral problems and how they are best treated.

Theories are not to be casually discarded as obstacles to dynamic action. The only theory that restricts freedom is the one invented by someone else and swallowed before it was cleaned, deboned, and had simmered a bit. While the eclectic shuns theory, the pragmatist uses it in creatively applied ways: "Pragmatism unstiffens all our theories, limbers them up, and sets each one at work" (James, 1907, p. 46).

Pragmatism and Group Work

Pragmatism is the philosophy that undergirds any integrative synthesis. One of the major disadvantages of any eclectic system is its emphasis on technical rather than on theoretical aspects of practice; its focus on divergences rather than convergences; its language of "collecting" rather than "blending," "selecting" as opposed to "synthesizing," and "applying" rather than "unifying" the parts (Norcross & Glencavage, 1989).

An eclectic group leader armed with a collection of techniques but no unifying theory of practice can be a dangerous professional indeed. Such a clinician would intervene but would be unable to articulate what he or she is doing and, more importantly, *why* a particular technique was selected. Pragmatism encourages theoreticians and practitioners alike to consider borrowing concepts from many different approaches and synthesizing them into useful models of practice that guide professional decisions and interventions.

All researchers, theoreticians, and practitioners would agree that therapeutic groups progress through a series of stages, even if there is considerable disagreement as to how many stages there are and what they should be called. Some examples of this diversity are shown in Table 2-1.

There have been a number of attempts to synthesize the various stage theories into a coherent, integrated, developmental model (Corey & Corey, 1992; Gazda, 1989; McCollom, 1990; Rose, 1989; Yalom, 1985). Certainly, we can agree that there is more than just a beginning, a middle, and an end. It is not only optional but obligatory for advanced group leaders to create for themselves conceptual models of what they predict will unfold and how they intend to help that process along. Historically, group work

Table 2-1 Group stage theories

Bennis & Shepard (1974)	Cohen & Smith (1976)	Tuckman & Jensen (1977)	Beck, Dugo, Eng, Lewis, & Peters (1983)	Rose (1989)
Dependence/Flight	Acquaintance	Forming	Initial assessment	Orientation
Counterdependence	Goal Ambiguity	Storming	Group identity	Preliminary work
Resolution/Catharsis	Group transference	Norming	Cooperative work	Conflict
Enchantment	Defensiveness	Performing	Cohesion	Resolution
Disenchantment	Reality strengthening	Adjourning	Intimacy	Secondary work
Consensual Validation	Norm crystallization		Commitment	Termination
	Distributive control		Self-confrontation	
	Experimentation		Review	
	Group potency		Separation	
	Termination			

arose from the need to provide therapeutic learning experiences that closely parallel experiences in the real world. As such, experimentation, creative innovation, and the scientific application of practical intervention strategies have always lent themselves particularly well to group settings. Helping structures that have been traditionally designed and restricted to a solo instructional system are becoming increasingly flexible in their application to groups as well.

A few years ago, for example, it was inconceivable that the treatment of sexual dysfunctions could ever have been done in groups. Because clients experience such embarrassment discussing their sexual problems and because the therapy takes a fairly individualized, prescriptive form, it was never imagined that a group could be an appropriate place for treatment. But resourceful and pragmatic practitioner/researchers have been particularly flexible in adapting sex-therapy strategies to the group treatment of premature ejaculation (Kaplan, Kohl, Pomeroy, Offit, & Hogan, 1978) and orgasmic dysfunctions (Schneidman & McGuire, 1978). Similarly, behavioral science literature is making increasing reference to the use of groups with a wide variety of purposes, goals, and populations. The group leader unrestricted by the bounds of a parent discipline, or even by the walls of an office, ventures out into the world prepared to help its inhabitants on their own territory.

There is great historical precedent for the marriage between the philosophy of pragmatism and the practice of group work. Kurt Lewin, J. L. Moreno, and many of the founding parents of the group movement were incredibly flexible and open in their orientations. Counselors and therapists operating on the front lines know that the cardinal rule in running any group is to come armed with an agenda for action but prepared to throw it out if circumstances change. There are too many unpredictable variables and individual needs to have a plan for The Group. You can pay attention to what has been going on—the dynamics and interaction. You can do your homework and be prepared, anticipate potential problems, develop strategies for handling them, rehearse your opening lines, and then suddenly—before there is a chance to pick up where you left off last week or to get a progress report from clients—a crisis arises that needs immediate attention. So much for your agenda.

Perhaps the luxury of operating from a closed system that restricts available choices and interprets all behavior in terms of a unique jargon is not affordable when many people are being helped at the same time. Perhaps the theories of group treatment are not yet as elegant as their individual cousins. Whatever the reason, group leaders must be flexible and open in their approach, aware of subtle changes and responsive to them.

What if, as scientist/practitioners, we could formulate a philosophy that can change to fit the requirements of the job?

Basic Premises of a Pragmatic Approach

There Is a Distinction between Absolute Truth and Relative Truth.   Absolute truth is an ideal to be pursued, a life goal that can never be reached. All theory is regarded as tenuous; human constructions are subject to constant revision in light of further data. The only truth we may be absolutely certain about is the inevitability of death. Nevertheless, a pragmatic group leader would find it crippling to make sweeping generalizations about human behavior. Although it may be relatively true that *some* people's problems stem from a faulty self-concept or that *some* people suffer from irrational beliefs whereas *other* people are victims of environmental manipulations, it would be a gross oversimplification of reality to believe that any single factor is the absolute contributor.

Are there any absolute truths about conducting therapeutic groups? One basic rule that might come to mind is that nonverbal attending behaviors are crucial to developing rapport, thus creating the cardinal maxim for practice: always maintain eye contact with group members. However, this principle of interpersonal communication could conceivably be reversed for maximum therapeutic benefit. A group leader may deliberately *avoid* eye contact as a way to extinguish approval seeking in a particular group member. Even the most basic so-called universal truths of the profession—such directives as "never give advice"—are relative to time, place, and circumstance. They are no more static than the rest of Dr. Einstein's universe.

Pragmatism Is Concerned Only with Useful Knowledge That Can Be Applied Directly to Practical Situations.   Theorizing about physiological indices of stress may be a fascinating study of the human condition, but unless the group leader can put such information to clinical use, its functional utility is worthless.

Following hours of group observation and equipped with the results of research available on the subject, the astute pragmatist can distill useful information to aid his or her work. Diagnostically, the therapist could note frequency of eyeblinks as a measure of member anxiety (Stern, Bremer, & McClure, 1974) or use eye-movement patterns to determine whether a client would respond better to visual, kinesthetic, or auditory imagery (Bandler & Grinder, 1979). The group leader who systematically collects useful data and stores it for later application would continuously monitor all perceptual input systems, asking the crucial question "How can I use this?"

Books, films, television, parties, any possible source of information about how people function in groups is a legitimate building block in the pragmatic approach. All personal experiences are valid shapers of professional effectiveness, especially in psychological helpers. The group leader who can draw on past associations of feeling shy and socially inept will find such empathic experiences valuable in helping clients open up in groups. The group leader who has made a systematic study of interpersonal approach patterns in shopping malls can apply such data toward promoting group intimacy more effectively. All group leaders could profit from a more systematic application of pragmatic philosophy, studying the world to find what it can teach.

Pragmatism Is an Empirically Based Philosophy, Steeped in the Scientific Method.   Knowing that there is a statistical difference in trust dimensions (as measured by frequency of "I feel" statements) between groups that received a particular treatment and groups that didn't is a wonderful piece of news, particularly if you need significant results to get a dissertation completed or an article published. But such studies are of minimal value to the group leader confronted by the angry stares of ten skeptics who believe that confidentiality is hogwash.

The philosopher/scientist is interested in useful research that allows him or her to make accurate predictions about the likely consequences of any action. The group leader is also interested in what can safely, reliably, and effectively be used to help a client reach a specific goal or to create a special climate in a given group. One way to accomplish those ends is to become familiar with what tends to work with most people in similar situations. Large-sample research is an excellent source of data for such purposes. But another way of reaching situation-specific goals is to collect data for that given set of circumstances, predict the desired outcomes, create an intervention that is most likely to produce desired results, implement the strategy, and assess its impact.

This systematic study of micro- rather than macrochange is the foundation for intensive design research. It is ideally suited for the pragmatist in that the best features of humanism and behaviorism are melded into a form of practical experimentation. The strategy is distinctly behavioristic in flavor with its strong emphasis on specificity, observability, and measurability; yet it is also solidly humanistic because of its in-depth study of a single case. Graphs, anecdotal material, or changes in the slope or acceleration of plotted lines instead of parametric statistics are relied on in the analysis.

Ironically, single-subject design research originated in B. F. Skinner's experimental assessments of intervention effects (Frey, 1978). Although it is a primary tool of the behaviorist interested in measuring change over time, it is the antithesis of what has become traditional, well-controlled, group-based research. Instead of large random samples comparing their behavior with the behavior of those who have received no treatment and then making inferences to a single case, intensive research studies an N of 1 and makes inferences to people in general.

The pragmatic group leader may also structure important studies in his or her own backyard. The most significant research is that which has the most impact. If a clinician reads about an experimental study that produced relevant, useful data, the best possible way to put the results to work is to replicate the study as intensive design research with his or her own groups. Similarly, case study investigations become the pilot programs for more massive research efforts at a later date.

Pragmatism Is Above All Pluralistic in Its Orientation.   "American pragmatism has fostered an *empirical* respect for the complexity of existence requiring a *plurality* of concepts to do justice to the diverse problems of mankind in its evolutionary struggles" (Wiener, 1949, p. 191). Critical common sense is used as a basis for operational, piecemeal analysis of how things and people work. The method is adapted to the subject matter until tests of verifiability can determine the meaning of an idea.

The use of any technique is sanctioned, regardless of its theoretical origins, but within the context of an articulated philosophical rationale that is flexible, encompassing, useful, and personally designed. Milton Erikson, the virtuoso therapist and hyponotist, believed passionately in the pragmatic approach.

> You need to extract from the various techniques the particular elements that allow you to express yourself as a personality. The next most important thing about a technique is your awareness of the fact that every patient who comes to you represents a different personality, a different attitude, a different background of experience. Your approach to him must be in terms of him as a person with a particular frame of reference for that day and the immediate situation. (Haley, 1968, p. 530)

For one particular group situation, a soft manner, quiet voice, low-key leader role, and lots of reflection might produce the most responsive involvement. For the same clients at another time (or a completely different group composition), the most advantageous strategy might be the use of direct confrontation, dramatic role plays, an authoritarian leader role, and behavior modification technology.

The Group Leader Formulates a Defensible Rationale for Every Intervention Used.   Since the goal of therapeutic groups is to help clients make constructive changes in their lives, therapists are interested in developing reliable tools for facilitating such progress. The key to any systematic attempt at group leadership is the consistent replicability of the tools that are used.

Just prior to any therapeutic action—whether an attempt to focus counseling content, to disperse conflict, to offer support, or to facilitate insight—the group leader would internally ask three questions: "What exactly appears to be happening?" "What specifically do I wish to accomplish?" "How will the intervention I'm about to use meet my desired goals?" If the answers are abstract, vague, or reduced to elusive intuitions, the group leader will closely scrutinize personal motives. Preferably, such an assessment is done as the process occurs; more likely it will be done during the convenience of an after-group "autopsy."

Such a detailed analysis of so-called gut realities will help make them more precisely implemented at future times but will also help stifle leader self-indulgence. Before using self -disclosure to build trust or model openness, for instance, the leader can ask himself or herself: "Am I doing this to help a group member or to make myself look good? Am I telling this anecdote to illustrate a specific point (if so, which one?) or to entertain myself? Am I confronting this client because he is genuinely disruptive to the group process or because he irritates me?"

In addition to censoring inappropriate verbalizations, defining the rationale for action allows the leader to accumulate a wider choice of strategies by filing away for retrieval those that have consistently worked before in similar circumstances. It also allows the practitioner to reveal the mechanisms by which change occurs in the group. Since group members often function as assistant leaders and are also committed to learning how therapy works so that they can change themselves in the future without having to return to the group, it is advantageous to share with them the reasoning behind a mysterious action.

If the group leader were spontaneously to stand up and dance around the circle of chairs, tapping each person on the shoulder while offering feedback, it would probably be helpful to share the rationale for doing so: "I am attempting to breathe some life into this group. People are acting bored and lazy. By varying my vocal pitch and nonverbal movements, I immediately captured your attention. Notice that you are all sitting up straight now with animated expressions on your faces."

The Pragmatist Is Versed in an Interdisciplinary Perspective of His or Her Chosen Profession.   The advanced group leader, in addition to being familiar with the theory and research of psychology, education, and related social sciences, would also have a broadly based understanding of the various branches of philosophy. Since the pragmatic group leader would be reluctant to embrace any single theoretical construct as the exclusive heir to truth, he or she must know the mechanics of personal theory building so that relevant and useful principles may be systematically collected from the universe of knowledge.

The sequential development of a theory-in-use that is applicable to group work usually begins with a fairly narrow adherence to an existing theory that has several attractive variables. The practitioner learns the necessary behaviors without a thorough understanding of their conceptual base and then readily applies the "party line." After this single theory is thoroughly accommodated into an existing philosophical framework, the group leader next moves toward bilingualism, or the ability to split allegiance among several attractive systems (Lancaster, 1981). The experienced group leader struggling for professional identity would next seek to explore higher levels of theoretical structure to resolve the intrapsychic conflicts that are irreconcilable at the practitioner's present level of primitive thinking.

As in the developmental sequences of all stage theories—like those of Freud, Piaget, Kohlberg, Erickson, Havighurst, Perry, and Loevinger—the group leader's philosophical progression moves in an orderly fashion toward higher levels of sophistication. As the pragmatic group leader begins to feel increasingly frustrated and restricted by the limitations of single-theory allegiance, more complex group dynamics, client concerns, and intervention problems will stimulate growth toward the next developmental stage in philosophic refinement. If an orthodox rational/emotive group leader, for instance, runs up against a client who is rational to the point of inhibiting spontaneity, the situation will call for borrowing strategies from other group work theories that more effectively facilitate the desired behaviors.

Once group leaders begin a systematic investigation of alternative helping strategies, a cognitive process begins to integrate this new knowledge into a unified system. At first, this multidimensionality will increase cognitive dissonance, thereby encouraging the development of a more concrete, pragmatic structure that will allow for the efficient selection of appropriate techniques "If . . . then" strategies help the group leader make simple decisions: *if* these conditions exist, these behaviors are demonstrated, and these goals are indicated; *then* I need to do these three things.

In the final stage of professional development, the group leader moves from a multimodal posture to the creation of a new system of order. From previous observations of group behavior, inquiry into existing theoretical explanations, integration of relevant knowledge, and testing of inductively reasoned hypotheses, eventually a new, personally designed philosophy will be deduced (Cattell, 1966).

The logic of this discovery process has been all but ignored by philosophers and scientists alike except for the early work of pragmatists such as Charles Peirce. Royce (1958) has drawn parallels between logical discovery, the final stage of professional development, and the methodology of multivariate statistics such as factor analysis. The spiral loops of identifying meaningful factors that account for the maximum variance among a number of diverse variables make factor analysis a suitable model for explaining how complex constructs evolve from the insightful progression of blurred covariation.

Constructive dialecticism permits group leaders to create their own pragmatic philosophies. Conceptual pluralism, synergism, relativism, probabilism, secular democratic individualism, eclecticism—these are the new watchwords of our profession. The basic tenets of philosophy and the operating principles of science can be merged effectively to create for each individual practitioner a truly functional pragmatic theory to guide leader behavior.

CHAPTER 3

How People Change in Groups

Human learning, an elusive and complex process that involves meta-morphic adaptation, has been viewed as essentially a survival function of the central nervous system (Anthony & Thibodeau, 1979). In the face of a constantly changing external world, the body's internal environment labors to maintain a delicate homeostasis. Various neurophysiological and biochemical processes in the brain coordinate their actions to gather, record, code, store, organize, and retrieve information about the external world. The organism then uses these data to better adapt to changing circumstances.

The same might be said about how and why people change in groups. No person ever really wants to change. A client with a happy marriage doesn't casually get a divorce, a perfectly satisfied employee doesn't quit a job, and a person who has discovered successful strategies for handling anxiety doesn't spontaneously throw them out the window just to learn new, improved coping mechanisms.

Group members *say* they want to change. ("I'm so unhappy, I wish I could be someone else." "I hate myself the way I am." "I really do have to start acting differently.") But what they really mean is that they want their group leaders to change them so that they don't have to do the hard work. The human organism does not voluntarily correct psychological imbalances; it is *ordered* to change because the host body and mind are too uncomfortable with the way things are going. In terms of energy expenditure and emotional investment, it is no longer economically feasible to continue chugging along at current unproductive levels. It hurts too much *not* to change. The person feels demoralized, hopeless, desperate. Something must be altered.

So much for one hypothesis about why people change. But an equally fascinating and more relevant question for therapists and counselors who attempt to promote change is "How and when does change occur?"

Variations of Change

A collection of people enters a strange room, each with a different set of expectations. They spend a few hours together in a circle, talking but mostly listening. They are not hooked up to electronic gadgetry, given pills to swallow, or subjected to surgical procedures to remove the offending problem. They simply spend time in one another's company, and somehow they feel better as a result. What is this magic that cures people of their suffering?

Any "normal" science can discover cause/effect relationships by isolating single variables that are suspected catalysts, subjecting them to intensive scrutiny and systematic manipulation, and then drawing inferences about their probable actions. The cataloging of neurotransmitters within the brain is an example of such an activity, one so significant that it often results in Nobel Prizes as rewards. From such investigations theories are born. The scores of substances that have already been identified, such as dopamine or norepinephrine, have scarcely scratched the surface of what is still left to learn. Current theories about the mechanisms regulating neurophysiology are so primitive that their authors are apologetic. Yet in our science of producing psychological changes—an infinitely more complex process than the anatomy of a single hormone or neurological system—theories of change flourish like hungry bacteria.

One theory claims that all group members make changes in their lives via resolving childhood conflicts by working them through with surrogate family members. Another theory tells us that it is the "atmosphere" in a group that becomes the central healing force, as if air rich in oxygen, nitrogen, or empathy helps people breathe more easily. Other theories claim that groups have "reinforcers" that, as do traffic cops, tell clients when to stop and go. Still another approach says that within a group of 10 people there are really 30 people who all act as their own parents or kids or other grown-ups do. Apparently these 10 or 30 people (depending on your perspective) all want to play games with one another, but the leader won't let them.

Theories have been advanced that say change occurs when group members, who are broken into pieces like shattered glass, become whole again. Another states that clients should talk to themselves more often, as do the people who wander around the streets of New York (which is where the author of the theory is from). Other change theories recommend that group members chant mantras, take off all their clothes, eat brown rice, roll into a ball, have their feet massaged, stick needles in their ears, pray for deliverance, take hot baths or do nothing at all.

Unfortunately, all the existing theories that attempt comprehensively to explain how people change in groups are in some way negligent. They all reflect the biases of their inventors (Palmer, 1980), who were blind to the work of others (Smith, 1975). They exhibit denominationalism (Stein, 1961), academic tribalism (DiLoreto, 1971), parochialism (Wolberg, 1954), cultism (Thorne, 1973), and religiosity (Ford & Urban, 1976).

It shows a gross misunderstanding and disrespect for the individuality of each person in a group to assume that all are there for the same purpose, that all relate to the world in precisely the same way, and that all learn and change by identical processes. Each client comes to a group with a different set of experiences, backgrounds, personality styles, goals, and cognitive patterns. People are so extraordinarily different from one another, even in their biological equipment, as to virtually defy classification.

Hence, any theory of human change, whether it is concerned with molecular alterations or behavioral metamorphoses, ought to be wide-ranging in scope.

It is hardly necessary to identify which theory is most powerful in promoting change: "A group experience resembles a therapeutic cafeteria in that many different mechanisms of change are available and each individual patient 'chooses' those particular factors best suited to his or her needs and problems" (Vinogradov & Yalom, 1989, p. 28). In a group of young children, for example, one girl seems to profit the most from the cathartic opportunities of disclosing her pent-up feelings of rage and fear associated with previous sexual abuse. A boy who has been friendless and isolated thrives on the opportunities to learn some social skills. Another boy appreciates most the interpersonal intimacy and closeness that has developed in the group, feeling part of a cohesive unit. Still another gains the most from vicarious learning resulting from observing others engage in desired behaviors.

Every theory appears to be an adequate explanation for the actions of its creator. It is probably true that a sizable part of the population does change as the result of expressing honest feelings, whereas another group of people (or perhaps even the same people) can change by altering their thought patterns, confronting their repressed desires, or structuring their environments. These multiple factors responsible for facilitating change may be identified from the literature.

Vive La Différence!

No two individuals are precisely alike. Ask any shoe manufacturer, dentist, or fingerprint expert about the differences in human beings. "Typical" hearts, stomachs, kidneys, and other organs exhibit a staggering diversity of shapes, sizes, and levels of function. In the nervous system—the main mechanism of perception and communication, containing all that may be described as consciousness—there are also many individual differences. In a comprehensive study of human physiological differences, Williams (1971) concludes that there really is no "average" person. The sensations of sight, hearing, taste, hunger, the needs for sleep and stimulation, the experiences each person has of the world are quite different phenomena.

If people are so different in the specific chemical compositions of their bodies, why should they be any more alike in the ways they learn, change, or grow? Is it any more valid to assume all people learn by modeling, or by reinforcers, or from unconscious motives, or through catharsis, or by expression of feelings, than it is to erroneously believe that all people have the same "normal" body temperature, react the same to medications, have a 30-gram thyroid, engage in sex three times per week, or perhaps think identically?

The Matrix for Change

Two major methods have been used to identify the therapeutic factors that operate in groups: retrospective client self-reports and critical incident reports completed at the end of sessions. Both lines of investigation are limited in that they tend to isolate discrete variables (catharsis, cohesion, and so on) rather than deal with complex interactive effects. Nevertheless, until we can devise more elaborate ways to identify how therapeutic elements in groups interact with one another, instead of dealing only with specific components such as feedback (Kivlighan, 1985; Rhode & Stockton, 1992) or indices of dominance (Lichtenberg & Knox, 1991), we are left with the alternative of listing factors individually.

Many researchers, writers, theoreticians, and practitioners think in terms of the conditions and therapeutic factors conducive to change in groups rather than in terms of any single school of thought. This *facilitative factors approach*, which seeks a fuller explanation of how and why group members change, has been advanced by several authors attempting to reconcile contradictory points of view. Although it is highly unlikely that any one of the following variables adequately explains how and why people change in groups, it is probable that most of them are quite influential. The matrix for change depicted in Figure 3-1 includes those factors that researchers and practitioners have found to maximally create and maintain the conditions that contribute to change.

The statistical science of factor analysis was spawned to provide mathematical models for explaining psychological theories (Harmon, 1967). Simplification of complex human processes is the goal of factor analysis, which describes meaningful categories by determining the principal factors that maximally account for the variance (communality plus uniqueness) of a contributing variable to its total model. A *factor* is a condensed statement of linear relationships between relevant variables that represent the actual reality of a complex psychological phenomenon (Eysenck, 1967). Factors are true variables that stand for the underlying theoretical constructs of

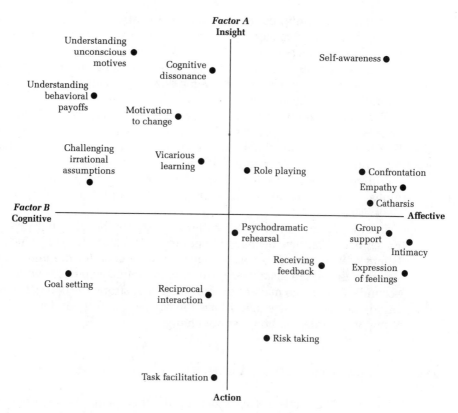

Figure 3-1 Factor Matrix for Change Variables in Groups

human action (Royce, 1967). The sum of all possible factors would thus constitute a perfect explanation of how several different variables are related to one another.

In the process of human change, there are a number of plausible factors that account for its action. If most of these "parts of the whole" could be gathered together to describe how change occurs in groups, a geometric model could probably be constructed in which the factors could represent, mathematically as well as symbolically, all known variables. Gorsuch (1974), for example, describes an orthogonal component model in which variables are graphically plotted as points, and then two factors optimally are added to the cluster in an attempt to illustrate the relationships among the variables.

For example, in the case of variables that lead to change in groups, several points can be displayed graphically according to their relationship to two primary dimensions. In Figure 3-1, Factor A represents "Level of Insight" versus "Level of Action"; Factor B describes a continuum of "Cognitive" versus "Affective" response styles. These quadrants were originally developed by Frey (1972) and later adapted by Hansen, Warner, and Smith (1980) for explaining group counseling theory. In this context, they are used as examples of how two factors can be portrayed as a basis for explaining the interrelationships among all relevant variables. Unfortunately, the process of change in groups is considerably more complex than can be described adequately by only two factors. Even a dozen factors could not account for all variance in the equation.

The factor analytic approach is consistent with the overall theme of this book, which attempts to integrate the major principles from various sources that best account for therapeutic change. Just as the preceding chapters have presented assumptions with which most practicing group leaders could agree despite their theoretical differences, this chapter presents a global view of change that is both generally applicable and specifically delineated.

In any model, however, no matter how comprehensive and detailed, a generalized overview of change in groups may not apply to any single case. Client change often involves exchanging the logical for the unreasonable. At other times, the discrete steps in this model may all occur within a few seconds. Finally, no matter how confident and strong the collective human mind may feel, we may never have the capacity to fully understand something as complex as how people change.

Overview of Change in Groups

Bloch (1986) has attempted to identify the therapeutic factors operative in group work. Although his research rests on the questionable premise that there are a finite number of elements distinguishable from one another by virtue of their highly specific effects on the group member, the author was able to describe what he considers to be the elements that produce the most significant therapeutic effects.

I believe that the process of group work is so complex as to defy complete description and that therapeutic factors are so interactive in their effects that it is impossible to truly isolate them as singular variables, much less measure their impact on a given group member. It is nevertheless helpful to review the elements common to virtually all leadership approaches.

A number of writers such as Corsini and Rosenberg (1955), Yalom (1975), Hill (1975), Trotzer (1977), O'Connor (1980), Hansen, Warner, and Smith (1980), Kottler (1983), Lieberman (1983), Corey (1990), Fuhriman and Burlingame (1990) have attempted the systematic taxonomy of therapeutic ingredients in groups. By combining, blending, and synthesizing elements presented by each of these authors, we end up with a fairly comprehensive model of how therapeutic groups operate and what are the factors contained within these experiences that promote constructive changes.

Stages of Change

The following outline delineates five general change stages subdivided into discrete, sequential steps, beginning in Stage I with pretreatment variables that operate in clients' heads before they ever enter a therapeutic group. The client's initial mind-set, for example, will be influenced by such predisposing variables as genetic determinants, physiological functioning, developmental stages, and frustration tolerance. Precipitating factors, catalytic events, characteristic thinking patterns, and expectations are all part of pretreatment variables.

An exploration phase (Stage II) is part of any helping system, although its length will depend on whether the group leader is psychodynamically or behaviorally inclined. After self-defeating behaviors are defined, members enter Stage III, in which behaviors are understood as to their payoffs, consequences, and other insight variables. Stage IV factors involve formulating and applying an action plan of intervention that will be evaluated and modified in Stage V. These identical process components, although labeled differently by individual helping systems, nevertheless have more in common than has previously been acknowledged.

Stage I: Pretreatment

1. Origin of concern
   a. Predisposing variables
   b. Precipitating factors
   c. Catalytic events
2. Mind-set
   a. Cognition
   b. Affect
   c. Behavior
3. Development of symptoms
4. Initial recognition of difficulty
5. Decision to seek help

Stage II: Exploration

6. Client expectations for change formulated
7. Discomfort intensified
8. Scene setting
9. Placebo for favorable prognosis planted
10. Trust building
11. Leader-modeled disclosure
12. Risk taking
13. Exploration of client world
14. Catharsis

15. Group support and initial feedback
16. Mutual identification, sharing, and spectatoring

Stage III: Insight

17. Challenge of irrational assumptions
18. Confrontation with inconsistencies
19. Realization of hidden and unconscious motives
20. Understanding behavioral payoffs and their consequences
21. Reassurance and peer support
22. Generalization to other behaviors

Stage IV: Action

23. Motivational support
24. Decision to change
25. Commitment to group
26. Brainstorming of alternative courses of action
27. Information giving and guidance
28. Goal setting
29. Formulation of plan
30. Reality testing
31. Rehearsal
32. Constructive feedback
33. Psychological homework
34. Commitment to action
35. Closure
36. Real-world practice

Stage V: Evaluation

37. Progress report
38. Additional input and modifications
39. Reinforcement
40. Finger on the pulse

Stage I: Pretreatment.   1. *Origin of concern.* A disaster occurs: an earthquake, a war, a famine, a flood, a cosmic accident. People die. The landscape is irrevocably altered. Some of the victims are crushed both literally and figuratively. Then the survivors clear their vision and attempt to cope with the consequences. Some will shrug indifferently while others will wail in helpless misery.

Why is it that people react so differently to identical crises? A death in the family can cripple some mourners for an agonizing decade of grief, whereas others bounce back after a weekend of hard crying. One woman will be driven to the brink of suicide over the shame of rape, whereas another will think of the episode as a painful ordeal that can be overcome. A divorce, a loss of income, an illness, a sexual dysfunction, or an exploded dream catalyze major negative consequences for some people; others find ways of constructively using such concerns as growth forces.

It appears that each individual's unique constitution acts as a predisposing variable for reaction to personal troubles. Depending on the body's chemistry, hormonal balance, genetic determinants and physiological functioning, a person is more likely to react to certain stimuli in certain ways than in others. Although no conclusive evidence supports the notion of "alcoholic genes," "depression DNA molecules," or "schizophrenic neurons," there is growing data supporting the hypothesis that much of human behavior may be controlled by underlying biological processes. At this time it would be very difficult to determine whether a bad temper is caused by predisposing "anger genes" (such as those popularly believed to accompany red hair) or by environmental influences. It is nevertheless significant to note that a wide range of reactions to the same stressful situation is possible.

Genetics and physiology may indeed play a causative role in client concerns, just as developmental stages probably exert their influence. An adolescent who is struggling through Piaget's period of formal operations, Kohlberg's stage of conventional morality, and Erickson's conflict of identity versus role confusion is likely to react to a crisis situation very differently from a man living through Levinson's Age-50 transition in middle adulthood. All these factors, including other relevant predisposing variables such as one's characteristic frustration tolerance and stable personality traits, will dramatically affect performance under fire. Even sleep patterns, energy level, body image, and self-concept will influence the total behavioral scheme.

A person's readiness to change is another important predisposing factor. The life work of Jean Piaget, Jerome Bruner, Arnold Gesell, and other developmental theorists indicates that people must reach a certain point in their personal-problem evolution before change can readily occur. Self-discovery depends not only on people's conscious willingness but also on their capacity to change. Bruner (1963) believed, however, that readiness could be taught by providing the client with prerequisite skills necessary for higher order functioning.

In one group led by two beginning leaders, it was evident that a volunteer willing to use group time was not immediately forthcoming. The leaders felt uncomfortable waiting for someone to volunteer, but they didn't quite know how to select an appropriate member on whom to focus. It hadn't occurred to them that they could search their memories for past content areas elicited from each client during preliminary exercises, nor could they think of a rationale for choosing any particular client with whom to explore. Instead they determined to let fate decide who would have the first honors, and so they randomly focused on a group member who had been silent. Dick, a very accommodating young man, dutifully responded to the query with the statement that he had had a problem but that it was now worked out. The co-leaders decided to pursue their quarry, mistakenly believing that he wanted help but was too shy to ask for it.

Dick felt hurt because a friend had ended their relationshp as a result of a solitary incident over which he had had no control. An hour was spent attempting to help Dick express his resentment, rehearse a confrontation scene, and get reactions from other participants. Throughout the counseling, Dick patiently repeated that he felt his problem was already resolved, although it was evident to others that there was much residual frustration. The problem was isolated, a plan was formulated, everything was taken care of except one thing: Dick didn't feel ready yet to confront the issue head-on.

Since he had been involuntarily selected, Dick had no power to control his progress. He knew that change would eventually become necessary, but he needed more time to mobilize his resources, build his energy, and heal wounds before he could bid for group time. Because he had been forced to participate before he was ready, Dick's forward momentum was stalled; he backed further into his shell. The other group members also left the session feeling frustrated because they perceived that valuable time had been wasted and that, given enough chance, several of them would have volunteered to work on concerns that needed more immediate attention.

2. *Mind-set.* The human mind perceives and responds on a number of different levels: thinking, feeling, and acting. In addition to catalytic events, predisposing variables, and precipitating factors, the client's initial mind-set will strongly determine how she or he responds to a crisis. Individual group members who prefer to reason and think analytically will *act* differently from those who prefer to feel intensely and emote spectacularly. Bandler and Grinder (1979) made some stunning observations on the unique perceptual mind-set of persons who may prefer to relate to the world from primarily an auditory, visual, or kinesthetic mode.

People who believe that their feelings must be spontaneously expressed before they can find relief will respond to their personal concerns a bit more dramatically than will those who view their behavior as the logical product of environmental and intrinsic reinforcers. Similarly, group members who believe that behavior is caused by feelings that are in turn caused by thoughts will naturally focus on cognitive aspects of the situation.

The human mind, notwithstanding the sameness of its physical components, is managed differently according to individual style and mind-set. There appears to be a relationship between anticipatory cognition and subjectively experienced disappointment if expectations are not met. Thus, a person who dwells endlessly on a future goal, whether a desired job or an important date, will be more disappointed than a person who minimizes anticipatory thoughts and feelings. If circumstances don't turn out as hoped, a high-expectation mind-set will program a drastic emotional response—

depression, anger, anxiety. A person who avoids unrealistic expectations will therefore experience less emotional trauma.

Although cognitive style contributes greatly to the development of behavioral symptoms, alterations in mood also affect stressful situations. When a person is having a bad day or is short of patience, it takes far less to ignite the fuse. These obvious factors, combined with physiological developmental, and psychological processes, all interact to produce the first signs that change is imminent.

3. *Development of symptoms.* The first indicators of underlying emotional distress often show themselves as physical symptoms. Before potential group members ever begin to realize that a presenting problem is severe enough to seek outside help, they will notice the occurrence of certain physiological and behavioral changes. Dilated pupils, rapid heart rate, nausea, diarrhea, dizziness, stomach cramps, and cold feet may accompany feelings of anxiety; depression may cause insomnia, loss of appetite, lethargy, or loss of sex drive (Bockar, 1976).

Symptoms are signals that something is wrong, just as pain tells us of possible physical injury. Whether the group leader is inclined to treat behavioral symptoms (such as drug abuse) as the "real problem" or views them only as surface cues of some underlying problem, the client will initially notice feelings of discomfort and will be highly motivated to reduce their level of intensity.

4. *Initial recognition of difficulty.* Here is an excerpt from a group member's journal:

In my former work situation as a salesman among a jungle of aggressive peers and complacent clients, my task was to apply appropriate ass-kissing behaviors as I deemed necessary to attain a particular client's "friendship," and hence business. I worked with peers I despised as whimsical prostitutes willing to do or say anything for money. I worked under supervisors who knew less than I about human nature and with clients who suck the blood from those who call on them. To compound matters, I had a strong psychological dependence on my boss—my own father. I felt totally alien and apart from those I worked with.

I gave in to the security, to the future, to the financial rewards of my work. I felt drugged senseless by outside forces that I allowed to control me. I looked around me at all of my working peers and their deluded bliss and realized that I could no longer hide from the inevitable—as much as I dreaded making changes, for the first time, I understood that *something* would have to happen.

When a symptom becomes unbearable and the person cannot discover ways to keep things under control, there is realization that a problem will not go away by itself. The change process begins with the first recognition that some alteration is necessary. Whistling in the dark won't dissolve the monster, procrastination and avoidance won't stop it from recurring.

Tristan has noticed that the more he tries to gain on all the tasks he feels he must accomplish, the further he falls behind. He cannot decide between using his Sunday afternoon to winterize his house, visit his mother, finish his school reading, complete a report for work, or catch up on his correspondence. So instead he watches a football game on television, feeling very guilty that he will now never finish what he needs to do.

The lists he has created make him feel even worse; he gets a stomachache every time he sees the schedule taped to the refrigerator door. Tristan's frustrations build and his symptoms of distress grow, affecting his friendships, his enjoyment of leisure time, and his self-concept. The difficulties multiply like malignant cells out of control, polluting every aspect of his life with which they come into contact.

5. *Decision to seek help.*

- "I can't afford it."
- "Why am I so weak that I can't solve my own problems?"
- "Other people will think I'm crazy."
- "I don't have the time."
- "I can't open up in front of a bunch of strangers."

Yet Tristan decides to join a therapeutic group anyway because his level of desperation and desire for relief outweigh his apprehensions. He is nervous, excited, fearful, optimistic, worried, reluctant, confused, skeptical, determined, and relieved all at once. Fluctuating in his decision to seek help, he consults friends and family and finally decides there is no use postponing what must be done. It is time to stop peering over the edge; the tiger, chasing him in circles, is catching up. "Perhaps a group experience will be the answer I've been looking for," he ponders, "but I doubt it."

Stage II: Exploration.   6. *Client expectations for change formulated.* Before clients arrive at the therapist's door, they have formed an impression of what they believe will happen. Because most group leaders know the dangers of ignoring expectations for treatment, they usually start intake interviews by exploring client perceptions. This fishing expedition is often amusing in the strange, diverse, and unrealistic comments it elicits. The layperson generally knows little about how groups work except from the distortions of gossip, sensational literature, and the media. Assuming that clients agree to be completely honest regarding their intentions for attending a group, we might hear responses such as the following:

Rose: I don't feel so good. I don't have any friends. I'm lonely. I want you to wave a magic wand so that my life will be perfect. Guys will start calling. Someone will offer me a good job. Please make me happy.

Donald: I was hoping to meet some girls because it is hard for me to get dates.

Randolph: My mother made me come. She says I got problems. I'm hoping you can convince her that there is nothing wrong with me.

Terry: My doctor says he won't give me any more drugs unless I come to this silly group. That's cool. I don't mind. As long as he keeps the pills coming, I'll sit here forever. What? You want to know what I think will happen? That's easy. You'll talk a lot. We'll pretend to listen, then we'll make up a bunch of garbage to tell you. And you'll act real pleased, but you couldn't care less if we live or die.

Lynn: I guess I'll tell you my problems and then you'll tell me what to do.

Fran: We'll play games and stuff. Tell stories. It'll be real fun. I can't wait to give massages.

These unrealistic expectations are counteracted through role induction methods—preparing participants for how to get the most from the experience. Strupp and Bloxom (1973) prepared an orientation film for new members explaining what happens in a group and what are appropriate roles. Although both their study and a follow-up study (Hilkey, Wilhelm, & Horne, 1982) demonstrated that prepared clients were more satisfied with their group experience than were those who did not view the film, this satisfaction did not necessarily translate into better outcomes.

7. *Discomfort intensified.* As participants wait for the group to get going, their levels of tension, anxiety, and perceived threat will rise. Fortunately, these are precisely the conditions that lead to further dissatisfaction with the self in its present state. The more uncomfortable a person becomes with recurrent self-defeating behaviors, such as shyness, fear of taking risks, or hesitance to open up and trust others, the more willing that person will be to do something to change the status quo. Withdrawal and passivity are certainly viable options, but, under the effective leader's direction, the cognitive dissonance can be reduced through constructive action.

The initial discomfort that group members invariably feel when confronted with the prospect of interacting with strangers acts as a further motivating force to ensure that they will follow through on their decisions to change. Unless anxiety reaches too far, in which case panic reactions may significantly inhibit any progress, intensified discomfort will often make clients more ready to take necessary risks to restore psychological equilibrium.

8. *Scene setting.* The group leader begins to set in motion a series of planned actions that are likely to facilitate desired changes in clients.

Logically, the first task is to establish ground rules that will lead to efficient performance. Issues of confidentiality are usually discussed. Rules are explained pertaining to fees, breaks, smoking, and attendance.

Most therapists also make a great effort to describe what is likely to happen in the group, and what are appropriate roles both for the leader and participants. The therapeutic process is often explained in reassuring terms, giving clients an overview of how change occurs. This preliminary description often acts as a predictor, in confident terms, of what will happen and how exactly it will occur. Since client expectations have already been elicited, it is now time for the leader to give realistic predictions.

9. *Placebo for favorable prognosis planted.* The expectation of success is a strong healing force. The repeated testimony of others who report how greatly they have been helped, coupled with the leader's confidence and positive expectation, sets the stage for maximum potential change in a group.

Jerome Frank (1974) draws a compelling analogy between the change forces that operate in contemporary therapeutic groups and those of a past era. The primitive faith healers were readily able to persuade large crowds to have conversion experiences by instilling powerful expectations of what could happen. Jefferson Fish (1973) has capitalized on this faith inspiration by describing a procedure of "placebo therapy" that structures group members' beliefs to maximize the sense of drama and impending magic that will occur. The charisma of an astute leader creates a powerful religious fervor in the flock; the faith of the people around each client acts as a social norming mechanism.

Most practicing physicians will sometimes have to practice deliberate deceit when a patient cries for unneeded medication. Giving the person in pain a sugar pill while commenting "I know this will make you feel better" has helped millions of sufferers find relief. The ethical considerations involved in deliberately misleading a patient are believed by some to be relatively less important than providing the unneeded medication or sending the person home empty-handed.

Nonmedical group leaders don't have to wrestle with ethical conflicts related to the use of placebo drugs, but we do make use of the same psychological principles when we plant a favorable prognosis: "This group is a great place to be. You made a very intelligent decision when you chose to come here. In fact, you are well on your way to making progress already, as evidenced by your commitment to work on yourself in this group. I have helped many people, just like yourselves, work on resolving their concerns. I believe I can help you as well." If we are worthy of the trust that clients place in our hands, we can deliver what we claim.

Instilling and maintaining hope in groups can be accomplished in a number of ways, beginning with the very first phone contact with a prospective participant. It is during this initial encounter that we communicate our strong belief in what we do—that it works quite well and would most likely be helpful in this situation as well. Couch and Childers (1987) describe those leader strategies that involve accentuating the positive features of group activity. Whenever a member improves in an appreciable way, the leader draws attention to this progress and encourages others to do so as well.

Trent has been feeling and acting quite hopeless in the group, dragging others down into the abyss of his despair. Those members who have been making fairly consistent, even dramatic progress are starting to feel guilty when they talk about their successes. Trent just stares at them with puppy-dog eyes, tears welling up in them. He feels utterly without hope, and this despondency was potentially contagious.

The leader, taking a cue from the literature on the importance of counteracting hopelessness (Corey & Corey, 1992; Yalom, 1985), decides to address this problem as a priority.

> **Leader**: Trent, I would like to compliment you on the progress you have been making lately.
>
> **Trent**: Huh? (*Other members also seem surprised by this comment; one person even starts to giggle.*)
>
> **Leader**: You seem taken aback by my observation.
>
> **Trent**: Nothing has changed. I've been coming here for seven weeks and . . .
>
> **Leader**: I know it must feel to you as if you are just as depressed as ever. However, in a number of small and subtle ways, I can see and hear a difference—nothing dramatic and nowhere near where you would eventually like to be—but, nevertheless, there are already small signs of progress. Would you be interested in hearing what many of the rest may have noticed?
>
> **Trent** (*hesistantly*): I guess so.
>
> **Leader**: That doesn't sound very convincing. Maybe you don't want to hear that you have made any progress. Then you would have to give up that cocoon of helplessness you are so wrapped up in.
>
> **Trent**: Maybe you are right. If you, or anyone else here, has seen any improvement, I sure would like to hear. I mean . . .
>
> **Tina**: You don't whine so much. Oh, don't misunderstand me; you still whine and complain quite a bit. It is just that you don't whine as often or for as long as you used to.
>
> **Trent**: That's just because you guys interrupt me whenever . . .
>
> **Karyn**: I notice that you've become more creative in the ways you try to not hear what is said to you. Just now Tina gave you a compliment that is utterly truthful. When the group first started, you were so clumsy in trying to weasel out of responding. Now you are much more inventive in making up reasons why you can't—er, *won't* change.

> **Brandon**: I like your shoes.
>
> **Trent**: Oh, well thanks.
>
> **Brandon**: I'm serious. What your shoes represent to me is that you care more about your appearance. And if you care about how you look, then you must have some minimal concern . . .

Granted, the members are reaching very deep in order to find something in Trent about which to feel optimistic. Yet, by accentuating what is positive, they are doing what is imperative to counteract hopelessness. Many clients believe that their role as a group member is to recite a litany of complaints about everything in their life that is going wrong. By forcing them to focus instead on ways that they are improving, we reorient their cognitive activity to a more balanced perspective.

10. *Trust building.* In her book on the roots of group therapy, Greenberg-Edelstein (1986) identifies the single most powerful therapeutic element to be the genuine feelings of caring that group members feel and express for one another. Drawing on evidence from both biology and history, she views reciprocal nurturance as the greatest hunger among members of our specie. Clients come to groups longing to satisfy this need for belonging.

Glantz and Pearce (1989) draw similar conclusions about the functions of therapeutic experiences, although they rely primarily on evidence from sociobiology. Noting that the history of human beings is dominated by tribal lifestyle wherein everyone belonged to a cohesive group that provided mutual support, Glantz and Pearce view the prospective client as searching to reconnect those close affiliations.

No longer are we part of a community in which everyone is responsible for and accountable to everyone else. The tribes have been disbanded. Extended families are separated by vast distances. Children are raised by babysitters rather than by relatives. We are all strangers to one another, lost and lonely, craving intimacy and closeness with others. Therapeutic groups thus provide simulated re-creations of a tribe, a place to belong where members support and stand up for one another. Groups are the closest thing that we have to an environment of reciprocal nurturance where everyone can feel safe and secure.

Cohesion is the glue that holds groups together—that makes them safe enough environments in which to accomplish therapeutic work. Greenberg-Edelstein (1986) believes that reciprocal nurturance is the single most important thing that happens in a group. When a person feels part of a cohesive group and experiences complete trust among peers, he or she is more willing to venture out of the protective shell that prevents constructive action.

Cartwright (1968), in his seminal study of how trust and cohesion develop in groups, considers trust and cohesion to be the major incentives for disclosing oneself, taking risks, or completing tasks. However, a number of authors (Gladding, 1991; Miles, 1957) also point out that trust and cohesion can be a mixed blessing, creating dependency, a reluctance to share negative feelings, and an emphasis on harmony over constructive work.

Initially, client change efforts are made to please others—the leader, other members, a lover, or a friend: "I'll become different to make *them* happy." But such an attitude is only one step removed from a previous strategy that had worked even less efficiently: "If only my mother/spouse/friend would change, then my life would be fine!" Eventually most group members work through their self-defeating approval seeking into a more internally based motive. Until that occurs, however, it is important that each client perceive other group members as attractive and trustworthy (Cartwright, 1951; Cartwright & Zander, 1968). Ohlsen (1977) recommends that group leaders increase their group's attractiveness by first screening members to include those who communicate effectively and are nonjudgmental and then dealing initially with client problems that imply that relatively healthy, well-adjusted, prestigious persons participate in group work.

11. *Leader-modeled disclosure.*

"I dare you."
"Double dares go first."

A person asked to try something risky is unlikely to take your word that nothing disastrous will happen. Any intelligent human being, before taking a plunge into a strange body of water, is going to do several things: (1) test the temperature with an exploratory toe, (2) scan the surface for dangerous obstructions, (3) check out the bottom for jagged rocks, (4) estimate the depth, and (5) watch others go first to see whether they're attacked by sharks. Only then will the cautious person take a few deep breaths and jump.

Group leaders usually pacify preliminary fears by initially demonstrating that risk taking is necessary and even attractive. In an introductory exercise through which the leader wishes to elicit personal information without the usual nonsense people reveal at first encounters, the leader will find it advantageous to model the kinds of disclosures that are most helpful.

"As the leader of this group, I will not use your valuable time to meet my own needs. Any time I share something about myself, I will deliberately do so to illustrate a point or to make it easier for you to respond. For instance, in this introductory exercise, it is *very* important that we hear honest self-descriptions that will help us all to know you well enough so that we can get down to the work at hand. This involves some risk, and so naturally you will want to hedge your bet by introducing yourself in the safe way you would at a cocktail party—telling us your age, marital status, occupation, place of birth, and other meaningless details we will learn anyway as a function of being around you. Instead, I would like you to introduce yourself in a uniquely personal way, perhaps sharing how you intend to use this group, what most people don't understand about you, or how you got to be who you are. Let me show you what I mean.

"I am basically a happy person, not because I was born this way but because I've worked hard on myself over the years. Actually, my progress began in a group very similar to this one when I was having incredible problems overcoming feelings of dependency on my father, trying to separate what I wanted to do with my life as opposed to what he wanted me to do. Since that time I have lived through some hard times—the deaths of several people I love, setbacks in my work—and I still do a lot of approval seeking to get people to like me. I am pretty good at identifying these concerns in myself whenever they crop up, and I know what to do to work them through. It's just that sometimes I feel too lazy. In this group, I hope to teach you similar skills for changing the parts of yourself that you don't like."

It is because even advanced group leaders sometimes misunderstand or misuse self-disclosure that we must emphasize what it is *not*: mechanical, a purging of confessions, excessively revealing, self-indulgent, or overly dramatic. Rather, self-disclosure is clearly related to the purposes and goals of the group and must be appropriate in length, content, and timing (Corey & Corey, 1992).

12. *Risk taking.* The first major step toward change is to encourage group members to get their feet wet. The risk taking that usually occurs during the exploratory phase of group work involves a public commitment in which (1) vulnerabilities are admitted, (2) helplessness is shared, (3) the desire for a new way of being is declared, (4) intimate thoughts are revealed, (5) preliminary intercommunication is begun, and (6) dreams for a better life are disclosed.

During this critical stage we attempt to disguise how difficult risk taking can be. We pretend that revealing oneself is as natural as clamming up, and so we deliberately act casually to put people at ease. We gear up our optimal levels of acceptance, respect, unconditional positive regard, warmth, and empathy to make participant risk taking appear to be easy. It's a good thing, too. Taking risks *is* synonymous with change.

As long as a person avoids, fears, or otherwise feels intimidated by a particular situation or kind of inner experience, he or she will continue to be controlled by it. Hanna and Puhakka (1991) thus nominate "resperception," or resolute focused attention on painful experiences, to be a significant therapeutic ingredient of any form of psychological healing. It forms a bridge between relationship and technique in that clients are encouraged and supported to face their concerns directly. It is the deliberate and constructive attention to a problem, a circumstance, that is even more likely in group settings where members force one another to look at what they are avoiding.

13. *Exploration of client world.* What is the minimum amount of data that needs to be collected from a given client in order to begin therapeutic

interventions? At the very least, an exploration of the presenting concerns, how they are specifically manifested, and how they affect the group member's total functioning must be systematically accomplished. Some group leaders need to be given a lot of information; others favor using personal digging strategies that they feel will best elicit valuable data. Everyone wants to get a firm handle on exactly what the client-in-focus feels is most disturbing.

Data might be collected on childhood traumatic experiences, relationships to parents, or developmental crises. Other group leaders might focus on mental status examination variables, such as assessing intellectual functioning or reality testing. Medically trained group leaders may want to check out urinary frequency, weight loss, fatigue, constipation, and appetite disturbances.

Every group leader has favorite exploratory questions on a variety of relevant issues. "When were you first aware of this problem?" "What would you guess is behind this conflict?" "What have you tried to do so far to work on this concern?" "How are you feeling right now?" "What are your favorite defensive strategies when you feel threatened?" "How do you believe we could best help you?" Some therapists don't find it necessary to gather any information at all—just a clear statement of the presenting problem. In any event, before change efforts can be accurately aimed, a preliminary target must be set up. Although the initially stated concern rarely ends up being the real problem, it is a starting point for further investigation.

14. *Catharsis.* It was Freud's original intent that his "talking cure" would form the basis for a new therapy of the mind. The ego and its defense mechanisms form a protective barrier, an immunological system, that fights off undesirable elements from releasing psychic energy stored up in the unconscious and the repressed id. Today, the orthodox psychoanalyst, as well as most types of group leaders, agree that Aristotle's concept of *catharsis,* or purging of the spirit, serves a useful purpose for clients, although it can sometimes be used as a ready excuse for therapists who don't know how to do anything else.

Haley (1980) cynically gives this advice to therapists who understand the scientific basis of diagnosis and research, know the theories of personality, development, and general systems, and understand how to pass licensing or school tests but cannot figure out how to cause change in clients: when in doubt, cathart. "The general procedure used by most experienced therapists who don't know how to cause change is to encourage the client to talk and talk on the gamble that this will cause improvement" (Haley, 1980, p. 386). Strangely enough, this *does* appear to have beneficial effects in a great many cases. As soon as group members begin to share their concerns, the fears diminish and warm feelings of relief wash over.

When group members share in great detail the disturbing elements of their lives, their frustrations and disappointments, or their self-defeating behaviors, the group leader will inevitably rely on therapeutic interventions such as active listening to encourage the full expression of these thoughts and feelings. And it is true that an expression of serenity often accompanies release of this previously stifled bile.

Whereas at one time such group approaches as primal therapy (Janov, 1970) and psychodrama (Moreno, 1957) elicited catharsis as the main focus, group practitioners now capitalize on catharsis primarily as an intermediary step to facilitate insight (Slavson, 1969) and help clients feel better (Weiner, 1977). Divesting *catharsis* of its psychoanalytic origins, practitioners now prefer the term *expression of affect* (Bond, 1983). It is still clearly an important factor in groups, especially by allowing clients to say whatever they think and feel yet still feel respected and accepted afterward (Long & Cope, 1980; Posthuma, 1989).

15. *Group support and initial feedback.* It is just after an intense verbal barrage that a group member most needs to be reinforced for taking interpersonal risks and disclosing difficult material, and it is at this point that structures for providing feedback are ordinarily employed. Clients receive supportive messages (and sometimes constructive suggestions) that their teary-eyed behavior was both appropriate and productive. This critical incident is also a time for reflection. The group-member-in-focus sighs in relief with the realization that the first great obstacle has been surmounted.

Carin, for instance, feels better, not only because she finally told caring people about what has been plaguing her all these months, but because she has had the first definite signal that help is forthcoming. The other group members did not laugh. On the contrary, they indicated great warmth, kindness, and empathy, even unrestrained admiration because she had taken a great risk by disclosing her personal feelings. Carin beams, gathering strength for the next round of tension. But the other group members begin to squirm because they realize that Carin had been speaking for them as well.

16. *Mutual identification, sharing, and spectatoring.* Human beings seem to have a morbid fascination for watching others in trouble. In the Roman Coliseum as in the Superdome, we pay extravagantly to support gladiators engaged in real or mock fights. Spectators get vicarious thrills imagining that they are the heroes struggling in a land-acquisition game like football or in a soap opera that makes our own troubles seem minor. Our expressways get clogged when accidents occur, not so much from wrecked cars as from curious onlookers who slow down hoping to catch a glimpse of blood.

In therapeutic groups, the thrill in watching members with conflicts comes not from the attitude "better you than me" but from the powerful realization that we all share similar concerns. Cohesion develops during this phase. People start to feel closer to one another, to lose their sense of alienation as they identify with a common issue. After all, what person has not had problems controlling negative habits, fears of failure, sexual fantasies, and other prevalent themes?

Every time a person makes a statement, shares a fear, or is addressed by the leader, everyone else internalizes the implications, asking: "What does this have to do with me? Do I have a similar concern? How can I apply similar principles to my own life?" It is strange that by watching other people change, we in turn change as well. When exploration of any client concern is completed, every person in the group has identified similar issues, shared them aloud, and offered support to the client struggling to change.

Stage III: Insight.   There are a number of different ways of approaching insight in groups: as an understanding of behavioral consequences, as an awareness of cognitive or affective processes, or as an interpersonal awareness. Yalom (1985) talks about "interpersonal insight" as distinguished from the usual self-understanding to which therapists and counselors refer. Specifically relevant to group situations, interpersonal insight allows clients to learn so much more about themselves than an increased awareness of their own life situation; they also increase their understanding of their own behavior in relation to others. They become aware of the characteristic interactive patterns by which they relate and respond to others.

Cal, for example, had been struggling in individual sessions for several months with little discernable progress. He had learned a tremendous amount about himself and the origins of his symptoms but had changed very little in his life—especially in his impoverished relationships with co-workers, friends, and family. After only a half-dozen sessions in group, however, there have been some fairly dramatic changes in Cal's behavior as a direct result of his interpersonal insights. He has learned about how others see him, how he comes across during moments of stress. He has learned about his defensive style of warding off intimacy. Most importantly, whereas his therapist had been unable in individual sessions to help Cal see how he turns others off or drives them away, group members have been successful in helping him to realize what he had been doing.

Fortunately, the advanced group leader is not restricted to only one insight strategy but may use a combination of consciousness-raising interventions, depending on what the situation calls for and what the client specifically requires or is likely to respond best to. The issue is not so much which approach to group member insight is preferred as it is how to help translate these awarenesses into constructive action. On the matrix for change in Figure 3-1, the opposite ends of the theoretical pole are represented by group strategies that emphasize either "Insight" or "Action." Many group leaders unconditionally accept this dichotomy, aligning themselves either with an approach that focuses on plans, techniques, and other action strategies or with an approach that encourages self-awareness, discovery, exploration, and self-understanding. The proponents of insight assume that knowledge of the problem will make it go away. On this issue, David Viscott comments:

> Understanding how and why you are a rat won't change the fact that you're a rat who irritates the hell out of people, unless you do something about it. Some patients who use therapy to get a complete understanding of everything in their life and still don't change can and often do use theapy as a weapon. (Viscott, 1972, p. 114)

The compromise position taken in this book and emphasized in the following stages is that *insight is a useful but insufficient condition alone to produce change.* By teaching group members a set of practical skills without helping them understand how and why these skills work, we deprive members of the opportunity to create their own strategies for handling new concerns in the future. Insight strategies, on the other hand, may be wonderfully enlightening in that they provide a form of relevant education; however, they may, at best, merely waste time and, at worst, disorient and confuse. If the group leader first incorporated only as much functional insight as is necessary for clients to understand how and why they are having difficulties and then focused on practical action strategies for changing specific behaviors, a perfect balance would be achieved.

17. *Challenge irrational assumptions.* As a starting point, it is sometimes helpful to highlight the underlying self-sabotaging assumptions that result in undesired behavior. Albert Ellis (1977a) identified many of the themes that pervade irrational thinking, such as exaggerating reality, demanding that the world be different, or judging others or oneself according to absolute standards. Whether sympathetic to the methods of rational-emotive therapy (RET) or not, one cannot be blind to the usefulness of adapting parts of the theory to promoting self-understanding. Ellis (1974), for instance, identifies several crucial insights that he believes group members must have before permanent change can occur. Clients are thus helped to understand that it is their thoughts that trigger unwanted feelings and that these may be altered by challenging the underlying irrational assumptions.

Although the RET clinician makes deliberate, repeated, and systematic interpretations of certain irrational assumptions, all group leaders do essentially the same thing, though less rigidly. When a group member talks of being consistently late because his job keeps him from being punctual, we begin to question the validity of this faulty assumption. When another client complains that she can't help being promiscuous because she has Italian blood on her father's side, we challenge that assumption. And when a group member expects everyone else to devote unlimited time every session to working on a single concern, that unrealistic assumption is examined. The fact is that all practitioners have a favorite list of recurrent assumptions that they are fond of challenging to initiate the process of insight.

18. *Confrontation with inconsistencies.* The self-understanding process that begins with an analysis of illogical thinking patterns continues when discrepancies in behavior are pointed out. With great diplomacy, clients are helped to examine their statements within the context of other messages they have communicated. The skilled Gestalt group leader is fond of isolating examples in which a client's words say one thing while body language communicates quite another. Other times, group members will contradict previous statements with verbalizations that are inconsistent. In any case in which group members act, think, or feel in ways that appear to be shallow or deceiving, the therapist will attempt nonthreateningly to bring such behaviors to conscious awareness.

There are, of course, distinct differences between how people see themselves, how others see them, how they believe others see them, and how they really are. Internal congruence, consistency between internal and external behavior, and authenticity are the universal goals for most group leaders working with clients. Yet, when interactional inconsistencies enter the picture demonstrating discrepancies between what people say, what they really mean, what other group members believe they heard, and what was actually said, the potential for exhibiting congruence and consistency is significantly reduced. Joseph Heller's *Catch-22* presents a hilarious dialogue typical of interpersonal incongruence.

Clevinger one day stumbled during a march and the next day found himself confronting a court martial and charged with "mopery, . . . being a smart guy, listening to classical music," among other things (Heller, 1955, p. 77). The following vignette, with all its comic absurdity, is only slightly exaggerated compared to some of the communication styles we encounter in groups. Clevinger, attempting to defend himself before the tribunal, finds an interpersonal logic different from what he is used to.

"Just what the hell did you mean, you bastard, when you said we couldn't punish you?"

"I didn't say you couldn't punish me, sir."

"When?" asked the colonel.

"When what, sir?"

"Now you're asking me questions again."

"I'm sorry, sir. I'm afraid I don't understand your question."

"When didn't you say we couldn't punish you? Don't you understand my question?"

"No, sir. I don't understand."

"You've just told us that. Now suppose you answer my question."

"But how can I answer it?"

"That's another question you're asking me."

"I'm sorry, sir. But I don't know how to answer it. I never said you couldn't punish me."

"Now you're telling us when you did say it. I'm asking you to tell us when you didn't say it."

Clevinger took a deep breath. "I always didn't say you couldn't punish me, sir." (Heller, 1955, p. 79)

Only after such gross inconsistencies are confronted can group members and the client-in-focus hope to proceed toward deeper levels of mutual self-understanding and then move on to the action stages of change.

19. *Realization of hidden and unconscious motives.* We are again indebted to the work of Freud for popularizing the role of the unconscious mind in conscious actions. The human brain is so mysterious, who can really claim to understand its complex modus operandi? Who really knows just how important the unconscious motive (if there is such a thing) is in creating problems or affecting change? It is better to be safe than sorry.

Milton Erickson had little tolerance for dynamic techniques of interpretation that bring repressed material to the surface, but he did have great respect for the power of the unconscious mind to promote necessary changes. He would therefore bypass the alert brain and speak instead to its dormant counterpart, sometimes producing magical effects. For patients resistant to hypnosis, Erickson might tap the unlimited powers of the unconscious by asking it direct questions and getting answers.

> Does your unconscious mind think that you can go into a trance? [Further elaboration is offered:] Consciously you cannot know what your unconscious mind thinks or knows. But your unconscious mind can let your conscious mind discover what it thinks or understands by the simple process of causing a levitation of either the right or left hand. Thus your unconscious mind can communicate in a visibly recognizable way with your conscious mind. Now just watch your hands and see what the answer is. Neither you nor I know what your unconscious mind thinks, but as you see one or the other of your hands lifting, you will know. (Erickson, 1967a, p. 37)

This pragmatic application of therapy for the unconscious often produces dramatic results, although it still doesn't provide conclusive evidence for the existence of surreptitious motives tucked deep in the cerebral cortex. If, however, we assume that hidden and disguised motives *do* exist, then we would be well advised to spend some time helping to make these thoughts and feelings more explicitly understood.

20. *Understanding behavioral payoffs and their consequences.* From medical literature, we learn of a phenomenon known as *secondary gains* that describes the indirect advantages of a patient's illness (Stern, 1964). As every hypochondriac well knows, sick people get a lot of attention and pity. They have a ready-made excuse for procrastination, bad temper, any abusive behavior. They can't help it, they're sick; they have a right to feel bad.

In the therapeutic self-understanding process, clients are introduced to the concept that *all* their behaviors have secondary gains, positive as well as negative consequences (Dyer, 1976; Greenwald, 1973). These payoffs create a vicious cycle that makes the job of changing that much more difficult to accomplish. In theory, the idea of teaching clients to understand the payoffs of their behavior is fine. In practice, however, the execution can be a bit more complicated.

In one group, a father was on the brink of tears describing a letter from his daughter informing him that she was dropping out of college to get a job. The daughter explained that she was sick and tired of being told what to do with her life and wished to be left alone. The father was riddled with guilt. Conceivably, he could be feeling proud that his daughter had the courage to do this difficult thing, but both pride and his daughter were the furthest things from his mind. He was playing back the record of his encounters with her and all the things he had done wrong. He shouldn't have pushed her so hard. He should have spent more time with her. He shouldn't have gotten the divorce or let her go so far away to school. It was all his fault; he had ruined her life, and now he would have to suffer for these unpardonable sins.

The group leader implemented a strategy in which he asked the father to repeat the stem sentence ''The great thing about feeling guilty is, . . .'' and members of the group would help him list possible payoffs that prevented him from changing his feelings (Dyer & Vriend, 1980).

The great thing about feeling guilty is:

- you can torture yourself for errors you feel you made and hope that this suffering wipes the slate clean.
- you can bloat your sense of self-importance. After all, you are totally responsible.
- you can avoid thinking about your problems as long as you focus on your daughter's.
- you can convey to others how much you care for your daughter in being so willing to take the blame for her actions.
- you can feel like a victim betrayed by an ungrateful child.
- you can get lots of sympathy from others because you act as if this tragedy happened to you.

In this group, the technique worked flawlessly. When I had the opportunity to practice it at a later date, however, it happened to be during counseling with an individual client. She was duly educated about how and why payoffs work, and she could readily see how important it was to understand them. But when it came time for her to finish the stem sentence and she was predictably speechless, I nervously looked over my shoulder for help from group members and recalled that, alas, we were alone. It was then that I determined to learn the common behavioral payoffs for every self-defeating action.

Basically, most examples of client suffering exhibit five common themes that therapists can isolate to facilitate the process of self-understanding. These themes are:

- procrastination
- avoiding risks
- retreating from the present
- avoiding responsibility for one's actions
- avoiding work or having to change

By making hidden secondary gains more explicit, we essentially deny group members their well-worn excuses for resisting efforts to change.

21. *Reassurance and peer support.* Along with the gift of insight is the associated pain of self-revelation. It hurts to discover how blind we have been, how ignorant and unaware of ideas that now appear obvious. In addition, understanding how and why personal troubles have been so persistently bothersome leads inevitably to the conclusion that some action must be taken. There is no longer any place to seek refuge. Excuses for avoiding change now sound so feeble that not even the client believes them. Before panic can set in and the flight impulse becomes too strong, the group's support system once again takes prominence. Members draw on their vast reservoir of concern and empathy to offer reassurance to their peer who is struggling with novel learnings. Thus, the group becomes a surrogate family that provides opportunities for participants to rework family-of-origin issues, complete with parent figures and sibling relationships, giving members opportunities to respond differently and receive support and feedback (Fuhriman & Burlingame, 1990).

22. *Generalization to other behaviors.* One final flash of insight is necessary before the change process moves forward toward concrete action. Most behavior is representative of a theme prevalent throughout a client's total being. If Fred has difficulty developing intimacy with other group members, he probably has similar problems of mistrust in other relationships. He avoids taking risks in his job, preferring predictable routines to more innovative productivity. He rarely deviates from his usual paths of travel while driving. He avoids unfamiliar parts of town, reasoning that if he had car trouble he would be stuck without help.

In short, Fred realizes that his drive for self-reliance and avoidance of any possible vulnerability, to which his behavior in the group attests, is altogether typical of his style. Finally Fred not only gains insight into the self-defeating mechanisms that keep him hanging back in the group but also learns that he engages in similar behavior throughout his life. The same irrational assumptions, closed-circuit traps, behavioral payoffs, and hidden motives that sabotage his efforts to change within the group hold true for actions outside the group as well.

Stage IV: Action.   23. *Motivational support.* The transition between insight and action-change processes, however discreetly they are implemented, will inevitably produce ambivalence and resistance in the client. With the realization that there is no turning back to the previously ineffective coping strategies coupled with the increased self-knowledge as to why the self-defeating behaviors have persisted, the client understands that a great many things will have to change. As attractive as the new order of thinking appears, however, the client also wistfully reminisces about the old self being left behind. There is also the significant prospect that what lies ahead will involve excruciatingly difficult efforts to put the accrued insights to work.

The group leader attempts to be helpful by being more nuturing and supportive, acting as the coach to a dozen cheerleaders who simultaneously cry "You can do it!" After a while, even the client will begin to believe it.

24. *Decision to change.* Just as much energy is expended to *evade* making decisions as in dealing with them, no matter how impending, crucial, or dire the consequences may be (Janis & Mann, 1977). And no wonder: there is always so much to lose. No matter what decision is made, there is always the possibility of committing the eighth deadly sin—making a mistake.

The decision to change ought to be the logical conclusion of the previous group work stages, which involved a sort of brainstorming. This problem-solving procedure, originally developed for use in industrial settings by Clark (1958) and Osborn (1963), has been found to be an optimal strategy for increasing productivity and creativity (Bayless, 1967; Parnes, 1967). Brainstorming, which has been used to invent such consumer products as the flashcube, has wide implications for the decison-making that occurs in therapeutic groups. The accepting, open environment, high motivation of participants, and emphasis on free thinking provide a perfect setting for committing oneself to constructive action.

25. *Commitment to the group.* There is nothing like a public statement to commit oneself to a course of action. With the possible exception of politicians, who give themselves permission to change their minds according to where their support is coming from, most people find that by verbally disclosing their intentions they will find it difficult to deviate from their course of action. The motive to change increases proportionately with the magnitude of commitment. If a group member vehemently tells many people that she intends to quit her job and try a new career, it is unlikely that she will be able to avoid that path should she change her mind in midstream. Too many people are watching.

Before clients commit themselves to change, they must be reasonably certain that they are doing so for themselves rather than to please significant others. At this stage in the change process, the commitment usually takes the form of a client voicing the results of his or her decision making in a way similar to the declaration of commitment that took place earlier when group participants shared the concerns with which they were having trouble coping.

In one group, before Aaron had the opportunity to formulate a systematic plan of attack, he spontaneously decided to declare that he was going to make some changes in his life. Preoccupied with his own thoughts, even while attention was focused on another group member, he blurted out in the middle of a reflective pause that he would have some good news to report the following week. The group leader redirected the focus to the original client, promising to get back to Aaron's outburst but never had the time to do so. Nevertheless, the next week, in spite of getting no specific help, Aaron made his dramatic report.

> **Aaron**: You may not believe this, but in the last week my whole life has changed. I decided that I had had enough of living a sham, being dependent on people around me. After the last group meeting I wanted to back down but realized that I had already committed myself to act, even if you didn't know exactly what I was going to do. At the time, I didn't either. Anyway, today you are looking at an unattached, unemployed, but very happy person. This week I broke my engagement, quit my job, sold all my possessions, told my parents to leave me alone, and decided to start my life over again.

26. *Brainstorming of alternative courses of action.* In the process of change, group members help one another to expand the choices available to them. All therapists attempt to remove obstructions that limit a client's perceived options in the world. Although these obstructions may include distortion of reality, "disasterization," lack of confidence, impoverished perceptual fields, unrealistic expectations, or inhibition of destructive emotions, the goal of all psychological treatment is to give clients alternatives to their self-defeating strategies.

A group setting is particularly facilitative in this regard, because the collective experience of a number of individuals is sure to generate viable options. Group members are trained to think scientifically when asked to reason through the decision-making process in an analytic way. Janis and Mann (1977) go so far as to specify seven major criteria that should be considered in "high-quality" decisions. The client should:

1. review the widest possible range of alternatives available, initially including even far-out choices in the hope that they could turn out to be feasible.
2. examine the desired objectives and the implications of each alternative for the client's personal value system.
3. systematically consider the positive and negative consequences that could conceivably result from each choice; Goldfried and Goldfried (1980) further recommend looking at both the personal and social consequences of each action as well as proposed short-term and long-term effects.
4. explore any relevant information that might shed light on alternatives.

5. integrate new information.
6. reexamine the consequences of each alternative.
7. develop contingency plans to cope with known risks and hazards.

Many group members experience a liberating feeling just knowing that other choices exist. There is a great difference between choosing to stay in a frustrating job or marriage and feeling trapped as if there were no other viable option. Bateson, Jackson, Haley, and Weakland's (1956) concept of the "double-bind" that drives kids into schizophrenia is an extreme example of the *logical* results of a lack of perceived choice.

Okun and Rappaport (1989) describe one possibility of this trap: a family consists of a girl, her mother, and father. The parents constantly nag the daughter about not showing them enough affection. Whenever she attempts to show affection, the parents scream at her for invading their privacy. When she retreats to show consideration for their privacy, she is berated for ignoring them and not showing affection. The girl is only 10 years old and so cannot leave the home. What choice is there for her except schizophrenia? When group members feel similarly trapped, we teach them that their own limiting state of mind creates the problem. By expanding the range of possible alternatives, we free clients from the slavery of the status quo.

27. *Information giving and guidance.* When E. G. Williamson, C. G. Wrenn, and Donald Super were in their prime, group work was synonymous with giving advice and instruction. For educational and career planning, there were few better ways to impart useful information than in a group setting in which discussion could take place.

In most therapeutic groups today, there comes a time when the leader and members offer constructive guidance to one another. If a member is seriously considering going to law school, it would be appropriate for relevant information such as potential job opportunities to be imparted. If a recently married person who is having conflicts in her relationship is seriously considering divorce, it would be helpful for her to understand what the process will involve.

Group guidance can be particularly valuable in the area of sexual dysfunction. In the instance of one couple, the wife felt frustrated because the husband was perfectly content until she complained. One day, while watching a talk show, the woman heard a sex expert casually mention the topic of female orgasm. The woman was dumbstruck: "Women have orgasms too? Oh my God, there's something wrong with me. I better get some help."

Reluctantly, the husband accompanied his distraught wife to the therapeutic group and eventually their problem came out. When questioned about what sex was like for them, the woman replied with embarrassment: "I don't know. Just like everyone else, I guess. Usually I'll be doing housework, watching TV or something, and he will clear his throat and point his finger toward the stairs. Then, you know, I pull down my pants and he undoes his zipper and puts it in me. How long does the whole thing take? Quite a long time, sometimes even a few minutes." When the laughter subsided and then stopped abruptly as group members realized she was serious, helpful information was provided on the importance of foreplay (including the revelation that such an activity exists). Simply revealing some tenets of basic sex education was enough to resolve their problem.

28. *Goal setting.* When all possible courses of action have been narrowed to a few viable options, the client's goals are specified according to his or her value system, constitution, and desired consequences. Again, the development of an appropriate goal involves the interactive contributions of all participants. It is to be hoped that this goal represents the logical culmination of all previous therapeutic efforts. Ideally, it should be as realistic as possible so that the client may have the greatest probability of success in reaching desired outcomes.

The formulated goals also function as a pretest for evaluating the relative success of the treatment plan. For this reason, group member goals should include a systematic format in which the overall group goals are specifically defined as individual subgoals for each participant, behavioral objectives are defined, priorities are ordered, and incomplete objectives are eliminated (Ryan, 1973). The group leader's task at this juncture is to ensure that momentum is carried forth to accomplish the stated goals (Krumboltz & Potter, 1973).

29. *Formulation of plan.* As a direct result of the previous decision-making, alternative-generating, and goal-setting procedures, group members are now prepared to aid in the formulation of a therapeutic plan designed to resolve the stated concerns. Such a blueprint might take the form of skill acquisition, structured risk taking, response decrement, environmental alterations, cognitive restructuring, or response increment (Gottman & Leiblum, 1974). In any case, the clients determine the strategy that is most likely to lead to a satisfactory conclusion.

After considering several viable options, Angela has decided that confronting her boss with a complaint will do no good since this supervisor has not responded well in the past to even the gentlest constructive criticism. Going above her supervisor's head would probably only make things more tense. Practicing assertive skills in the group and confronting other members in a nonthreatening manner would be good practice, but Angela is already an accomplished confronter. Finally it is determined that the best strategy would be to focus on Angela's internal behaviors—her unrealistic expectations, demanding attitude that others live by her rules, and perfectionistic standards. Angela decides that she could profit by learning to relax, to calm herself down when she feels herself losing her cool with the boss. She could practice dealing with her supervisor in the same manner she has been but *feeling* differently about the experience.

30. *Reality testing.* As an extra check on the plan's suitability, Angela and her co-members critically pick apart the program's components. They predict the likely consequences; they determine risks, short- and long-term benefits. In this process of reality testing, it is discovered that at weekly departmental meetings it would be unrealistic for Angela to keep her mouth shut and concentrate instead on doing her own excellent work; she feels morally bound to try to change aspects of the work situation that are not in the employees' best interests. It is not realistic for her to be exclusively concerned with her own frustrations because she feels a sense of responsibility to help her less articulate colleagues, who would suffer even more without her support. These reality-testing dialogues enable group members to make some necessary revisions.

31. *Rehearsal.* The greatest overall benefit of group work is the emphasis placed on the realistic practice of self-enhancing behaviors. As an experimental laboratory with controlled conditions, the group setting provides clients with structured rehearsal sessions. Criticism and other self-indulgent practices are minimized. Attempts are made to make these therapeutic simulations as much like the real world as possible.

In psychodrama and role-playing techniques, the group leader acts as director, setting the stage, helping the client to cast antagonists and to write the script (Moreno, 1964). Group members are allowed spontaneously to confront their real conflicts in a reasonably safe situation; their performances may later be analyzed by their understudies and the director.

Rehearsal of internal behaviors, such as of Angela's goals, may also be practiced before the client is thrown to the wolves. Participants may keep a journal to practice thinking in new ways, internalizing novel ideas, and combating inhibiting fears. One group member used her journal as a vehicle for imagery rehearsal, practicing what she would say to herself and to her husband when they met in divorce court.

32. *Constructive feedback.* Originally adapted from cybernetics by Kurt Lewin during the very beginning of the group movement in the 1940s, feedback implies a direct communication between input and output. It is what permits group members to alter their behavior in light of new information, and it is considered one of the essential features of therapeutic groups (Jacobs, 1974; Morran, Robison, & Stockton, 1985; Rhode & Stockton, 1992; Rothke, 1986).

Feedback is what Vinogradov and Yalom (1989) describe as "corrective emotional experiences," in which clients' maladaptive behavior is reacted to by others in the group. When received, feedback provides clients a more objective image of how they come across to others. This is the essence of interpersonal learning—what many group members consider to be the single most helpful therapeutic process in groups (Freedman & Hurley, 1980), especially when members feel understood during the process (Anderson, 1985).

Rehearsing new skills is meaningless unless group members can learn how well or badly they performed and how their behaviors may be made more effective in the future. Feedback is used to reinforce desirable actions while extinguishing others, such as yelling, that consistently create problems. Rehearsed feedback is also helpful for providing data on the effects the client has on others when certain behaviors are used. It motivates group members to continue trying the things that tend to work.

Feedback from the group leader or other members should follow certain guidelines.

1. It should be clearly expressed in terms and language to which the client-in-focus can best relate.
2. It should be expressive and personalized so that it does not come across as a cliché or stereotype.
3. It should be concise, reducing the essence of a message into efficient words.
4. It should be as specific as possible, labeling the target behaviors and supporting them with examples.
5. It should be given as soon after the rehearsed behaviors as possible to maximize reinforcement principles.
6. It should be given with a specific rationale in mind such as to point out an inconsistency or offer a suggestion.
7. It should be honest, avoiding watered-down truths, predictable statements, or comments designed to score approval-seeking points.
8. It should be diplomatically confrontive, straightforward without being needlessly provocative. The delivery of the message is at least as important as its content.
9. It should be sensitively expressed, capitalizing on empathy variables like kindness, respect, and acceptance.
10. It should include both constructive criticism and constructive support rather than being given in a context of positive and negative.

The use of feedback in groups is limitless. It is one of the best services provided throughout the sessions and various therapeutic stages because it is so rare to get helpful, honest feedback in the real world. Perhaps the most difficult task is for the group leader to elicit constructive feedback that meets the above criteria.

33. *Psychological homework.* Homework is an unfortunate word, evoking images of forgotten assignments, teachers' red-marked corrections, and repetitive busy work. It is not unknown for a group member to flush in indignation when a careless leader comments: "That's an area you could work on. Why don't you do that as a homework assignment for next week?" Just as students "forget" to hand in their papers or recklessly scribble some half-hearted last-minute effort, some clients act similarly, usually because

of a lack of commitment to complete something that another person has authoritatively assigned. When assignments are mutually determined and the reasons behind the work are clearly understood, the successful completion of tasks is more likely.

We are well aware of the intrinsic difficulties in practicing group work: that our clients often become dependent on us or become group junkies; that they learn to perform like zoo animals, acting only when there are spectators throwing peanuts; that the hard-fought effects of therapy are short-lived. To counteract these problems, the therapist attempts to structure ingenious ways to get clients to work on their own time, practicing in their worlds, where it counts, what they have learned in the group. "Thus, practice leads to improvement, and improvements leads to increased practice" (Palmer, 1980, p. 174).

To facilitate the transfer of learning from the group situation to the client's world, group members are helped to create and follow through on homework of a special kind. These assignments should be self-initiated (Cormier & Cormier, 1979), be mutually negotiated with the therapist and other members (Dyer & Vriend, 1977), and involve fairly attainable and realistic tasks. They should contain a "do statement" specifying what the task is to be and a "quantity statement" declaring how often the behavior will be practiced (Shelton & Ackerman, 1974).

34. *Commitment to action.* Once insight into the concern is gained, goals are set, a plan of action is established, relevant skills are rehearsed, and outside work is determined, a final commitment is made in the group to follow through with stated intentions. Mutual support and discussion usually result in several other members making silent or public commitments to initiate desired changes. Clients who are competitive by nature, or who constantly compare themselves to others as a yardstick for measuring their own self-worth, will now use their neurotic drives for productive purposes:

> **Thoughts**: What a boring group tonight. I've been sitting here for the past two hours talking to myself just like this. I can't believe Nadine is finally going to get off her butt and read her husband the riot act. So he is selfish, demanding, spoiled, and insensitive. Big deal. I wonder if she realizes what a good thing she's got going? I wouldn't take that crap if someone treated me that way. Except from my mother. So she gets a bit carried away sometimes. It's not so bad. I can live with it. I'd just love to see a weakie like Nadine try and tell off my mother when she gets in one of her moods. Actually, it might be quite a show. Nadine has fire in her eyes that has never been there before. Well, hell, if she can do it, so can I. Maybe it's time for me to finally tell my mother to get off my back.
>
> **Said Aloud**: Yea, I have something I could work on too.

35. *Closure.* Closure comes next—the end of the session. We learn in graduate school that closures should be perfectly timed and paced. First we tie up loose ends, then elicit summary statements from clients concerning what they learned and what they will work on between sessions. After the debriefing and gradual decompression adjustment to re-entering the real world, we give our final speech, timing its end with the sweep of the second hand so that members leave the group with a sense of completion.

Inadvertently, however, we have also discovered advantages to another form of closure: none. Because we forgot to watch the time and a crowd of people is clamoring to use our room, we are forced to interrupt interaction in the middle with an apology: "I'm sorry, folks, but we seem to be out of time. We'll pick up with this next week." The clients, of course, grumble; they feel as if they've been left hanging on a hook. But then a strange thing happens: as dissonance rises, group members think about the group proceedings more often than usual during the week. They must resolve their own closure in the face of many dangling ends that don't fit together.

There is thus a rationale for choosing a method of closure, depending on intended goals. Tying things in a neat package or deliberately programming a healthy amount of chaos may each serve clients well.

36. *Real-world practice.* This, the most important part of therapy, does not occur in the group. The rehearsal is over, and the live performance begins before an intensely critical audience. If preparation has been sufficient, the clients will successfully complete their therapeutic tasks, internalize novel ideas, apply their newly acquired skills, and practice thinking in more fully functioning ways. The use of adjunct structures, such as those described in Chapter 14, are also helpful at this stage.

Stage V: Evaluation.   37. *Progress report.* Before any new business is taken up, the group leader will check out and evaluate the progress of group members who previously received counseling time. Clients will report what they have worked on, to what degree they have met their objectives, and how they feel about their experiences. "Are you on the right track?" "Which parts were most difficult for you?" "What unexpected problems did you encounter?" "How do you feel now about what you have done?" "What do you plan to do next to follow up on this progress?"

38. *Additional input and modifications.* Seldom do things go according to plan, no matter how meticulous the preparations. Unexpected variables always crop up. People never seem to cooperate as they are supposed to. At this stage, the leader and group members briefly offer input and elicit client reactions to departures from the intended path. "Just how effective were the planned interventions in light of your goals?" "Are your goals still the same?" "What modifications in your plan are necessary?"

Ordinarily, a transition will be made from this externally framed evaluation pattern to a self-monitoring orientation in which group members may now independently follow and control their own progress. Gottman and Lieblum (1974) favor the use of tools such as "The Annotated Record," studying concomitant variations in graphic displays, Stewart Charts, or even calculating autocorrelations to determine the specific impacts of planned interventions. Group leaders less behaviorally inclined will devise similar strategies to ensure that group members follow through on their initial work.

39. *Reinforcement.* In addition to the self-satisfaction that results from accomplishing a difficult task, group members receive healthy doses of peer respect and praise. Sometimes it is just the anticipation of how great it will feel to tell group members about how well you performed and to acknowledge their laudatory comments that will act as a final impetus for implementing difficult changes. The reward-enriched milieu of a group allows the "cure" to be maintained throughout subsequent sessions.

40. *Finger on the pulse.* Subsequent sessions will provide numerous additional opportunities for group members to refine and practice the behaviors they are working to master.

Chapter 3 has aimed at integrating the most prominent and useful learning theories into a comprehensive, flexible explanation of how people change in groups. The action-theory-in-use is no more or less than a functional description of what most group leaders do in their groups. It is not itself a static, stable concept but a metamorphic phenomenon. When group leader personality variables, training experiences, goals, and unique group member needs and interests are added to the formula, the theory of change takes on quite a different surface structure, with its own language, techniques, and preferred strategies. But the underlying structure of most group approaches remains the same. This final chapter of Part I completes discussion of the interwoven threads that bind group helping systems together.

PART II

Dimensions of Advanced Group Leadership

There are certain attributes of the leader, specific reasoning processes, and appropriate roles that are most likely to promote desired outcomes. Therapists who are effective models; who capitalize on imitative learning processes; who skillfully use their bodies, language, and the ways they live their lives as examples of a masterful existence will ultimately enhance the power of their interventions. The specific ways in which leaders communicate their modes of thinking and reasoning, their methods of dealing with problems and conflict, and their styles of interacting with clients or colleagues can better provide groups a therapeutically charged atmosphere.

CHAPTER 4

Following the Leader

A tribal ritual among certain South American societies is literally to eat the brains, and thereby the spirit, of enemies defeated in battle. These people believe that consuming the courage and knowledge of their vanquished foes enhances their prowess as warriors. In modern Western society, we worship our heroes instead of eating them. Recording artists, movie stars, athletes, and writers are paid seven-figure yearly salaries to act as heroes for us. We seek their autographs, pay homage to them, and glorify them to a level above our own. To select and follow heroes or mentors appears to be a human drive.

A *mentor* is a wise adviser, a guide, a sponsor, a teacher of the protégé, a transitional figure who encompasses the virtues of competence, wisdom, ethics, and success. Levinson believes the mentor relationship to be crucial to an individual's development through the seasons of life: "The relationship enables the recipient to identify with a person who exemplifies many of the qualities he seeks. It enables him to form an internal figure who offers love, admiration, and encouragement in his struggles" (Levinson, 1978, p. 334).

Therapeutic Modeling

The importance of the roles that significant models play in people's lives cannot be underestimated. Whereas reductionist learning theorists would have us believe that the human race is shaped by satisfiers, reinforcers, need hierarchies, antecedent determinants, or all varieties of different stimuli-response chains, many other powerful forces facilitate human growth and development as well. In addition to the genetic scripts that program how humans evolve and the sequential stages of cognitive reasoning of which developmental theorists are so fond, there are other, intuitive answers to the question "How did I get to be who I am?"

We are all constantly on the lookout for new people to admire, to learn from, to study, and to imitate. Merchandisers, fashion specialists, and marketing personnel understand this, playing up to the compelling attractiveness of models in the media who are deliberately created to exhibit the dimensions of power that Bandura (1977) has found most seductive. Thus, models displaying their nurturing capabilities are hired to attract attention to aspirin or laxatives. Paid actors dress up in white lab coats with an assortment of pencils in their pockets, a stethoscope around their neck, and proclaim "Tests in a major hospital found—." However silly their appeal, we *do* buy their products. Models who exhibit striking physical or sexual power command even more attention and influence. The basis for modeling theory is that group members are exposed to demonstrations of desirable behaviors, which members then rehearse, are coached in to make adjustments, and then are given feedback on their performance of them (Rose, 1989).

In a narrow sense, therapeutic modeling in groups can be regarded as an extension of social learning theory. The group leader attempts to maximize attentional, retentional, and motor reproduction processes that occur in imitative learning mechanisms. Once a client has been motivated to observe the modeled behavior and is helped to retain the image and to rehearse it symbolically, the pathway is cleared for actual execution of the duplicated behavior in real-life situations. This paradigm is familiar in the group helping model, since members are regularly encouraged to experiment with new skills they have witnessed within the safety of the group. Psychodrama and role playing aid rehearsal efforts; support and feedback from peers act as reinforcers to perpetuate the imitated behaviors and to facilitate the internal cognitions necessary for generalization and integration to occur.

A group is, by its very nature, a special arena for modeling and imitative learning to take place. This is most likely to occur when group members (1) are helped to develop skills in observation and imitation, (2) receive incentives for imitating others, and (3) have opportunities to observe, interact with, and practice new behaviors under the supervision of desirable models (Bandura, 1969; 1977). Although group members can (and often do) serve as models for one another, it is primarily the responsibility of the group leader to serve this role, since he or she has greater reinforcement power than anyone else in the group (Cooke & Appolloni, 1976; Edleson & Rose, 1981).

Modeling can occur both spontaneously and incidentally, and as part of a deliberately planned and structured program. Examples of the latter include such structures as:

- acting out rehearsed role plays that emphasize important themes (Edleson, 1979)
- performing rehearsed vignettes that highlight relevant principles that have been discussed (Rose & Edleson, 1987)
- showing videotaped models of desired behaviors, such as social skills (Hazel, Schumaker, Sherman, & Shelton-Wildon, 1981)

- using videotaped segments of appropriate and inappropriate behaviors to teach discrimination abilities (Creer & Miklich, 1970)
- employing self-modeling techniques or "interpersonal process recall" by videotaping group members engaging in helpful behaviors
  and then playing the tapes back in session to review constructive
  actions (Kagan, 1973)
- prescribing certain videos or television shows as homework to
  observe effective models in action (Rose & Edleson, 1987)
- using puppets and animated characters with young children to
  model appropriate responses to certain situations (Cartledge &
  Milburn, 1981)
- creating written scripts of ideal behavior to employ in situations of
  conflict (Sarason & Ganzer, 1969)

Historically, every therapeutic pioneer from Hippocrates to Freud has
made systematic use of his or her personality as a means of encouraging
mimicry by clients. The use of anecdotal material so common to the psychoanalyst, the use of self-disclosure by the Rogerian, and the use of semantic
demonstrations by the rational-emotive group leader are all examples of explicit modeling in action. Regardless of historical theoretical affiliations,
all group leaders today tell "therapeutic" stories, construct metaphors, and
relate successful encounters showing that their methods work. Most group
leaders rely on role playing as a major strategy to demonstrate appropriate
skills for effective living, hoping that group members will incorporate the
strategies by having observed them. They also believe in one of the principal strengths of group work: while one client is receiving specific help,
most of the others are learning by watching.

That group members make constructive changes in their lives merely as
the result of observing others doing so seems to be a very tenuous assumption. Yet we notice that often it is the participants who say the least that
grow the most. While one client tearfully relates her struggle to break free
of her husband's dominance, the others sit quietly. She promises to make
some changes during the coming week—to assert her independence, confront the insensitive spouse, to think differently about her situation—yet
she returns having had only minimal success. The real magic of the situation lies in what the other clients have to report.

> **Member:** Well, at the time, last week seemed incredibly tedious to
> me. I kept wandering and drifting, looking at my watch, hoping the
> session would end. It wasn't until I got home that I realized how
> closely her situation parallels mine. I guess I was afraid to pay at-
> tention because while you were talking to her, you were talking to
> me, too. Well, anyway, I sat down with my wife and straightened
> some things out. I'm tired of being pushed around, too!

Strangest of all is that we take these incidents for granted. The veteran
is seldom surprised when people on the right make an about-face although

the leader is talking to someone over on the left. Putting therapeutic modeling to work in groups has become automatic. The group leader rarely makes a conscious decision to model a little here or a little there. The subtle and spontaneous aspects of one's personality, the personal effectiveness that is displayed by one's characteristic style, are as much facilitative forces as the most deliberate technical intervention.

A Fully Functioning Model

The single thread that binds together all effective group practitioners is certainly not their unanimous allegiance to a particular theoretical approach. At first glance, master group leaders such as Fritz Perls, Eric Berne, Carl Rogers, and Albert Ellis would appear to have little in common. Their therapeutic goals, favorite techniques, underlying philosophies, and leader roles contradict one another. Yet they all project to their clients an image of a formidable individual who is fully in charge of his personal world. They exude self-confidence, expertise, worldly experience, and serenity.

Carl Rogers is the prototype of a warm, sensitive, caring, and genuine human being, precisely the characteristics he considers to be crucial to the therapeutic relationship. Albert Ellis seems always to be rationally engrossed, the epitome of an internally controlled, logical person who can cure himself of any emotional suffering. Freud, Adler, and Perls were also incredibly dynamic personalities, scientists who took great pains to practice what they preached. Their legacy to contemporary group practice is found in the behavior of every effective group leader. Behind every exciting, beneficial group experience is an energetic, knowledgeable, skilled, and enthusiastic leader.

There is consensus among a number of group writers and researchers on what are the ideal characteristics of effective group leaders (Corey & Corey, 1992; Grotjahn, 1983; Kottler, Vriend, & Dyer, 1974; Posthuma, 1989; Trotzer, 1989). Most of these traits are similar to the ideal qualities of therapeutic practitioners in general that have been described extensively (Beutler, 1983; Carkhuff & Berenson, 1977; Corey, Corey, & Callanan, 1993; Decker, 1988; Frank, 1973; Garfield, 1980; Kottler, 1991); but there are nevertheless some special attributes that distinguish group specialists from their brethren. These would include such things as: an affinity for and attraction to group environments; special cognitive styles such as the ability to process multiple stimuli simultaneously and sort through information to find the most significant focus; interpersonal attributes similar to those of superlative teachers, who can facilitate classroom environments; and greater adaptability and flexibility to change directions fluently, depending on what is happening.

Personal mastery is a relative concept, one that takes into consideration the potentialities, goals, expectations, resources, and limitations of any given individual, although there is a consistent image regarding what constitutes the characteristics of such a person. The personally masterful group leader is one who has attained a state of fluid movement through life, who works toward higher levels of proficiency in every human action, who is always involved in a process of formulating goals to work toward. This group leader is the kind of person toward whom others gravitate because of a reservoir of inner strength, quiet competence, and compassionate spirit.

What is personal mastery but the development of skills necessary for a happy existence? A personally effective human being is in control of his life, goals, dreams, and destiny. This is what Abraham Maslow (1954) meant by the term *self-actualized*, what Fyodor Dostoyevsky (1864) described as a person of "acute consciousness," and what Ambrose Bierce (1911) defined as a "fool":

> A person who pervades the domain of intellectual speculation and diffuses himself through the channels of moral activity. He is omnific, omniform, omnipercipient, omniscient, omnipotent. It was he who invented letters, printing, the railroad, the steamboat, the telegraph, the platitude, and the circle of sciences. He created patriotism and taught the nations war—founded theology, philosophy, law, medicine, and Chicago . . . In the morning of time he sang upon primitive hills, and in the noonday of existence headed the procession of being. His grandmotherly hand was warmly tucked in the set sun of civilization, and in the twilight he prepares Man's evening meal of milk-and-morality and turns down the covers of the universal grave. And after the rest of us shall have retired for the night of eternal oblivion he will sit up to write a history of civilization. (Bierce, 1911, pp. 43–44)

Personally masterful therapists are busy persons, intensely concerned with their well-being and that of their fellow humans. They are action-oriented truth seekers who pursue the unknown and take productive risks in the search for a more satisfying life. Most important, they are in a continual state of improved change, ever working to become more personally effective.

In addition, there are some corollary assumptions implicit in the personal mastery model.

1. The more personally skilled group leaders become, the more professionally effective they become.

2. The group leader is in a constant state of change, as are all group members. Each client concern and interaction conflict forces the leader to look inward, asking the question "Have I worked this problem through for myself?" While using group time to work through personal struggles is clearly unethical, the group leader cannot help but use the time between sessions to personalize relevant struggles to bring them toward successful closure.

3. The more effective group leaders become at solving personal problems, the better teachers they can be at facilitating such outcomes in clients. The

group leader should have learned ahead of time how to work through any concern with which a group member may have difficulty.

4. No mere human has ever reached perfection. Every group leader ought to be engaged in a rigorous self-training process aimed at teaching higher levels of personal mastery. Identifying behaviors in need of improvement is the first step in making constructive changes. The following list of characteristics will aid group leaders in self-evaluation.

Self-Confidence

What makes advanced group leaders most effective is their comfort with and high-level functioning during spontaneous occurrences. In part, this is the result of what Grotjahn (1983) describes as the group leader's "schizoid" features—"that is, in being able and willing by nature to split himself and endure contradictions" (p. 295). This splitting takes place when we are able to understand each group member through projective identification while retaining our own sense of identity. The deep-level understanding that results is what allows the experienced leader to "shoot from the hip" and usually hit the target.

Group leaders who have faith in their therapeutic powers transmit this contagious attitude to their observant clients. Therapy takes place between two believers (Fish, 1973). Before group members can realistically hope for progress, they must fervently believe in the leader's skill. A level of self-assurance balanced by realistic modesty seems necessary to gain and keep a client's confidence. The group leader should therefore feel a strong sense of mission in this work, an attitude reflected in personal style. Introducing a technique with "I believe this will help you considerably" will produce more dramatic results than a hesitant alternative such as, "I'm not sure, but I hope this will work—if we're lucky."

Risk Taking

Because all change involves risk, a good portion of time spent in groups is centered on activities designed to facilitate risk taking in a safe, secure atmosphere. Sharing personal secrets, giving feedback, committing oneself to a goal, or (for some clients) even talking aloud results in accelerated heartbeats. For a group leader to expect clients to unburden their troubles or undrape their vulnerabilities without being a world-class expert in this difficult life skill is to practice hypocrisy. A person skilled in risk taking welcomes the mysterious and unknown, actively initiates new relationships, abjures superficial communication, and willingly experiments with new behaviors. Such group leaders are admirably equipped to help clients take the plunge because they actively practice constructive risk taking in every facet of life, from discovering new roads for travel to finding higher levels of intensity in love relationships.

Humor

The person who can create and bring humor to life is one committed to joy. Therapeutic groups are notoriously serious places, full of tears, gut-wrenching pain, and the molted skins of people struggling to become whom they are not. The group leader who can appreciate the folly of human existence, the silliness of so many human actions, the sublime and ridiculous in his or her own behavior as well as in other people's behavior is well prepared to lighten the load of client suffering. To appreciate what is funny is one thing and to laugh at oneself is still more admirable, but to actively create humor in groups is crucial to helping people keep their problems in perspective.

Flexibility

The flexible mind is one without a vested interest in retaining any attitude, value, thought, feeling, or behavior. Such a mind argues only with itself, is open to all possible alternatives, and has no desire to convince other minds of its rightness. Its possessor will try any means available (as long as it is morally responsible) to accomplish a goal, and, if no acceptable solutions to a problem readily occur, it becomes a matter of routine to create a new pathway to truth. The flexible mind does not worship strategies that have worked previously but is constantly searching for more efficient and effective means for solving life's problems.

Creativity

Albert Einstein described creative people as those who are unable to understand the obvious. They are continually searching for original paths to take. They are intellectually playful, exploring ideas for their own sake or to see where they lead. Creative persons are more sensitively attuned to their environment, more perceptually aware of subtle events around them. Nonconforming individuals frequently refuse to play by conventional rules but are constantly experimenting with novel approaches to making their lives more efficient. They are rebels, sometimes "troublemakers," because of their persistence in pursuing truth to its conclusion regardless of the consequences. Creative group leaders leave every session bathed in sweat, having exhausted themselves to find new ways of energizing, motivating, and facilitating client growth.

Internal Discipline

The psychologically independent person is one free of conventional schedules. Since there are too few moments in the day to enjoy life to its fullest, sleep becomes an enemy to such a person. Sleep is practice for death, and boredom is just another way that people sleep through their waking moments.

The internally disciplined individual is totally absorbed in work and play and is capable of resisting approval-seeking behaviors or any dependency on a person, routine, or habit. This person is in charge of his or her body, telling it what it may eat, when it may sleep, and how it must perform despite destructive temptations. The capacity to resist enculturation and societal demands that are not personally meaningful are other components of internal discipline, as are the ability to get things done and the dedication to pursue productive activities in the face of seductive distractions.

Flow

When a person becomes so immersed in the present moment as to lose the sense of time and of self, experiencing floating action without thought, heightened awareness without effort, that is *flow* (Csikszentmihalyi, 1975). Between boredom and anxiety, between relaxation and alertness, lies the capacity to flow, to experience each waking moment to its fullest. Maslow, who described such intrinsically satisfying moments as "peak" experiences, noticed that self-actualized persons release their creative spirit during periods of special wholeness. The Asian understands this concept as Ki; the Western mind thinks of it in terms of living totally in the present moment. For clients who escape into a past of guilt, trauma, or self-defeating patterns or who "futurize" with worry and fantasy, the group leader can be a powerful model of someone totally centered in the here and now.

Free of Negative Emotions

Group leaders must be experts at helping clients rid themselves of self-defeating emotions such as anger, depression, shame, jealousy, guilt, worry, self-pity, and frustration. The internally controlled person is immune to the panicky fluctuations of mood to which the helpless are afflicted. Neither the weather nor other externally caused events and human actions affect the balanced emotional stability of one who is in charge of thoughts and feelings. Freedom from extreme negative emotions means continual internal ruddering to make certain that personal conflicts are worked through and that active steps are taken to keep a realistic perspective in focus. Negative emotions are not foreign to the personally masterful, but such persons have the skill to ensure that upheavals are mild and short-lived.

Logic

Logic is the systematic application of reasoning to interpret and make sense of the world. With the human heritage of belief in magic and spiritualism, the subjective nature of perceptual systems, and the wide range of individual differences, very few people reason in the same way. Nevertheless, the group leader, above all else, must be a clear thinker and systematic problem solver who can sort through the confusing maze of human action to isolate relevant segments for scientific analysis and intervention.

Honesty

An adjective that often precedes the noun *honesty* is *brutal*. Outside the confines of a therapeutic group, people are little interested in hearing the truth. They prefer to be slightly deceived, subtly misled, or told a few white lies because the truth usually hurts. It is difficult to be direct, to tell people exactly how they come across. It is even more difficult to be diplomatically confrontive. The scrupulously honest person feels compelled to speak his or her mind but can do so with enough sensitivity to avoid triggering defensiveness. But the honest person refuses to dilute the truth, even if it means listeners will not like what they hear.

Of course, honesty can also be used to punish and intimidate group members, as well as be employed carelessly without regard for its healing effects. That is why this attribute must be tempered with the good judgment to know when and how to be honest in a therapeutically useful way.

Energetic Enthusiasm

In a study of eminent thinkers of the past century, Goertzel, Goertzel, and Goertzel (1978) found a striking pattern among the world's great scientists, writers, artists, and politicians: none of them slept very much. They had unbounded energy to pursue their goals, taking time out for rest only when their bodies were driven to exhaustion. The zest with which one pursues a vocation, the excitement that one feels for living, the enthusiasm and energy evident in one's voice and manner are the most compelling evidence of an effective model. This excitement is transmitted like electricity vibrating in the atmosphere, prompting others to tap greater energy resources.

Compassion

Although Rogers and Carkhuff restrict their discussions of therapist personality to clinical dimensions such as empathy, unconditional positive regard, acceptance, and genuineness, a far more important characteristic is evident in dedicated helpers. Compassion is that uniquely human quality of feeling an affinity for all others in the world. A concern for others' welfare, a love for all people, a respect for individual rights, an individually principled concept of morality, and a great sensitivity to the suffering of others are all part of what it means to be compassionate. A compassionate person offers aid for internal satisfaction rather than for monetary gain or to win points in heaven.

Modeled Messages

There are a number of ways in which a group leader capitalizes on modeling influences as therapeutic tools. It can even be argued that everything a group leader does is an example of covert modeling. From the deliberate use of self-disclosure to the more subtle forms of cued reinforcement, the therapist communicates the force and power of his or her personality. Although most modeling occurs on unconscious levels, the group leader is nevertheless studiously observed and imitated by attentive protégés. We would therefore be well advised to spend far more time and energy attempting to make such learning mechanisms more explicitly pointed. Following are a sampling of group leader techniques that capitalize on modeling effects.

Watch Me

In psychodramatic role reversal, the group leader alternates between demonstrating effective interaction strategies and providing supervised experiences for the client to practice new skills. According to the prescribed formula, a client is given an opportunity to recount relevant background information, such as the exact nature of the conflict, accompanying trepidations, previous experimental outcomes, capsulized portraits of antagonists, even details regarding where the confrontation might occur, including the most realistic arrangement of a stage set.

Next, the client-in-focus, who (let us say) is consistently trapped into arguments during every family visit, selects the players who will act out a representative conflict situation. The client may be asked to choose group members who most resemble her mother-in-law, husband, and other characters, or volunteers may be recruited for these parts. In either case, the scene is set, positions are taken, and the action begins.

> **Client**: Hello, Mother. I hope we're not late?
> **Mother-in-law**: As a matter of fact, you are. I just know the roast is burned. I knew I shouldn't have trusted you again.
> **Client**: But Mother, I told you—.
> **Father-in-law**: Never mind. Let's sit down to eat.
> **Client**: But I tried to explain—.
> **Mother-in-law**: Explain? There's nothing to explain. My son was never late until he married you.
> **Client**: As a matter of fact, the reason we're late is because your son decided he had to watch the end of the football game.

The destructive interaction pattern between the client and her in-laws is already evident. After group members conduct an analysis, offering suggestions, analyzing motives, and exploring client feelings, the group leader proposes that characters assume their parts once again, this time with the client watching the proceedings as an observer.

Client (*played by therapist*): Hello, Mother.

Mother-in-law: You're late again, you know.

Therapist: Yes, actually I do realize we're 15 minutes past the time you expected us. That's why I gave you an estimated time of arrival.

Mother-in-law: You gave me no such thing! Hubert, did she tell *you* that?

Father-in-law: Not that I remember, dear.

Therapist: Mom, Dad, this seems to be getting out of hand, and we've only just walked in the door. I wonder if I might talk to you both for a moment?

Mother-in-law: Well, what about? I'm very busy. The roast is already ruined. I don't know what I'll serve for dinner.

Therapist (*stepping out of role and addressing client*): What did I do that was different from your approach?

Client: For one thing, you didn't lose your cool. You also didn't get defensive or try to hurt her back.

Therapist: Yes, and I also set her up to confornt the issue head-on instead of playing games. Why don't you jump in now and deliver the speech you've been practicing all along? Say the things you've always wanted to tell her. But remember, stay calm as you saw me do. Don't let her ruffle your feathers.

The psychodramatic encounter is now programmed to allow for further role reversals. Each time, the group leader can highlight a particularly effective behavior that can be used to defuse an explosive conflict.

Specific, personally masterful behaviors pervade the group leader's style. The message "watch me" is communicated whenever the leader steps in to redirect the focus of counseling content. When intervening with the statement "Perhaps you could be a bit more concise in giving us this background," group members may be thinking to themselves, "I must remember to do that more myself when people start rambling." When the leader interrupts a member who, in sharing his feelings repeatedly uses the pronoun *we*, by asking, "Are you speaking for every person in this room?" the modeled message gets clearly understood by others who may realize that they too can use this technique to stop others from speaking for them without their consent.

Other "watch me" messages include memorable verbalizations such as the following:

- "That's an excellent question. Would anyone care to answer it?" (*To be used when you can't or don't want to answer the question yourself.*)
- "You say you don't know what you would do. Well, what would you guess you might do?" (*To be employed when a person refuses to take a stand on an issue.*)
- "Who says life is fair?" (*To be asked of a victim of self-pity.*)

- "What do *I* think of you? How does that make a difference?" *(To be used to short-circuit approval seeking.)*

Clients will tend to remember and use the responses their leader employs effectively in the group. Through osmosis clients become more proficient at important life skills such as "keeping the ball in the other person's court" or never feeling ashamed about something in oneself that is impossible to change.

There is, of course, much more to the imitative learning approach than committing a few magic words to memory. Nonverbal gestures of self-confidence, tranquility, and competence are also transmitted. Group members attempt to resolve their initial discomfort and anxiety by creating a semblance of structure in what appears to be a chaotic situation. They become possessive about their physical space (their chair), exercising a territorial imperative. They also look to the leader for appropriate cues, imitating the leader's posture, language, even gestures. Shapiro reports on one group

> led by a colleague who had a habit of rhythmically stroking her long hair during periods of silence and high tension. By the fourth week of the group all six of the female group members were stroking their own hair the same way. This was even true for one woman who had short hair and who in effect was stroking hair which would not be long enough for years! (Shapiro, 1978, p. 130)

One of the distinct advantages of group work is that it allows clients to receive training as helpers at the same time that they are working through their personal concerns. One of the best possible ways to learn a skill such as reflecting one's feelings is by first watching a master demonstrate the behavior and then having readily available opportunities to practice it. A therapeutic group provides just such a workshop atmosphere.

Both subconsciously and deliberately, group members learn communication skills that are part of the leader's repertoire—to use confrontation non-defensively, to simplify the complex, to summarize, to describe things concretely, and to interpret the meanings of behavior. It is the group leader's "chairside manner," the cool, calm style, that keeps clients intrigued enough to keep learning. Once the group leader has earned the group members' respect as an invaluable resource person and consultant, modeling strategies fall easily into place.

Since what a client does outside the sessions is far more important than what goes on within the group, the therapist can use modeling capabilities to structure beneficial homework assignments. Modeled demonstrations in the field act as transitional learnings to form a bridge between group work and the real world. Milton Erickson was an absolute wizard when it came to programming therapeutic incidents for his clients. He had been known on several occasions to take his clients by the hand and lead them through forays into the "combat zone." Whether to a bar, a restaurant, a party, or a walk through the park, Erickson would creatively structure situations that allowed him to model appropriate behaviors and then to prod his clients to try them out.

There are a host of possible field trips that the creative group leader may incorporate into the treatment plan. A group of chronic overeaters may be taken to a tempting restaurant to demonstrate useful strategies for ordering healthfully from the menu. The group leader can model the pace of the meal, emphasizing a slow, savoring approach to eating. Overeaters learn by observation to be more selective about what they put into their mouths.

A group of shy participants may be taken to a social gathering, asked to observe the leader approach strangers and deal calmly with rejection, and then encouraged to initiate conversations themselves. A group of 4-year-olds can be led to a local playground and taught the basic concepts of sharing and respect for property by modeled demonstrations.

Whether in the group or in the field, the modeling group leader indirectly offers this advice: "Watch me. Words lie but actions don't. Observe what I do and how I act. What you see in me is the best I have to offer you. Reject the aspects of my behavior that you find counterproductive, but watch carefully. Those skills I have that you admire, those things I do that you wish you could apply, those behaviors that you want to adopt for yourself— take them! They're yours for the asking."

Listen to Me

The theoretical works of Ellis (1977a), Meichenbaum and Goodman (1971), and Bandler and Grinder (1975) focus largely on the language people use to describe events. Meaning is derived from an interpretation of objective occurrences by subjective internal sentences. The ways in which people talk to themselves and the language they use to communicate with others predispose them to think in rational or irrational patterns. This cognitive-based approach to explaining emotional suffering has helped even the psychoanalyst, existentialist, and humanist pay a lot more attention to the structure of syntax, choice of vocabulary, and semantics, regardless of their avoidance of the rational philosophy and technique.

A great deal of semantic modeling occurs in any group in which clients spend time listening to their leader. Characteristic speech patterns, favorite expressions, and even vocal intonations are unconsciously imitated. The group leader concerned with logical precision of language is careful to speak in terms consistent with reality-based constructs, thus modeling effective ways to think aloud. If members of a group are particularly uncommunicative, uncooperative, and resistant during a session, the leader may choose, instead of an angry, scolding outburst, to demonstrate by choice of words that he or she is constructively working on the inner frustration.

> **Leader:** At first I really *made myself feel* upset at all of you because I felt that my time was being wasted. Then I *said to myself*, these

people are not here to please me; I'm here to help them. *I told myself* to stop feeling self-pity and to get busy trying to initiate some action. *I helped myself* to feel more relaxed by realizing that your actions are not part of any conspiracy against me; this is a problem *I created for myself* by distorting what actually happened.

The language-sensitive group leader corrects exaggerations of reality that are prevalent in client speech. What group members say indicates how they characteristically think about their life situations. In response to the statement "My lover puts so much pressure on me that I am trapped in the relationship," the group leader might ask, "Don't you mean 'I am putting so much pressure on myself that I am trapping myself in the relationship'?"

Ellis and Harper (1975), Bandler and Grinder (1975), and other writers offer several specific examples in which other modeling language interventions might be appropriate.

Client: I feel awful.

Therapist: I want you to say instead: "I feel awful when I don't get what I want."

Client: But if I do assert myself, I will surely hurt her feelings.

Therapist: *You* will hurt her feelings, or *she* will hurt her own feelings?"

Client: This is just so depressing.

Therapist: *This* is so depressing, or are *you* making yourself feel depressed over this situation?

Client: I'm shy.

Therapist: You mean: I act shy whenever I am with a group of strangers who are older than I am.

Client: I really should buy her a present.

Therapist: Should? Who says you should?

Client: I must finish whatever I start.

Therapist: Must? You will die if you don't?

Client: I have to get this job.

Therapist: I don't recall seeing that among the Ten Commandments. Perhaps you mean: I would *prefer* to get this job, but if I don't I guess that will be another example of something I wanted but couldn't get. Oh, well.

Client: Obviously, this is a waste of time.

Therapist: To whom is it obvious?

Client: I can't just move out of the house.

Therapist: You *can't* or you *choose* not to at this time?

Client: It is terrible that this happened to me.

Therapist: Is it really *terrible* or only inconvenient?

Client: I'm just no good at asking girls out on dates. I've always been that way.

Therapist: You've got date-inhibiting genes? Don't you mean instead: Until now I have never learned to ask girls out on dates, but I may decide to learn that skill in the future?

Self-Disclosure

The use of self-disclosure in groups is probably the single most abused therapeutic intervention. Group leaders who like to hear themselves talk; who, because of ego deficiencies, attempt to impress clients with their prowess; or who use group time to meet their own needs are acting unethically. Yet every leader is periodically guilty of sharing personal information or a story that is really intended not to help clients feel more comfortable but to help him or herself feel more at ease. In answer to the internal question "What do I hope to accomplish by sharing this with members of the group?" we sometimes have no defensible rationale.

All self-disclosure involves the sharing of personal information, but there are a number of specific intentions for initiating this modeling technique. Leader self-disclosure can be used to facilitate client personal sharing on the same level or to develop better rapport by reducing the psychological distance between therapist and clients. It can be used to create a more open group atmosphere; to convey warmth, genuineness, and empathy; or to change clients' perceptions about their behavior. It can be employed as a morale booster to convey messages such as: "I'm OK, you're OK," "Be like me!" "You can do it, too!" or "This really works."

In a community mental health center located on the bottom floor of a housing project, a dozen therapists declare their resolve to reach more of their disadvantaged constituency. They have all been in practice for several years, some of them for a few decades. Although they work and live on the outskirts of the island city of Singapore, most of them have been educated in the United Kingdom or the United States. Those who have studied at their own national university are nevertheless quite familiar with the universal standard texts in the field.

As do counselors and therapists in our own part of the world, these practitioners feel frustrated by their meager resources with which to help the children and families who seek their services. They are understaffed, underpaid, and overworked. Furthermore, they do not believe they are making a dent in the overwhelming needs of their citizens. Individual and family sessions are their standard treatment modalities, since the values of Chinese, Malay, Indian, and other ethnic groups are most compatible with these orientations. They have experimented with running groups as a way to reach more people, but, alas, the requirements for "public" self-disclosure and sharing mean a loss of face for those who reveal too much.

Kia-su is a Singaporean term that refers to the competitive drive of people to make themselves look good at others' expense. This national tendency makes group work in this country a potential nightmare. Already reticent to self-disclose because it might appear as bragging or self-indulgence, Singaporean group members also invest much energy into figuring out ways to make sure that *what* they say and *how* they say it presents them in the best light. Even the slightest possibility of the perception of failure or weakness must be avoided at all costs.

The rules that apply to members also apply to leaders. If the group leaders are seen as losing face, then they will not command enough respect to be influential. How, then, are these dedicated professionals supposed to introduce group work to a culture that holds values that discourage public intimacy?

It is the hallmark of our specialty that we must be innovative, flexible, and quite creative in the ways we work—perhaps more so than for other treatment modalities. This certainly proved to be the case with the staff of this Singaporean clinic, who did find a way to incorporate groups into their work by applying the following strategies.

Defining group work as a private setting. Participants are informed that when confidentiality is enforced, groups are *not* public encounters. Thus the usual rules for conduct, and the norms of kia-su, are suspended temporarily.

Including more structure. Participants expect group leaders to be experts, and as such, leaders should provide guidance and advice. After a period of time in which the leader dominates, process interventions that involve members could gradually be introduced.

Modeling of leader disclosures. Participants come to see that if someone of the leader's stature can self-disclose or confront someone gently, others have tacit permission to do so as well.

In any capacity in which self-disclosures are used to model appropriate behaviors, leaders ought first to ask themselves "Whom will I help by sharing this? How will it help them? Is there another intervention that might accomplish the same goal without focusing on me?" Such self-monitoring activities will ensure that the leader will be spotlighted only in the specific instances when this is effective for promoting client change.

I Am What You Wish to Be

"I am an extremely happy person. You'll almost always see me smiling because that's how I feel inside. I rarely get angry, feel depressed or frustrated, sad or jealous, or experience negative emotions. I make things happen in my life, rather than waiting for relationships or events to come to me. I am very productive, sleep only about five hours a night, and yet know how to feel relaxed and forgive myself when I don't complete all self-assigned tasks.

"I am constantly searching for areas of my behavior to improve. For instance, I am too impatient, and sometimes I push people a little too much. But I have the skills and knowledge to work through virtually any personal concern. I know how to make depression or boredom go away. I can appreciate privacy but am rarely lonely. I am always in some stage of setting goals for me to work toward.

"I used to be a pitiful creature: helpless, dissatisfied, and depressing to be around. But then I went to work on myself. I practiced new skills I'd learned in the group, worked on new behaviors between sessions, talked to myself in my journal, in my head. I worked hard to get where I am now. It's no accident, act of fate, or coincidence that I feel as good as I do. I am the one responsible. So can you be responsible for your growth!"

The preceding introduction illustrates how a group leader uses self-disclosure to transmit some powerful modeled messages. By candidly and confidently revealing personal strengths and successes, the group leader clearly communicates "I did it! So can you. I dare you to be like me." Positive self-disclosure conveys the image of a group leader in charge of self. The dimensions of power in modeling that Bandura (1977) believed crucial to successful learning transfer are strongly implied in positive statements about oneself that exude expertise, competence, confidence, and nurturance.

I'm Human, Too

Negative self-disclosures can also be therapeutic, although they rely on an opposite strategy. To develop rapport with group members, to close the psychological distance between master and disciple, to increase the sense of perceived similarity between client and therapist, the leader must model messages that emphasize his or her essential humanity. It is crucial for clients to understand that their leader is prone to error, failures, mistakes, and miscalculations, just as they are.

Shame, for example, is easier to bear when a person whom you admire and respect shares something apparently shameful without embarrassment: "Yes, I was once caught stealing as a child. I got a job in a drugstore so that I could get some birth control devices that I was too young to purchase. When they caught me, I wanted to die."

The group leader is as error-prone as the rest of the human race. Acknowledging past mistakes while at the same time highlighting acceptance of one's limitations is an instructive attitude to demonstrate for group members. The fear of failure is a crippling, self-defeating behavior that sabotages any attempt at experimentation or risk taking.

Leader: I approached the first waitress for a date, and she immediately turned me down. It didn't hurt as much as I thought it would. What the heck, what did I have to lose? So I walked up to another attractive waitress, who also declined a date but was a little more diplomatic. I then realized for the first time that no one could ever reject me again. To refuse a date is not to reject me as a person. Only I am capable of rejecting me, because that is more a state of mind than of circumstances. I felt so freed that I approached two more waitresses, both of whom also said no. The funny thing is that when I walked out of that restaurant, dateless after four attempts, I never felt better in my life!

The group leader gives permission for others to feel vulnerable or admit weaknesses by demonstrating that such behavior is not incompatible with pride. It is perfectly all right to cry, to hurt, or to be confused.

I'll Give You a Cookie

The spectator effects of group work make it ideally suited for emphasizing the social aspects of reinforcment. Observers tend to increase the frequency of behavior that they see being reinforced in others.

> To cite but a few examples from laboratory studies, people will adopt high performance standards that reduce self-gratification, they will select non-preferred foods, they will sacrifice material goods, they will divulge personal problems, and they will pursue formerly resisted courses of action more readily if they see models praised for exhibiting such conduct than if models receive no recognition for their actions. (Bandura, 1977, p. 119)

Since the principal object of therapeutic groups is to get people to experiment with new behaviors that they previously have been inhibited from trying, vicarious reinforcement is among the best tools available to the group leader. Participants can be clearly rewarded for engaging in socially approved ways: "Sam, it was fantastic watching you in action. I really respect the courage it must have taken to share that with us."

Socially undesirable behavior may also be vicariously extinguished through the use of modeled punishment. Particularly in beginning group sessions, when clients are learning ground rules and acceptable behavior, leaders will rely on subtle forms of shaping procedures to help facilitate a fully functioning group. After a group member offers unsolicited advice to another, the leader may intervene: "Dana, how was it helpful to you to hear Kevin tell you what he would do in your shoes? Oh? It wasn't helpful? You resented him for taking the focus off you, and, besides, hearing his advice doesn't help you to think for yourself?"

When one client becomes verbally abusive to another, vicarious punishment will act as a deterrent to future transgressions. Modeling of this sort provides indirect information to observers about how they may and may not act. Although it does not work quite as effectively as more experiential forms of modeling, vicarious reinforcement will motivate people to persist in their change efforts, even in the face of failure, when they witness others being similarly rewarded. Bandura (1977) also believes that vicarious reinforcement can reduce group members' inhibition levels and increase their influenceability potential. Observing a peer undergo threatening confrontations without adverse consequences, even producing favorable results, increases the probability that others will imitate this modeled behavior.

Once Upon a Time

Many group members feel stuck in a rut with little hope of ever stopping their wheels from spinning. Some come from economically and culturally deprived backgrounds whereas others come from homes in which there was little emphasis on the stuff from which dreams are made. With underestimated potential, underdeveloped goals, and an overall attitude of indifference, it is difficult to make significant progress toward desired achievements. Kids who get off to a bad start, with a poor record of academic achievement and/or behavioral problems, want to give up; adults with physical/psychological disabilities may succumb to self-pity. Group leaders are hard-pressed to invent ingenious ways of pulling the unmotivated out of the muck.

One energizing force involves recruiting models from the past. Throughout history, people have overcome long odds to make significant contributions to humankind. The lives of these admired people may be effectively displayed so that group members can profit from the inspiration. That a creative genius like T. S. Eliot was the victim of depressive bouts that forced him into seclusion, or that Al Jolson, Muhammad Ali, Bob Dylan, Ingmar Bergman, and Babe Ruth were all budding juvenile delinquents, has instructive value for people trying to overcome similar problems. Tennessee Williams recovered from a year-long illness only to develop a debilitating shyness that lasted the duration of his childhood.

These and other testimonies from famous people act as a powerful means of modeling effective behavior. The hero worship of celebrities that goes on in our society makes it even more difficult for the average citizen to be content with an ordinary existence. We are trained from an early age to pay homage to the wealthy and famous, and our heroes become our models.

It is often helpful to point out the fallibility of those we admire. It makes them more approachable, easier for us to relate to. From a systematic study of biographical literature, the group leader may select the life of a famous person, a powerful model, to hold up as a blueprint for group members to emulate.

- A group member who acts extremely withdrawn and shy in the group can be told of Albert Einstein's reluctance to circulate among strangers.

This man, the first to be nominated as prime minister of Israel, fought a lifelong battle to learn even the most basic social rituals.

• Bertrand Russell's struggle with the meaning of love throughout his 98-year life offers a potent example of someone who took personal responsibility for his happiness, juggling relationships, affairs, and marriages to satisfy his longing for a compassionate, sensual companion.

• Charles Darwin, perhaps the most radical and independent scientist in recorded history, experienced such guilt when trying to sever his emotional dependence on his father that he was prepared to cancel his voyage on the HMS *Beagle* as a naturalist and become a country clergyman if that was his father's preference.

• To the young person entering a new profession with many obstacles, the group leader may mention the tribulations of Vincent Van Gogh: "Here was a man who had the dedication and commitment to pursue a career in which he rarely received emotional support. He stood alone, suffering day after day of isolation, never once selling a painting in his lifetime. And you've just used 15 minutes to lament that a whole week went by without your having made a single sale."

Ernest Hemingway's bouts of alcoholic depression, Sigmund Freud's stoic tolerance of chronic pain, André Gide's search for his homosexual identity— all can be brought out as models of attempts to cope with difficult challenges. If history has any real value, it is for us to learn from the lives of those who have gone before us. How have the self-actualized heroes of the past coped with their personal handicaps? What can they teach us today?

The Complete Model

It is not enough for the advanced group leader to remain current only with the literature of counseling and psychotherapy. Professional journals and new texts have much to teach us about theoretical innovation, improvements in behavioral intervention technology, research in group dynamics, and refinement of group techniques; but group leaders belong to a profession whose relevant knowledge transcends academic demarcation.

The study of philosophy allows the group leader to reason critically and to investigate issues carefully. The different branches of philosophy—logic, ethics, ontology, epistemology, metaphysics, and kineology—all help the trained mind approach the sensitive problems of human existence with clarity. Philosophy helps the group leader select the best questions to ask, even if it provides few answers.

The social sciences, humanities, human physiology, linguistics, even the performing arts all help to make group leaders more worldly in running groups. The more experience they collect, the wider will be the range of knowledge from which to choose the best intervention. Dedicated group leaders who travel around the world are exposed to different cultures and customs. The skilled traveler learns to communicate on a variety of levels, to initiate helpful relationships, to appreciate the subtle complexities of the environment, and to adapt readily to changing circumstances. Even tourist photography trains one to pay attention to detail and composition, to examine the world through a sensitive, artistic eye. All such life experiences make a group leader better able to relate to a variety of persons and to understand a broader range of human problems.

In a sense, we have been in a continual state of rigorous training for our profession since birth. We remember and know how to use the critical incidents of our childhood. We recall our significant learnings vividly and are able to pass on valuable insights. The first bicycle ride without training wheels, the first kiss, the first stay away from home, and other critical incidents give us the background to understand the personal meaning of such events for others.

Voracious reading is another means by which advanced group leaders pursue their education. Novels, poetry, plays, biographies and other nonfiction give us glimpses into the motives and thinking processes of distressed characters. Dostoyevsky teaches us about existential suffering, Salinger instructs us in adolescent development, Doris Lessing helps us understand depression. Films and television add visual and auditory stimuli to the study of human conflict. In short, the more intensely group leaders experience life, the better they become in dealing with intensity in others. By studying the lives of famous people in addition to in-depth analyses of their own lives, group leaders can help clients select models more intelligently.

CHAPTER 5

The Power of Language in Groups

Whereas neurologists, cardiologists, internists, and surgeons have electro-encephalograms, blood tests, biochemical analyses, and biopsies to aid in their diagnoses, group leaders have nothing but their sense organs and a few primitive psychometric devices. There are no technological aids to bail them out of trouble. They have their minds, their training, their intuition, and a propensity for the masterful manipulation of language. They are neither technicians nor scientists; they are communicators. They cure with the power of language.

Language is both a formal system of verbal expression and a description of behavior in flux. Since its birth in the fifth century A.D., the English language has continually changed to reflect new thinking and more modern concepts. Language evolves as words are manufactured, borrowed, assimilated, and blended from other sources.

Language is phenomenally responsive to change. The language of Chaucer bears little resemblance to that of the contemporary Hollywood street person cruising Sunset Strip. Through mispronunciation of words, shortcut speech patterns, or even blends (*clap* + *crash* = *clash*; *flame* + *glare* = *flare*), our language changes. We readily steal words from other languages and call them our own. *Tycoon* comes from Japanese; *rocket* from Italian; *salt* from Old Norse; *emotion* from French; *boss* from Dutch; and *skunk* from Algonquian Indian (Farb, 1974).

Syntactical aspects of different languages are indicative of underlying cognitive principles unique to each national heritage. When learning a Romance language, for instance, one of the most difficult concepts for English speakers to grasp is the subjunctive mood, which changes the tense of subordinate clauses ("It is necessary *that you pick me up*," or "*I wish that you would come*"). In cases of expressed doubt, desire, denial, negation, emotion, preference, insistence, regret, or impersonal situations, respect for logical relationships is indicated by implying that because we wish something to occur doesn't necessarily mean that it will occur. In English, the subjunctive is becoming extinct. Except following the words *may* or *might* ("that he may live forever") or expressing conditions that are contrary to fact ("If I were a rich man"), this tense has largely been abandoned. One wonders what impact these omissions have on our thinking processes.

Perhaps our language is contributing to the prevalence of externally controlled people, avoiders of responsibility, and psychologically dependent individuals. Whereas in English it is common to hear illogical utterances such as "he made me so angry" and "she worries me to death," indicating speakers who are not in charge of their emotional states, Spanish makes use of reflexive verbs for similar statements. This linguistic structure forces speakers to take responsibility for their own internal processes and self-initiated actions, turning passive actions in English into active states in Spanish. The verbs *to be angry* and *to worry*, for example, are expressed quite differently in Spanish reflexive verbs. *Enojarse* literally means "to get yourself angry"; *preocuparse* means "to worry yourself." Quite legitimately, responsibility for these internally manufactured states is placed within the sphere of the speaker's ultimate control.

Many English-speaking group members could profit from thinking reflexively or subjunctively—that is, abdicating unrealistic expectations for controlling other people's behavior and taking more responsibility for their own. Subjunctive tenses could express more logical ideas:

> "If I were only a man *(but I'm not)*, I wouldn't take so much flak."
> "I prefer *(but I'm only expressing my preference)* that you visit me tomorrow."
> "I insist *(but I can't make you)* that you stop calling me for help."

Reflexive verb uses could also be used to focus responsibility more legitimately:

> "I *frustrated myself* when I didn't get the job."
> "I *woke myself* up at 6:00, *worried myself* about being late, and then *made myself* cry because I couldn't *make myself remember* where I was going."

The Logic of Language

Language is a means of communicating thoughts through symbols that have a degree of permanence in time and a discreteness in space. According to Bertrand Russell (1961), this utility is both indispensable and dangerous, for language, unlike mathematics, is relatively imprecise. It describes objects with definitions that are unsupported by the laws of physics. What precisely are *time* and *space*? Can they be seen or touched? How do we know they really exist?

We speak of "time," apparently understand its meaning, even pretend it exists in the world. But we often forget that such abstractions are created within the human mind. They help ease our intolerance for ambiguity, the frustrations of the unknown. In a sense, then, we invent our realities through language. We speak of things like cohesion, trust, norms, power, relationships, dynamics. We invent ideas like "super-ego," "mind," "personality," "neurotic," and wear them like the emperor's new clothes.

> Language continually asserts by the syntax of subject and predicate that "things" somehow "have" qualities and attributes. A more precise way of talking would insist that "things" are produced, are seen as separate from other "things," and are made "real" by their internal relations and by their behavior in relationship with other things and with the speaker. (Bateson, 1977, p. 67)

Language represents only one aspect of reality—a symbolic map of the territory, the coding into words of actual things in the world. This verbal portrayal may be consistent and logical, or it may exhibit dimensions that are quite unreal.

Bandler and Grinder (1975, 1979) distinguish between the deep structure and the surface structure of a person's communications, suggesting that verbalizations seldom accurately convey their intended messages. For instance, a group member might say "I'm sick and tired of people laying a bunch of crap on me all the time," when what he really means is "I don't like it when my wife constricts my freedom by giving me orders about how I should spend my time on Sundays." The concepts *people, bunch of crap,* and *all the time* not only fail to convey the real meaning behind the communication but also fail to specifically provide a useful perspective on reality.

Words are the symbols we use to express ideas, which are abstractions of our thoughts and feelings, which are in turn the result of how we perceive the world. There is thus a funneling effect that converts the nature of reality into a more progressively diluted form, each step in the conversion losing a degree of accurate representation from its predecessor.

The technique of active listening, the main mode of helping, is a process of ignoring surface statements and discerning their underlying affective messages. By decoding or interpreting what people say aloud to mean something quite different, we help them become more whole (in Gestalt language), more congruent (in Rogerian terms), better ego-integrated (in psychodynamic phraseology), more rational (in the cognitive-behavioral system), or operating from a less impoverished model (in neurolinguistic programming language). These therapeutic goals, and the labeling processes used to reach them, can be substantially diverted from course if the group leader forgets that the "language map" is not the same as the "territory" it represents.

Group Leaders as Language Coaches

Group leaders must upgrade professional speech to the level of current research and clinical expertise. Imprecise language not only indicates faulty reasoning on the therapist's part but also can lead clients to deny responsibility for their actions because "The Family" is at fault.

The reality therapist, in groups or in any setting, is interested in capitalizing on the intricacies of meaning contained in each word of the question "What are you doing?" Wubbolding (1988) explains that until clients can be helped to specify which behaviors and choices are blocking desired needs, clients will find it very difficult to pursue what they want. Group members are thus helped to attend to, and use the language of, self-responsibility: "What am I *doing* that is getting in the way of what I want?"

It can be therapeutically beneficial for leaders to help clients see themselves as unique individuals within their larger family systems. Speaking about what "we believe" or what "our family feels" can be corrected by determining whether the speaker is expressing the true beliefs of all persons present and is doing so with their consent. Interventions such as the following might be implemented.

> **Therapist**: Hector, your father just said that all of you are dissatisfied with the way things have been going lately. Is he speaking for you, too?

> **Therapist**: Cynthia, I notice that you keep using the pronoun *we* and glancing at your husband each time I ask you a question. I wonder how *you* feel, compelled to include his opinion with yours, and how he feels having you answer for him.

It would also be advantageous for therapists to obliterate "we-oriented" thinking from their own conceptual vocabulary. If therapists could avoid reducing individuals to categories or labels, the focus of therapy would be on treating people and not on treating just their relationships. A marriage, family, or group exists to serve the needs of the people in them. Once the relationships become destructive and self-defeating, a therapist can intervene to enhance the quality of communication among people, teaching each person either to act in a more fully functioning manner with family members or to make decisions regarding reduced quantity of interactions. In either case, the family or group does not change; the individual people do.

It must be said that many implicit rules of therapeutic groups are conducive to fakery, and first among them is the unique language system.

> **Bertha**: I experience you as hostile.
> **Irving**: Oh, yeah? You're just projecting.
> **Leader**: I hear you both saying that you're angry.

Jargon often gets in the way of honest, natural communication, because before group members can spontaneously emote, they must first dress their naked feelings in suitable clothing.

> **Clem**: I think you're full of ostrich manure.
> **Leader**: Don't you really mean "I *feel* you're full of ostrich manure?"

Alan Watts (1966) lists seven basic rules of interpersonal engagement that can be adapted by group leaders.

A double-bind game is a game with self-contradictory rules, a game doomed to perpetual self-frustration—like trying to invent a perpetual-motion machine in terms of Newtonian mechanics, or trying to trisect any given angle with a straightedge and compass. The social double-bind game can be phrased in several ways. (p. 67)

- *"The first rule of this game is that it is not a game."* The group leader perpetuates this contradiction with the statement "Let's pretend this is real." Group members then imagine that others are their mothers or bosses, and speak to them *as if* they were. They play feeling games and interaction exercises all the while they pretend that they aren't really playing games at all.
- *"Everyone must play."* It doesn't matter whether the clients are convicted murderers serving six consecutive life sentences, students who are "encouraged" by their teachers to participate in the program, or parents who threaten their kids with a choice of solitary confinement or a group, let's pretend we all want to be here. Since everyone is here anyway, I would like to ask you all to share your perceptions of one another. But, of course, you don't have to participate unless you want to.
- *"You must love us."* We're all such nice people, so caring. We really like you a lot. We have empathy, unconditional positive regard, acceptance, respect, and genuineness. You must love us, too.
- *"You must go on living."* Isn't life grand? It is so full of freedom and choices. Even when your body is riddled with cancer or your mind is preoccupied with depression and pain you must go on living.
- *"Be yourself, but play a consistent and acceptable role."* If you can't act naturally in this group, where can you feel comfortable? Right? Just be yourself . . . as long as we can predict what you're going to be and approve of that self.
- *"Control yourself and be natural."* Smile into the camera. That's right. Look as if you're having a good time, or at least learning something. Wipe away those tears; they're ruining your make-up. OK now, ready?
- *"Try to be sincere."* Even if you don't know how to act sincerely, fake it. We'll never know the difference.

Group members have also created unique linguistic structures to represent their thinking symbolically. Clients thus believe in abstractions like "shyness," "trauma," and "depression" and allow these words to influence how they think, feel, and act. Rather than acting as elected delegates to represent ideas, words *become* ideas. Group members speak of their "unassertiveness" as if it were a genetically transmitted disease. They ascribe their problems to "fate" or the "unconscious," but what these abstractions mean depends entirely on the user's perceptions. We may, in fact, apply any number of verbal labels to our observations, each the product of perceptual/cognitive/affective processes.

Ellerbroek (1978), for instance, was interested in the psychodynamic effects of language on acne. Because the names we choose to call a thing are optionally determined, acne can be called a "disease," a "normal condition," a "sign of stress," a "dermatological problem," "a curse," or "a kind of chosen behavior." Ellerbroek explained to his patients that acne results from a *feeling* of being picked on, a depressive reaction, a psycholinguistic pattern, and he was therefore able to treat pimples psychologically.

A. J. Ayer, the logical positivist, attempted to dispel fuzzy thinking and communication by bringing language under the umbrella of empiricism. By applying the criteria of verifiability to test the genuineness of statements, Ayer (1952) was able to distinguish three types of proposition in the world of discourse, all of which can be considered as nothing more than probable hypotheses. All statements made, whether analytic, synthetic, or judgmental, are factually significant only to the extent that they may be verified by any given person. This linguistic assumption fits well within the philosophy of pragmatism and the practice of group work. All statements may be formulated in different linguistic patterns and may be interpreted in the unique language of each client.

Acting essentially as a language coach, teaching clients to change the descriptors they use of the world (Shands, 1970), the therapist must be particularly concerned with the precise use of language and its power to influence. The philosopher Ludwig Wittgenstein believed that the problems of philosophy (and therefore of the world) are essentially confusions in the use of language. One goal of therapy, then, is to clear away defective linguistic usage in communication processes (Chessick, 1977).

The Language of Emotional Expression

In discussing the affective dimensions of language in social contexts, Hayakawa (1964) describes the power of several communication devices to exaggerate, to command attention, or to send a message more forcefully. The group member may hide in a forest of abstraction or venture forth in a web of allusion. For the group leader, the tasks of language sensitivity are twofold: first, to diagnose affective messages hidden in the content of discourse, and second, to communicate subtle verbalizations by means of a variety of delivery modes.

The use of *metaphor*, for example, is the bread and butter of group interaction language. At the most elementary level, it is the most powerful of affective descriptors: "I'm so sick of this crap I could die!" First cousin to metaphor, but less confrontive in demonstrating parallels between unrelated subjects, the *simile* also carries much emotional weight in its descriptions: "Can't you take charge of your life? You're acting like a half-fucked fox in a forest fire."

What of the shock value of so-called dirty words (a metaphoric value judgment in itself)? Words, of course, have no emotional valence except that which the listener reads into them. The shock value of certain scatological terms arises from their taboo. Their utility derives from their emotionally descriptive implications.

For group leaders, the first problem of emotionally descriptive language is the presence of discrepant experiences in the use of obscenities. Some group leaders claim that the prolific use of such language is therapeutic because it enables the therapist to speak to clients as they speak to themselves. After all, a person who drops an anvil on his foot is unlikely to think: "Oh, gee whiz. What a shame. I just smashed my foot into a bloody pulp." But group leaders prone to the use of swear words may alienate clients so offended by the medium that they can't hear the message. And for group leaders who themselves find such words distasteful, there is the risk of communicating nonacceptance to group members who pepper their talk with an occasional expletive.

Several other linguistic devices of emotional expression affect a person's relative perspective. These include *personification* ("This school system really pisses me off with its self-righteous rules") and *allusion*, an abbreviation of images. For more complex feelings, language can create incongruent comparisons to deal with shades of affect or ambiguous arousal. The use of irony, pathos, and humor are helpful in this context.

There are also many cases of language abuse in therapeutic groups as the result of emotional factors. Since we are often unaware of how we speak, our language can act as a hidden obstacle to effective thinking. We respond unconsciously to certain words, depending on our prior experiences with them. *Shirt*, for example, seems an innocuous word unless one has prior experience with Hitler's "Brown Shirts." So, too, words like *kike*, *nigger*, *Communist*, or *psychotic* have other than neutral connotations.

Huppe and Kaminsky (1962) identify several common language errors that occur in forms of emotional communication and to which therapeutic group work is highly susceptible. Clients will rely on emotional but illogical language practices as resistance tactics. Unless these emotional arguments are countered by group leaders who are skilled at recognizing and disputing them, it is unlikely that lasting changes will occur.

Abusive Uses

The first in a series of language errors that results from emotionality is *character assassination*. Whereas previously this has involved questioning race, religion, or profession as an invalidating factor, group settings commonly evoke the misuse of psychological jargon: "How can *you* tell *me* what to do; you're the one with the inferiority complex."

Group members may defensively attempt to destroy one another's views by criticizing their origins. In the *genetic fallacy*, the content of a perceived attack is ignored while focus is placed on distracting variables. The client can therefore totally refute any validity in a threatening statement: "No wonder you're off base; look where you got your information."

Any of several emotional appeals can also be used. In an *appeal to the people*, a client may seek to gain validity for expressed ideas by consensual methods. If group member unity can be swayed to support the deviant position, the client reasons that arguments will carry greater weight: "We all know this. We've seen you do it." In the *appeal to pity*, the speaker uses arguments top-heavy with emotional seductiveness. Sympathy is aroused by appealing to listener emotions: "You just *have* to help me. I can't do it all myself. Just do it this time to get me started."

Appeal to a higher authority is among the most tenaciously resistant arguments to the therapist's counterlogic: "But my minister says . . . ," "But Freud didn't believe that . . . ," "But that directly conflicts with the Bible . . ." Finally, the *appeal to force* is a favorite tactic of childhood, as when a youngster threatens "I won't be your friend if you don't loan me your bike." In groups, the threat takes a similar form: "Maybe I won't come back next week unless . . ."

Faulty generalizations are evident when group members base all-inclusive assumptions on a sample of one, erroneously believing all cases to be identical: "My Aunt Minosa got better by trying this idea; I don't know why you won't try it, too."

The *post hoc ergo propter hoc fallacy* involves a confusion in causal relationships in which, for example, recency is assumed to exercise the most important effect on behavior. Skinner has explained how superstitions develop through precisely this same mechanism. If one happens to do well on an exam using a particular pen, the pen takes on lucky qualities.

> **Client**: My wife ran out on me just because I quit my job.
> **Group leader**: Sure, one event happened to occur right after the other. However, it appears that your wife left you because you've been a drunk for the past two years.

A favorite stall tactic is the use of *circular reasoning*. To the child who asks why little girls don't have babies, the mother replies "Because they're little girls, honey. That's why."

> Sometimes an argument is quite complex and then it is more difficult to check for circularity: "Freud claims that we are often frustrated because our sex drives are blocked and they become blocked because we are thwarted in our desires." The circularity here may be difficult to discover until "frustrated" is seen to have the same meaning as "thwarted in our desires." (Huppe & Kaminsky, 1962, p. 202)

Another filibuster maneuver is the one of *irrelevance*—that is, the speaker attempts to cloud the issue by bringing in distracting variables: "Maybe what you say is true, but I don't see how it can be proved. I remember once when I saw Buckley on TV—have you ever seen this guy? He's got this style that's fantastic.''

In the use of *imperfect analogy*, verbal reasoning goes something like this:

1. ''You and I are similar.''
2. ''When I had problems in school, so did you.''
3. ''Just before my latest divorce, my wife started complaining about not having enough freedom.''
4. ''Your wife is now asking for more freedom.''
5. ''Therefore, you're going to end up with a divorce, too.''

The *misused metaphor* relies on inappropriate pictorial phrases and vivid language to presume parallels between unrelated things. For instance, based on only two of a person's qualities, she or he is called ''a monster.''

Mind reading (''They think I am terrible''), *prophesizing* (''I will never get the job''), and *centering* (''The teacher always tries to humiliate me'') are also quite common among group members who are significantly exaggerating their predicaments.

All these abusive uses of language appeal to emotional factors in communication. They form incomplete representations, semantic deletions, and impoverished surface structures. They violate the linguistic rules of well-formedness and semantic relationships (Bandler & Grinder, 1975).

In the course of evolution, the intonations of phonemes (as heard, for instance, in infant babbling) have become associated with various emotions rather than with any content (Lacan, 1968). When emotion becomes intentionally directed toward an object, the child is born into language. ''The relation of language and emotion thus constitutes an evolutionary advance: to use language—the abstraction of underlying systems—to change those systems'' (Kellerman, 1979, p. 258).

The relationship between emotional states, their representative cognitions, and expressed language has become the foundation for two quite popular approaches to therapy. In neurolinguistic programming, group participants are taught to attend more consciously to the deeper structures of language. Syntax and logical semantic relations are formed to represent true experiences more accurately. By avoiding semantic deletions, distortions, ambiguity, nominalizations, generalizations, and other illogical linguistic structures, group members are able to change their models of the world, hoping to introduce more options and choices into their repertoire (Bandler & Grinder, 1975).

In rational-emotive therapy, group members are also instructed to eliminate irrational language from their internal vocabularies. According to this theory, the language that people use in their self-talk as well as in communications reflects an underlying pattern of emotional/cognitive disturbance (Ellis, 1977a). Illogically based statements such as ''I can't stand it,'' ''I must do it,'' ''I'm a louse,'' and ''He made me angry'' are therefore altered to reflect more accurate representations of concepts: "I can stand this but I don't like it," "I choose to do it," "I've done a few lousy things," "I made myself angry over what he did."

Such theories have brought about the precise phrasing of therapeutic comments to imply that impending changes among group members are not only possible but likely.

Guidelines for Group Leaders

"Just as a mechanic carries around a pair of pliers and a screwdriver for use in an emergency—just as we all carry in our heads tables of multiplication for daily use—so can we all carry in our heads convenient rules for extensional orientation" (Hayakawa, 1964, p. 314). Hayakawa's introduction to the rules of logical communication offers the group leader a mind-set for applying the guidelines of effective semantics. To ground us in reality, to prevent mindless behavior, to avoid illogical verbal solutions, the following rules are suggested.

1. *Words are not things.* Alfred Korzybski was among the first philosophers to help untangle the confusion between thoughts and their symbolic codings in language. His famous dictum "the map is not the territory" suggests both the incompleteness of the spoken word, in that it does not represent *all* the nuances of a thought, and the assurance that some parts of the whole will inevitably be lost in the coding and transformation from an abstract image into a concrete medium.

Language is therefore a convenient approximation of an idea, a classification or naming such as a map represents, but it is not itself the territory it describes: "It is necessary to be quite clear about the universal truth that whatever 'things' may be in their pleromatic and thingish world, they can only enter the world of communication and meaning by their names, their qualities, and their attributes" (Bateson, 1977, p. 68).

Group leaders must therefore use their symbols well, employing precise, descriptive language to convey their ideas. Group members, too, speak in symbols of their thoughts, often saying much more or much less than they mean. They may follow counterfeit maps, hastily scribbled, expecting to reach a destination that is impossible given the limitations of their internal cartographers, who may draw what they *see* but not see what they draw.

Jean Piaget observed that children operate from false maps, and he attempted to explain why they consistently experience perceptions inconsistent with reality (as *we* know it). Children can cheerfully describe the moon following them over their shoulders or how a nickel can be worth more than a dollar because it is heavier.

Clients, too, use their language to inadequately describe the territorial images in their brains. We dutifully attend to these communications, yet never assume that they are anything more than approximations of the intention.

The meanings that words have for us are not necessarily the meanings *in* clients. The high frequency of clarifying and restating leader interventions attests to this sensitivity.

2. *Meaning is determined by context.* The phenomenology of an individual's background and unique perceptions determine the precise meaning of a verbalization. The statement "you're bad" can have quite different meanings with only the minority status of the speaker rotated as the independent variable. A black adult or Catholic priest could thus intend two very different interpretations of this moral judgment—the former, highly favorable in its recognition of "coolness"; the latter, an indictment of sin and moral transgression.

A Singaporean psychologist who counsels in Mandarin has found it necessary to adapt a number of concepts to the Chinese way of looking at things. She had learned in Gestalt training in North America that when a client says "I can't," the phrase should be changed to "I won't." Her Chinese clients, however, had no idea what she meant, since the Mandarin language does not differentiate between these expressions the same way that the English language does. *Can't* and *won't* mean the same in a culture where freedom, independence, and *self*-responsibility are a lot less important than collective obligations to the family and society.

3. *Distinguish differences in "truth."*

Wachtel (1980) suggests that communicators should encourage clients to think in terms of unlimited choices and alternatives for the future. He compares the difference between static confrontations such as "you are a person who has difficulty speaking" and interventions such as "sometimes you talk more easily than at other times." This principle can be taken several steps farther in groups by ensuring that interpretations and confrontations include the following elements:

- The assumption that most behavior—emotional, cognitive, and motor—is varied and inconsistent: not "You are passive," but "Occasionally in the presence of threatening persons like myself, you *act* passively."
- The assumption that actions do not have a life of their own but are the result of people's deliberate or unconscious intentions. Group members are responsible for what they think, feel, and do: not "What

you just said made me angry!" but "I just made myself angry over what you just said."

• Interventions include *specific* data regarding the target behaviors. The difference between "Sometimes you talk more easily than at other times," and "Whenever Francine has finished talking or she glares at you, you inhibit yourself from talking" is that the latter feedback provides useful, specific information that can be acted on.

• The assumption that verbalizations have a specific rationale. While shooting from the hip sometimes produces the most dramatic effects, almost all interventions have specific rationales in a group leader's head, *whether they can be articulated or not.* It is a good idea to encourage group members to query leader interventions whenever they are confused—both to expose the apparent magic of actions and to train clients to think analytically. The message to them is: *before* you do or say something likely to bring about mushroomed results, anticipate the likely consequences.

4. *The use of colorful language.* People tend to remember ideas that are either novel to them or potentially useful—those that have a high stimulation valence. We plant metaphorical phrases as time bombs, set to go off when clients slip back into mediocrity outside the group. We also like to model the intrinsic beauty of language, respect for the order of words. All clients leave our groups better able to communicate, more fluent in their expressive powers.

5. *Group leaders, whenever possible, avoid the use of depersonalizing jargon.* Too many experts are insensitive to their audience—physicians when they tell patients they have some tongue-twisting condition that could easily be described in five-letter words, or mechanics when they authoritatively diagnose a car as having some strange syndrome of engine disturbance.

6. *Sexist and class-discriminating terms are avoided.* In what has been the fastest growing cultural change in human history, dating a mere 30 years since the civil rights and women's rights movements began in earnest, our language already reflects the new order. Words like *mankind, manpower, freshman, coed,* and *housewife* are rapidly becoming obsolete. Stereotypic expressions, biased statements, insensitive verbal transgressions have no place in therapeutic groups.

7. *Group leaders should use language that is precise, direct, and behaviorally descriptive.* On the one hand, it is of paramount importance to avoid misinterpretations that result from muddled language. On the other hand, it may sometimes be expedient to speak ambiguously about an idea to permit multiple, personal interpretations among participants. Among therapists, a favorite riposte to a request for clarification is "What did you think I meant?"

Yost, Beutler, Corbishley, and Allender (1986) devised a structured cognitive approach to treating elderly, depressed adults in group settings wherein they were taught to speak differently about their plight—both to others and to themselves. The whole focus of the group experience was targeted around working with language, especially with expressions representing cognitive distortions. Some of the more useful interventions that were modeled in the group included the following therapeutic responses.

Group Member Lament	Therapeutic Response
"I'll never get better; my situation is hopeless."	"Try, 'This is very difficult for me, but with patience and hard work, I *will* improve.' "
"Life just isn't the same anymore and I hate it."	"I think you mean to say changes are sometimes disorienting but can be interesting at times."
"I have nothing to live for and nobody who cares about me."	"I wonder if some of you in this group could help her restate that feeling more accurately."

This progression of leader-modeled cognitive interventions eventually guides group members to a greater awareness of their language. In particular, Yost and his associates list a number of therapeutic questions that encourage group members to monitor the ways they express themselves:

- *What is the exception to this generalization you just made?* Nobody cares about you anymore? There is no one alive, no one in this group, no person you know *anymore* who has any feelings toward you?
- *What might you reasonably expect?* You said you should be able to grasp this stuff more easily and quickly than you are. In what ways are you being unrealistic in your demands?
- *Where is the evidence that this is true?* When you say that things are hopeless, you are implying that you have made no progress and never will. How is that statement faulty?
- *How are you exaggerating the significance of what took place?* Is this really the tragedy you are making it out to be because your daughter won't visit you as often as you would prefer?
- *What is the positive side of this situation?* It is certainly inconvenient that you will have to give up some of your privacy when you get a roommate, but what advantages are there to this situation?
- *What is another possibility?* You have concluded that Mildrid won't speak to you because she is a "stuck up old prune" who thinks she is too good for you. What else might explain this conflict between the two of you?

Cognitive approaches to group work are, by their very nature, language oriented. The same could be said for Gestalt, Adlerian, or Reality methods that have their own systems for monitoring language related to self-responsibility. The fact of the matter is that experienced group leaders cannot afford to affiliate themselves with allegiance to only one theoretical system. What makes group leaders advanced in the first place are their flexibility and willingness to take the best from all possible options and synthesize them into a unified conceptual paradigm.

Words to Avoid in Therapeutic Groups

Words, in and of themselves, are neither good nor bad. Nevertheless, some words that clients commonly use act as symptoms of underlying illogical, distorted, or irrational thinking patterns. Most experienced group leaders have trained themselves to monitor client speech patterns and language usage, both to collect meaningful data about how clients characteristically speak and to attend more closely to the subtleties of communications. Sometimes a little bell rings in our head, an alert that some principle of reality has been violated.

There are words, usually indicative of cognitive distortion, that make it much more difficult for group members to experience change. These words thrive on the force of externally controlled factors such as fate, luck, "it," or "them." An attitude of resignation, despair, and hopelessness sets in when one verbalizes statements that imply "I can't help it, it's not my fault."

Rudestam (1978) cataloged the semantic structure of language used in therapy. Studying the works of Perls, Korzybski, Bandler, and Grinder, he constructed a pathological vocabulary that clients use in their fuzzier thought processes. To these sources can be added the contributions of Ellis (1974), Beck (1976), Rose (1989), and several of my own ideas. The following dictionary calls to attention unproductive words and errors to be avoided in group work.

Fair

The question "Who says the world is fair?" echoes through the offices of therapists throughout the world. This expression of confrontation was among the first attempts by professional helpers to challenge the erroneous assumptions of stated language. Obviously, if the world were a fair place, people would treat one another with respect. There would be no crime, poverty, or sickness. All people would get what they want; they would also get what they deserve.

Unfortunately, however, this is not the case. Neither an Eleventh Commandment, the Bill of Rights, nor the Magna Carta guarantees that people will get everything they want whenever they want it. To shout "foul!" is to complain unrealistically that the universe has not complied to one's special wishes.

Sometimes clients need to be challenged: "I guess this is one of those times when you didn't get what you want. Has that ever happened before? Is it likely to happen again? Are you so special that because you don't believe things are fair, they should therefore change, and the world should transform itself so that your life will be easier?"

Platitude

"These troubled times call for men of stature," said the therapist to the midget. By borrowing someone else's tired and trite formulation of language, therapists can conceivably conduct an entire group session without uttering a single original statement. Tyler and Thurston (1977) offer such classics for the platitudinal counselor as: "It takes two to tango" (for the schizophrenic); "Don't take life too seriously; after all, you'll never get out of it alive" (for the client with existential angst); "Take two aspirin and call me in the morning" (for the suicidal group member). Platitudinal comments spare us from having to *think* about what we really have to say. It also helps clients feel as if they are insignificant repositories for other people's trash.

Luck

Someday there may prove to be a reality base for ideas such as luck, fate, Karma, coincidence, and astrological signs. However comforting it might be to believe in such external forces, for the most part, these concepts only make inertia and proscrastination a lot more likely. As empiricists and scientists, we model for our group members the qualities of logical analysis. "Where is the evidence that these concepts exist? And even if they do exist, how is it helpful for you to believe in them?"

Group members who habitually use these words often admit that they exercise little control over their lives—they are puppets, victims of some mysterious force. They renounce responsibility for their actions and defer their fate to something outside themselves. The swift and certain answer to a claim of luck or fate is to vigorously challenge its actual effect on outcomes: "Are you saying that the reason you run such a successful business today has nothing to do with your personable style, your instinct for taking advantage of ideal situations, your willingness to take risks, but only because you are lucky? I wonder how that belief comforts you?"

Need

To *need* something is to require it for continued physical survival. The only things we ever truly need are oxygen, nourishment, and shelter from the elements, although a case could also be made for sex and human touch. No one ever needs anyone or anything else. A great many things in life are desirable, wantable, preferable, or terrific, but none is actually needed. People whose *needs* go unfulfilled experience panic and fear; unsatisfied *wants* only produce discomfort or inconvenience.

Whenever group members use the word *need*—as in "I need this job" or "I need feedback from the rest of you"—they are helped to substitute the words *want, prefer,* or *desire.* It is no great catastrophe to do without a thing we might *prefer* to have in life; after all, we've been disappointed many times before. But the deprivation of a need implies torture or death.

Can't

> **Client**: I *can't* come to the group today.
> **Group leader**: You *can't* come today? I see. You mean you're either chained to your bed or in an advanced state of coma?

This little helping verb, so anonymous when buried in a sentence, is among the most abused of all words. *Can't* relinquishes one's power and control. It means that one is unable to do something. To say "I *can't* get a job" is very different from saying "I don't know how to get a job" or "So far, I've been unable to find a job." Similarly, "I *can't* confront him in this group" is different from "I *won't* confront him," "I *choose* not to confront him," or "I don't *want* to confront him." In reality, there is very little one *can't* do in this world if one is willing to suffer the consequences.

Never

First cousin to *always* and *forever*, *never* is an overgeneralization that exaggerates reality. The use of these words leads to a false sense of hopelessness. Who can say what might happen in the future? "Perhaps you may not feel happy very often in the future, but you would have a bitter task ahead if you were *never* to feel happy again, not even for an accidental instant, and were *always* to feel depressed."

Because these words reinforce a sence of helpless resignation (Why try since you will *always* be this way?), the client's motive to change becomes handicapped. By altering *never* or *always* to the more flexible *sometimes* or *occasionally*, people admit that they can function effectively in some situations: "Much of the time I feel slightly depressed, but sometimes I feel quite good."

Expect

Expect goes hand in hand with disappointment, for the latter is not possible without the former. The amount of time spent anticipating an event is directly related to subsequent disappointment if the event does not turn out as *expected*. To minimize expectations is to reduce or prevent disappointment in the future.

It is one thing to attempt to predict future occurrences but quite another to indulge in fantasies that only preempt what one hopes will occur. How bored one feels, how much one lives in the future and in fantasy, how much one tries to control and anticipate, will all contribute to the frequency of *expect* in one's vocabulary. The oracle on the mountain advises "Expect nothing, and you will never be disappointed."

Must

The use of *must* implies a demand that things be a certain way; it is a command to the universe to pay attention and cooperate extra hard with one's wishes. Ellis (1977a) coined the memorable term *musterbation* to highlight the frenzied self-abuse people subject themselves to when they publicly or privately declare that they deserve some result. As children pout when they don't get their way, grown-ups unrealistically order the world to deliver on demand. Group members play variations on the linguistic theme: "I *must* do well." "Other people *must* treat me fairly." "I *must* get my way." The obvious retort is that time-tested strategy perfected in childhood: "Who says?"

Problem

Problems usually have solutions, and people who have problems spend their time trying to find solutions to them. They mount a mission in search of the Holy Grail, Truth, or some such answer that will disperse this storm cloud forever. Since problematic people, by implication, are inadequate, inept weaklings, it is highly unlikely that the search will lead to a satisfactory result.

Only in mathematics do problems have single solutions. Geometric theorems can be proved, algebraic equations may be factored; sums, dividends, and products can be calculated to find solutions to problems. In group work, the words *concern* or *trouble* can be substituted for *problem*. Concerns don't necessarily imply that something must be rectified or that there is a single answer that will fix things.

I'm

These two letters and apostrophe have kept more people from changing than all the excuses in the world. Short for "I am," *I'm* is a self-defining descriptor that irrevocably reduces the totality of a human being to a convenient label. "I'ms" are overgeneralizations, oversimplifications, and more: they offer a flawless excuse for running in place. When "I'm shy," I am blessed with a condition as certain as "I'm North American" or "I'm 30." "I'm shy" also brings with it "I'm always shy, I was born this way, I will always be shy, I can't help it." Statements can be rephrased in a way that implies control, temporary states, and situation-specific behavior: "I *act* shyly," "I *behave* shyly."

Maybe

Maybe, perhaps, I think so, I guess, possibly, I don't know are all safe ways of avoiding a commitment. They are evasive words that group members use to back out of tight situations. When these ambiguous responses are used, the group leader has to work extra hard to get some clear declaration of opinion or intent. Shown here is a typical evasive dialogue that can sometimes be stopped through persistence.

Group leader: How do you feel right now?
Client: Kinda strange.

Group leader: Strange meaning nervous?

Client: I guess so.

Group leader: What is going through your head that is making you feel strange?

Client: Um—Ah—

Group leader: That you aren't in control of this situation?

Client: Yeah, maybe.

Group leader: And that you don't like being in this vulnerable situation?

Client: You could say that, I guess.

Group leader: Well, what do you believe will happen next?

Client: I don't know.

Group leader: What do you imagine is in store for the future?

Client: I just can't say. How should I know?

Group leader: Take a wild guess. What do you guess is going to happen next?

Awful

When something is awful, nothing could ever be worse. *Awful* or *terrible* implies that some catastrophe has occurred that the person cannot survive. The use of these words usually involves an exaggeration or distorted perception in which the person feels both frustrated and helpless. Therapeutically, it is helpful to confront the client's ungrounded assumption that things are, in fact, awful.

"If it is awful that you flunked your class, what then would we call it if you had been permanently kicked out of school? And if you were kicked out of school, that would not be terrible either, since there is always something worse that could occur. Certainly, this is inconvenient, embarrassing, frustrating. But, *awful*? It is very difficult for you to prove that anything is ever totally bad."

Made

The misuse of verbs creates an unhealthy distortion of reality in which cause/effect relationships become confused. Since one's own neurons and synapses, the stuff from which feelings are constructed, are inaccessible to others in the world, it is difficult to believe that anyone can *make* another feel anything. Short of physical contact, feelings are self-manufactured states.

When language signals that cognitive distortions are going on inside a client's head, the group leader vigorously challenges the rational base for the distorted beliefs: "He *made* you cry. How exactly did he do that? Do you have a 'cry button' on your forehead that he can push at will? Did he reach inside your brain, perhaps through your mouth or ears, twist a few neurological connections, and thereby make you cry? In fact, you did it to yourself *after* you heard what he said."

It

The use of ambiguous pronouns like *it, they, we,* and *people* send incomplete messages to listeners. The full meaning of a thought, its depth, detail, and totality, is left unsaid. The deeper meaning, the significant parts of the communication, are the features of the statement that the group leader can work on.

> "When you say that people in general don't like you, which people are those? Every one in the Western hemisphere? Everyone you know? Or just your younger brother?"
>
> "You just used the pronoun *we*. Who, exactly, are you speaking for beside yourself?"
>
> "*It* really got to you? How exactly did *it* do that, and which *it* are you referring to?"

Wrong

"Right," "wrong," "good," "bad," and other value judgments imply that there is some absolute standard of measurement by which all behavior in every culture may be assessed. Except for those who endow a book, like the Bible or the Koran, with such divine power that each word must be interpreted literally by a single preacher, there is no touchstone for determining whether anyone else's behavior is absolutely right or wrong.

One behavior might be better than another, more productive or effective relative to some other choice; but to label someone or something good, bad, right, or wrong is to live out Sartre's credo that all humans "desire to be God." Even if such a deity exists, it is unlikely that He sits in the sky with a blackboard keeping track of our good and bad thoughts. Only when the language of value judgments has been eliminated from group members' vocabularies can they hope to be accepting of one another.

> "Who says that it is *wrong*?"
>
> "How do you know that it is bad for him just because it is bad for you?"
>
> "Who are you to judge everyone in the world, calling them immoral because they don't act as you would like?"

The preceding entries certainly do not constitute an exhaustive list, but they do provide a sampling of the kinds of destructive language that signal reality distortions and obstacles to change. They are vocal symptoms of underlying cognitive and affective processes. Language is, after all, about the only thing we have to work with. Group leaders help people change by listening and talking, using language with scalpel-like precision.

The experienced group leader can always become a more expert communicator, a more fluent poet, and a creator of therapeutic images. Watzlawick (1978), however, emphasizes the greater need for therapists to speak their clients' language rather than forcing clients to learn to speak theirs. The reason that traditional therapies take so ridiculously long, he suggests, is because clients are expected to master a foreign language before they can be helped. The therapist can use language, as a chameleon changes color— to suit the environment.

> In other words, the therapist not only does his utmost to arrive at an understanding of the client's values, expectations, hopes, fears, prejudices—in short, his world image—as quickly and as completely as possible, but he also pays attention to the *actual* language of his client and utilizes it in his own verbalizations. (Watzlawick, 1978, p. 140)

People can be pragmatic in their choice of language and flexible in changing their speech. Their vocabularies, which give concrete labels to abstract ideas that are cataloged in the brain, change easily with the times. For these reasons, the group leader may concentrate on changing the behavior of group members by changing the language they use to describe their worlds.

CHAPTER 6

Macro- and Microdiagnostics

There is a story about a billion-dollar luxury liner, outfitted with every possible appointment, convenience, necessity, and designed to gratify every decadent demand that could possibly be of interest or use to its several thousand prominent passengers. This floating Taj Mahal, booked solid for months by wealthy citizens and cargo exporters, exhibited a phenomenally delicate profit margin in which time was equivalent to money. For this great ship to sit idle for even an hour, much less for a day or a week, would cost the company millions in delays, late penalties, and inconvenience for everyone concerned.

Every effort had been made to ensure that the ship would operate at peak efficiency. The engine room had as many backup systems and fail-safe mechanisms as an *Apollo* rocket. No quality had been overlooked in building the most reliable, durable mechanical equipment money could buy. The engine room was staffed by officers, experts, and mechanics from around the world. Each stood vigil in a gleaming white uniform looped with gold braid and brass buttons. Computer systems, draped in pastel plastics and steel, lined the walls. Nothing could possibly go wrong.

Except that the ship's engines somehow would not start. The crew had tried everything to remedy the situation as the passengers paced restlessly for an hour, then two. The captain frantically wired around the world for advice, getting nothing in return but sympathy. So the great ship stood idle in its berth. Experts and engineers were at a loss as to what to do next. Finally, an officer recalled hearing about a mechanic who could fix anything. For 60 years he had repaired broken engines of every sort, although his methods were alleged to be somewhat unorthodox.

After scouring the dockside streets, the crew finally located the weathered old man in a bar. Creaking slowly to his feet, he agreed to help solve their problem and shuffled to the scene, pushing a wheelbarrow full of greasy tools. He entered the engine room, surveyed the scene, and ordered everyone to give him room. Like a rat, he scurried from one end of the room to the other, feeling parts, smelling the air, nodding absently to himself.

After several tense minutes the observers grew restless. The old man's staccato grunts became more urgent as he settled into a corner of the room with hundreds of brightly color-coded pipes spread in every direction. Selecting an obscure pipe, he studied its shape and form for a moment, then returned to his wheelbarrow to search for the correct tool. Finding an immense monkey wrench, he strolled over to the pipes, reared back with his wrench, and, to the astonishment of everyone, gave one of the pipes a great whack. The shudder reverberated along the gleaming metal until, a minute later, the engines sputtered, hiccupped a few times, then settled into a gentle purr.

The old man was embraced by the other engineers, and the captain solemnly approached to offer his gratitude. As the ship finally began to get underway, the captain took out the company checkbook to pay the mechanic. "How much do we owe you?" he asked. "$50,000," replied the old mechanic. The captain sputtered: "You old crook, how dare you overcharge us for the little you did. For an expenditure this large I must clear the amount with the owners. You'll have to submit an itemized statement."

The mechanic nodded, found an old scrap of an envelope in his pocket, and scribbled his bill:

Mechanic's Bill for Fixing the Ship

Hitting the pipe..$10.00
Knowing where to hit the pipe...........................$49,990.00

Total..$50,000.00

Philosophers, engineers, surgeons, mechanics, plumbers, and group leaders are all skilled diagnosticians who find out exactly what is wrong, how it happened, and what needs to be done to put it right. But all the skills of a mechanic or techniques of a group leader are useless without the knowledge of precisely where and how to "hit the pipe." In the case of group leadership, diagnosis has a special value in identifying individual (microlevel) as well as collective behavior (macrolevel) patterns. Economists, too, think in terms of macro- and microlevel concepts—respectively, that which affects a whole system and that which affects any component of the universe.

Haley (1976) thinks of macrodiagnostic labels as the crystallization of a repeated sequence of behaviors within a social organization, such as a family unit or group structure. He believes that the therapist must be included as part of the presenting problem, since she or he formulates and defines the issues in diagnostic terms. According to Haley, these professionally created problems make human dilemmas chronic by constructing a group system that encourages conformity to expected norms. A schizophrenic residing in a hospital, for example, will experience a lot of trouble by failing to live up to the staff and ward rules for appropriate schizophrenic behavior.

> The nurse just now picked up one of the sheets I have written. She read it—looked at me oddly—and asked what in the hell I thought I was doing. And because she expected an answer in keeping with my strange occupation—I did not have the heart to disappoint her. So I gave her an answer that fitted. I told her that I was Shakespeare, the reincarnation of Shakespeare trying to sidestep a strait-jacket. (I'll admit that I feel queer enough to be the reincarnation of something but I doubt if Shakespeare would claim me.) But hurray! She came back down the aisle with a whole ream of paper and said to me: "Go to it, Shakespeare." (Jefferson, 1964, p. 13)

Group leaders use methods of reliable diagnosis much different from those operating from, say, a hospital staff approach. It is crucial for group leaders to be able to label client self-defeating behaviors, not for the sake of pigeon-holing a person into a discrete category, but to get a handle on specific problem areas as a prerequisite for systematic change efforts. This process of microdiagnostics gives the group leader a much more comprehensive framework for understanding and practicing effective therapeutic observations.

There has been an increase in the popularity of differential therapeutics (Beutler & Clarkin, 1990; Dies, 1992; Frances, Clarkin, & Perry, 1984) and technical eclecticism (Howard, Nance, & Myers, 1986; Lazarus, Beutler, & Norcross, 1992) as a way to conceptualize client concerns. These models stress the importance of accurately assessing the specific needs of each group member and delivering specialized treatments to address particular problems. Although this conception is better suited to individual formats, the idea behind this thinking is that different modalities (group, family, individual) are best for certain clients; different kinds of groups (experiential, goal oriented, and so on) are best for certain client needs; and even within the same group, particular members require different kinds of interventions (confrontation, support, and so on) to benefit best.

Whereas *microdiagnostics* deals with labeling individual client actions, *macrodiagnostics* is concerned with the larger processes that help the leader assess what is going on in the group. What can the heavy silence mean? What effects are minicoalitions having on total group functioning? Why can't things seem to get started? These and similar critical questions permit the group leader to think macrodiagnostically while analyzing significant themes as they arise.

In macrodiagnostic considerations of general living systems theory, Miller and Miller (1983) explore the ways in which the functioning of therapeutic groups is an extension of the organization of each component of the universe. This is true whether we are looking at any level of living systems: cells, organs, organisms, organizations, societies, or planets. They all organize themselves in ways to take in, process, and put out matter, energy, and/or information.

To apply living systems theory to group work, the advanced praciitioner must attend to a number of processes, specifically to identifying structures and subsystems that would evolve among members. Just as the family therapist looks carefully at boundaries, coalitions, and power hierarchies within the family system, the group leader explores various group structures and processes, including but not limited to:

- how group members make decisions
- how information is processed
- what boundaries are in place that divide, filter, and restrict information
- how subsystems function in relation to one another
- communication patterns
- cultural/ethnic values in place
- assigned or adopted roles
- controls and sanctions to pressure conformity
- equity of need satisfaction
- balance between individual and group goals
- developmental evolution of individual and group stages
- conflict resolution
- metaphoric/symbolic messages

In each of these areas, the group leader continually makes diagnoses and reassessments regarding the current level of group member functioning. This labeling process helps the advanced practitioner make adjustments in methodology to reach desired goals more effectively.

The Functions of Labeling

The computer was designed by the human mind. It makes binary decisions by placing a single datum into a particular category based on some classification overlay. Things may fit over here in this round hole or over there in that square hole. If we should come upon a thing that fits in neither one hole nor the other, we may create a third, triangular hole, or we may squeeze, mold, or reshape the mutant thing until it fits into one of the existing holes.

Humans are by nature schematic beings whose brain capacities function according to the limitations of the available classification systems. When the child creates a cognitive category indicating that big, brown four-legged animals with tails are called ''cows'' and is then confronted with a thing called a ''horse,'' the mind is forced to broaden its classification scheme to include the new element of the class. ''The division of the perceived universe into parts and wholes is convenient and may be necessary, but no necessity determines how it shall be done'' (Bateson, 1977, p. 42).

There are many examples to support the human need to classify parts and wholes into convenient, orderly systems, even in the field of mental health. The first cave people were able to determine who among their citizens was strange enough to warrant drilling holes in their skulls to let the demons escape. The ancient Egyptians diagnosed female mental dysfunctions on the basis of uterine positions; the patient would later be treated by having her vagina fumigated. The Babylonians relied on the goddess Ninkharsag and her eight assistant gods to recognize disease syndromes. The physician Empedocles of Sicily diagnosed imbalanced humors of yellow and black bile, phlegm, and blood. The Hippocratics and their methods of clinical medicine initiated the first comprehensive mental disease classification system that included personality and behavioral characteristics.

Throughout history, until Emil Kraepelin (1856–1926), practitioners had sought creative ways to identify patterns of mental sickness. A favorite clinical diagnostic process of the Dark Ages was to initiate "trial by water" (any "patient" who drowned was a witch) whenever a person exhibited deviant behavior sufficient to draw attention. In recent years, we have had Sheldon's ectomorphs, mesomorphs, endomorphs, and other body types as diagnostic correlates. Before that, phrenology, palm reading, and astrology were all in vogue as diagnostic devices. A brief history of psychiatry, psychology, and education is, in fact, an account of the evolution of more accurate, consistent, and valid diagnostic schemes.

But diagnosis is not just used for convenience or because it is aesthetically pleasing to have people grouped in neat little places. Diagnosis is the process of understanding the client, "a system of classification that the therapist uses to establish goals and select the most advantageous base for promoting learning" (Robinson, 1978). Shertzer and Stone (1980) summarize the further functions of diagnosis:

- to make predictions about client behavior so that a plan can be formulated that will fit with anticipated outcomes
- to summarize client issues, their causes, and abnormal features based on observable characteristics
- to determine the unique personality dynamics of each case
- to identify skill deficiencies in client functioning
- to understand the significance of client behavior
- to create working hypotheses that aid this understanding of another individual

Diagnostic thinking is the culmination of deductive reasoning to reach conclusions that will guide leader behavior. Therapeutic diagnosis is essentially a process of problem formation in which the client's concerns are simplified to manageable levels by reducing the significant variables to the lowest common denominator without sacrificing their essential qualities. For example, a group member could complain of the following behavioral symptoms:

1. compulsive drive to achieve straight A's in school
2. perfectionist standards and expectations for friends and lovers
3. bouts of depression after events that should have been exciting (exams, dates, new experiences)
4. reluctance to cooperate with early therapeutic efforts, although verbalizes a great desire for help
5. has very few friends and, although lonely, does not approach interesting strangers
6. feels trapped living at home; quarrels with family but can't find affordable housing
7. is almost always in control of social conversation, leading the discussion and introducing the topics
8. is extremely skilled at communication and extraordinarily perceptive regarding others' feelings
9. engages in a lot of approval seeking with group leader, showing off superior mind
10. acts condescendingly toward a group member of the opposite sex
11. is the only group member who preferred not to receive feedback in the introduction exercise
12. acts moody in the group whenever another person reports substantial progress
13. is fantastically insightful in understanding the origins and payoffs of the presenting concerns but balks at the prospect of talking in terms of goals
14. refuses to do any psychological homework between sessions
15. is extremely supportive, caring, and helpful to group members perceived as less intelligent and capable
16. withdraws when faced by confrontation; will not fight back

This is only a sampling of possible cues indicative of the client's characteristic behavior. We could also mention a variety of other data, which may or may not be relevant, such as how other group members react to the client or what the client has done previously to cope with difficulties. But let us assume that these 16 behavioral symptoms are those most important to the situation (an invalid assumption in reality, when we never know whether we have accumulated enough background). The group leader must now decide which symptoms are the most significant. Based on the available evidence, what may we logically conclude is the most reasonable diagnosis of this client's principal problem? We don't care to categorize or classify; we only wish to label specifically the main concern in need of resolution.

Themes of approval seeking, psychological dependence, and externally controlled thinking are all prevalent here, as are attitudes of perfectionism and a fear of failure. Following intensive, in-depth scrutiny, the diagnostic arrow eventually pointed toward the client's reluctance to take risks of any kind. She had programmed her life and relationships to maximize security and predictability, preferring to remain alone rather than to risk feeling vulnerable. She worked methodically in school, not because she enjoyed learning or wanted good grades, but because she needed the structure and routine of compulsive studying. She avoided parties or any social setting where she had to relinquish total control. Within the group, she resented anyone who was willing to take risks because risk taking reminded her of her own inadequacies.

The clinician is in the unenviable position of playing detective to determine which pieces of evidence are important, which symptoms need further investigation, what variables are confounding the picture or masking actual circumstances, and what causal relationships are involved in the situation. In this problem-formation, the therapist can as easily complicate the existing difficulties by misjudgment, oversimplification, and illogical thinking as reconcile the conflicts. In the words of Lord Berkeley: "We first raise the dust and then claim we cannot see" (Watzlawick, Weakland, & Fisch, 1974).

The most difficult aspect of trying to determine what is going on in a group at a particular moment in time is that the process is affected by what each member is thinking, feeling, and doing; whether these reactions are a result of what just took place or whether they are reverberations of some personal factors. Any group event can be interpreted in many different ways, depending on the stage of group development, the content of discussion, the quality of interaction, the meaning ascribed to each action by each member, and the psychological distance between and among participants, as well as on a host of personal variables such as individual perceptions, attitudes, and values (Roark & Radl, 1984).

As therapists, we attempt to sort out this maze of confusing stimuli and find or create some meaning to the action. The degree to which our inferences are accurate is based on our ability to know what is going on inside each participant. Freeze a moment, *any* moment in a group session, and there will be an assortment of individual reactions to what is going on. In one moment, for example, Ned is speaking about his problem of talking too much. Tanya is trying to get Mona's attention, rolling her eyes skyward in exasperation. The leader notes this reaction but misreads Mona's blank response as agreement when, in fact, she is rehearsing something else that she wants to say later. In her absent-mindedness, Mona leans too far forward, completely enthralling Tom in a forbidden view down her blouse. Tom is now gone in his own world, which is just fine with him because he was bored anyway. Toni is listening carefully to Ned's monologue, nodding compassionately as he speaks. Dan sighs in frustration, disgusted with how Toni is encouraging Ned to keep talking.

If this is the reality of what is taking place inside each participant's head during one frozen moment, the leader's (or any other outside observer's) view of events bears a rough but incomplete approximation of phenomenological accuracy. The leader can see the general boredom and malaise among the members and may even catch Tom peeking down Mona's blouse. But nothing indicates either the extent to which Mona is distracted or the fact that Dan is becoming increasingly agitated. This represents the unfortunate diagnostic limitations that a group leader must contend with in trying to infer what is happening at any moment. This is why, in the words of Roark and Radl (1984, p. 203), the group leader's main jobs is "to keep members from being lost in this maze of inferences and to help them express, respond, and understand their actual needs and concerns." Since we can neither read minds nor be expected to interpret behavior accurately all of the time, it is crucial that we enlist the help of group members to be responsible for "diagnosing" and expressing their own internal processes.

"Dislabeling" Effects of Diagnosis

Bakker (1975) claims that the main reasons clients don't change have less to do with clients than with our "dislabeling" conceptions and interventions. If a chronic patient makes remarkable progress just after entering psychotherapy, we sometimes tell ourselves that the changes weren't real—just a temporary symptom alleviation to avoid confronting deeper issues. We contribute to the myth that change is difficult and unlikely when we focus on stable personality factors that can no more be altered than can one's physical appearance. When medical-model concepts are applied that emphasize disease processes, change to counteract the supposed degenerative effects is quite difficult.

The standard psychiatric labeling process involves considerations that are designed not only for the patients' benefit but also for the convenience of insurance companies, hospitals, research directors, and the practitioner. The "game" is to pick a 5-digit number from the *Diagnostic and Statistical Manual of Mental Disorders* (DSM-IV) that can be plugged into the appropriate blank spaces on the Blue Cross forms. No treatment begins, no help is offered, no therapeutic wheels are set in motion until the medical establishment is first satisfied in its craving for a diagnostic number.

It's hoped that this microdiagnostic process involves a detailed examination of mental status, a series of structured interviews, psychological testing, a developmental case history, medical and neurological examinations, and finally a differential diagnosis that covers the diagnostician in case the best-guess judgment is wrong. The clinician collects all the available symptoms and then attempts to arrive at a label that best summarizes most of them. That no three diagnosticians can reliably agree on the same diagnosis, or even on the same observable symptoms, for the same patient supposedly speaks more for clinical inadequacies than of any deficiency in the system. A client's bestowed label depends very much on the biases of the diagnostician, the prestige of the patient, how other people have reacted to the patient's behavior, and the societal norms that vary across race and culture.

In diagnosing diagnosis, Small (1978) concludes that it suffers from the same maladies that afflict disadvantaged clients—malnutrition, prejudice, identity confusion, and lack of dignity.

Kogan (1959) found that a diagnosis may be expressed in terms of the equation:

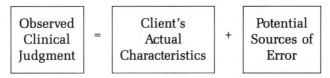

$$\boxed{\begin{array}{c}\text{Observed} \\ \text{Clinical} \\ \text{Judgment}\end{array}} = \boxed{\begin{array}{c}\text{Client's} \\ \text{Actual} \\ \text{Characteristics}\end{array}} + \boxed{\begin{array}{c}\text{Potential} \\ \text{Sources of} \\ \text{Error}\end{array}}$$

where "potential sources of error" could be influenced by any of the following variables (Stuart, 1970):

- the clinician's expectations
- the clinician's theoretical orientation
- the clinician's personal biases
- the clinician's inaccurate observations
- the clinician's illogical reasoning
- the client's inconsistent behavior
- the client's socioeconomic background
- the client's personality style
- the client's perceived similarity to the clinician
- the client's attitudes toward treatment

There is one additional problem in the use of traditional methods of diagnosis: the proliferation of "psychoese" language. Rosen (1977) coined the word *psychobabble* to describe the overuse of nonsensical words for classifying feelings and thoughts. Now, Rosen laments, people no longer feel depressed, they are "bummed out"; they aren't tense but "uptight"; not inhibited but "hung-up"; not fearful but "paranoid"; not strange but "schizzed-out."

Unfortunately, therapists in general and group leaders in particular are responsible for encouraging this practice. Benshoff (1978) offers a whole glossary of confusing terms that we model to our clients. When we say "meeting your own needs," what we really mean is "You are not acting as we want you to." When we say "share," what we really mean is "spill your guts." When we ask for a feeling, what we really want to see is an emotional reaction. "Shaking with terror or sobbing with disappointment are two good responses, and throwing up is always acceptable" (Benshoff, 1978, p. 165). It's not that we so much enjoy speaking in the riddles of verbal fashion, nor do we consciously create a vocabulary full of clichés, simple typologies, and phrases. It is rather that it is easier to borrow other people's language than to create our own.

Della Corte (1980) believes that the labeling craze is more than just a current fad. As is slang, psychological jargon is deliberately ambiguous, permitting its use in any situation with satisfying results. It allows the communicator to sound knowledgeable and up-to-date, yet makes it possible to alter the meaning of words after the fact. But Della Corte contends that the terminology also serves several useful functions. It provides an important illusion of diagnostic validity, but, more crucially, it promotes a feeling of cohesiveness among the people who speak in common tongue. For instance, after singer John Denver graduated from a group, he was interviewed by *Rolling Stone* and gave the following account.

> How far out it is to be a bird and fly around the trees. I am what I've always wanted to be and that is the truth. And I think—in fact, it's not what I think, but I observe that if people were to really take a good look at themselves, they are exactly the way that they have always wanted to be. . . . My experience is that if I can tell you the truth, just lay it out there, then I have totally opened up a space for you to be who you are and that it really opens up all the room in the world for us to do whatever we want to do in regard to each other. If I don't like you, I'll tell you. And that's great. (Rosen, 1977, p. 28)

This illustrates the power of group settings to indoctrinate participants into their language systems. Group members have a sense of belonging; they are part of a special club with its own fraternal codes and communication. It feels good to be able to recognize predictable behavior patterns, match them with a memorized label, and play amateur psychosleuth when the diagnosis is yelled aloud:

"You're 'parenting' again."
"Quit being a Manipulative Monopolizer."
"Your 'Hostile Child' is showing."
"If you weren't so 'passive/dependent,' you wouldn't have this problem."

Somewhere in the back of the group member's head something clicks into place and the diagnosis is confirmed: "So *that's* the name for what you were doing" (as if by giving a name to a thing we unravel its mysteries).

We have many names to call group members who do not meet our expectations or who have unusual ways of "cooperating" with treatment. The most benign are *resistant* or *reluctant*, but the literature abounds with other words to describe them: *hateful, abrasive, impossible,* or *obnoxious.* So-called difficult group members "are often just people with problems that are more complex than we usually confront and with an interactive style that is different from what we might prefer. Calling them names only disguises the reality that resistant clients are attempting to tell us about their pain, even if their method of communication is sometimes indirect and annoying" (Kottler, 1992, p. 39).

Diagnostic Alternatives

Stuart (1970) claims that the principal problem of current diagnostic practices is that they are based on "Aristotelian rather than Galilean logic, which results in the postulation of entities which cannot be shown to exist" [p. 75]. Stuart further specifies intrinsic weaknesses in the system where (1) the diagnosis is made in the context of a threatening situation; (2) the discrete categories are not mutually exclusive; and (3) the categories are so complex as to defy reliable application.

One of the most startling shortcomings of the DSM-IV is its almost total disregard for interpersonal behavior and social-psychological variables. Since group leaders are largely concerned with interpersonal behavior, the psychiatric nosological system is virtually useless as a functional tool. All the interpersonal approaches to diagnosis that we have inherited from Horney (1945), Berne (1966), Sullivan (1947), Adams (1964), Bales (1970), Ohlsen and Pearson (1965), and Hill (1971) have been ignored in the current system, leaving group leaders to fend for themselves.

Begelman (1976) has compiled an exhaustive list of criticisms against traditional psychiatric diagnoses that yield, in the opinion of Adams, Doster, and Calhoun (1977), surprisingly little useful information about the client's behavior. The reliability of the system has been questioned by a number of researchers (Rosenhan, 1973; Temerlin, 1975; Zigler and Phillips, 1961, 1965; Zubin, 1967). It fosters a disease concept of emotional concerns, giving the client an excuse for remaining helpless: "It's not my fault. I've got an anxiety neurosis. No wonder I can't relax." It presumes that everyone with the same label has the same problem, a misconception that sabotages any effort to individualize therapy. The labels become stereotypical and stigmatizing. They dehumanize the patient and have a strong bias toward searching for pathology. Finally, Begelman (1976) and McLemore and Benjamin (1979) point out that psychiatric labels have little value for establishing prognoses, constructing treatment plans, or even predicting behavior.

There are a number of other diagnostic models that are probably more appropriate for group settings than the medical model favored by our mental health system. Table 6-1 describes several other models that offer several advantages by minimizing pathology and maximizing complete behavioral descriptions of client experiences. Developmental and phenomenological models help us assess individual group member issues, and behavioral and systemic diagnostic perspectives aid us in the macrodiagnostic process of understanding interactive effects.

To counter the limitations of traditional diagnostic practices, McLemore and Benjamin (1979) recommend using an interpersonal model that takes into account the client's functioning within a social context. This has obvious advantages for practitioners working in group settings in allowing the interpersonal diagnosis to include: (1) a focus on social behavior rather than on disease, (2) a relatively stigma-free description of behavior, (3) more reliable and consistent applications, and (4) implications for prescriptive therapy within an interpersonal context. The authors then formulate the beginnings of a working model in which a group member's behavior is labeled in terms of its effects on self and others.

Table 6-1 Diagnostic models

Model	Primary Structure	Sources of Information	Advantages	Disadvantages	Treatment Implications
Medical	Discrete categories of psychopathology	Data-based quantitative research	Organization of etiology, symptom clusters, and prognoses	Categories not as discrete and reliable as needed; reduction of individual to a label	Application of treatments to diminish symptoms and cure underlying illness
Developmental	Predictable stages of normal development	Case studies; qualitative and quantitative research	Aids in prediction; emphasis on healthy functioning	Stages overlap and are difficult to assess; not a universal system	Identifying current level of functioning so as to stimulate growth to next stage
Phenomenological	Complex descriptions of the person while minimizing use of labels	Qualitative research; personal experience	Captures essences; flexibility	Subjective biases and distortion	Use of self as instrument to establish relationship and understand client's world
Behavioral	Specific description and identification of behaviors and reinforcers	Direct observation; quantitative measurement	Very specific and descriptive	Misses complexity of human experience	Set specific goals to increase or decrease target behaviors
Systemic	Contextual descriptions	Family history; direct observation	Views bigger picture of issues	Negates individuality	Work within family structure

Source: From Kottler, J. A. & Brown, R. W. (1992). *Introduction to therapeutic counseling*. Pacific Grove, CA: Brooks/Cole.

McLemore and Benjamin illustrate this model with the example of a parent who routinely uses power tactics on a child (*hostile blame—interpersonal*). The child internalizes the hostility, creating guilt. The guilt, now interpersonally diagnosed in the context from which it developed, can be effectively countered by the group leader who uses *empathy* and interjects intrapsychic healing forces such as *support*. This interpersonal diagnostic system can therefore be reliably applied to predicting consequences as well as to understanding etiology.

Virginia Satir (1972) developed a diagnostic system that also lends itself well to interpersonal group situations, particularly in family therapy and in analyzing macroconcepts and interdynamics. Satir's patterns of group communication include those who are *placaters*, who avoid conflict at the cost of their integrity; *blamers*, who attempt to show strength by placing the focus on others; *computers*, who rely on intellectual, ultrarational ploys to hide vulnerability; and *distractors*, who make us dizzy with irrelevancies. Ineffectively run groups would therefore exhibit these incongruent communication styles in conjunction with closed-system rules and restrictions.

Other interpersonal classifications, such as those by Gladding (1991) focus more specifically on group member behavior than on style or personality. Such a distinction is crucial to avoiding the *dislabeling* process of typecasting personalities rather than focusing on what people do. The therapeutic implications are, of course, that once self-defeating behaviors are productively labeled, they may be changed. Personalities, style, nature, and disorders imply a degree of stability and permanence that would therefore resist alteration.

The following behavioral labels represent a meaningful selection of common self-defeating behaviors found among group members. Only after these difficulties are clearly and specifically identified, *with the client involved in the self-diagnostic process,* can the group leader hope to go to work on them. This summary of dysfunctional behaviors is therefore converted into the labels to which clients can most easily relate. These labels include microdiagnostic (intrapersonal) as well as macrodiagnostic (interpersonal) behavioral indices.

Intrapersonal Behaviors

Procrastination: Acting as if, by waiting long enough, a concern will go away by itself.
Behavioral example: a group member repeatedly declares that she wishes to make certain life changes but never seems to have the time to act.

External Control: Demonstrating a lack of control over emotions, behavior, or oral habits.
Behavioral example: "I just can't help it. The depression just came over me."

Living in the Past: Hiding from the present by using the past as an excuse for the way one is.

Behavioral example: "But I've always been this way. I've never been good at speaking up in groups."

Self-Pity: Feeling sorry for oneself and helpless to do anything about it.

Behavioral example: "I wish, just once, I could get a girl to go out with me again."

Guilt: Punishing oneself for some regretted misdeed in the past.

Behavioral example: "If only I could have known, maybe she'd be all right today."

Worry: Spending time thinking about future things that could happen but over which one has no control.

Behavioral example: "What if it rains during the picnic? I don't know what I would do."

Psychological Dependence: Demanding that the world be a certain way in order for one to be happy; having life ruled by external schedules; having attachment to another person that involves needs rather than wants.

Behavioral example: "I can't just go out and get a job unless my husband gives his permission."

Rigid Thinking: reluctance to give up untenable positions, having a vested interest in certain ideas; getting into hopeless verbal battles.

Behavioral example: a group member who has a difficult time changing views or admitting that she or he is wrong.

Ethnocentricity: Judging the world and other people's actions according to a narrow, personal value system.

Behavioral example: a group member who criticizes another for acting differently than she or he would act.

The methodology for diagnosing any of these phenomenological patterns is usually done within the context of an exploratory behavioral assessment in which the group leader attempts to get a handle on the nature of the presenting concerns. Both Lazarus (1973) and Kanfer and Phillips (1970) developed a seven-component assessment paradigm based on the client's behavior, affect, sensation, imagery, cognition, and interpersonal relationships. The diagnostic framework incorporates an analysis and clarification of the client's problem, an assessment of motivation and reinforcement levels in the client's life, a reading of biological and social/cultural experiences, as well as an analysis of the client's self-control, social relationships, and physical environment. All these factors together form a meaningful diagnostic pattern that not only summarizes the exact nature of client difficulties but also implies the best therapeutic alternatives for treatment.

Gottman and Leiblum's (1974) problem-assessment strategy involves treating client symptoms not as important in themselves but as warning flares that therapeutic efforts are necessary: "A good assessment should suggest hypotheses for intervention and not merely result in categorization or labeling" (Gottman & Leiblum, 1974, p. 25). They therefore contend that client diagnosis ought to include the following questions:

- How and why did the client decide to seek help?
- What has the client already attempted to do to resolve the problem?
- What are the client's expectations for treatment, including leader and group member roles?
- What is the client doing that she or he should not be doing because it is disturbing to others?
- What is the client doing that is disturbing to self?
- What are the client's operating assumptions and cognitive structures?
- Is the presenting concern interactive in nature? Who else is involved?
- How often, when, and where does the presenting concern arise?
- What reinforcers and maintenance variables are perpetuating the client's self-defeating behaviors?
- What events and experiences in the client's past are relevant to the current problem?
- What are the client's characteristic functioning levels in life skills (sleeping, eating, loving, sex, integration skills, appearance, moods, energy level)?
- What are the client's behavioral assets, deficiencies, and abilities?

Any of these diagnostic systems, or even a traditional mental status examination, requires that the clinician think analytically to isolate significant variables for further investigation. The intrapersonal behaviors also form a backdrop for understanding the broader macrodiagnostic concepts found in interpersonal behaviors.

Interpersonal Behaviors

Approval Seeking: Deliberately or unconsciously speaking or acting to win the leader's or other members' good opinion, even at the expense of one's personal convictions.
Behavioral example: whenever a client speaks, he makes eye contact only with the leader.

Mothering: Acting as a rescuer and nurturing figure to reduce one's personal level of discomfort over conflict.
Behavioral example: "I wish you'd stay off Michael's back. Can't you see he's had enough?"

Politicking: Speaking for others in the group without their consent.
Behavioral example: "We don't like the way things have been going."

Boring: Speaks in a monotone with little animation; prone to rambling about inappropriate irrelevancies.
Behavioral example: "I guess—I don't—have—much—to say."

Jesting: Inappropriately making jokes and clowning to win attention, disrupt group focus, or shrug off a painful confrontation.
   Behavioral example: a client starts laughing hysterically, making funny faces of rejection right after receiving direct confrontation.
Withdrawal: Passive behavior characterized by silence, blank expression, and escape defenses.
   Behavioral example: throughout a session, one client scoots back chair, stares out window, and doodles on paper.
Martyrizing: Taking on the image of a sufferer who has no choice but to shoulder the burdens of the world.
   Behavioral example: repeatedly complaining about how miserable life is but doing nothing to change the situation.
Interrogating: Excessive aggressive questioning with an implied demand for the "right" answers.
   Behavioral example: "Why are you so weak you can't face up to me?"
Monopolizing: Self-centered rambling, storytelling, and talking to the point where it is difficult for others to have group time when they want it.
   Behavioral example: "Did I ever tell you about the time—?"
Shrinking: Playing pseudoleader by dispensing advice or overintellectualizing.
   Behavioral example: "I think my problem is just a manifestation of the unresolved hostility I feel toward my father."
Evasiveness: Watering down the truth out of a fear of hurting others' feelings or from vulnerability.
   Behavioral example: "You want feedback? I think you're a pretty nice guy."

Broader Patterns

In addition to the interpersonal dimensions of macrodiagnosis, the group leader is also concerned with the broader patterns of group dynamics that predict future outcomes. The practitioner will want to identify aspects of collective behavior to prepare appropriate interventions for circumventing problems, to protect individual rights against pressure toward conformity, and to orient oneself, as a sailor would read the stars to make certain the voyage is on course.

The first signpost to assess is the group *synergy* (Cattell, 1948). What is the accelerated collective energy that is available in the session? Are participants focused on what is happening? Synergy is the productive cooperation among clients that maintains a harmonious atmosphere sufficient to meet individual therapeutic goals. Based on the attitudes, motivation, and behavior of all members at any given time, the total synergy of a group may be dynamic or in need of recharging. There is a contagious transmission of excitement that the group leader carefully monitors, occasionally intervening to keep productive energy flowing smoothly.

Interchange compatibility is a term coined by Schutz (1958) to describe the mutual expressions of inclusion, control, and affection among group members. To what extent are clients reciprocating interpersonal needs from one another? Who is giving and who is taking? Are exchanges roughly balanced as to which clients are offering support, taking risks, using group time, or giving feedback? If only a few members are receiving most of the help, doing most of the talking, or taking most of the time, the interchange compatibility factor is unbalanced. The group leader would then be signaled to spend more time drawing out other clients while keeping dominant members more in control.

All groups have subgroup coalition formations that must be identified for the purpose of determining their effects on total group member functioning. These interpersonal attraction/repulsion patterns could conceivably inhibit natural drives toward cohesion and mutual intimacy by setting up competitive factions. Who rescues whom? Who attacks whom? Which members are most similar-dissimilar? Who defers to whom? Who knows whom outside the group? What alliances affect group outcomes in what ways? What payoffs do participants accrue as the result of their joint actions?

The level of trust and cohesion must also be accurately read at frequent intervals. A high frequency of "we" statements, equal contributions, cooperative statements, expressions of liking the group experience, unprompted participation, and mutually supportive comments would indicate a group of individuals functioning at high levels in these dimensions (Krumboltz & Potter, 1973).

Any of these few macrodiagnostic targets or some of the predictable problems and critical incidents discussed in Chapter 7 require the group leader to be a special breed of diagnostician. There is a pragmatic motive to the labeling process. The therapist hopes to identify common themes and provoke client self-diagnosis so that a clear vision is provided of exactly where the therapeutic efforts are headed.

CHAPTER **7**

Critical Incidents, Predictable Problems

During the span of a human life, there occur critical periods in which specific biological, cultural, and psychological factors make their influences known. As these developmental factors arise, individuals must master a set of skills to resolve novel conflicts and adapt to crucial growth spurts or all future progress will become retarded (Havighurst, 1972). The infant who fails to develop emotional attachments to a parent, the child who does not learn socially acceptable ways to seek adult attention, or the adolescent who never masters abstract reasoning are all doomed to spend their lives in a state of compromised functioning (Erikson, 1963; Gazda, 1989; Ivey, 1991; Piaget, 1956).

Throughout its duration, a group goes through a series of predictable stages. In therapeutic groups, as in human evolution, progressive development leads to potential problems. Every experienced group leader comes to recognize these critical incidents that can so easily sabotage therapeutic effectiveness. Within a single instant, all our training and preparation must come into play; a split-second decision must be made as to the best way to handle the situation; and we must live with the consequences forever.

The instantaneous decisions that group leaders must make when confronted with critical situations in the field are not unlike those required of jet pilots. According to Tom Wolfe (1980), successful flyers all have an elusive but necessary quality called "The Right Stuff," which they must unhesitatingly exercise during a crisis.

> Being a fighter pilot . . . presented a man, on a perfectly sunny day, with more ways to get himself killed than his wife and children could imagine in their wildest fears. If he was barreling down the runway at two hundred miles an hour, completing the takeoff run, and the board started lighting up red, should he (a) abort the takeoff (and try to wrestle with the monster which was gorged with jet fuel, out in the sand beyond the runway) or (b) eject (and hope that the goddamned human cannonball trick works at zero altitude and he doesn't shatter an elbow

or a kneecap on the way out), or (c) continue the takeoff and deal with the problem aloft (knowing full well that the ship may be on fire and therefore seconds away from exploding)? He would have one second to sort out the options and act, and this kind of workaday decision came up all the time. [p. 26]*

Similarly, being a group leader presents a professional with more ways to damage other people's lives than our spouses, children, or clients could possibly imagine in *their* wildest fears. With reported "casualties" reaching as high as 47% (Gottschalk, 1966) or even 80% of participants (Lieberman, Yalom, & Miles, 1973), Hartley, Roback, and Abramowitz (1976) urge practitioners to become more aware of the variables that produce deterioration effects. Certainly, groups run by experienced and well-trained therapists have less potential for inflicting damage than do encounter groups led by laypeople. However, it is the critical incidents that short-circuit progress in groups—the problem clients, crisis stages, and pivotal moments—that will ultimately determine positive experiences in members, if their leaders handle them smoothly.

Just as jet pilots have less than a second to make a critical decision that will affect their immediate well-being, group leaders are regularly faced with conflicts in which their chosen course of action, selected within an instant, will ultimately affect the safety of a dozen persons in their charge. If a belligerent and abusive group member "comes barreling down the runway" determined to wreak havoc on unsuspecting peers, the leader must make one of three choices: (1) confront the client with the inappropriate behavior (and risk alienating, embarrassing, ridiculing, or damaging him); (2) ignore the behavior and attempt to extinguish the actions (and allow potential abuse to ripple throughout the group, destroying intimacy, cohesion, and perhaps the defenses of a vulnerable member); or (3) try to use the outburst as a stimulus for openly working through the issue (allowing the client to manipulate group time and draw attention to himself, inadvertently rewarding his deviance). There are perhaps a thousand other legitimate courses of action, but none that leads to a single, "correct" solution to the problem.

The purpose of this chapter is to reintroduce advanced group leaders to a catalog of the most common critical incidents that occur in groups so that they may better prepare themselves to handle anticipated problems as they arise.

Common Critical Incidents

A number of writers have constructed lists of critical themes requiring leader interventions, among them Cohen and Smith (1976), Corey, Corey, Callanan, and Russell (1992), and Yalom (1985). A group problem may be defined as

*From *The Right Stuff,* by T. Wolfe. Copyright © 1980 by Farrar, Strauss, & Giroux, Inc.

any interactive event, or result from such an event, that interferes with the completion of therapeutic tasks or the attainment of client goals. After presenting this definition, Rose (1989) then mentions some of the more common instances of such critical issues—low cohesion, an overly dominant member, a member's withdrawal from the group, excessive off-task behavior, destructive coalitions, overdependence on the leader, active conflict, and problematic group norms.

Edelwich and Brodsky (1992) identify some of the most common problem behaviors that group leaders must face on a regular basis.

- physical flight (absences, lateness)
- nonparticipation (silence, withdrawal)
- external focus (blaming, gossip)
- ventilation (grievances, anger)
- monopolizing (attention seeking, rambling)
- intimidation (emotional blackmail, verbal abuse)
- seduction (helplessness, eroticism)
- red crossing (rescuing, avoiding conflict)
- intolerance (peer pressure, prejudices)

Most noteworthy among the critical incidents are several significant nominations that must be handled with particular skill, sensitivity, and diplomacy. For instance, in every group there are a number of "firsts" that command the attention of every participant until they can be integrated into the existing scheme of things. Every novel stimulus requires that an organism adapt to the altered physical/psychological environment. The first time the therapist says "I don't know," shock waves ripple among the clients until they figure out the implications of having a leader who is less than perfect. Other firsts can be just as traumatic.

Some of the most important firsts and critical incidents are described here as they would arise chronologically in a group.

First Impressions

As group members first enter the room and begin to make themselves comfortable (and uncomfortable), they will check out the other members. On the basis of their perceptions and biases, they will form limited, narrow first impressions of one another: "That girl looks like she's mad at the world. I like that guy she's sitting next to, though he seems even more nervous than I do. I *know* I'm not going to like these older guys with their pinstripe suits and snotty attitudes. I wonder what these people think of me?"

In the initial encounter, group members will tend to write off those whom they perceive as different or strange and will attach themselves to a few persons who may hold values similar to their own. Coalitions are established that must eventually be expanded to reflect more open acceptance of all persons, regardless of their lifestyle preferences and personal traits. Clients will need to be helped to quickly move beyond superficial encounters and predictable small talk to deeper levels of honest communication.

Opening exercises designed to start the group with structured introductions often help dispel negative reactions because people usually become more attractive after they have made disclosures. Residual limiting impressions, those that were reinforced during the introductions, will dissipate further if participants are given an opportunity to express them aloud. In one such exercise, clients are instructed (on the pretext of remembering one another's names) to select the animal that a given person most reminds them of. After clients creatively introduce themselves, they are offered the chance to hear how they initially come across to others in the group.

> **Member**: Arthur, you remind me of a turtle. You seem quiet, lazy, unassuming. You are content to bask in the sun. Yet you love to swim and explore beneath the water where no one can see.
>
> **Member**: Nicole, my first impression of you is of a basset hound. You appear loyal, protective, cuddly. You're a good tracker with your nose to the ground. But you feel awkward, ungainly, and powerless, or at least you sit that way.

This exercise, or one like it, will get first impressions out in the open. It provides feedback to people in a relatively structured, nonthreatening manner. It helps clients (1) hear nondefensively how they come across to others, (2) become more accurate in interpreting others' behaviors, (3) get practice in giving constructive feedback, (4) become more congruent between the images they believe are projected and the ones that people actually see, (5) collect significant data about one another, and (6) be more accepting and flexible in their perceptions of others, more willing to appreciate individual differences (Brown, 1978).

Unequal Participation

Within minutes of the first group session, it becomes evident that the willingness of clients to participate is uneven. Some persons enthusiastically contribute all that is available to their consciousness while others pout, sulk, or cautiously wait to see whether disaster befalls those who leaped before they looked. Resentment builds in those who have given much but who don't see their partners reciprocate. Cautious and reserved members may resent those who "hogged" most of the group time, feeling that they would have spoken up if they had been given more time. Frustration levels increase as feelings of inadequacy become evident during introductions.

Often the leader will deliberately use a well-tested structured exercise that is designed specifically to ensure equal input among members. A leveling effect can be programmed into the introductory activity by providing specific instruction on appropriate behavior and by allowing all clients the same amount of time. A 3-minute timer can be used to encourage conciseness and meaningful introductions that include such basics as expectations for the experience, present feelings, stated goals, characteristic functioning patterns, troublesome behaviors, apprehensions, and predictions of what will occur.

In later stages of the group, unequal participation is confronted more directly by drawing out the passive members (while also protecting their rights to privacy) and encouraging overactive members to be more discriminating in their decisions to speak up. Generally, additional feedback is invaluable in this situation because passive members will receive support that their opinions are valued while overactive members will learn of specific instances when they ramble and focus on themselves. It is only when participation becomes equally distributed that feelings of belonging, identification, cohesion, and intimacy will develop.

Statement of Superficial Concerns

The inherent ambiguity of the group situation together with diversified client expectations lead to much confusion and uncertainty. Members may argue about the "real" purpose of the group, stalling progress until some unifying themes and common goals come into focus. Early attempts to resolve differences in interests, background, style, needs, and goals will be unsuccessful until a common language has been developed. The group leader works to restate and clarify client messages in a way that creates greater cohesion and mutual identification.

"When you describe your problems arising from being overweight all your life, I think that all of us could relate to the experience of being an outsider. I noticed Kevin averted his eyes, Samantha looked embarrassed as if she were self-conscious about her physical appearance, and everyone else sort of looked inward. When you mentioned that you were in this group, not because you're weird like everyone else in here, but only because you want to drop 40 pounds, I was again reminded of the concerns that most of you share in common. Your problem is not so much a matter of losing 40 pounds—I'm sure you've found a dozen diets that will help you shed the weight for a few months until you gain it all back—but rather a lack of self-control.

"You are a constant victim of the external world. You see a billboard and start humming the McDonald's jingle until you get to eat. You look at your watch and decide it's time to eat, whether you're hungry or not. I bet that this problem of being externally controlled is not limited to your overeating behavior, nor is it unique to you in this group. You've already said how easily you are hurt by others, a symptom of externally controlled emotions. Tabby and Nadine share that difficulty when they lose their tempers so willingly. And all the rest of you mention in some context how you aren't in control of your lives. To say that the only way you intend to use this group is as a diet support system is to grossly underestimate your own potential for change and the collective resources available here to offer assistance."

After clients initially state their reasons for joining the group, their goals, and how they intend to use their time, it will become evident that there are varied interpretations of what is expected. After the first go-around, some clients will have bravely volunteered deeply serious concerns—about their marriage, their sanity, or their sexuality. Others will decide to play it safe (or perhaps they just aren't skilled at self-diagnosis), declaring such goals as "I want to get my parents off my back," "I'd like to get a promotion in my work," or "I want to understand myself better."

It is the job of the group leader to universalize these concerns, translating each from a superficial, narrow orientation into one to which everyone can relate: "When you say you want to get your parents off your back, what you really mean is that you let others get to you. You're also not good at confronting people who abuse you. Does anyone else have a similar problem?"

Small Talk

Until group members learn the rules about appropriate topics for discussion, there is much rambling, small talk, and digression that is unrelated to therapeutic growth. Most people attempt to generalize their behavior in other group encounters, such as parties and meetings, to their actions in therapeutic groups. They have learned to wear plastic smiles, engage in trivial conversation, hide their true feelings, and play games of deception that are patently unacceptable in a counseling setting. If the group leader allows such chitchat to continue, clients assume they are acting as they are expected to act; but if the chatter is cut off and their usual defenses are stripped away, they begin to feel even more vulnerable. The group leader's task is to model appropriate socializing behavior that is sensitive, direct, and concise while encouraging members to avoid small talk. Silence is preferred over an incessant outflow of trivia.

Some clients will persistently bring discussion back to small talk about politics, baseball, soap operas, or the weather. It is only by educating them about how therapeutic groups are different from social groups, that clients will begin to realize how and why they waste valuable group time. After a while, participants will begin to monitor themselves with regard to trivial, distracting discussions.

Collective Silence

A beginner usually makes the mistake of assuming that all group members are part of an uncooperative conspiracy to resist treatment. Their lack of dramatic, *observable* behavior is interpreted as a sign of reluctance to participate. But since only one member can speak at a time, there is *always* group silence except for the voice of a single person.

Some members wait patiently, knowing they are not yet ready to contribute anything meaningful. Others are silent because they don't understand what is expected of them. At least one client will deliberately keep quiet just to see what the leader will do. Another might be working on a self-defeating behavior of talking too much and so refrains from making input. A few will be using the silent time productively to gather their thoughts, integrate new ideas, or formulate a plan. Someone else may be relaxing, resting, regrouping energy after a period of intensity. The point is that all choose silence for their own personal reasons.

The leader who approaches this critical incident with the goal of reducing his or her own discomfort is likely to find trouble along the way. Such an attitude might be expressed as: "I don't know what's wrong with everyone today. I thought we were making some headway; I guess I was wrong. That's O.K. if you just want to sit there, but it's such a waste of time."

It is almost always helpful instead to select one person (usually the client who seems most responsive at that moment) and address an inquiry in a more personal fashion.

> **Leader**: Manuel, I notice that you have been very quiet for the past few minutes. What would you imagine Chan and Louise are thinking about over there in the corner?
>
> **Manuel**: Uh—gee, I don't know. I was just thinking about whether I wanted to use group time tonight. I think Louise looks kind of bored because she keeps yawning and looking at you to *do* something. Chan just looks like he's daydreaming.
>
> **Leader**: Well Manuel, what do you think *we* should do now?

When working with a co-leader, it is tempting to drop the problem in his or her lap. (To the co-leader): "What do you make of this silence? I'm a little confused because a number of people look like they want to speak but seem to be holding themselves back."

However the problem is managed, it is the style of execution that is most important. The group leader wants not only to state that silent periods are acceptable, even desirable and necessary, but also to encourage risk taking by members who are too intimidated to speak their minds. By keeping their fingers on the pulse of each participant, leaders can readily interpret the meanings behind "silent action" and so gear their strategies to meet the requirement of each situation.

Functional Deafness

When few meaningful communications can be induced in the early sessions of a group, self-centered monologues become the norm. Clients unskilled at attending to one another will fail to give others their full concentration. Human relations specialists have always been fond of structuring exercises to enhance the quality of intercommunication. Participants may be paired off and requested to repeat verbatim everything that has just been said to them before they are allowed to respond. Advanced group leaders are usually able to intervene without seriously disrupting the flow of things: "Beth, before you continue with your anecdote, could you repeat what José just said to you?" Or in another situation: "As you were receiving feedback from the others, you acknowledged their messages before they were even warmed up. It is as if you were only pretending to appreciate their comments when actually you had no intention of giving their ideas consideration."

Often the problem must be brought out in the open by discussing how difficult it is to concentrate on other people's talk while at the same time you are rehearsing your own speech. The behavior can then be interpreted as a fear of saying the wrong thing, a case of performance anxiety that cripples one's attending powers.

First Angry Outburst

Even though we can predict that at some point during the early group sessions someone will have an angry outburst, the foreknowledge doesn't much reduce the startled response when the event occurs. We tell ourselves and our clients that spontaneous emotional expression is good, that it is an example of what we are here for—to work through negative feelings. Still, the first uncontrolled tantrum is almost always traumatic.

The angry person starts turning colors, the neck muscles stand out, and the energy builds to a very loud crescendo. The anger may be self-directed, resulting from frustration; it may be a hostile action to agitate or disrupt proceedings; it may be a definitive last-ditch defense against perceived attack; or it may be an honest acknowledgment that sore toes have been stepped on.

In whatever form and manner the first anger arises, the leader must deftly intervene to prevent casualties among other group members who are not prepared to handle the confrontation constructively. An explanation is in order in which the therapist simultaneously acknowledges the validity of the anger, gives permission for it to continue (unless it is grossly abusive), and reassures group members that the steaming client is indeed playing by the rules.

Once the anger has been labeled, the catharsis is redirected toward focusing on some resolution of the problem. The most important point is for the therapist to treat this spontaneous conflict in the same calm, accepting, controlled manner with which any other conflict would be resolved. After analyzing the reasons and motives behind the anger and working through destructive attitudes that were responsible for the outburst, as well as through any interaction variables with other members who were involved, the therapist can lead the client to express the anger more effectively.

Schuerger (1979) recommends guiding therapeutic anger by four means. (1) encouraging directness, honesty, and precision of expression; (2) making certain that complaints are specific and complete; (3) following through the anger with involvement in the conflict or with the target person(s);

and (4) teaching more socially acceptable alternatives for working through hostility.

A hard lesson that every schoolteacher must learn is that there is a fundamental difference between *being* angry and *acting* angry. In situations in which negotiation, pleading, and logical reasoning fall on deaf ears, an angry outburst is the only way to get people's attention enough to communicate that you are serious. However, when an angry display is called for—to stop a fight in the classroom or to get an insensitive group member to quit infringing on the personal rights of others—it is possible to do so without *feeling* out of control on the inside, even though you *look* out of control on the outside.

The group leader may choose to cap the erupting volcano with instruction on controlled anger—how group members can dissipate anger when they feel it rising, how they can express anger nondefensively, and they can use angry experiences for future growth.

Giving Advice

From movies and television, clients often acquire distorted expectations of what will happen in therapeutic groups. Since most people operate from a problem-solution orientation anyway, there is a strong drive to solicit and give advice as soon as the presenting concern is expressed. Group members feel pity, empathy for their friend in trouble. They want to help the person solve his difficulties in the quickest way possible—by dispensing advice.

Even before the concerns have been sufficiently explored, group members may jump in with "Have you tried . . . ," "If I were you . . . ," or "My advice to you is . . ." The advice givers feel great because they believe that they are *doing* something to resolve the ambiguity of the situation and make the pain go away. They breathe a sigh of relief: "Well, we fixed that problem. Who's next?" The client-in-focus, of course, loves the advice and soaks up as much of it as possible. One doesn't have to take responsibility for the advice's outcome when someone else offers it.

The group leader must step in during these early "home-remedy" swap sessions, explain how and why they are going on, and describe the reasons that they are destructive in the long run, even though they temporarily help everyone feel relieved: "Mickey, how is it helpful for you to hear these suggestions before you are done sharing what is wrong? And even if this advice is followed to the letter—you go home and say what they told you to—what will you have learned to do next time? You will have learned that when you have problems in the future, you find someone else who will tell you what to do."

Power Struggles

Power struggles begin in earnest once group norms become reasonably stabilized. Those who have initiated discussions fight for control, believing that they have contributed the most and so deserve recognition. Actually, the early initiators are smooth talkers, usually with experience in other groups. They are overly prone to giving advice to others based on the delusion that problems are easily solvable if only they can find the "right" solution.

Some members try to ace the leader out of the authority role, challenging actions and blaming mistakes, whereas others align themselves in a protective posture to defend the leader against all criticism. Clients try all their best tricks to win leader approval, some by demonstrating compliance and flexibility, others by being rebellious and independent. When they speak, all clients' eyes will be intently focused on the leader, looking for the slightest sign of displeasure.

Dependency issues come to the forefront, producing simultaneous resentment and relief. Clients expect the leader to take full responsibility for providing entertainment and so tend to hang back. The leader tries to extinguish such dependence by slightly withdrawing, allowing leadership spaces to be filled by those who want the responsibility. By voluntarily yielding power, the leader is automatically seen as less threatening. The power struggle takes a back seat once the aura of Godliness is stripped from a leader who is perceived as perfect in all ways. When limitations and weaknesses are willingly displayed, the leader is a less attractive target for hostile acts.

Acute Anxiety

When a person is matched to a challenge that is perceived as either too difficult or that requires the use of unavailable skills, anxiety results. The overwhelming, panicky realization that you might be in over your head, that things might get out of control and ultimately destroy your existence, is the subjectively experienced state of anxiety. It is not just a matter of *having* anxiety; but "*being* anxiety" (May, 1958).

The anxious person might start shivering with cold and sweat simultaneously. Breathing pace will increase, as will hand tremors, body shakes, and feelings of unsteadiness. Nausea, vomiting, dizziness, and choking sensations might also accompany the attack. A spectacle unfolds before the group. The anxious person, attempting to control the symptoms, finds that panic becomes even more pronounced as a breaking point is approached. It is frightening enough to brave anxiety within the privacy of one's own home or in a therapist's office, but to do so before a group of persons whose approval has become important is excruciatingly painful.

Freud (1926) was among the first to suggest that anxiety serves a useful function by acting as a danger signal that prepares the organism for combating threat. Like an athlete or a gladiator, the anxious person's body chemistry clicks into "fight or flight" gear, rushing blood to the muscles, stopping digestive processes, constricting blood vessels in the skin to minimize bleeding from injury, releasing epinephrine to open breathing tubes, increasing heart rate and oxygen flow, and dilating pupils to better perceive danger (Bockar, 1976).

Spontaneous anxiety, such as might occur in a group, can be triggered by a number of factors, the most common of which involves helping efforts getting too close to the mark before the client feels fully prepared to change. The instinctual "smoke alarm" that is supposed to warn the occupant of potential danger instead burns down the house (Hoch, 1950).

Beck (1976) describes the anxious client as someone with an "overactive alarm system," one who responds to the slightest hint of perceived danger by psychologically fleeing in panic, thus actually creating harm—a constant state of anxiety that prevents any possible change. Beck further conceptualizes anxiety as a thinking disorder that involves exaggerating or distorting reality, involuntary overvigilance, and "castastrophizing" about possible outcomes. When a group member with a low tolerance for frustration and impoverished interpersonal skills attempts to express ambiguous feelings or integrate confronting feedback from other participants, anxiety can arise.

Beck's assumption that the alarm is worse than the fire does little to appease the other group members, who don't know that World War III hasn't really started in their colleague's body. Wracking sobs, tears, moans of anguish can be traumatic for untrained spectators to watch. One client's anxiety becomes contagious and spreads throughout the group unless the leader can swiftly and confidently intervene to offer relief.

The use of meditation, relaxation, or hypnosis to dispel acute anxiety in groups is often helpful. Before any further action can take place, the client's fears must be pacified and the observers must be convinced that things are under control. Using a firm, commanding voice, the leader distracts the anxious client from panic feelings by directing attention to rhythmic breathing, a focal point to stare at, and/or the systematic relaxation of muscle groups.

One of the first groups I led contained a young woman who was devastated because her husband had run away with her best friend. She couldn't talk about the episode without crying. I was successful enough at calming her down so that I was able to use some imagery rehearsal. She visualized herself walking down the street, confronting her husband unexpectedly, and, before we had the chance to have her practice staying relaxed, she lost all semblance of composure. Her behavior became so dramatically tense and out of control that *we* started to panic. The other group members looked to me for reassurance and all I could offer was a sickly, apologetic smile.

Finally, I *pretended* to know what was going on and proceeded to administer psychological first aid until she was calm enough to continue the therapy at a *much* slower pace. Her message, however, was clear, and I remembered thereafter to follow the client's lead instead of moving at a speed that felt comfortable for me. Unfortunately, I can't give this anecdote a happy ending. The woman dropped out of the group the following week, explaining that the anxiety in the group was much worse than any of the fears within her own head.

Prejudicial Incidents

Once the ice has been broken and an atmosphere of honesty prevails, people are more willing to reveal their prejudices and biases toward those with a different lifestyle. Group members will choose sides: blacks versus whites, feminists versus male chauvinists, atheists versus believers, old versus young, rich versus poor, middle class versus social dropout. Since participants feel that permission has been granted to say whatever is on their minds, they open an attic of stored judgments about every conceivable ethnic, socioeconomic, racial, or religious lifestyle represented in the group. The magic words "You people" will then preface any number of creative combinations of abuse.

"You people are just looking for charity."
"You people are all a bunch of lesbians."
"You people don't care about anything except your damn possessions."

Sexist stereotyping, racial tensions, and other critical incidents that result from overgeneralized thinking are best handled by making the confrontations personally based rather than taking place on a cognitive plane. All the ignorance and rigidity that stems from a lack of personal involvement with the scorned population—the "Archie Bunker Syndrome"—are dissipated after people are given the opportunity to confront one another on a personal level.

In one group, in which sexist and prejudicial comments were creating further gaps in understanding and greater hostility, time was taken out to confront the problem directly. Everyone was instructed to role play the opposite sex and race. White females became black males, white males became black females, and so on. Discussion was then directed to a topic controversial enough to ensure that members would play their roles to the hilt and identify strongly with the experiences they least understood.

White males pretending to be black women complained that they felt exploited. Black women playing the roles of white men shared their frustration in not being able to find jobs because of reverse discrimination. Black males acting as white females disclosed their fears of being successful; they felt they were scaring away men. And white females, assuming the minds of black males, exaggerated all the ridiculous stereotypes—bragging about how large their penises were, calling out derogatory names, and expressing much anger at having been discriminated against. The result of this psychodramatic structure was a greater sensitivity and understanding of one another's unique positions.

Setbacks

After significant progress has been made, clients often regress to previous self-defeating behaviors when they are under duress. Group members' worst fears are confirmed—that any changes made are only temporary reprieves. Once a client backslides, all the other group members vicariously experience the setback, wondering when it will happen to them.

Sufficiently preparing participants for the realities of change—two steps forward, one step back—minimizes panic reactions. Confidence grows with the knowledge that even if a return to previously ineffective functioning should occur, the client can readily fight back to the new line of scrimmage just as before.

Somewhere during the middle of a group's life, once members have had a taste of personal mastery, the leader can deliberately provoke situations that require the use of newly learned skills. The clients can then practice recovery strategies within the safety and support of the group. Certain themes—for instance, the subject of death—become critical incidents by their highly emotionally charged nature.

Yalom (1980) sometimes introduces a dying cancer patient to a group of reasonably healthy individuals, hoping to provoke a confrontation with the inevitability of death. Instead of eliciting an atmosphere of morbid fatalism, however, the content spans the usual assortment of presenting concerns. In addition, at one time or another, each group member is given a bonus by facing his or her own death anxiety as both a participant in the struggle and as a spectator in the dying process of a peer. The concept of setback is reframed within a positive context, providing opportunities for flexing one's new-found strength rather than highlighting weaknesses.

"I Won't Be Me"

Grieger and Boyd (1977) have investigated common themes that clients use to dispute rational thinking in order to preserve their irrational ideas. Frequently, group members will "cop a plea" when a session gets too intense. Unless a leader is prepared to challenge vigorously the validity of statements such as the following, a critical incident will emerge that is very difficult to handle.

"This group is turning me into a phony."
"All this problem-solving stuff is making me into a talking computer."
"I don't recognize myself any more—I'm losing my identity."

As a last-ditch effort at holding on to "good old me," however pained, anxious, or depressed such a person was, the client will resort to uncompromising measures. It is as if the "new me," with all its competence and control, is too frightening to face: "At least when I looked into the mirror

I knew what to expect—those comfortable blotches, those bags under the eyes, that sour disposition. Now when I shave in the morning a happy face that I don't recognize smiles back. I'm not sure I like it either."

This cognitive dissonance can be dispelled by using the typically confrontive, logical responses of the cognitive/emotive therapist. Grieger and Boyd (1977) suggest responses like "How can you possibly be anyone else but you?"

> We ask the client whether he would lose his identity if he were required to change from being right-handed to left-handed. Then we show him that, although he would find it awkward for a period of time to switch handedness, he would with persistent effort use his left hand more often, more comfortably, and perhaps with more facility until it became "natural" for him. [p. 254]

Boredom

After working patterns have become established and group members can reasonably predict the outcome of each session, the following will typically occur. The leader will get reports from members, all saying how much they enjoy the group. People will fight over who gets group time. They will all do a little exercise to get their heads primed. Someone will cry; someone will laugh. A few people will get most of the attention. They will summarize what they learned, get feedback from others about how wonderful they are. Then an atmosphere of boredom may take over.

Unless there is a liberal dosage of spontaneity, humor, varied formats, unpredictable agendas, and a free-flowing, flexible structure to the group, clients will grow restless and lethargic. Boredom is the supreme enemy, the state of existence in which time moves intolerably slowly. When clients become bored, their perceptions of time in the group alter dramatically. Clients require a constant bombardment of stimulation to keep them occupied. They cannot stand being alone in a room unless the television or stereo is blaring. They can't eat without reading the paper. They can't sit still for more than a few minutes. Their counterparts, who are relatively immune to boredom, have a never-ending fascination for involving themselves in any activity. In the dentist's chair, they will count the hygienist's nose hairs. In a faltering group, they will have a list of favorite activities to keep themselves happy until things pick up. They might make odds on who will speak first or reflect on what is holding them back. However they choose to handle the situation, they obviously have skills that bored clients lack.

The beauty of group work is that the heterogeneity of participants encourages people to teach from strengths: "Kathryn, while you sit there restless, sulking, and yawning, staring out the window, wishing you were somewhere else, hoping that I'll do something to rescue you from this fate worse than death, Becky sits over there happy as a clam. I wonder why she is so content to enjoy her thoughts, why she gets herself involved when she is restless, when you are powerless to do anything but suffer boredom?"

Conflict and Resistance

In writing about the constructive nature of conflict in groups, Mitchell and Mitchell (1984) mention the importance of bringing up and dealing with undercurrent issues as well as the value of stimulating interaction. Of course, as a focal point, conflict may also lead to deterioration in trust and cooperation if not managed properly. To this end, the authors offer several recommendations, the most important of which is building from the onset of the group appropriate norms for confrontation. In fact, one of the things that distinguishes advanced group leaders from their less experienced peers is greater comfort with and confidence in dealing with periodic upheavals. This "calmness under fire" models for other participants the salient attitude that what is happening right now, although heated and passionate, is a constructive exchange that will lead to positive outcomes. This can only occur under the stewardship of an able leader who works to protect people against becoming casualties.

Group members often learn from such conflicts that: (1) confrontation, when communicated appropriately, can lead to tremendous growth; (2) resolution occurs only through collaboration and compromise; (3) avoidance or diminishment of conflict is often not helpful in the long run; and (4) there are as many different perspectives of what is going on as there are participants. For example, after speaking at length about her lifelong struggle to trust men, Samantha viewed her own disclosure as clear, cogent, and incisive. Li, however, thought Samantha sounded whiny and embittered, stirring up trouble by forcing the genders to choose sides. Nigel, who had been speaking earlier, thought Samantha was attempting to control the session and draw attention away from him. Felipe, on the other hand, felt profoundly moved by Samantha's story; he began examining his own trust issues toward members of the opposite sex.

After the session ended, other group members processed Samantha's comments as they walked out to their cars. They also reflected little consensus in their points of view about the relative meaning of this incident. Samantha was alternately perceived as bitchy, courageous, manipulative, and vulnerable.

Even the two co-leaders didn't agree on how they viewed Samantha's behavior. One leader thought Samantha's disclosure was a significant catalyst for future action in the areas of love and trust. The other leader felt that Samantha had diverted the discussion to avoid the more potentially frightening issues of self-destruction that Nigel had been on the verge of bringing up.

Because of the inevitability of multiple perspectives, Mitchell and Mitchell urge that advanced group leaders play an important role by synchronizing members in such a way that all participants can understand one another, even if they do not agree. This is especially important when one or more group members is attempting to play a leadership role within the group.

From their research on the structural development of groups and how and why difficulties arise, Beck, Dugo, Eng, Lewis, and Peters (1983) found four distinct leadership roles that emerge among group members. The *task leader* is usually the designated authority of the group, the one the therapist or counselor has empowered to act as the one in charge. This leader sets norms, facilitates equitable interaction, clarifies goals, and keeps discussions focused. This, of course, is the role we are most familiar with and the kind of group member we most appreciate.

> **Group leader**: We seem to be straying in a number of different directions right now and a number of you look confused.
>
> **Consuela** (task leader): I don't think we finished completely with Shirley's issue, and I would like to suggest that we help her find closure before we move on to someone else.

The researchers, however, discovered that virtually all groups have other kinds of leaders as well—individuals who can be of invaluable help or who can be major thorns in the side of progress. The *emotional leader* is the person who is most concerned with expressing feelings and eliciting the same from others. Ideally, this leader models openness, authenticity, and support.

> **Patty**: It's just so hard for me to admit that I'm so incompetent as a parent that I can't control my own kid.
>
> **Anton** (emotional leader): I can't tell you how much it means to me that you shared that. I feel so much closer to you now that you don't have to pretend to be so perfect.

In the worst case scenario, the emotional leader acts as a lightning rod, dispersing currents of intense feelings of anger or anxiety. Because this person is more affectively expressive than other members, he or she has the potential to stimulate greater cohesion and intimacy in the group or, on the negative side, to make the group a very uncomfortable place through inappropriate and frequent emotional outbursts.

> **Kim**: This isn't easy for me. I know that. But it's time for me to come to terms with the reality that there is a good chance I won't survive this surgery. It means—
>
> **Frank** (emotional leader): I'm sorry. I just can't help crying. I feel so awful for you.
>
> **Kim**: I don't need or want your sympathy. But I do need you to listen to me and not interrupt—
>
> **Frank**: There is no need for you to be so rude. I can't help it if I am so moved by—
>
> **Group leader**: Frank, you interrupted Kim again at an important point. Your input is valuable, and I know this is hard for you, but—
>
> **Frank**: (Breaks into tears.)

The *scapegoat leader* is the person in the group who is most different from the rest. He or she "marches to the beat of a different drummer," which can either be tremendously distracting or wonderfully enriching in terms of adding diversity to interactions. In his or her best role, this group member contributes by helping others expand their narrow views. Uniqueness, tolerance, acceptance, and individuality become issues that are explored thoroughly as a result of this leader's contributions. This person genuinely wants to fit in and will do so given sufficient help, acceptance, and encouragement.

> **Nate**: I really want to hear what you guys think about what I just said. Candy, why do you always just stare at me like I am an insect? You never say anything.
>
> **Candy** (scapegoat leader): I know my quietness bothers some of you. I just don't like to talk if I have nothing important to say.
>
> **Group leader**: Candy, it is perfectly all right for you *not* to talk, if that is your choice. I think Nate is asking specifically what you think.
>
> **Candy**: You say it is all right for me not to talk but then you tell me that I should. I thought you said it was acceptable in this group to find our own ways of expressing ourselves. My whole life, people have been demanding that I act in certain ways. For me to sit quietly and observe, participating when I want to, represents growth for me. I wish you would respect that and not just give lip service to the ideal.

In the worst case, the scapegoat leader becomes a destructive distraction, unwilling or unable to abide by even the most basic group norms and rules. He or she is more than one step behind the rest—a whole flight of stairs behind and likely never to get any closer.

> **Rikki**: I just had the most amazing revelation! Maybe it is not my parents who have been holding me back. I know you've been trying to tell me this for some time.
>
> **Group leader**: Stay with that idea. Talk some more about what that "revelation" means for you.
>
> **Peter** (scapegoat leader): My parents bug me a lot too. I wish they would just get off my back.
>
> **Group leader**: Peter, we can come back to that. For now, let's follow up on what Rikki was getting close to for the first time.
>
> **Rikki**: No, that's all right. Let Peter talk.
>
> **Peter**: Well, as I was saying . . .

The *defiant leader* can be the representative of the "constructive opposition," but most often this leader acts out his or her ambivalence about being in the group. Of all the kinds of leaders that emerge from among the group members, this one can be the most difficult of all to deal with. Such an individual may be determined to take everyone else on, to act out in ways to assert power and control, to engage in a strategy employed by the comedian George Carlin as an adolescent: "Since I was bored, why not deprive everyone else of their education?"

> **Group leader:** If it's all right with you, let's move on to something else.
> **Janis** (defiant leader): Who the hell died and made you Pope?
> **Group leader:** Excuse me?
> **Janis:** I said, "Why do you feel such a need to control us?" I thought you said we are the ones responsible for the group.
> **Group leader:** That is certainly true. In this case, however, I am helping to move things along. It seemed that things were dragging.
> **Janis:** So you, the all-knowing Mama, decided to rescue us from our own misery. Hey, what do you all think about our Great Leader, telling us poor deprived kids we are boring her?

Hopper (1978) prescribes working through group member resistance by the provision of sufficient structure and comfort in early sessions, by liberal leader modeling of cooperative group behavior, and by realistic expectations on the therapist's part for predicting when, how, and why such behavior occurs. A great many explanations are viable for a variety of motives behind resistant activities, which is why they are so difficult to handle. They are probably the most critical of all incidents that will occur in any group, assuming many disguised forms and having different labels. A group member may exhibit resistant behavior for any of the following 15 reasons.

1. The client doesn't want to be in the group in the first place but is only attending to satisfy the demands of someone else, such as a spouse, teacher, friend, or supervisor. Surprisingly, this is one of the easiest types of resistance to handle because the client is usually outspoken and honest about resentments. When external incentives for participation are hidden, however, the reluctance will take a more subtle and devious form.

2. Resistance is frequently an adjustment reaction to a novel situation. Therapeutic groups are strange places to the uninitiated. Only a fool would take the apparent concern, empathy, and safety at face value until phenomenological confirmations are experienced.

3. Under pressures to conform to group norms, all but the very meek feel the need to flex their individuality. Resistance can thus be an expression of rebelliousness, an unwillingness to be grouped as a part of the whole.

4. Much client anxiety may be centered on negative expectations of what the group experience might offer. The person who anticipates "mind games," hostility, "touchy-feely" exercises, and a dogmatic, rigid leader will be more likely to erect protective barriers. Even if projected negative outcomes don't materialize, the client will still resist, just to be on the safe side.

5. The unusual and flexible leadership style of most group leaders presents a confusing image to clients at first. Authoritarian, democratic, and laissez-faire behaviors might all be in evidence within a single hour. The

leader is definitely an authority figure to group members but a very unconventional authority nevertheless. However warm and caring, the therapist's actions still represent "the powers that be" to anyone who doesn't have power. Resistance can therefore be a testing of limits to carve out pecking-order roles. If there was ever a place to challenge authority by resisting compliance to expectations, a therapeutic group is the ideal.

6. Considering how few moments there are during the day in which a person is not an active participant of some group at work, home, church, school, or play, it is amazing that so many people have social fears of groups. Teachers, who spend their professional lives performing in front of groups, can reach a moderate state of panic when trying to speak up in graduate classes. Lawyers, physicians, and other human-service professionals who communicate with people all day long often clam up in a group situation. This fear of being judged by others and of interacting in groups sparks a lot of resistance in those who want to speak up but feel they can't perform adequately in front of their peers.

7. A corollary of the social-fear motive is resistance due to a fear of failure. Persons who are used to feeling totally successful in their chosen profession and their peer groups feel out of their element in a therapeutic group. They expend every ounce of energy trying to make themselves look good and logically spurn any opportunity that involves being spontaneous or unpredictable, in which perfect competence isn't guaranteed on the first trial.

8. The Great Unknown makes people think twice before they leap. Some group members become very slippery to avoid having to take risks. They will work diligently on self-awareness or insight, but when the time comes to apply new knowledge in the real world, they find their courage has left them.

9. Resistance can be a sign of someone who enjoys manipulating others. It is, after all, an attention-getting ploy that evokes emotional responses in other members and even in the leader. It is like a 2-year-old kid drunk with power from the realization that simply by uttering the word *no* he can send grown-ups into fits of desperation. The resistant client can stop leader actions dead in their tracks, collect laurels of pity from others, and at the same time feel like a poor victim who can't help the situation.

10. Every group member has formulated preferences for how she or he prefers all other participants to be and to act. When they don't cooperate according to the plan, resistance can be used as a way to punish offenders: "I'll show you all for not treating *me* right, acting as *I* would. I'll make you suffer. You know how excited you've been getting over the progress I've made? Watch this—I'll go back to the way I was."

11. Resistance can also be an act of jealousy to sabotage forward motion. Every time a group member makes significant life changes, it helps other clients feel more dissatisfied with their inertia. A client can then refuse to cooperate with group proceedings, knowing that by resisting she or he

no longer has to feel threatened by the rules the productive members are following.

12. The expression of ambivalence is not only evident in sabotaging other clients' progress in the group but is also strongly reflected in one's own attitudes toward changing: "I want to be different from what I am, but I don't really want to handle the consequences of this growth—having to be responsible for my life."

13. A group member experimenting with new behaviors experiences frustration similar to that of an infant trying to practice turning over. Like the infant, who will pout and fight after a desperate effort, the client will resist "handling" when his or her patience is worn thin. What looks so easy for the leader to do is impossible for the client to feel comfortable imitating. Resistance in this case acts as a warning to the therapist to back off until the client's energy supplies are replenished for a counterattack.

14. Resistance is also used as a pacing mechanism to stall for time. In the language of physics, resistance is the drag that slows down the force of movement. When change accelerates too quickly, the human mind will attempt to decelerate progress to more comfortable levels that allow breathing space.

15. Finally, resistance can be a strategy of personality style. Some people take pleasure in resisting *anything* because it is intrinsically satisfying for them to participate in conflict. They love the challenge of argument and controversy and will switch sides fluently, depending on which point of view offers the best opportunity for antagonism. Such persons resist because they are strong-willed enough to appreciate the stimulation that comes from locking horns with a powerful adversary.

In the next chapter, we will cover in greater detail the possible variations of difficult group members such as those just described and, in particular, what interventions are most helpful in neutralizing their toxic influence. In the context of common critical issues, the next subject we cover is collective group resistance.

Responding to Group Resistance

There are times when group members act collectively to resist the leader's efforts to facilitate the process. This sabotage may result from a deliberate conspiracy on the part of one or more participants to undermine the leader's authority, or, more often, may represent a shared desire on the part of many to avoid perceived risks.

Since conflict is the inevitable result of any group activity, Unger (1990) suggests that leaders plan for group resistance before it ever begins. One of the ways that he believes this preventive intervention is best done is by negotiating and clearly defining the contractual goals for the group so there is shared ownership of the rules. These might include a number of items, depending on the type of group. For example:

- that physical or emotional abuse will not be tolerated
- that each member will not speak for others without their consent
- that each participant will take responsibility for getting one's needs met
- that there will be an equitable distribution of group time, with each member getting a fair share
- that members will not be permitted to complain and gripe about things and people over which they have no control
- that members will be respectful and sensitive to others' rights
- that nobody will be pressured to do or say anything for which they do not feel ready
- that participants agree to reveal themselves in honest and authentic ways

This contract then permits the leader to enforce compliance to the agreed-upon rules without feeling defensive: "It would seem that your desire to talk about the weather and your vacations is a way to avoid following up on what happened last week. That is all right with me, but it violates the rules that all of you established."

Conflict and resistance are integral parts of almost any group functioning and, when successfully resolved, lead to greater cohesion and higher functioning. A number of conflict-management strategies suggested by Kormanski (1982), each with distinctive features and disadvantages, can be chosen, depending on the situation and on one's theoretical preferences. Some of these options are listed in Table 7-1.

Each of the leadership options summarized in the table is used in conjunction with others, and rarely in a pure form. For example, conflict erupts in a staff meeting because some members want to move the agenda along expeditiously while others are interested in debating some issues at greater length. In addition, the communication style among participants is quite diverse: a few are highly intellectual, even detached, dealing primarily with content; others are more process oriented and wish to address underlying relationship issues. The leader observes the interchange with half amusement and half frustration; clearly some resolution of this conflict is necessary if any constructive work is to be accomplished.

The leader first tries a *withdrawal* strategy, hoping that individuals will work out their differences on their own; instead, they escalate. Next, she tries *suppression*, using humor to play down the conflicts and trying to keep things task oriented. Then she institutes a combination of *integration* and *compromise* strategies to help staff members come to some consensual agreement. Because this group is a bit more dysfunctional than most and time is growing short, the leader recognizes that more direct, incisive intervention is indicated to keep people on track and minimize further casualties from the heated exchange. Once this structure is implemented, she is able to return to a less intrusive group management style.

Table 7-1 Conflict management strategies

Option	Strategy	Advantages	Disadvantages	Indications
Withdrawal	Moving away from or postponing conflict	Allows members to resolve own conflicts naturally; keeps leader out of foray; is benign first intervention	Not useful in crisis— ignoring conflicts that may escalate later	When critical information is missing
Suppression	Playing down conflict issues	Diffuses emotion; distracts attention from minor issues	Conflict may smolder; may be perceived as weak	When more support is needed before confrontation
Integration	Seeking consensus	Identifies new, creative solutions; facilitates team functioning.	Consensus difficult to achieve; takes a lot of time	When unity and cohesion building are needed
Compromise	Negotiating solution in which all factions give a little	Promotes cooperation and collaboration; win/win solution in which everyone profits	Dilutes individual preferences; agreed-upon solution may not be the best	When some members are not having needs met
Power	Deliberate influence of outcome through praise, arbitration, etc.	Best during crisis or when time is short; breaks deadlocks effectively	Can create resentment and rebellion against leader	When decisive action is called for

Source: Adapted from "Leadership Strategies for Managing Conflict" by C. Kormanski. In *Journal for Specialists in Group Work*, 7, pp. 112–118. Copyright © 1982 by the American Counseling Association.

In another study of how group leaders handle resistance, Spinal (1984) classifies the possible interventions into the following categories:

Intervention	Example
Directing the process	"What is your reaction to that?"
Directing the interaction	"Say that directly to her."
Commenting on the process	"We seem to be drifting a lot."
Clarifying the process	"Things seem different with only two of you contributing."
Validating resistance	"It's helpful sometimes for us to move slowly."
Confronting resistance	"You keep changing the focus off you."
Interpreting the process	"It seems difficult for you to talk about your feelings."
Setting limits	"You keep complaining about what others are doing to you."
Silent observation	"I'm comfortable waiting."
Task facilitation	"How might we move forward?"
Didactic intervention	"This is a normal and predictable stage."

Spinal concluded, based on her study of residential treatment groups for battered women, that resistance was most often mismanaged when leaders were too passive, or colluded with the obstructiveness through benign neglect. This behavior is usually less typical for advanced leaders who have learned early on that decisive action is often called for during critical times of significant resistance. This is true even if the action is a form of "strategic" withdrawal to allow group members to take more responsibility for enforcing appropriate conduct.

In addition to these process interventions, handling resistance also involves leaders' recognition of their own contribution to the problem. This may be caused by the leader's need for approval, feelings of inadequacy, unresolved personal issues, inconsistent enforcement of rules, or human error. Since impasses in group are, by definition, interpersonal problems, it is clear that there are some member/member/leader dynamics that may be altered through perceptual shifts in the way behavior is understood and responded to (Weiner, 1983).

Strategies for Handling Critical Incidents

There are other critical incidents and predictable problems that frequently occur: termination and re-entry problems, conflicting goals between leader and participants, degeneration of the group into a gripe session, or difficulties with oversolidarity in which the pervasive closeness that has

developed only confirms the suspicion that people outside the group cannot be trusted. All these incidents may be dealt with in a systematic fashion
that involves several sequential steps.

First, the group leader must be able to recognize critical incidents when
they are occurring. This macrodiagnostic process involves some fairly clear
notions regarding what exactly constitutes a critical incident. The operational definition will probably be consistent with one's theoretical framework. For example, one fairly pragmatic definition describes a critical incident as any observable, sufficiently complete client action that permits
inferences about that person or group process and requires some leader intervention (Cohen & Smith, 1976; Flanagan, 1954).

Second the group leader must be able to identify microdiagnostically the
specific variety of critical incident that is occurring by noting its effect on
individual members and their reactions. Cohen and Smith (1976) suggest
examining the context in which the event occurred, including precipitating
factors that led up to the incident, relevant background, group climate,
timing, and the intensity of member responses. The specific diagnostic
decision may then include figuring out what happened, why and how it
occurred, and whether a leader intervention is called for to resolve the
therapeutic issue.

Once the critical incident has been clearly dissected, the leader formulates
an optimal plan for creating therapeutic insight from the wayward ingredients that are prevalent. Consider a group in which one client is chronically
late for sessions. Other members become impatient and resentful. Soon
voices and blood pressures rise, and acceptance, tolerance, and politeness
decline. The leader takes a deep breath, offers reassuring words to the effect
that "We seem to have gotten carried away," then attempts to use the outburst as a constructive lesson for understanding effective confrontation.

In resolving interpersonal conflicts such as these, the practitioner will
want to clarify communication, structure specific goals satisfactory to all
parties, filter out distracting variables, and use compromise and consensus strategies to avoid win/lose situations (Frey, 1979). Critical incidents *are*
critical because they can be used for better or for worse. Rather than dreading
and avoiding them, the advanced group leader should calmly face such
predictable problems and sometimes even encourage their development,
secure in the knowledge that they can be transformed into stimuli for accelerated growth.

The critical incidents of therapeutic groups are very similar to the developmental tasks of individual human growth. Both natural processes arise
during certain predictable, invariant, sequential periods in the life of a
group or individual, the "successful achievement of which leads to happiness and to success with later tasks, while failure leads to unhappiness
in the individual [or group], disapproval by the society, and difficulty with

later tasks'' (Havighurst, 1972, p. 2). As the child must form meaningful human attachments in the first months of life; master basic survival skills in the first few years; build an identity during puberty; establish autonomy, responsibility, and involvement in adulthood; so, too, will clients go through a series of progressive crises which, after mastering the skills necessary to resolve the conflicts, will lead to greater personal mastery both as a group participant and as a human being.

CHAPTER 8

Working with Difficult Group Members*

In almost every group, there is someone who is a bit unusual, different from the rest. There appears to be an unwritten law of the universe that for every conglomeration of persons numbering more than a few who are gathered together for a common purpose under a set of rules, there will always be one person who, although well meaning and good natured, will have quite inappropriate behavior and responses. This person, for a variety of reasons, lacks basic skills for attending to group events and proceeds in a style that may be most generously described as eccentric.

Difficult clients in individual sessions are challenging enough for us to deal with; in group settings, their behavior is even more obstructive because of their contagious effects in interaction with other people. A client who is unusually manipulative, obnoxious, defiant, or withdrawn can wreak havoc in a group, sometimes even single-handedly destroying any semblance of cohesion.

The Limitations of Preliminary Screening

Although obviously prevention is the best solution to the problem of difficult group members—that is, using screening to prevent them entrance in the first place—often this is not feasible, possible, or realistic. First, people who are very good at being manipulative know how to make a good impression when it counts. Second, our diagnostic screening is not always very accurate; we can only search for the most obvious signs of pathology to disqualify candidates. Third, some clients do not actually become difficult until they enter the group arena and something in them is triggered by interactions that take place.

---

*This chapter is an expanded version of an article that will appear in the *Journal for Specialists in Group Work.*

I recall one client I was seeing in individual counseling who was absolutely delightful—dynamic, fun-loving, bright, expressive, an award-winning teacher. She was absolutely perfect for a group that I was running, so I invited her to participate. I could never have imagined, nor anticipated, what would take place after she arrived. I never had the slightest inkling that her behavior would alternate between hostility and sulking. At one point, several members politely but firmly informed her that she would have to leave.

The fourth reason that we cannot screen out difficult clients is the simple, practical reality that they are often the ones who most need the help. If we were to draw a profile of the ideal group client, it would certainly not be the sex offender or repeated drunk driver referred by the courts; yet these are the people who end up on our doorstep—defiant, resentful, and determined to make life as miserable as possible for everyone else. These are the kind of clients who are so obstructive that, for the sake of other members in the group, they must be screened out as soon as possible after their sabotaging behaviors are discovered (Gazda, 1989).

Defining the Difficult Group Member

Difficult clients have been defined by Smith and Steindler (1983) as those who attempt to take over and control the proceedings. More specifically, they fall into several categories identified by Kottler (1992) in a review of the literature on the subject.

1. those with chronic, uncontrollable diseases that impair interpersonal functioning
2. those who have hidden agendas they are unwilling to reveal
3. those who ignore appropriate boundaries
4. those who refuse to accept responsibility for their plight and who tend to blame others
5. those who are argumentative
6. those who fear intimacy
7. those who are impatient and unrealistic about what group work can do for them
8. those who are inarticulate or who lack verbal skills
9. those who are unduly literal, concrete, or who have an intolerance for ambiguity
10. those who are significantly divorced from reality
11. those who are "empty" inside and who are unable to access internal states
12. those who are despondent and express abject hopelessness
13. those with little impulse control who have explosive tantrums or outbursts
14. those who feel entitled to special privileges.

Examples of these categories of difficult group members are described in Table 8-1.

Essentially, then, we have certain expectations for how group members ought to act; they should be respectful of others, cooperative, responsive, grateful for help, and do what they say they will do. The more that a given client deviates from our prescribed roles and expectations, the more likely it is that he or she will be perceived as difficult by a group leader.

Characterologically Difficult Members

There are those clients who choose to be difficult, and then there are those who cannot seem to help the obnoxious ways they respond to others. In a study of characterologically difficult group members, Leszcz (1989) describes them as having the following features: a persistent view of relationships—in group, as well as in life—as internalized relations of the past; an inability to develop stable relationships with anyone; a reliance on primitive defenses; intense modulations of affect; oscillations in self-esteem from grandiosity to worthlessness; expression of rage in self-destructive acts; and fear of intimacy expressed as exploitation, engulfment, or lack of trust.

In spite of the extreme symptoms and volatile interpersonal style of these individuals, Leszcz advocates group work as the ideal "holding environment" for characteristically difficult clients. A group, after all, provides stable, affirming norms of conduct. Intense transference and idealizations are diluted. The difficult client has the opportunity to log interactive experience while receiving supportive yet confrontive feedback (Azima, 1986). There

Table 8-1 Profiles of difficult group members

Category	Characteristics
Chronic, intractable diseases	Organic brain damage; dementia; closed head injuries; attention deficits
Hidden agendas	Workers' compensation cases; civil suits
Ignore boundaries	Come late; skip sessions; take more than fair share of time
Refuse responsibility	Externalize blame; complain; focus on outsiders; deny progress
Argumentative	Enjoy verbal combat; abrasive; belligerent; demanding
Fear of intimacy	Reject help; withdrawn; withholding
Intolerance for ambiguity	Difficulty processing group experiences
Separated from reality	Paranoid; active hallucinations
Empty	Little capacity for reflection or introspection
Despondent	Actively suicidal; morbid; withdrawn
Impulse problems	Explosive; substance abuser
Entitled	Demand attention; narcissistic

are opportunities for positive attachments and, perhaps most important of all, the group meets the client's need for intimacy with little fear of abandonment. Groups, quite simply, shake things up more. They force the rigid client to give up characteristic self-defeating behaviors in favor of other alternatives (Wells, Glickauf-Hughes, & Buzzell, 1990).

People with severely narcissistic or borderline disorders suffer from isolation and self-preoccupation that distance them from others. The group is thus the perfect medium for bridging this gap in experience, even though feelings of both exhilaration and abject fear are likely to be aroused (Tuttman, 1990). Of course, as with all clients who exhibit rigid personality traits, character disordered group members will not do well, and may aggravate everyone else, if they exhibit paranoid traits, a low tolerance for ambiguity, extreme neediness, or a pseudointellectual style that blocks any affect (Horwitz, 1987).

Powles (1990) offers the following set of questions the group leader should ask before undertaking the task of including a characterologically difficult client, such as an individual with borderline features, in a group.

Is this client truly difficult? Labeling a group member as obstructive often represents more a statement about the clinician's own level of frustration than it does about the client's behavior: "Is this client manipulative and controlling, or am I just irritated because he or she does not meet my expectations?"

Should I work with this client at all? "Given a client's symptoms, needs, personality style, and accurate diagnosis, is he or she a good candidate for what I do and how I do it?" Some clients do not or cannot respond to any treatment; others are just not good candidates for the kind of group work that we do. I have, for example, referred to other professionals and settings more than a few clients who wished to join my group to deal with their problems of explosive anger.

What kind of treatment is best for this person? Individual or group? Structured or unstructured? Heterogeneous or homogeneous groups? Beginning or advanced? Insight or action oriented? Cognitive or affectively based? Group or leader centered? These and other questions help define whether a particular difficult client is well suited for a specific group setting. Such treatment planning decisions are based not only on the observation that a particular client may act out in group but also on the particular manifestations of potential obstructiveness—whether the person is prone to manipulation, control, narcissism, rigidity, withdrawal, or a host of other possibilities.

Difficult Members in Group Settings

Group Members Who Act Out

Since, by definition, acting out in groups takes place at a preconscious level, leaders attempt to intervene by increasing clients' awareness of their provocative, seductive, or aggressive behavior. One other option that is probably preferred is to structure things so that other group members help the person acting out accept responsibility for inappropriate behavior (Fenchel & Flapan, 1987). To structure group norms in such a way that obstructiveness, in all its many permutations, can be discouraged, leaders must have a thorough understanding of the specific dynamics of each difficult client that they may encounter. We begin with one of the most challenging of all such individuals—the group member who attempts to monopolize time and attention.

The Entitled Client.   So common is this type of group member that almost every standard textbook mentions something about how to handle the client who seeks to control the group (Corey & Corey, 1992; Edelwich & Brodsky, 1992; Gazda, 1991; Gladding, 1991; Yalom, 1985). The entitled or monopolizing group member is someone who has an ingenious number of ways of keeping the focus of group attention on him- or herself. Persistence and sheer single-minded devotion to self-centeredness can often compensate for a lack of variety in monopolizing methodologies. For example, a group member may respond to input from someone else by beginning with "That reminds me of the time. . . ." Filibustering is another common variety of group domination, in which the group member drones and rambles endlessly, ignoring others' frustration and boredom, even failing to respond to repeated intervention.

The entitled group member may be overtalkative and take more than his or her share of time for a number of reasons related to missing cues: a lack of interpersonal sensitivity or even some cognitive/perceptual deficits. Whether there is a cross-wired circuit in the brain or the phenomenon was learned, some people, no matter how often and vigorously they are confronted, seem to lack the ability to change their behavior.

There are many other reasons that certain people attempt to monopolize group time. They may feel a sense of entitlement, that they are more important than others in the group. In addition, they may enjoy a number of secondary gains from their behavior; they avoid intimacy by keeping others at a distance as well as feel a sense of power over the control that they wield.

Entitled clients beg convincingly for help and then reject or sabotage it. They come late to group sessions, or miss them altogether, and then expect everyone to accommodate them by using most of the time to bring them up to date. They must believe they are in control at all times and so will attempt to manipulate others to meet their needs on their own terms. They may be needy and demanding, whining and pathetic, using their feelings of omnipotence and entitlement to stave off the deep-seated pain associated with feelings of powerlessness (Boulanger, 1988). As long as they can control the proceedings of a group and the behavior of others (including the "omnipotent" group leaders), they have demonstrated—temporarily—their sense of power.

Initially, the group is a narcissist's ultimate fantasy—a stage on which to perform before a new audience, one composed of people who are easily seduced. Yet, with the leader's assistance, groups set firm limits and establish consistent consequences for people who take from others but who do not reciprocate. The very norms of therapeutic groups ensure that one's status and approval are based not on how much one talks but on how much one helps others. Since, as does any self-absorbed person, the entitled client must be taught the capacity for empathy, groups are especially fertile places for these skills to be learned.

Friedman (1989) recommends that, before any intervention is attempted with these group members (and intervention is clearly called for), the leader first take note of his or her own impatience level; sometimes group members talk a lot just because they have a lot to say and do not know how to express themselves succinctly. Once the behavior has been accurately identified, some form of *active* intervention is almost always required, even if it is to cue another group member to do the work: "Mario, you seem to be getting progressively more frustrated as Francine has been speaking. Tell her what you are feeling."

The most challenging part of any intervention with monopolizing clients (or with any difficult client, for that matter) is to retain one's composure and sensitivity. Whereas beginning group leaders will naturally be cautious —even hesitant—in any intervention, those of us with more experience recognize more immediately exactly what we believe is taking place: "Uh-oh, a monopolizer. The others are getting restless. Better stop this before it gets out of hand." Experienced leaders therefore are inclined to jump in more decisively—sometimes prematurely.

With any difficult group member, leaders have to assess both the consequences of the behavior on the member's own life and the effects this behavior has on others in the group. Leaders have a responsibility to give the monopolizer feedback on inappropriate or self-defeating behavior, but to do so in ways that are therapeutic for others.

Friedman (1989) further reminds us that the function of group work as a treatment modality is to facilitate interaction. Any client behaviors that inhibit that process must be stopped. The intrinsic difficulty of this simple imperative, however, is that monopolizing behavior (especially if it is characterologically rather than situationally obstructive) can be very firmly entrenched. For this reason, firm, consistent, and yet compassionate intervention is needed, in which the group leader limits the monopolizer's verbal domination, provides feedback in terms of its effects, and helps other group members assume responsibility for monitoring the behavior in the future. This last element is crucial to any group so that members can learn to apply what they learn in sessions to those situations outside the group in which they need to be more assertive with these who attempt to control them.

The Manipulative Client.   As is the entitled client, the "generically" manipulative client is after control. Often this group member, who appears defensive, self-centered, intense and who acts out in the group, is identified as having a borderline personality disorder (Friedman, 1989; Horwitz, 1980; Macaskill, 1982).

This diagnosis has a number of implications, both constructive and self-defeating. On the one hand, the borderline diagnosis sets in motion an extraordinary set of therapeutic limit-setting activities and mind-sets that help us minimize these individuals' danger to themselves, to others in the group, and even to ourselves. Once we think we are dealing with a borderline, we tend to react differently than we would otherwise.

On the other hand, calling a client a borderline personality (as well as a host of other names) can be a way that we express our cynicism, hopelessness, or even anger toward those who are not cooperating with our agenda. *Borderline* is the single most abused and least understood diagnostic label we have; often it is indiscriminately applied to any client we find irritating (Kroll, 1988).

Whether manipulative clients can profit from a group experience depends on how dysfunctional the clients are and what particular style of control is favored. Clients' threatening to kill themselves if they don't get their way is considerably more difficult to manage than are clients who are struggling to assert their will by threatening to pout.

Since manipulative clients thrive in an atmosphere of tension, conflict, hostility, and chaos, it is especially important for leaders to rely on confrontation rather than on interpretation as the preferred intervention (Friedman, 1989; Stone & Gustafson, 1982). Leaders will find it helpful to distinguish between situational versus characterological manipulation: is the client manipulative only in the group or in every aspect of life (Dowd & Seibel, 1990)? Concurrent individual and group therapy is also recommended, sometimes even including families in the adjunct treatment (Slavinska-Holy, 1983). It is crucial that leaders employ a set of rules that include setting firmer boundaries, employing more structure, not making exceptions, and limiting their own self-disclosure (Sklar, 1988; Warner, 1984). Related to this enforcement of rules is the need to keep in mind that the limit setting be therapeutic rather than punitive, triggered by our own frustration and impatience.

Finally, when working with entitled, manipulative, or character disordered group members, it is important that leaders confront their own issues by asking themselves a series of questions before any intervention is attempted (Gazda, 1989; Kline, 1990; Kottler, 1992):

- What am I feeling right now?
- What exactly is triggering these feelings?
- Who else seems to be having similar reactions?
- What am I doing to create or exacerbate the problems?
- What personal issues of mine are being triggered?
- Whom does the client remind me of?
- How am I acting out my impatience with the client's progress?
- What expectations am I demanding of this client?

In his group work with disturbed inpatients, Erickson (1984) viewed difficult group members less in terms of their behavior and more according to the leader's actions that led to the patients' obstructiveness. Specifically, Erickson felt that the group leader's passivity, rigidity, and mistimed or miscued interventions most often created problems among participants.

It is clear, then, that difficult group members are as much a matter of the leader's perception as they are members' actual behavior. Rather than labeling any group member as a problem, it is far more useful to look at the *behavior* as problematic (Friedman, 1989). When we assign clients names on the basis of a role they play (monopolizer, help rejector) or a formal diagnostic label (narcissistic, borderline), we begin thinking about them "as enemies to be defeated rather than as people in pain who are coping as best they can, even if their method of communication is sometimes indirect and annoying" (Kottler, 1992, p. 39).

The Silent Client.   The silent client can "speak" even louder than do those who monopolize in terms of drawing attention and disrupting group movement. There are four basic reasons that a client may remain aloof and "outside" the group: (1) a lack of trust in the leader, process, or other members; (2) a manipulative ploy to get attention; (3) an inadvertent style based on a client's state of mind (depression, schizophrenia, emotional devastation); and (4) a part of group member's family background or culture that taught him or her not to break the image of appearing healthy.

Silent behavior has a profound effect on others in the group, as it brings out sympathy and concern as well as anger and feelings of inadequacy: "We are a failure as a group as long as one among us is so disengaged."

As recommended with the monopolizer mentioned earlier, Friedman (1989) urges the leader to find out what the silence or withdrawal means: Does the person wish to join in but does not know how? Is the behavior within voluntary control? What is the silence or withdrawal communicating? Is there an endogenous or organic process operating in the client? What are the motivational and secondary gains underlying the behavior? When has he or she demonstrated minimal responsiveness, and to what, when, and to whom specifically? What is this person being asked to do that is beyond his or her present capability?

The key to these and any other questions that come to mind is to find some leverage for engagement, even if it is a token gesture. Once the meaning of the behavior is identified, whether as a form of defiance or of protection, efforts can be made to address these issues more directly. When members are involuntary participants in the group, forced to come against their will, withdrawal or silence is one of the few ways that they can assert themselves.

Corey, Corey, Callanan, and Russell (1992) point out that silence in a group is not necessarily a defense; it can just as often be a learned response of being polite or deferential. Corey and his colleagues offer a number of possible ways to intervene that are typical of the creativity group leaders show in their efforts to equalize participation.

- *Interpret the behavior in terms of its effect.* Silent behavior can be used as a form of punishment, hostility, or withdrawal, each of which signals different underlying intrapersonal dynamics and interpersonal consequences.
- *Examine the silence in a cultural context.* Among some ethnic groups, silence is considered the most appropriate way to show respect for others.
- *Confront the silent member.* Invite feedback from members as to their reactions.
- *Create a structure more conducive to participation.* Form a circle composed only of the more silent members in which they are the only ones permitted to talk.
- *Work with the silent members.* Focus on those clients and stay with them until they have been drawn out.
- *Schedule an individual session.* As with all problem members, consultations can often be helpful to explore what is getting in the way.

In the most extreme case, the silent, withdrawn group member can also be showing signs of depression and suicidal potential. Hipple (1982) ran a group in which every participant had suicidal intent as their primary issue. Even with this high-risk population, Hipple reported that the group provided a degree of support, security, and understanding that could not be met in other ways. To capitalize on these benefits, however, the group leader must be well versed in the intricacies of working with severely depressed individuals. This expertise includes being especially vigilant to signs and symptoms of danger as well as being proficient in metabolizing the strain of being around so many dependent and despondent people at the same time. Hipple further recommends that leaders of such groups adopt a more active, directive role than usual and be willing to intervene decisively when the situation warrants it.

Groups with Multiple Difficult Members

Yalom (1983) describes some of the special problems that emerge as a result of working with a severely disturbed clientele. Dramatic outbursts are likely. Inappropriate behavior is commonplace. People routinely fall asleep, "chase their tails," or inexplicably bolt from the room.

Yalom cautions that running such groups require a different mind-set than does leading those with relatively normally functioning individuals. Yet his primary words of advice also have applicability to any setting: *anything dramatic that takes place can provide useful stimulation for work in the group.* One of the outcomes of group work is that participants become more reflective about their own and others' behavior. Interpersonal events—

any event, whether common or bizarre—presents a stimulus for people to react to.

Among the most difficult clientele to reach in group settings is the elderly, especially those suffering from depression, Alzheimer's, and dementia. In their group treatment program designed specifically for this population, Yost, Beutler, Corbishley, and Allender (1986) demonstrate the usefulness of adapting structures to fit the particular needs and capabilities of their clientele. There is nothing that dooms a group more quickly than asking participants to do things that are beyond their abilities.

In groups of depressed elderly clients, leaders created a structure that took into consideration: (1) their short attention span, (2) their preference for living in the past, (3) their difficulty in organizing their thoughts, (4) their tendencies to ramble, (5) their poor thought retention, (6) their adopted sick role, (7) their attitudes toward doctors and the medical system, (8) their characteristic interactive patterns with cohorts, (9) their lack of psychological-mindedness, and (10) their value system that was established seven decades earlier.

This exhaustive list of group member characteristics thus allows the leaders to plan a therapeutic experience that compensates for weaknesses that would ordinarily disqualify these clients from consideration in group treatment. Of course, of high priority would be to combat the self-sabotaging, internal messages that block growth and change. Among those beliefs that are most common in this population are the following.

"I'm too old to change my ways."
"I never asked for help in my life, and I'm not about to start now."
"You're too young to know anything that could be helpful."
"Nobody cares whether I live or die."
"If I tell these people my secrets, I'll be shamed."
"If I join this group, it just means I'm crazy."

There are many disadvantages to working with homogeneous groups of clients who share similar problems; for instance, they tend to gang up against the leader and protect one another from having to change. Since they all present the same complaints, group sessions can turn into gripe sessions. Furthermore, such groups sacrifice some of the excitement and dynamics that come with a diverse composition spanning the ranges of age, socioeconomics, culture, and presenting complaint. Although cohesive and trust elements build more quickly in homogeneous groups, it is difficult for people with the same dysfunctions and weaknesses to help one another.

In spite of these problems, some groups of homogeneous difficult clients, such as the depressed elderly mentioned earlier, are ideal settings in which to help people move along at a realistic pace. Obviously, members of such groups will be more tolerant and accepting of one another's foibles than would be the case if younger, healthier people with intact memories were included.

Berg and Landreth (1990) even recommend groups as the treatments of choice for the elderly, since the group is the ideal environment for combating loneliness, for providing support for declining physical prowess and accompanying illnesses, and, most of all, for providing opportunities for networking.

A group format constructed specifically for a particular difficult population—whether they are the depressed elderly, addicts, or spouse batterers—allows the leaders to concentrate on those clinical skills, group structures, and process interventions most likely to be successful. For example Yost and his associates (1986) discussed how, in their program for the elderly, it was necessary for group leaders to utilize interventions such as the following.

- "I wonder, could you summarize the main point of what you are trying to say?"
- "Rather than focusing on the past, what would you change about the present?"
- "How could you say that differently, so that you sound more hopeful?"

This format also allows co-leaders to help one another monitor their own levels of compassion, patience, and empathy—qualities that are at risk with difficult client populations. As the Yost and associates program did include cognitive methods at the core, strategies were devised to confront the group leader's own defeatist beliefs: "I'm just kidding myself thinking these people will ever get better. They all have one foot in the grave anyway." Internal interventions can take the form of: "Who am I to judge what is a worthwhile quality of life? Aren't these people entitled the opportunity to better their situations? Haven't they earned the right to be treated with dignity and respect?"

Although we are speaking about the special problems in working with an elderly population, the same principles apply to any homogeneous group of difficult clients. If you conjure up an image of some of the more amusing possibilities, picture such a collection of people with explosive personalities or borderline features or clients who are passively withdrawn, in advanced states of denial, or who all despise authority figures. These groups would be quite a handful and would have the potential for deviant norms to develop easily. Still, such clinical situations invite experienced group leaders to invent creative means by which to work around the deficits and design potent, individualized group experiences by taking into consideration the cultural, familial, and environmental context for their inexplicable behavior.

Difficult Behaviors in Context

In one group I was leading in an ethnically diverse region (Hispanic, Native American, and Caucasian), a Native American woman was perceived by others as presenting a major obstructive force. She appeared quite hostile and critical, especially in reaction to anything said by one of the white group members.

This negative attitude was becoming a problem for the group, disturbing the already tenuous balance of cohesion that had been negotiated by people of very different value systems. Even when the woman was challenged to contribute to the group by another person of her tribe, she remained resolute in her sometimes passive, sometimes overt aggression. She carried a chip on her shoulder and fully intended to make the life of everyone in the group as miserable as her own.

It is perhaps understandable that, as the group leader, I was becoming more and more frustrated with the woman who was disrupting my group. During an individual session with the woman, I finally learned the context for her difficult behavior. "When I was a child I was taken away from my family and put into a government school. From the day I set foot in that school, I was made to follow rules that made no sense to me. I could not see my parents or my sisters. I was deloused, forbidden to speak my own language, forced to pray in a strange religion, and punished for all manner of offenses, such as speaking during mealtime. I was teased mercilessly by the other children because I had no clothes of my own. I was beaten as punishment for running away. Finally, at age 13, I ran away for good and became a prostitute—the only way I could support myself. For stealing my childhood I have never forgiven the white people. I have spent my life in helpless rage for the way our people have been dishonored."

The members of the group, of course, had no idea what this woman had lived through. To them, she merely appeared to be a bitter woman who was determined to be difficult. Once we understand the context of a client's obstructive behavior, once we are able to focus on what they do that we dislike rather than writing them off as incorrigible, we are much better able to show patience and compassion and to offer assistance in a way that limits their acting out and yet still protects the rights of others.

Managing Difficult Group Members

Most difficult clients remove themselves from a group when they realize that they are unwilling or unable to live up to the group norms or meet the leader's expectations. Since roughly 25% of people who begin groups drop our prematurely (Yalom, 1985), this exodus of some clients presents a challenge to any group leader to see that group cohesiveness and stability are not compromised. Whether the disruptive client stays in the group or elects to leave (usually in a dramatic way), other members may feel their experience is devalued and their closeness to others is impeded. The initial relief of having a difficult member gone is replaced with feelings of anxiety, abandonment, and rejection (Vinogradov & Yalom, 1989).

When the disruptive member elects to stay in the group, even the advanced leader will have his or her hands full trying to keep things under control—both internally and externally. Once it is determined that it is indeed the client's behavior that is the problem rather than the leader's overreactions, some intervention is definitely called for. Kline (1990) recommends that the following principles be used during this therapeutic action.

1. Filter out any contamination (residual anger, frustration, impatience, hurt) that may impact on the effectiveness of whatever you do.
2. Model the kind of appropriate, clear, direct, and sensitive communication you would like to see; reinforce that behavior in others as much as possible.
3. Present immediate feedback as to the impact of the disruptive behavior.
4. Help the client accept responsibility for the choice to act in dysfunctional ways.
5. Identify any hidden agendas on the part of the problem member and make them more explicit.
6. Involve the other members in the process of responding to disruptive behavior.
7. Use individual conferences to consult with a member who is not cooperative. Consider other therapeutic alternatives.
8. Try to treat any disruptions as potentially constructive opportunities for learning and growth.

This reframing of dramatic, distracting incidents as potentially useful helps the group leader think in terms of what can be done therapeutically to process what is happening. Yalom (1985) describes a number of cases in which particularly difficult and disturbed clients act out in a group. He responds to the individual with firm yet gentle confrontation but, more importantly, addresses the other members as if something helpful would naturally come from the incident.

Dalia "manipulated" her way into the group by repeatedly nagging her individual therapist to allow her to join. Since he was reluctant to give his approval but also did not wish to alienate her, he suggested she speak directly to the group leader, certain that she would be turned down. Dalia approached the group leader with the introduction "My therapist thinks it would be a good idea if I joined your group." One month later, she had become any group leader's worst nightmare.

While others sat by and watched their cordial relations disintegrate, Dalia was truly in her element. She interrupted and cut off members, ridiculed others who tried to muzzle her, even confronted the leader every chance she got. The group was losing its focus and momentum.

Once the group leader was able to regain his composure, he was able to reframe the interpersonal dynamics triggered by Dalia as an opportunity for growth. Many of the group members had been struggling with issues of passivity in their lives, and here was another instance of that taking place. This time, however, instead of talking about what people were doing to them outside of the group, they could respond to what they were allowing to transpire right before their eyes.

Of course, Dalia elected to leave the group after limits were installed and her behavior was consistently confronted by others. Even if she was not helped by her group experience, most of the other members ultimately benefited from her presence.

Leaders' Contributions

Although this chapter has focused on the special problems in working with manipulative, entitled, or character disordered group members—as well as on operating with homogeneous populations such as the elderly—the same principles apply to any difficult clients. These clinical situations invite group leaders to invent creative means by which to work around the client deficits and design potent, individualized therapeutic experiences.

We have an obligation to protect the rights of other group members, a responsibility that can only be applied through consistent limit setting and compassionate yet firm intervention. Most of all, group members perceived as difficult require honest and caring feedback from others to help them act in ways that are both in their own best interests and consistent with healthy group norms. This requires that group leaders demonstrate tremendous flexibility, patience, and a willingness to look at their own contributions to conflicted group interactions.

CHAPTER 9

Compatible
Co-Leader Functioning

The co-therapy model in which two clinicians work simultaneously with the same group of clients has been considered the cornerstone of therapeutic work by a number of prominent practitioners (Goulding & Goulding, 1991; Napier & Whitaker, 1988). Yet, there has always been resistance to the idea of using two leaders in a single group. Critics warn that the partnership is more for the benefit of therapists than that of clients (Haley, 1976), that it can set up destructive competition (Balgopal & Hull, 1970) and toxic relationships (Corey, Corey, Callanan, & Russell, 1992).

Opposite sex co-therapists may indeed struggle with the temptation of sexual entanglements that can result from their special intimacy. Failure to address physical attraction issues between each other can lead to a number of problems—a distortion of therapeutic clarity and purpose, triangulation with another member or one's own spouse, and confusion in messages to members who are struggling to deal with trust issues in relationships (Courville & Keeper, 1984).

In a survey of the membership in the American Group Psychotherapy Association, respondents cited a number of other concerns related to co-leadership models, including power struggles over who will do what and when it should be done; lack of congruence or parity between partners; and communication problems when leaders are moving in different directions (Roller & Nelson, 1991). Posthuma (1989), as well, warns of the competitive temptations inherent in any professional partnership. These can stem from interpersonal dynamics between two individuals struggling for recognition or even fighting for member approval: "Which one of us do you like better?" The competition can be further exacerbated by the inevitable conceptual and value differences between two leaders who have their own strong ideas about the best ways to do things.

Advantages of Co-Leadership

Advanced group workers have co-led and will continue to do so because they recognize certain therapeutic advantages that are not possible during solo leadership, even though research has not conclusively demonstrated this superiority. Co-leader relationships become dysfunctional when one or both partners are oblivious to the issues highlighted previously or are unwilling or unable to work them through. In these cases, the facade of cordial respect is dropped and leaders begin acting toward each other as bickering spouses or siblings, a situation that group members from dysfunctional families will recognize.

Friedman (1989) even wonders why, in the absence of any empirical research (although there are numerous anecdotal reports) demonstrating the inherent superiority of co-led groups over those with a single leader, this model persists at all. His answer is that even if it isn't any better for clients and it does have some additional problems, it is for the leader's benefit that co-leadership is often preferred. It is certainly true that many experienced leaders attribute their high morale, continuing growth, and avoidance of burnout to their willingness to work in tandem with compatible colleagues (Wylie & Markowitz, 1992). Other distinct advantages are also evident.

1. Group work has been criticized for affording individual members less opportunity for therapeutic time. When a 1:1 ratio between client and therapist is increased to a 10:1 ratio, there are bound to be people lost in the shuffle. Whereas a client in individual counseling has the luxury of being an "only child" commanding the therapist's total attention, the client in a group setting is only one of a dozen competing siblings. In a 2-hour group of 12 participants, each member is entitled to an equitable share of only 10 minutes. Two group leaders, however, can ensure better coverage and more efficient use of therapeutic time. One leader can choose the primary responsibility of making certain that each person has an opportunity to speak.

2. Two co-leaders allow for differences in personality and style, ensuring maximum contact with culturally different and individually unique participants. Co-leaders are thus able to increase the range of the resources, knowledge, and skills available (Nelson-Jones, 1992). Co-leadership is probably the only way to provide sufficient support and supervision to low-functioning clients, such as those manifesting psychotic or borderline symptoms; this structure allows the leaders to maintain their own emotional stability in the face of annoying, intense conflicts (Feilbert-Willis, Kibel, & Wikstrom, 1986).

Co-leaders are able to complement each other by picking up on things the other might miss. In a testimony to the power of this model, one therapist describes several examples of how her co-leader provided additional support: "I would notice Fred's many negative statements about his wife while my co-leader would then reflect his feelings of ambivalence relative to the marriage. My co-leader would speak to Isaiah's attempts to meet women; I would note his loneliness. While he would facilitate a dialogue between Kate and Jesse, I would observe the other group members' reactions and facilitate their input, or comment on what I noticed about the interaction. The combination of the two of us was unbeatable."

With mutually vigilant partners, the biases, prejudices, weaknesses, and shortcomings of each therapist can be minimized. Co-leaders become responsible to each other for their actions, in addition to each's societal, institutional, group member, and self-responsibilities. This added safety feature may even further reduce the frequency of casualties.

3. Shapiro (1978, p. 157) believes that "every group can be conducted best by more than one therapist" because the co-leader becomes a "reality-based sounding board for the other partner." Group work can be a lonely business. The constant pressure, repeated conflict, and highly charged atmosphere can wear down even the most hardened professional. The use of co-therapists minimizes omissions, subjective distortions, and mismanagement of tricky situations (Russell & Russell, 1979). Diagnoses can be better targeted, interventions can be better timed, and group time can be better spent.

4. Rosenbaum (1971) has noted that having two leaders is more convenient for clients, giving them better value for their money. If one therapist is sick, on vacation, late, or tied up, the other can take over. Or if one leader is having a tough day, is run-down, or feels temporarily lethargic, the partner can keep the level of enthusiasm up. Far from encouraging a therapist to "slide" and lazily defer decisions and actions to a peer, co-leadership involves shared responsibility for more territory. There are fewer excuses for making mistakes or overlooking valuable content when double the resources are available.

5. Many novel ideas expressed in a group are initially rejected because they seem so foreign. Two leaders can endorse each other's verbalizations, reinforcing and supporting the attempts of each at motivating client change. After one leader introduces a concept, confronts a client, or initiates a process intervention, the second leader may choose to offer supportive examples and substantiating data. Each intervention becomes more powerful when implemented with forceful consensus.

"I noticed that you had a smirk on your face while my partner was explaining the ways you deliberately seek attention in the group. I, too, have observed you in action. Earlier today, for instance, whenever you spoke, you would only make eye contact with me and ignore everyone else. Even when I averted my gaze, you would stare at my forehead rather than talk to anyone else. It is as if my opinion is the only one that counts."

6. Many counselors and therapists shy away from running groups because of the strain on their attention span. It is virtually impossible for a solo leader to fully attend to every subtlety requiring individual focus. In addition to possessing the skills and knowledge necessary to counsel an individual in the group, the therapist must also continuously take the pulse of every other member. The single leader's brain easily becomes overloaded with busy signals.

"I've got to press Sandra harder. She's slipping away with her typical game-playing manners. Perhaps I could—. Oops. Why is Rob squirming over in the corner? Did I hit one of his nerves? There go those giggling guys again. I better interrupt them before they begin their distracting jokes. Where was I? Oh, yeah, I was formulating a plan to motivate Sandra. But she keeps looking to Jody and Melanie for approval. I must break that destructive bond between them; they keep protecting one another from any growth. And there's Cary acting bored again, dying for attention. I've got to ignore him and get back to the problem at hand. But what *is* the problem at hand?"

Two leaders working in tandem can systematically divide the duties that require a leader's attention. While one therapist is leading an exercise, the other can help to moderate. While one is talking, the other can be scanning member faces for reactions. While one is preoccupied with counseling a client, the other can divide his or her energy between cueing other members to respond, making sure they stay involved, and objectively assessing the progress of interventions.

7. With co-leaders, clients can experience support and confrontation simultaneously. There is a greater willingness to accept constructive feedback when it is offered nonthreateningly. It is therefore possible for one therapist to circumvent a client's defenses and resistances by playing a nurturing, soft role at the same time that the partner is pointing out inconsistencies in that client's behavior.

> **Co-leader A**: I can really feel for you; I know it hurts. I can see by your tears how much pain you are in. It is so overwhelming to be in the single world again, forced to fend for yourself. You wonder if you'll ever find a lover again.
>
> **Co-leader B**: Yet feeling sorry for yourself won't make things any better. Wishing and hoping for deliverance won't make it happen. You keep blaming yourself for everything you might have done differently if you had had another chance. But there is not another chance for your wife to come back. That's over forever. And I am sitting here wondering why week after week you play these same games. The tears, the dejected, pitiful looks, the same old stories. We've heard them over and over again. What does it take to get you to work and create a new and better life for yourself?

Co-leader A: I know that was difficult for you to hear, but perhaps she is right. You know that we care for you, that we hate to see you suffer like this. How do you feel now? What are you thinking?

8. There are special advantages in applying the co-leader model to marital and family therapy, which is, after all, just a form of group work in which all participants are related. The therapeutic coalitions that inevitably form within family therapy structures can be brought out more flexibly by two therapists. Lantz (1978b) recommends establishing affiliations with particular family members to facilitate interpersonal structural changes. He suggests that one therapist can deliberately flirt with a spouse of the opposite sex as a way to get the other, more reserved spouse more involved. In another situation, the other therapist may act as a scapegoat by deliberately mimicking a family member who is being picked on, thereby taking the pressure off the badgered person and redirecting it toward himself or herself.

9. The likelihood of group member identification and compatibility with the leader is increased if there are two options available. When co-leaders are of different sexes and represent different ethnic and socio-economic backgrounds or personality styles, group members can gravitate toward the person they perceive as being most similar to themselves. It is generally agreed, for instance, that sex therapy with opposite-sex therapists is effective because the leaders can model a positive couple relationship at the same time they make it easier for the husband and wife to relate to their own sex (Masters & Johnson, 1970; Wolman, 1976).

In a study demonstrating the effects of a dual therapy team on improving marital relationships, Epstein, Jayne-Lazarus, and De Giovanni (1979) found that couples learn more adaptive communication roles and constructive conflict resolution by observing the modeled behavior of male-female co-therapists, particularly when the relationship they demonstrate is compatible with client expectations. Other writers recommend that healthy relationships be systematically modeled by co-therapists to encourage complementary sex roles, flexible attitudes, and appropriate dominance patterns in couples (Rice & Rice, 1975; Sonne & Lincoln, 1966). Finally, co-led groups can be designed advantageously for specialized client populations, such as children from broken homes, who have never seen authority figures interact in a free and open manner (Zimpfer, 1971).

10. The dilution of authority between two group leaders can make it easier for members to feel less rebellious and threatened. The team provides a model of healthy, ideal relationships between powerful, respecting persons. Other advantages of using two leaders include spreading out dependency effects in clients and mutually sharing the burden of working with depressed, lonely people.

In summary, co-led groups have the potential to be more dynamic, safe, exciting, and interesting for clients and therapists alike. Most of the disadvantages of co-led groups arise from the unproductive relationship between therapists (Davis & Lohr, 1971; Galloghy & Levine, 1979; Gans, 1962). Unless the partners can work as a complementary team, much group time can be wasted in power plays, bickering, and mutual sabotage.

"Two heads are better than one as long as both are working" (Galloghy & Levine, 1979, p. 296). When there are inequalities of roles in dominant/submissive patterns or when relationships become confounded with personal conflicts, there is bound to be trouble. Fortunately, most of the disadvantages and dangers of co-leadership can be minimized, if not eliminated, by taking precautions in the selection and preparation of an effective partner.

Co-Leader as Trainee

Since its inception by Hadden (1947) a half-century ago, co-leadership has been the preferred model used by advanced practitioners to train less experienced ones. Some writers such as Roller and Nelson (1991), however, do not consider such unequal collaborations to be true co-therapy because both partners are not functioning as *co*-leaders as much as they are acting as supervisor and trainee. They therefore suggest the Spanish derivative *nequipos* (unequal team) to connote partners working together but representing different levels of experience and authority.

Whether co-leaders must be equals in order to meet the strict definition of the term is beside the point; the reality is that, most of the time, advanced practitioners will be working with a partner who is less experienced. Except in situations working with beginning practicum students or interns, co-leaders usually make an effort to present themselves as co-equals. Group members, of course, will be able to discern quite easily which partner knows more, can do more, and seems to be more in charge. But that is fine; what is most important is *how* the co-leaders model their relationship in the group, by being mutually respectful and cooperative.

When advanced practitioners function in the role of supervisors as part of a nequipos team, the following suggestions are recommended (Bernard, Babineau, & Schwartz, 1980; Kottler & Blau, 1989; Roller & Nelson, 1991).

1. *Address the protégé's fears of failure.* "What if I don't have what it takes? What if I make a mistake? What if I hurt someone? What if I am not doing enough?" These are but a sampling of some of the internal doubts that run through the beginner's (and many advanced practitioners') mind.

2. *Make it safe for the protégé to make mistakes.* Learning comes from experimentation and constructive risk taking. It is important to provide sufficient support for the less experienced co-leader to practice what he or she has learned.

3. *Help the protégé process what was learned from miscalculations and misjudgments.* Review each session with an eye toward constructive suggestions that are framed in nonthreatening ways.

4. *Model an honest confrontation with one's own imperfections.* Demonstrate a willingness to solicit feedback from your partner and openly disclose those aspects of your leadership you are working to improve.

5. *Monitor the usual errors of beginners.* These may include being too passive, taking too much responsibility for outcomes, showing difficulty following or tracking proceedings, tolerating silences poorly, or exhibiting a lack of confidence.

6. *Confront approval seeking as well as competition.* Since co-leaders should be modeling effective cooperation between partners, attempts should be made to address dynamic issues between them.

Co-leadership also affords beginning practitioners the opportunity to work under close supervision while learning to develop their own style. In one permutation of this model described by Miller and Williams (1989), the more experienced co-leader functions as an assistant coach who provides instant feedback, suggestions, and support to the less experienced leader. Sitting by his or her side, the assistant coach is positioned to whisper words of encouragement or wisdom into the co-leader's ear. This is actually a more intrusive version of the absentee-cueing system in which the coach sits on the other side of a one-way mirror and speaks to the co-leader through a wireless microphone (Cohn, 1973). Regardless of the assistant coach positioning, he or she is able to offer a number of helpful cues (Kottler, 1977).

Directional cues: "Redirect the focus back to the conflict."
Supportive cues: "Great job!"
Pacing cues: "Slow down a little."
Process cues: "Notice their avoidance of intimacy."
Time-keeping cues: "Begin to work toward closure."
Timing cues: "Confront him now."
Content cues: "Pick up the reference to guilt."
Skill cues: "You might try role playing."
Interpretation cues: "You are being tested."

In each case, it is important for the advanced group leader to be concise and sensitive to the other leader's feelings of being critically evaluated. When this system is used in its best form, the beginning leader eventually comes to hear the "coach's" voice as an extension of an internal voice inside his or her own head.

Choosing a Co-Leader

Choosing a co-leader, like selecting a spouse, is too often a random process. Therapists and counselors are more often matched according to convenient considerations, such as friendship or the proximity of their offices, than by any systematic rationale.

Lang and Halperin (1989) describe the dynamics of what occurs between two leaders, the "courtship and competition" that inevitably takes place, as a unique kind of marriage. They recommend a deliberate, prolonged, and structured courtship before this marriage, one in which co-leaders discuss their attitudes, values, and preferences related to their work; their relative comfort with anger, structure, or self-disclosure; their clinical strengths and weaknesses; technical issues related to absences, rules, money; how disagreements and conflicts will be resolved; specialized roles each will play. These pregroup orientation sessions are best followed by postgroup processing in which differences are discussed, feedback is shared, and group events are analyzed and understood. Without such systematic selection and preparation of co-leaders, chaos can prevail.

For example, in one doctoral-level group internship, partners were paired randomly. Because Joelle and Jay happened to be sitting across from one another, they were chosen to be a team to lead a group of sophisticated students. With five minutes during the break to plan their strategy, the co-leaders naively believed they were ready to take on the task. "After all," they reasoned, "we're intelligent, sensitive people. We're doctoral students in counseling. We know our stuff and what to do."

The group began smoothly enough with Joelle and Jay returning attention to a member who had received help during the previous session. After the report was completed, they began to search for another candidate who wished to use group time. As frequently occurs, a great silence fell as members checked out one another to determine who would volunteer next. Growing nervous, Jay resorted to a strategy that he had relied on many times before; he picked a person who he thought might want to use the group time: "Gerry, I notice you're getting fidgety, as if you want to speak up but are a little apprehensive. I remember a few weeks ago you were complaining about how powerless you felt at home. Is there anything I can do to make it easier for you to talk?"

But before Gerry could respond, Joelle interrupted with her agenda: "Perhaps it would be better to wait for someone to *volunteer* to use the group rather than one of us doing the selecting. People should take responsibility for their own behavior in here."

More silence. Jay leaned back, crossed his arms, and waited.

"Well then," Joelle interjects, "perhaps we should try an exercise designed to get things moving. Why don't we go around the group—."

"Excuse me, Joelle," Jay interrupts exasperatedly, "but I thought that we'd already selected a client who might like to go to work. Gerry looked as if he was just ready to jump in when you interrupted him. Judy and Geoffrey also look like they'll be ready with a little prodding. Why waste time with an exercise?''

Joelle angers visibly. "We didn't select a client, *you* did. Furthermore, it isn't our job to pressure people to perform. They must go at their own pace. If you weren't so authoritarian. . . ,'' and so forth.

To quote Napier and Whitaker (1972, p. 498), ''you need to get married before you have children.'' Particularly in marriages of convenience, or when co-leaders have been involuntarily assigned by supervisors, there will be much strife until partners work out their differences. In spite of their problems, Joelle and Jay probably could have functioned effectively as a team had they sufficiently prepared each other, communicated at length about their preferences, and compromised on certain basic assumptions.

A number of researchers and practitioners suspect that most of the potential dangers inherent in group work are determined by how irresponsible, aggressive, and incompetent the assigned leader is. Most of the potential abuses of co-leader functioning are similarly determined by the quality of therapist matching (Roman & Meltzer, 1977).

In their study of the phases that co-leaders go through while working together, Dugo and Beck (1991) formulated a developmental model of how this unique relationship evolves. In the four beginning stages, the leaders (1) create a contract with one another, specifying assigned roles, (2) form a team identity in which mutual respect is demonstrated, (3) build team functioning, which leads to (4) developing closeness with one another. In the next phase, co-leaders (5) define their respective strengths and weaknesses, which evolves into (6) exploring possibilities for reworking the original contract. The latter stages involve (7) supporting self-confrontation, (8) integrating new insights, and (9) closing issues related to separation.

From Lennon & McCartney and Rogers & Hammerstein to Woodward & Bernstein and Masters & Johnson, all successful teams have had essentially identical qualities. World-class doubles tennis partners can anticipate each other's moves with uncanny accuracy; they know exactly where each partner will be positioned on the court at any moment. Tag-team wrestling partners well understand their limitations and physical endurance; they know when to rest and let the other partner take over. Master bridge players can read the subtlest signals in a partner's face so that they can expertly play into each other's hand. Co-authors tend to choose their partners on the basis of complementary experience, style, temperament, and skills. Selecting a compatible co-leader for group work should not be a random process any more than should choosing a partner in any other important endeavor.

As to specific requirements in co-leader matching, Corey and Corey (1992) warn that the decision should be based on a lot more than personal attraction. Trust is an essential element. The partnership should be an open relationship, a model of constructive compromise. There should be a great willingness to learn from each other. Co-leaders should be extremely flexible in their style and orientation to maximize the advantages of matching complementary personality styles—perhaps pairing a spontaneous person with one who is more reflective and deliberate.

Mutual respect is important so that co-leaders feel safe in disclosing their fears, limitations, and weaknesses to each other. Only by being aware of mutual strengths and limitations can co-leaders know how to best utilize them (Gans, 1957). Once relevant variables are matched according to these established criteria, co-leaders can then form a meaningful division of labor.

Issues for Preplanning

Co-led groups can be potentially frustrating experiences for all parties concerned, even when the leaders genuinely like and respect each other. While one therapist is heading in one direction, attempting to facilitate a group member's insight, the other therapist may be pursuing a different goal, thereby short-circuiting both helping efforts (Edelwich & Brodsky, 1992). Clients can be caught in the middle of a psychological tug-of-war that determines who will win a senseless power struggle.

> **Group leader A**: And so it is very important that you practice being more assertive when—
>
> **Group leader B**: Even more important than the practice, you absolutely *must* stay in touch with your feelings. Do you know what I mean?
>
> **Client**: Yes, but—
>
> **Group leader A**: Let's give you an opportunity to practice being assertive right here in group. Pick out someone—
>
> **Group leader B**: —whom you have strong feelings for and share them with that person.
>
> **Group leader A**: Actually, I was about to ask her to confront her boss in a role-play situation.
>
> **Client**: I'm confused.
>
> **Group leader B**: Yes, that's apparent. That's why I want you to work through the confusion before you confront anyone.
>
> **Group leader A**: But first shouldn't we help her to. . .

In addition to struggles of competition between leaders, most conflicts and inefficient functioning are the result of inadequate preparation on the leaders' part. Just as a vocal duet must rehearse endlessly or as tennis partners must devote hours of practice to learn each other's moves, so must co-leaders negotiate their roles ahead of time.

During preliminary planning sessions, co-leaders can decide who will open the group and who will close it, who will take responsibility for timekeeping, and other practical functions. At this time, co-leaders should negotiate their roles, deciding who will specialize in particular strategies or conflicts. Specific procedures should be standardized and instructions for implementing psychodramatic structures talked through.

There can also be considerable discussion of a philosophically compatible format that is flexible enough to allow for individual differences in leader style and background. Although working only with identical theoretical affiliates is unnecessary, it is probably counterproductive to pair an orthodox psychoanalyst with a radical behaviorist. Mixed marriages work quite well if both co-leaders are open, flexible, and motivated enough to learn from each other. Actually, the greatest benefit for therapists in the co-leader structure is that it not only allows for but also maximally facilitates an open exchange of ideas. A therapist cannot help but increase his or her repertoire of group skills as the result of observing and working with a respected colleague.

A part of initial planning sessions can be devoted to learning how each other's minds characteristically function: ''What do you do when a group member refuses to participate? How do you handle silence? What goes on inside your head when you are waiting for responses? How do you anticipate dealing with conflicts between us that arise in the group?''

At this time, one therapist may cue the other to observe leadership behaviors, paying particular attention to a skill that is being refined: ''After the group I'd appreciate your assessment of my ability to stay neutral and not inadvertently let my biases slip. Please watch me carefully in this regard, since I have been told before that I tend to shape clients to answer questions the way I have in mind.''

In pregroup briefings, co-leaders may create a set of signals between them as an abbreviated private language system. Standard cues can be developed for pacing time, switching counseling focus, or indicating future direction; specific signals can be selected for temporary communication channels. If one leader, for instance, wants to be monitored on a tendency toward rambling, the co-leader can, during appropriate instances, unobtrusively signal to bring this behavior to attention. Another prearranged hand movement might indicate the beginning of a planned sequence to focus on a particular group member or group exercise. Other nonverbal signals can be developed to communicate other messages:

- ''I don't understand where you're going.''
- ''Help me, I'm stuck.''
- ''Keep it up; you're doing fine.''
- ''Start to wrap things up.''
- ''Lighten up; you're pushing too hard.''
- ''Let's try something else.''

Prearranged signals can be augmented through prerehearsed strategies in which co-leaders discuss how they will handle predictable critical incidents. At this point, leaders should also discuss the structure of sessions and screen prospective clients together. Favorable, cooperative expectations can be set up in clients ahead of time by arranging conferences with co-leaders. The therapists can then compare notes on each participant as a means of understanding how each leader thinks, conceptualizes behavior, and would proceed with the case. They can share initial impressions of clients, discuss anticipated special problems, rehearse how they might work with them, and create compromise strategies with which both partners would feel comfortable.

An egalitarian co-therapy relationship is established by formal and informal channels of communication, mutual acceptance, and shared mutual responsibility. This alliance simultaneously permits both individuality and the opportunity for each to help the other grow (Getty & Shannon, 1960).

Tandem Techniques

Together with the increased popularity of co-therapist structures comes the advent of new helping technologies specifically designed for this medium. Just as violin concertos are composed differently from piano sonatas, co-led groups require specialized structures if they are to function effectively and capitalize on their intrinsic advantages. Although some minor style adaptations are necessary when therapists work with partners, equally important is the mastery of adjunct leadership techniques that are ideally suited for co-led groups.

The co-leadership model is not merely a technique that is used for particular purposes in a group; rather, it is a *relationship* between two professionals that demonstrates high levels of cooperation, congruence, balance, and crystal-clear communication (Roller & Nelson, 1991). Goulding and Goulding (1991) elaborate on the intangible aspects of therapeutic partnerships: "If you define *technique* as a trick or artificial maneuver, then good and effective co-therapy can never be a technique" (p. 197). It is first and foremost a *public* relationship.

Across-the-Group Communication

The first of these tandem strategies evolves from the open relationship common among co-therapists. There comes a time when one partner doesn't understand where the other is going or when one leader becomes confused by events that have developed or experiences frustration over intense resistance. In such instances, the leaders may decide to communicate to each other across the group. The dialogue may be initiated for a number of reasons, most notably to share thinking aloud.

> **Co-leader A:** Miriam, we've been working with Gail for the better part
> of an hour, and I've yet to see much progress. Every time we get close
> to the root of things, she backs down. I can't decide whether we

should move on to someone else while she rests, or whether she is actually inviting us to push harder.

Co-leader B: I agree, Ronnie. This is getting us nowhere. Personally, I think Gail is having a great time playing games with us, though she's probably unaware that they are games. Let's confront her directly and force her to make a decision.

Gail, of course, attends carefully to this interaction, gleaning insight into her behavior, and then has sufficient time to prepare herself for the next phase. The other group members listen to the interchange carefully. They learn a lot about how the therapist's mind functions, how it analyzes problems and comes to a resolution. As they become more fascinated with the process of group work, with the skills of promoting insight and action, they also grow more proficient at applying the concepts to themselves.

Communicating across the group also allows leaders to synchronize their actions. It often happens that one therapist will begin a series of interventions on the basis of a hunch. When the direction is not readily apparent, the other therapist is left behind. This problem can be overcome by sharing the agenda aloud.

Co-leader B: Ronnie, follow me for a moment. I have an idea I want to try. While I work with Laura, Phyllis, and Jeff, I want you to note their reactions throughout the encounter. I think you'll catch on soon enough, as will the rest of the group.

Intragroup leader communications can also be initiated for pacing reasons or to confront behavior in an indirect, nonthreatening manner.

Co-leader A: I notice that this side of the group is getting bored. Shall we liven things up a bit?

For whatever reasons across-the-group talking is used, the result is usually desirable as long as leaders have a specific, defensible rationale for doing so. Certainly, co-leaders can operate more efficiently as a team when they keep each other informed. And clients definitely appreciate the opportunity to watch their leaders demonstrating their most open, genuine, and honest style.

Psychodramatic Duets

J. L. Moreno was fond of employing co-leaders in psychodramatic routines. One therapist would work as a director, structuring the role-play situation; the other would act as an "auxiliary ego" to the principal protagonist. Since the time of Moreno's original work, practitioners have become quite inventive in using multiple group leaders in psychodramatic strategies. A co-leader may reflect different aspects of a client's personality—acting as a hostile double, as either the "rational" or the "feeling" self, or may choose to mirror the client's true intentions by means of exaggeration.

Group leader: What then, Isaac, would you really like to do?

Isaac: I just don't know.

Auxiliary ego: *(standing behind shoulders)* I really do know, but I'm afraid to say.

Isaac: Well, maybe I'd like to try something different for a change.

Auxiliary ego: I'm sick of my life the way it is but I feel trapped— like I don't have a choice.

Group leader: What would you like to do differently?

Isaac: I just don't know!

Auxiliary ego: *(makes sounds of chicken clucking with arms flapping)*

Isaac: I *do* know exactly what I want, but if I say it out loud you'll throw it back in my face if I back down.

A strategy suggested by Getty and Shannon (1960) utilizes "participating ego" and "observing ego" roles to allow the temporarily less active leader to assist all other group members in becoming more aware of how proceedings are affecting them. While one therapist becomes totally immersed in helping a client work through a concern, the "observing ego" works in a supporting manner to keep others involved. Each person's nonverbal behavior can be closely and continuously scrutinized for responses to stimuli. When appropriate, they can be cued to share their personal reactions as feedback or empathy to the client-in-focus.

Dyer and Vriend (1973b) describe "role working" psychodramatic structures in which co-leaders take on the parts of guardians of Heaven and Hell. Group members are required to explain why they deserve entry, thereby evaluating the meaning of their lives. Other imaginary scripts can be enacted in a courtroom where co-leaders become prosecuting and defense attorneys while group members play jury and witnesses to the hypothetical crime— usually some irrationally guilt-inducing incident. Scenarios could similarly be played out in other creative settings in which co-leaders take complementary therapeutic roles. Sacks (1973) describes an additional 80 possible strategies through which co-leaders can capitalize on auxiliary ego techniques.

Subdivided Groups

Lantz (1978b) describes a group technique that was created specifically for co-leader functioning. Using one-way mirrors that allow unobtrusive observation, a co-therapy team can facilitate better understanding among family members by allowing them to watch and analyze one another in action. While one therapist directs communication among family members as they bicker and fight, the other can sit with the rest of the family behind a one-way mirror so that they may gain insight into interaction patterns. The observing therapist can thus help family members make sense of what they witness, interpreting incomprehensible actions, answering questions, and leading discussions about inner reactions felt during the sequences.

In one family therapy group composed of divorcing couples and their children, the parents stayed with one group leader while their children went with the other into the observation booth to watch the proceedings. Most of the parents felt inhibited by the children's presence, although they knew it was important to openly discuss the impact of the upcoming divorce. This compromise arrangement was structured to allow the parents to verbalize concerns for their children's welfare as well as for the forthcoming drastic changes in their own lives.

During one heated discussion, the parents were sharing their misgivings about being single parents. How would the kids react to dates being brought home? How would they adjust to the absence of their other parent? Meanwhile, just a few feet away, on the other side of the mirrored wall, the children had questions of their own. Why did Mommy and Daddy stop loving each other? How come they were yelling at each other? The patient and understanding co-leader can help appease the children's fears by addressing their apprehensions. The dialogues that were initially stimulated by this twin-group structure can be continued when they meet again in the whole group. Each co-leader brings a unique perception of the experience, and each group member has an honest appraisal of the conflicts involved.

The same principle can be applied to any group in which there is an apparent crack in cohesion. For example, if age factors, gender conflicts, racial tensions, or attitudinal variables enter the picture as devisive forces, the group could be temporarily split with each co-leader running a smaller unit to deal with the issues. Inhibitions would thereby be reduced, and participants might feel more comfortable getting themselves started in a smaller, more homogeneous group. Once stated goals are met, co-leaders can once again merge their efforts to heal the deepening gulf among participants.

Fishbowl structures can also be employed, in which an inner group takes turns with an outer group in actively pursuing intense interactions. While members of group A explore their feelings of frustration at being misunderstood, members of group B observe the session as their leader programs them to watch for certain things or whispers to them. Afterward, group B members can take center stage to talk about their observations while group A members become active spectators.

Dual Gender Structures

The co-leader format has become standard operating procedure for helping couples with sexual dysfunctions. Masters and Johnson (1970) pioneered the dual-gender therapist approach as a way to ensure that both husband and wife would have a confidante to relate to in the discussion of sensitive and embarrassing issues. It is generally easier for a woman to relate to another woman when discussing her inability to reach orgasm, just as most men feel more comfortable talking to a male therapist about a problem in maintaining an erection. Although there have been no well-controlled studies to date that clearly demonstrate the superiority of either dual-gender therapist teams or co-led groups over single-therapist formats, group leaders find much intuitive appeal in pursuing the team approach.

In a couples group in which clients complain of male-oriented sexual dysfunctions, such as impotence and premature ejaculation, the problems of wives as well as of the husbands can receive balanced attention from male-female co-leaders, as the following illustrates.

Male client chorus: This is so humiliating to talk about. Our masculinity is compromised, our feelings of human competence are completely demoralized. We can't even satisfy our wives, take care of them in bed, much less satisfy ourselves. We wish they weren't so demanding all the time. We're so afraid of failing that we're bound to fail every time we try.

Female client chorus: It's so frustrating to get all worked up and then be left hanging because they can't perform. They never had this problem before, why now? Is it something that we're doing? We thought we were attractive enough women, but now we even question our abilities. They make us so angry that it's not even worth trying any more.

Male co-leader response to male chorus: Your sense of masculinity is totally tied up in your sexual performance? Are you competing on a football field? Have you never made mistakes before, performed less than your expectations? How can you possibly expect to relax in bed and enjoy sex when every thought revolves around: "My God, what if I can't do it. She'll make fun of me. That would be terrible. Boy oh boy, do I hope this works *this* time. I wonder if this means I'm gay? A *real* man could take care of business. I've got to do it this time, I've just got to."

Female co-leader response to female chorus: I never realized you all were so powerful that you take responsibility for your husbands' actions as well as for your own. Of course you take this personally. And, yes, you *do* feel guilty. You wonder if there's something wrong with you because your husbands want to forget that the problems exist while you say that sex is important.

Male-female leadership partnerships also work well with adolescents who are experiencing identity confusion. Boys and girls should all have significant role models to emulate. At the same time, they could learn to relate better to the opposite sex under the tutelage of their therapists.

In one group of 15-year-olds, the theme had been centered on the frustrations of being dishonest. The girls complained that when they found boys they liked, they were forced to play passive, eye-batting games until the boys finally got the message to approach them. The female leader asked why they didn't take more initiative in self-disclosing ways. When the girls complained that the boys would only panic and run if the girls were to take the lead, the male group leader used self-disclosure to show how enjoyable it is to be approached once in a while instead of always having to take responsibility for the way things go.

Guest Co-Leaders

For a group with the right sort of composition, the possibility exists of introducing an occasional guest co-leader who has expertise in some needed area. Presumably this guest would neither be resented nor destroy cohesion if a fairly well-developed, secure atmosphere already existed and if all persons involved were adequately prepared.

A co-leader might be recruited who has specialized knowledge of human sexuality or of career decision making, depending on stated needs. Theme sessions could be structured around topics such as logical thinking processes or the spirit of Zen. In every case, the regular group leader(s) provide continuity while the guest co-leader(s) add diversity and excitement.

Guest co-leaders add a unique dimension to the group process. Clients often find that it is worth sacrificing a little intimacy by bringing in an outsider if the person is sensitive to their needs, has a low-key approach, and can be a compatibly functioning partner with the principal therapist(s).

Co-Leader Interviews

Self-disclosures can be even more potent therapeutic devices in tandem structures. When two therapists know each other intimately, are familiar with each other's background and experience, then their mutual awareness can be put to work in illustrative ways. Co-leaders can cue each other or conduct mini-interviews to elicit significant material and model openness: "Ivan, when you hear Cheryl talking about her guilt in not being a perfect parent, what comes to mind? I recall that you lived through the ultimate parental guilt trip when your daughter tried to kill herself. How did you handle yourself?"

Another example demonstrates the manner in which group leaders can effectively and indirectly self-disclose helpful anecdotes.

> **Co-leader A:** I notice that Bruce keeps coming back to the kids as his main excuse for staying in the marriage. He seems to believe that by being a martyr and living with a woman he doesn't love, he's somehow doing the best thing for the kids. Your parents were divorced when you were quite young. Did the experience traumatize your life?
> **Co-leader B:** No, quite the opposite. It was only *after* my parents split up that things got better. I saw my father more often because he didn't

have to escape from the house any longer. When my parents started dating other people, for the first time I saw grown-ups kissing and hugging each other. Until that point, I had assumed that all husbands and wives show their love by slamming doors in each other's face.

Interviewing techniques can also be used as a method of clarification. One leader may ask the other to elaborate by drawing out comments, asking for supporting examples, or even embellishing the original ideas. Leader communication will be more clearly understood when co-therapists monitor each other's language, asking for further interpretation or clarification when necessary.

Playing Doubles

Napier and Whitaker (1972) compare co-led groups to the bilateral partnership involved in doubles tennis. While one player falls back to take the long shots, the other rushes to the net to take most of the short interaction. It is rare for both to work simultaneously on the same shot. Generally, turns are alternated according to one's preferences and present position on the court.

Most interrogation teams well understand this idea. Often, one group leader will deliberately specialize in a complimentary, nurturing style while the other will choose to be more engaging. After one partner works aggressively to jar information loose, the softer, consoling partner will then offer comfort. Once the people on the other side of the net alter their style, defense, or attack, the group leaders can flexibly change their team functioning to throw a lob, ground stroke, or volley.

Rice, Fey, and Kepecs (1972) identify six co-leader style options. The *blank screen* leader is passive, anonymous, and safe, rarely taking any risks or being provocative. The *paternal* therapist is objective and businesslike, inclined to analyze the past. The *transactional* leader is much more casual, spontaneous, and present-moment oriented, while the *authoritarian* leader is goal oriented and structuring. *Maternal* therapists are highly verbal, supportive, and interpretative, and *idiosyncratic* therapists are critical, conforming, and programmed.

Each of these co-leader styles is, of course, interchangeable, depending on circumstance and mood. Some therapists prefer partners to be similar in style, thereby ensuring compatibility but sacrificing variety; others enjoy partners with different but complementary styles. In tennis or in group work, a doubles team works well together when both players can flexibly change their styles to fit the needs of the situation.

Debriefing

In addition to the sizable advantages to clients, the co-therapy model offers many educational benefits for group leaders. Indeed, the most prevalent use of co-led groups is in counselor/therapist training programs in which clinicians can receive hands-on experience while under close supervision. Even for group leaders with roughly equal status and experience, there are ample opportunities for mutual growth. Regular debriefings should therefore be scheduled to process the events of the previous session. This is most often done on an informal basis. As the last client leaves, the co-leaders inevitably pivot on their heels and ask, "So what did you think?"

In the debriefings, co-leaders will first want to critique each other's performance as honestly as possible, giving specific, constructive feedback about interventions that appeared helpful, wasteful, or harmful. They will next check each other out as to behaviors that were not understood. Certain "lessons for beginners" will predictably crop up if one of the leaders is a student, intern, or less experienced clinician. The supervising leader might point out the following common mistakes:

- not sufficiently scanning client nonverbal behaviors to interpret reactions
- being too passive, safe, and timid about getting involved
- acting self-indulgent by rambling excessively or using self-disclosure inappropriately
- following own agenda so closely that actions were in conflict with co-leader
- staying on a superficial level by not sufficiently exploring the individual or group dynamics
- speaking in a monotone, showing little enthusiasm or excitement
- wasting valuable group time by letting clients engage in intellectual small talk
- not using co-leader enough in supportive ways
- using too limited a variety of interventions, mostly restricted to reflections of feeling and summarizing responses
- trying to solve problems too quickly because of own discomfort with ambiguity
- becoming too interrogative, bombarding clients with inappropriate questions
- allowing clients to use general pronouns like "we" and permitting some clients to talk for others without their consent
- permitting clients to use the group for griping about things and people that can't possibly be controlled
- rarely helping clients focus on concrete goals that they could commit themselves to work toward
- becoming too intolerant of silent periods, forcing people to talk before they felt ready
- not attempting to generalize the stated concern by drawing in other participants and looking at common themes
- asking clients "why?" when they didn't yet understand what the problem was, much less have an answer

- not managing time properly, allowing a few people to dominate and then focusing disproportionately on one idea
- reinforcing precisely the behavior that needed to be eliminated

For experienced group leaders, who make fewer mistakes of this sort, debriefing sessions might be devoted to analyzing group dynamics and identifying possible therapeutic goals for each client. As the pathologist conducts an autopsy to figure out what caused a body's death, co-leaders can use their debriefing sessions to identify cause/effect occurrences or circular casualty dynamics. With each hour that they work together, co-leaders can become even more growth-committed, questioning their actions, noting their effects, and filing for later use those techniques and skills most likely to produce positive results and calculated therapeutic risks.

PART **III**

Advanced Group
Leadership Strategies

*As group members learn from us, we learn from them. Each group session
pushes us to become more knowledgeable, more skilled, more effective. Our
continual state of self-training helps us make our own personal and professional lives more satisfying. As our expertise grows, so do the standards
we have for our actions.*

*Beyond the basic group leadership skills are many advanced strategies
that flexibly allow intervention on more complex and creative levels. The
advanced group leader will borrow any and all useful techniques from a
variety of approaches, adapt them to specific situations and clients, and
refine them until they are thoroughly integrated into his or her personal
structure.*

CHAPTER 10

Productive Risk Taking

Freedom and anxiety are intertwined. With freedom comes choice, and with choice comes the realization that there are no right answers, no guaranteed solutions, only viable options. The more options available to a person, the more freedom that person has. And freedom posits taking absolute responsibility for one's life. According to Sartre (1957), humans are condemned to freedom because, once thrown into the world without a choice, they become responsible for everything they do: "It is therefore senseless to think of complaining since nothing foreign has decided what we feel, what we live, or what we are" (p. 53).

Only later does it occur to us that freedom begets responsibility, which begets risk, which in turn begets anguish. This angst can be combated only by exercising one's freedom, by taking risks and choosing actions even though they may be wrong. "The first act of freedom," William James (1908/1950) wrote, "is to choose it."

Even suffering can be deliberately chosen. The ultimate freedom is to exercise one's will in the face of logic and reasoning, to fight determinism to the last breath, even if it means choosing suffering. In Dostoyevsky's *Notes From the Underground* (1864/1960), the protagonist does just that—stubbornly risks his sanity to choose emotional pain.

> Twice two makes four seems to me simply a piece of insolence. Twice two makes four is a pert coxcomb who stands with arms akimbo barring your path and spitting. I admit that twice two makes four is an excellent thing, but if we are to give everything its due, twice two makes five is sometimes a very charming thing too.
>
> And why are you so firmly, so triumphantly, convinced that only the normal and the positive—in other words, only what is conducive to welfare—is for the advantage of man? Is not reason in error as regards advantage? Does not man, perhaps, love something besides well-being? Perhaps he is just as fond of suffering? Perhaps suffering is just as great a benefit to him as well-being? Man is sometimes extraordinarily, passionately, in love with suffering, and that is a fact. (p. 209)

The anxiety that results from the choice—no, the responsibility—to take risks is the principal focus of therapeutic groups. Helping clients involves bringing together intention, will, and risk (May, 1969). A client's wishes and desires are transposed onto a higher level of consciousness, the motive to act, which is then converted from the decision and will to change into the actual risk of changing.

Risk taking is central to all that changing involves. Unless one is prepared to take chances, to experiment, to try out new strategies, to look into the unknown and pursue what lies ahead even though one is hesitant and afraid, then all the talk is meaningless. Since risking necessarily involves the possibility of loss or injury, there is justifiable hesitation on the part of the client to minimize adverse consequences such as heightened vulnerability, rejection, reputation damage, or loss of self-esteem.

It is part of informed consent that we educate clients about the risks they may encounter as a result of participation in a group. This is especially true with regard to the possibilities of confrontation, emotional outbursts, coercion, and judgmental comments that could occur (Corey, 1990). There are other risks associated with participation in such an enriched, potent atmosphere, an environment that often facilitates some dramatic changes in a relatively short period of time. That is why I begin a group with the following warning: "This is not a place that you will want to return to unless you are utterly serious about making some significant changes in your life. There is no way that you will be the same person that you are now after this group is over. Think long and hard about whether you are prepared to live with the consequences of making yourself into a different, more fully functioning human being." This serves partially as an introduction to my informed consent statement and also as a way to enhance positive expectations and placebo effects. Clients still need to be informed that "Nonetheless, client risk taking is basic to group therapy, for it generates the here-and-now material that is a prerequisite for meaningful interpersonal transactions" (Bednar, Melnick, & Kaul, 1974, p. 34).

Groups are natural places for therapeutic experimentation because group members are more likely to make riskier decisions there than they would alone, both to increase their status and to diffuse responsibility (Brown, 1965; Shaw, 1981; Stoner, 1968). The group is an ideal environment with built-in dynamic support systems to encourage risky behavior. These inherent pressures can be naturally fermented by the leader without artificially introducing any foreign ingredients. People are more willing to share self-revealing information to others who have taken similar risks (Jourard & Jaffe, 1970; Worthy, Gary, & Kahn, 1969), and they are much more willing to do so after an introductory group discussion focusing on a sample of risky problems (Clark, 1971; Pruitt, 1971).

The desire to win peer approval, plus the competitive nature of most people, helps to encourage a contagious risk-taking effect in groups. Furthermore, when individuals are given feedback indicating that their level of risk taking is not up to par, they become more revealing. This "risky shift" phenomenon has helped to explain why group decisions are generally less cautious and conservative than individual decisions (Runyan, 1974; Spector, Cohen, & Penner, 1976; Stoner, 1968). Whether because responsibility is more diffused, because riskiness is a cultural value, or because adventurous group norms force compliance, there is much evidence to suggest that group settings are ideal for promoting risk-taking behaviors (Shaw, 1981).

Our society generally places a highly favorable and prized value on risk taking (especially if the results are profitable). Our most glorified heroes tend to be explorers (Columbus, Magellan, Neil Armstrong); radical writers and artists who risked peer disapproval and ridicule to make their statements (Freud, Van Gogh); scientists and philosophers who were ahead of their time (Einstein, Russell, Galileo, Socrates); and daring military geniuses (Napoleon, Alexander, Eisenhower). We admire risk taking in others even if we are afraid of it in ourselves.

When group members discover that they are far from the risk-taking norm, the value most prized in a therapeutic group, dissonance is heightened until they change in a direction more consistent with the adventurous status quo. To create a favorable impression in others, clients must become more risky in order to demonstrate that they are part of the "in-group."

Much of what group work accomplishes is to provide a safe structure for participants to practice taking risks. Whether a decision needs to be made, a confrontation must take place, or a new skill is to be learned—whenever change occurs—an element of risk is involved. The Great Unknown beckons: I dare you. To the rear lies all that is secure and predictable, safe and comfortable, however self-destructive such inertia might be; ahead, somewhere in the darkness, lies truth. Maybe.

Inhibiting Influences

Even the most reluctant of group members will readily agree that risk taking is absolutely necessary for any change to occur. Perhaps a dreaded confrontation will have to take place, or a new job is just beyond the horizon. Loneliness can be countered only by approaching attractive strangers socially. There is no shortcut to eliminate the inevitable risk that accompanies an exploration into the Great Unknown.

One primary goal of the group leader is to promote an atmosphere of low extrinsic risk so as to minimize subjectively experienced intrinsic risks (Niles & De Voe, 1978). Initial sessions do not provide a natural environment for relaxing and expressing deep feelings. Members are uncertain what will happen and how they should respond. They are threatened by the faceless strangers, intimidated by the imposing leader, repulsed by certain peers, and fearful of what they might have to do. Altogether, initial group sessions can be intimidating for clients very eager to experiment with new behaviors but desperately afraid that others will disapprove of them.

Several inhibiting influences sabotage risk-taking efforts in groups and in group members' minds. People avoid taking risks, for example, because of the neurotic payoffs they receive. They don't have to work hard at changing. They can feel sorry for themselves. Their psychological maintenance system ensures that they can remain safe. Once these factors are identified, specific strategies can be used to neutralize their negative effects. In the Japanese martial art Aikido, opponents' aggressive energy is countered with balanced movements that turn the force against them. Similarly, the oppositional dynamics in groups that make risk taking appear so ominous can be harnessed for constructive purposes to make the work more fluent.

A client's readiness to take risks can therefore be encouraged by the natural pressures in groups that create more dissonance in self-satisfaction levels. The more internal conflict that is intensified by group interaction, honest feedback, and other factors, the more willing, even desperate, the client becomes to change the status quo. It is only when one looks in the mirror with total disgust that one is sufficiently motivated to do something about the false image. The following variables are additional inhibiting influences common to group settings. Only after each has been identified can group leaders take steps to neutralize their effects.

Fear of Consequences

The most readily apparent inhibitor to taking risks is that of the perceived consequences. Before taking any action, especially one that involves unknown factors (such as how others might react), people spend considerable time estimating probable and possible outcomes. Group members tend to exaggerate what could conceivably occur and to magnify the potential dangers. They often inflate their sense of self-importance, believing that everyone else has nothing better to do than constantly scrutinize their behavior. In actuality, the worst possible reaction would be that members don't do or say *anything*.

There are also realistically projected consequences, the likely outcomes of which make an action a bad risk. Backgammon, for instance, requires that a player calculate all possible outcomes from an opponent's throw of the dice and then make the most aggressive move on the board that has the fewest *acceptable* risks. Essentially a symbolic form of interpersonal risk taking, backgammon trains the mind to consider what can be gained versus what can be lost. The aggressive player who takes frequent *calculated* risks will always win over the more cautious player. The key, of course, is to help group members assess probable outcomes realistically and to encourage them to operate on those assumptions.

The fear of consequences can be minimized by keeping the fear within acceptable parameters. Byrd (1974) developed certain rules of risk taking for middle-management executives, professionals who tend to play it safe even though personal promotions and company profits are based on taking frequent calculated risks.

The first rule is never risk more than you can afford to lose. When a client asks ''What is the worst possible thing that could realistically happen?'' the disasters enumerated are much less horrendous than what had been anticipated. A client reluctant to take a new job fantasizes about all the possible catastrophes that could occur as the result of the career change; but when pressed to specifically verbalize what could happen, she finally admits the worst outcome: if the job doesn't work out, she might have to search for another. Realistic potential losses can be predicted fairly accurately from available data. Once decisions are made as to what a person is willing to sacrifice, behavior that stays within those acceptable limits can be planned.

The second rule is not to risk a lot for a little. If potential gains don't far exceed anticipated losses, it hardly seems worth the effort to take the risk (although ''high-rollers'' will opt in favor of the unknown whenever there is a tie, just because it is fun for them to confront the unknown). A moderately satisfied group member who has earned the respect of peers by speaking with care and deliberation is unlikely to throw her respected style out the window in favor of a more spontaneous, impulsive manner (at least until she understands that it is better to have more choices than fewer choices).

The final rule of risk taking is an integrative application of logic and emotion, of Western and Eastern thought, of physics and Tao, of right and left cerebral hemispheres: put your trust in the odds *and* your intuition.

All-or-None Law

An individual's willingness to take risks is also stifled by distorted views about what risk taking involves. The human propensity to think in dichotomies has no basis in reality except perhaps in physical laws, such as the absolute minimal threshold necessary for a nerve impulse to be conducted. This all-or-none law may apply to a circumstance such as being pregnant (as one cannot be ''somewhat'' or ''partially'' pregnant), but it has no place in the conception of risk taking. When a group member reasons that the only two options available are either to clam up or to self-disclose unreservedly, the likely course of action is clear. For this reason, clients must be helped to dispel their absolute notions in favor of seeing behavior along a gradual continuum.

Bednar, Melnick, and Kaul (1974) identify levels of client risk along a developmental scheme, beginning with self-disclosure, the least threatening variety; then moving to interpersonal feedback, which requires considerably more skill yet involves less predictability of outcome; and finally coming to group confrontation, the highest possible level of risking. Group confrontation, in which a member shares dissatisfaction with a current activity, can virtually explode with negative consequences. Everyone could unanimously boycott the outspoken member, ridicule his or her opinions, and use the outburst as an excuse for devious psychological torture. Worse, the person could be totally ignored.

These different levels of risking can be ordered on a gradient so that the therapist may progressively encourage low-level toward high-level risking, slowly inoculating participants' exposure to perceived danger. In this way absolutism is replaced by relativism, allowing more possible choices for client action.

In one introductory group exercise used to establish cohesion and intimacy swiftly, participants are requested to share a meaningful secret about themselves that no one else knows. This can be done anonymously on paper, thereby minimizing the level of risk, or it can be done aloud in which clients admit their secrets. In either case, the group begins on an intense note because the content involves deep issues and all participants are given the opportunity to "get their feet wet."

By far the riskiest secrets were those concerning sex; secrets about expressing violence or fears of being insane were also considered difficult to share. In their study, the researchers asked college-age group members to write anonymously the one thing they would be most afraid to reveal aloud. They collected 359 secrets on a staggering array of subjects that people consider risky to disclose, a conclusion not altogether surprising. Experienced group leaders continuously observe clients sweating and stammering for five minutes before they finally reveal the "terrible secret": "I once fantasized that I was the opposite sex." Other supposedly risky secrets included "I'm on the pill," "I'm lost and lonely," and "I'm bored with my social life."

The ten secrets that were considered to be the riskiest (as judged by four independent reviewers with an inter-rater reliability of 88%) were ordered as follows:

1. I have had an incestuous relationship with a member of my family.
2. I have been in a mental institution.
3. I have V.D.
4. I masturbate almost every night.
5. I have homosexual tendencies.
6. I sometimes feel I have to kill someone.
7. I once jacked-off in the grad reading room of the library.
8. I deal and take speed.
9. I am constantly toying with the idea of killing myself.
10. I stole half of my books from the bookstore.

Knowing what most people regard as risky disclosures is helpful to group leaders so that we may gently ease them into the content of sessions without frightening them too early. When we model examples of risky disclosures, we can select topics that we know are very difficult to share to lay the groundwork for others to respond on intense levels.

Fear of Failure

Throw a frisbee and a dog will leap into the air, stretch its mouth open, and try to catch the spinning disc. If the dog should miss and land sprawled on the ground with the frisbee bouncing atop its head, what would happen next? The dog would probably not whine, cry, pout, and feel sorry for itself. It would not develop performance anxiety and become so hypersensitive that it could never again go after a frisbee without crippling self-doubt. The dog would probably wag its tail, pick up the frisbee, and return enraptured to the human for another toss. But when humans don't live up to their expectations, when they make mistakes or miss an opportunity or act less than perfectly they think of themselves as failures (Dyer, 1976).

Individuals naturally differ in their propensities to take risks; also, great variation exists in the degree to which people will make rational choices. People who are preoccupied with winning approval and who have a high fear of failure are less able to adjust their risk-taking strategies to fit situational requirements; they will consistently act inappropriately conservative or reckless. Those who are less concerned with group members' opinions will make more intelligent decisions about when and how to take a risk (Bern, 1971; Kogan & Wallach, 1967).

The alternative to a failure-avoidance orientation is to behave without accompanying self-judgments. The group leader must work with clients to wipe out anticipatory regrets that inhibit experimentation. A group atmosphere conducive to risk taking is one in which the possibility of failure does not exist. People either do or they don't do, period. In one exercise, adolescents were given practice at handling rejection and eradicating the word *failure* from their vocabularies. They were instructed to ask one another for things they knew they would never get and then to remain calm in the face of disappointment. If, when they took interpersonal risks, the worst thing that could occur was not that they could fail but that the other would not respond, then they felt more free to take risks.

Inhibiting Stress

It is well known that whereas a little anxiety improves performance of a well-rehearsed task, too much anxiety can result in stage fright. Unfortunately, the situational factors prevalent in therapeutic groups may produce toxic levels of stress that curtail risk-taking actions. The pressures to conform, performance anxiety, comparisons to peers, approval seeking, and other group norms are all anxiety-provoking stimuli. Hypervigilance is also evident in group situations in which a person enters a state of helpless panic in the face of an oncoming threat with insufficient time to prepare evasive action. For the same reason that people may freeze during a fire escape or other group crisis, group members may allow the prospect of an impending risk to cripple thought processes and constrict effective strategies for countering the threat.

A favorite method for teaching reading to first-graders used to be to arrange the children in a circle (the teachers must have heard from psychologists that circles, like pyramids, have healing properties) and then to have them take turns reading a story aloud. However benign the intention, the result of this exercise (as I recall it) was that each child would wait in panic, counting the number of places until his or her turn, and then fall apart from stress when the cue finally arrived. Another effect was that as soon as your turn was over, you could daydream for the rest of the period while your friends suffered the wait.

Novice group leaders often make the same mistake in their efforts to expose clients to taking risks. When an introductory exercise requires people to tell something about themselves each in turn around a circle, clients usually spend the time rehearsing their introductions instead of attending to others. After their turn is taken, they will spend the rest of the hour patting themselves on the back with relief.

The inhibiting stress can be intensified or diminished through the use of structure, depending on when and how it is introduced. Early group structure in which expectations, goals, and roles are clarified helps to make risk taking easier (Bednar, Melnick, & Kaul, 1974). When clients understand what is appropriate behavior, how the group process will emerge, and what is likely to happen, they are a lot more willing to take therapeutic risks (Goldstein, Heller, & Sechrest, 1966).

We can soften the impact of anxiety-provoking stress by preparing participants for the experience. For instance, giving constructive feedback to one another reduces stress by providing certain guidelines for diminishing the ambiguity of the situation. Risks can be structured according to spontaneous circumstances where rehearsal anxiety won't get in the way: "Just now you gave me that look where you stare down at me as if I were a bug you want to squash." Structure can involve specific declarations of risk: "When I get home tonight, my husband will be dozing in front of the television. I'll explain to him that I'm uncomfortable and dissatisfied with the amount of work he does around the house and then negotiate a more equitable arrangement."

Providing minimum structure works to reduce inhibiting stress; so does encouraging familiarity and intimacy. If people can be helped to feel more comfortable, they will be much more willing to try out new behaviors.

Degree of Comfort

At the other extreme, feeling *too* comfortable with oneself may also diminish a person's motive to take risks. As noted earlier, people don't change as long as they are minimally comfortable with the way they are. Often group leaders must intensify the dissonance in people so that they will work to reconcile their inner conflict between the status quo and the desired future. Group members are not likely to take risks until they feel externally, or preferably internally, pressed to do so.

Many group techniques are designed to make clients feel uncomfortable with their ineffective selves. Once the ball is rolling and a few courageous clients jump in with both head and heart, the others begin to notice how attractive the risk takers are. They may at first be resentful and later jealous, but eventually they are respectful of their more venturesome colleagues. "If they can do it, so can I" is the hoped-for conclusion they will reach.

In one group, a middle-aged man listened restlessly to the tearful complaints of a college student who had just broken up with her boyfriend. Apparently, they had been dating since high school and had settled into a fairly comfortable routine. Eventually bored with the relationship, the girl decided to break it off even though she was giving up some great times. "What has this to do with me?" wondered the older gentleman, suddenly aware that he was feeling hot and sweaty. "After all, my marriage has been good for the past 24 years. We've raised two pretty nice kids. We have a nice house, kind friends, and we're very considerate of each other's needs. But this girl gets rid of her boyfriend just because she doesn't love him intensely. What the hell *is* love, anyway? That's the stuff you see in movies!"

Another group member supported the girl by disclosing that he had wanted to do the same thing with his lover. He had lived with his first and only gay lover for some years until he, too, had settled into a comfortable but dependent routine. It had taken him almost six months to work up the courage to leave. "I really admire your spirit for not letting things drag on. There was a great temptation for me to wait until I could find another lover before I left my old one. What you're doing takes a lot of strength, especially when what you're leaving is so convenient."

The older man now begins to sweat profusely. His heart pounds. Finally he speaks out: "Is it really so terrible to have a comfortable marriage? I mean, sure, some things are boring and predictable. We have sex every Wednesday and go out for dinner every other Friday. We go to sleep every night after the late news, though on Mondays we sometimes watch a talk show. Sure, it's gotten to be a drag. I don't believe I've loved my wife for 10 years. But is it really worth giving up a 24-year investment just because it isn't all that exciting? Well, maybe it is. What should I do?"

This man's discomfort was multiplied in direct proportion to the risk taking going on in the rest of the group. As others shared their apprehensions, it became more acceptable to admit his own fears. Finally, he was motivated to risk opening up because his discomfort had become intolerable. Keeping his secret safe did not seem all that attractive compared to the great relief he could feel on unburdening his soul. The more honestly he spoke, the more quickly his temporary comfort level reached a point of equilibrium, at least until he decided to retreat once again to his delusional safety.

Illusion of Safety

Just as the ostrich that buries its head in the sand believes that because it cannot see danger, danger will not see it, people deceive themselves into believing they have invulnerable protection against the outside world. By having convinced themselves that they are safe, they need take no risky action that could jeopardize the present, temporary tranquility.

One such victim of the safety illusion was Doug, who had worked as a top executive for a major corporation for almost a decade. During his career ascent, pushing for innovative changes, he had of course made enemies. Now Doug was unhappy in his work: his actions were constantly countermanded, his opinions were ignored, and he was rendered powerless by people both above and below him. But Doug was reasonably comfortable. He had a pension plan. He liked his neighborhood. His office was attractive, and over the years he had made some fine friends. If his job wasn't the best, at least it was secure (or so he would tell himself on declining every job offer that came along). Finally, everything collapsed around him. He was pushed out of his position and forced to resign, and at 55 years of age he felt too old to start over. The illusion of total safety crumbled. Doug had waited too long, deceiving himself that taking risks was not necessary because his position was unassailable.

So many group members list and total their blessings, then spread them around as reminders of how good things really are. In reality, however, the only thing that one can logically expect is the unexpected. The only true safety is in the knowledge that one is fully prepared to give something up if a productive risk becomes necessary. But believing this and selling the idea of risk taking to clients are quite different matters.

Selling Productive Risk Taking

Jerri was extremely resistant to taking risks of any kind, finding it much easier to comply with her parents' and friends' expectations than to search for meaningful goals of her own. Whenever she "accidentally" took a risk, such as confronting another group member or approaching a stranger at a party, she would deny that the action was a risk because it wasn't all that difficult to do. She eventually verbalized a risk that she wanted to take badly enough to place herself willingly in a vulnerable position. Although she desperately feared rejection, she was eager about the prospect of initiating a romantic relationship with a man with whom she had long been smitten.

When queried by group members as to what exactly she had to lose by approaching the man, Jerri was silent for at least two minutes before finally admitting that she was stumped. She felt frightened that he might ridicule her brutally, although she knew that he was a sensitive man who liked and respected her. At worst, he might express a willingness to keep the relationship on a friendship basis, which at least would reassure her that he liked her for her mind rather than for her body. If he should respond with romantic overtures, her wish would be fulfilled. Either way she couldn't lose.

Jerri was now able to think of risk-taking experiences as opportunities to enhance, rather than to destroy, existing security. By holding back, she was cheating herself of growth experiences and depriving her loved ones of seeing in her an independent spirit that had lain dormant for so long. In retrospect, Jerri laughs at her former reluctance to initiate risks.

In the group session that had made the difference, all action had been suspended. Not only was her progress stopped dead, but all forward movement in the group had halted. Everyone had started playing it safe, engaging in polite conversation, dutifully saying the right thing when called on to speak. Typical of most groups, a period of temporary cowardice had developed. Clients had mentally counted their chips and decided that mediocrity isn't so bad after all, at least when considering the alternative.

It was quickly determined that the fear of risking was the pervasive theme. All the symptoms were evident: a high frequency of artificial flattery, warning looks of "don't tread on me," evasiveness, reluctance to declare goals, contentment with the status quo, increased fear of leader interventions, and much protective defensiveness. Although individual members commonly exhibit these behaviors, rarely does this coward's plague strike all who are present at once.

A radical procedure was needed. Members were once again beginning to enjoy the false sense of security that comes from hiding. The group leader decided to try a scolding approach, a minilecture intended to remotivate clients toward action, reminding them why they had joined the group in the first place. The purpose of such an impassioned speech is to highlight all the crucial elements of the change process that are involved in attacking the path of most resistance—taking productive risks.

Perhaps the most difficult task for group leaders is to sell productive risk taking to clients. To gear up for a dramatic pitch seems eventually to be necessary in every group. Usually there has been some impasse and people have begun more skillful dodging. Conversation has become safe and predictable, involving low-risk topics or those that have been previously brought up. Sometimes clients will revert to their old standard defenses: "I just don't have anything to work on right now. My life is going pretty well."

Particularly in the early sessions, members will exhibit much reluctance as they cautiously test the water. Stubbornly they cross their arms and demand: "Prove to me that any of this will make a difference. Why should I go out on a limb when it can so easily break off?" At this point the ball is in our court. It is up to us to recruit potential risk takers to take the plunge.

A Hard-Sell Speech

Sometimes it becomes necessary to give a hard-sell speech, one of the few times we resort to lecture tactics as a matter of choice. If pep talks work well when coaches give them to athletes as a motivating force, why shouldn't they also work for us? Occasionally I catch myself checking whether the time is right and the players are ripe for such a pitch. I take a deep breath, bore holes in their heads with the intensity of my gaze, and then deliver one of my favorite therapeutic speeches, usually intended to shake group members out of their inertia.

This speech always contains certain elements, although its form may change.

1. It must be entertaining.
2. If long-winded, it is for the purpose of repeating important themes.
3. It makes things seem easy.
4. It is educational and informative.
5. It is self-disclosing. I admit that I have the same concerns, but
6. I did something about them.
7. It is not *too* scolding in its tone.
8. It gets clients enthusiastic about starting on their productive risks.

The following is a sampling of the marketing strategy I employ to sell risk taking to group members:

"How many times have you found yourself trapped in a boring, entirely predictable conversation? When was the last time a friend asked your opinion and, instead of giving it to him honestly, you told him only what he wanted to hear? How long ago did you last approach an attractive stranger? When was the last time you did something completely new, something that you had never tried before? How many times have you stifled yourself from speaking your mind in here? When is the last time you took a risk?

"There are different kinds of risk taking, some of them productive and others potentially harmful. Jumping out of an airplane without a parachute, getting into fights, and ridiculing others are examples of the latter. Productive risk taking, on the other hand, usually takes the form of expanding or broadening one's experience for self-growth. Although taking the risk itself is often not pleasurable, the satisfaction of trying something new is. Taking risks is exhilarating. It is no accident that so many people like to gamble, drive fast, or play dangerous sports, although even more people experience the dangers vicariously through books, TV, and movies.

"Productive risk taking helps you overcome fears, develop self-confidence, and enlarge your life experiences. Examples include risking the disapproval of others by doing what you want; risking honesty and sincerity when you reveal yourself to others; risking discomfort, inconvenience, or rejection by becoming intensely involved with another; risking failure by trying something new; or risking change by ridding yourself of self-defeating behaviors.

"What is risky for one person is not necessarily so for another. To some people, ending a long relationship, a marriage, or a friendship is the most difficult task imaginable. Others fear quitting a job or starting a new life.

Still others avoid failure at all costs. Think about what *you* are most afraid of risking. Is it meeting new people? Becoming intimate with someone in or out of this group? Ridding yourself of your dependencies? Trying something new? Exploring the unknown? There is a sign that you can use as a reliable guidepost as to what is risky for you; when your stomach feels queasy or your legs feel jittery because you're trying to avoid doing something that you really want to, that's an indication a risk is in sight.

"It's easy for me to recall those painful images of the past when I struggled to pursue the unknown—times when all thought and activity seemed suspended, waiting for me to make a decision. The same process occurs in everyone. I would think of something that I really wanted to do; but before I had a chance to carry out my plan, I would scare myself senseless with all the things that could go wrong, all the disastrous results that could occur as a consequence of my bumbling ineptitude. Of course, the disaster that I imagined, even if it did arise, could never be worse than all my self-inflicted misery, lamenting what a spineless jellyfish and gutless wonder I was for giving in to my fears. One incident that recurred throughout my college years is still a source of inspiration to me. You will all be able to see a little of yourselves in me.

"The setting is a small midwestern university. I am in my dormitory room, the lights dimmed, seductive music in the background. Although my roommate conveniently left the room an hour earlier, I am not alone. An attractive female companion is sitting next to me, discussing the cafeteria food, her art history course, and plans for the future. I'm not listening. Instead, I'm thinking how much I want to kiss her. At least four times my mind orders me to make a move, but my body fails to obey. I am crippled by my thoughts: 'What if she hates me and slaps me in the face? What if she doesn't like it and thinks I'm inept?' Or the worst thought of my adolescent naivete: 'What if she *does* like it? Then what do I do?'

"Inevitably my self-debate would end in an ultimatum to myself. I would begin a countdown from ten as I prepared—nine, eight, seven—to kiss her gently on the lips—six—and hold her in—five—my arms. I always—three, two—chickened out before I got to one. Then the real self-abuse would start. Eventually I became so frustrated and angry wih my behavior that I decided no rejection from anyone else could possibly hurt more than my own self-condemnation.

"After years of practice at taking risks, I am now better equipped to deal with others' disapproval of me as well as with breaking down my own resistances. Today, if I were to encounter a potentially risky situation, such as wanting to try or say something I've never attempted before, and I feel myself hedging and backing away, that would be a signal for me to go forward and conquer my fears. I remind myself of all my past hesitations and what they cost me. Then I convince myself that the only way I will ever become more effective in my life is by mastering new behaviors instead of mindlessly reworking old ones.

"Right now, think about the risky things you've wanted to do for a long time but continuously put off because of fears. Is it making a career switch? Telling someone what you really think? Speaking up more honestly in this group? Sharing something personal for which you are afraid others will condemn you? Whatever it is, you are probably giving yourself a lot of excuses for not taking action.

"You like your security, safety, and predictability no matter how miserable or ineffective you are. Taking risks means changing in some ways, having to learn something new, and that's hard work. Sure, it would be nice to be a fully functioning, happy individual who is in control, but not if you have to work for it. You'd prefer to sit back and wait for some magical transformation to take place in your mind, making you into the person you'd really like to be. After all, you've believed for a long time that you'll always be as you are, and there's very little you can do about it.

"Forget that nonsense that you are controlled by your past. So what if you were toilet trained too early or saw your aunt naked in the shower. You have many good excuses for the way you are and the reasons you got that way; but your past will continue to shackle your present moments and future efforts as long as you believe that you are powerless to change. Avoid taking risks, experimenting with new behaviors, really working on yourself to grow and you will remain the same inert, predictable, listless self. The choices available to you are only as limited as your imagination. If you choose to alter dissatisfying aspects of your behavior, this commitment will help motivate your journey.

"Think again about the things you don't like about yourself, behaviors you would like to change, anything from being overweight to feeling excessively guilty. Whatever the undesired behavior, you've learned to live with it. It brings comfort because it resembles a stable character trait. After all, you've always smoked, worried, been dependent, fat, unhappy, or nervous. Why change now?

"Why, indeed? Because you lead a basically boring existence. Your life routine runs like clockwork. Why should you risk what you have for something unknown? I could give you many reasons, but they are all my own motivations for structuring new experiences in my life, discovering novel solutions to problems that confront me. I cannot do your work for you, nor can I convince you to make your life more exciting and meaningful.

"It is totally up to you. The next time you catch yourself censoring risky thoughts or hesitating to speak up in the group, ask yourself what you really have to lose. Question your motives for playing it safe. Take a deep breath and then plunge in. It is *only* by taking risks that you can ever expect to make changes in your life. If you don't venture forth in this group, exploring new territory, encountering people more intimately, you will be condemned to a life of stale mediocrity. The choice is yours. Now, does anyone have anything to say?''

If the minilecture has had its effect, group members start to get fired up. They also feel a little guilty for hanging back, but the momentum has begun. Since risk taking involves a response inhibition behavioral model rather than a response deficit model, a great part of the group leader's work involves coaching clients to do what they have already learned to do selectively since birth. Promoting risk taking is among the most difficult challenges for group leaders. Clients fight back every inch of the way, forcing leaders occasionally to wonder why they must sell an idea that is so obviously beneficial.

Feeling Alive

In varying qualities and quantities, risking is part of every human endeavor. Taking a risk requires choosing among several possible courses of action, any of which may bring about consequences that leave the individual worse off than before. All living is uncertain, unpredictable, uncontrollable, hazardous. The only risk we never have to choose is our own mortality.

To live a life without risks, without deciding or choosing, is to live a life unfulfilled, an empty existence with neither responsibility nor freedom. Therefore, the most meaningful of activities that a group leader can perform is to train clients to become more willing participants in the risk-taking process (but without unduly pressuring them, as was evident in the vignette). Once inhibiting influences are removed and clients are prepared to make intelligent choices, motivated to act on their honest intentions, encouraged to experiment with unknown factors, and immunized against crippling disappointments, only then will they truly come alive.

CHAPTER 11

Creative Metaphors

Most of the service professions rely on an impressive armory of technological gadgetry for helping their patients. Dentists have their little mirrors, X-ray machines, cavitrons, nitrous oxide, and miniature picks and shovels to mine tooth decay. Neurologists rely on brain scans to aid their diagnostic decisions; cardiologists use electrocardiograms; and internists know just the right questions to ask and places to feel to determine what ails their patients. Once the problems are identified, they may be dispensed quickly with a few injections, pills, or a surgeon's scapel. Voilà! The appendix is removed, and, with it, all the accompanying discomfort.

As group leaders we have no stethoscopes or tongue depressors with which to probe client problems. There are a few psychological tests to administer, but MMPI profiles or Myers-Briggs scales are nothing compared to the cold, calculating efficiency of a radiologist's analysis. With a few notable exceptions, we have no pharmaceutical weapons to combat our clients' problems of loneliness, boredom, shyness, poor grades, existential angst, or nosy in-laws. Group leaders have no surgical procedures to remove psychological malignancies. We cannot dissolve psychic pain with any proven laboratory strategies, nor can we reliably produce similar outcomes using any application of technology. To serve our clients, we have only our minds and our skill at communicating what is in them. The use of language, the ordering of words into meaningful sequences, is virtually the only means available for therapists to help people change in groups.

Human beings most often think in terms of images and stories. Robert Frost believed that "all thinking is metaphorical." H. Parkhurst claimed that "any supreme insight is a metaphor." Kenneth Burke agreed: "Whole works of scientific research, even entire schools, are hardly more than the patient repetition, in all its ramifications, of a fertile metaphor." C. S. Lewis repeated the theme: "All our truth, or all but a few fragments, is won by metaphor" originally proposed by Nietzsche: "To know is merely to work with one's favorite metaphors. . . . And what therefore is truth? A mobile army of metaphors. . . . Truths are illusions of which one has forgotten that they are illusions'' (Schibles, 1972). Haley (1968) believed that all client concerns are stated metaphorically: the phobia, the depression, the confusion are symptomatic analogies of a deeper coping struggle.

We dream of intricate plots while asleep and construct elaborate fantasies during idle waking moments. The ability to reason in abstract images appears to be a uniquely human trait. Bateson (1977) related the anecdote of a computer that was asked by its programmer whether it could ever think like a person. The computer printed out ''That reminds me of a story.''

The informal, free-flowing tale told by a guru, the formally constructed image used by a minister, the bedtime story with a moral told by a parent, the symbolic image created by the psychoanalyst—all are examples of therapeutic stories in action. Such images, whether in the form of metaphor or anecdote, are among the most powerful tools that group leaders can use.

Therapeutic Metaphors

> Water—the ace of elements. Water dives from the clouds without parachute, wings, or safety net. Water runs over the steepest precipice and blinks not a lash. Water walks on fire and fire gets blisters. Stylishly composed in any situation—solid, gas, or liquid—speaking in penetrating dialects understood by all things—animal, vegetable, or mineral—water travels intrepidly through four dimensions, *sustaining* (Kick a lettuce in the field and it will yell ''Water!''), *destroying* (The Dutch boy's finger remembered the view from Ararat), and *creating* (It has even been said that human beings were invented by water as a device for transporting itself from one place to another, but that's another story). Always in motion, ever-flowing (whether at steam rate or glacier speed), rhythmic, dynamic, ubiquitous, changing and working its changes, a mathematics turned wrong side out, a philosophy in reverse, the ongoing odyssey of water is virtually irresistible. (Robbins, 1976, pp. 1–2)

The ever-present, everlasting, ever-adapting nature of water. Water is part of the composition of all living things. It is a silent witness in all human acts. It cares nothing about money, who is president, whether you live or die. Water endures; it will flee your body after it has outlived its usefulness. Water feels no guilt or anger. It shrugs its indifferent shoulders to war and famine. It knows no pain; it expresses no sympathy.

The 80 years or so that we temporarily inhabit this planet as living beings are but an infinitesimal speck in what Carl Sagan (1977) terms the ''Cosmic Calendar.'' When you consider that the water molecule has been around for several billion years, what difference can it make what you do with your ridiculously short life of several decades? If you think it is a long time until your next birthday, consider how long you will be dead. One hundred years from now, who will care whether you were divorced, lost your job, or even existed? Will water care when your heart stops beating?

Put your hand on your heart. Feel it beating, pumping blood throughout your body. It's a living organ that is destined to wear out after beating about three billion times in your lifetime. That seems like a lot, but you've already used up a billion of your allotment. Even now, while you've been daydreaming, another few thousand slipped by, gone forever. How long did you sleep last night? That's about 30,000 heartbeats. And how many moments have you thrown away feeling sorry for yourself, steeped in depression? Each time your heart beats, you lose another second of your life, forever.

The monk, the guru, the master, the shaman, the healer, the teacher, the therapist and group leader all instruct by metaphor. By spinning tales of what other people do, the therapist introduces his clients to the realities of hope. "His metaphors and parables make it necessary for the pilgrims who would be disciples to turn to their own imaginations in the search for meaning in their lives" (Kopp, 1972, p. 13).

Images of water and of heartbeats create powerfully influential and enduring thought patterns. Each time group members become aware of their hearts beating, they are reminded of how they waste their present moments in needless suffering. Every time they think of water cascading down a waterfall or feel it massaging their bodies in the shower, they are reminded of nature's indifference. Whenever they inflate things out of proportion to reality, imagine disaster or worry, or take anything too seriously, they can think humbly of water and heartbeats. These enduring metaphors act as time-release medications, flowing through the bloodstream long after the group sessions have ended.

Stories need not even make sense to be effective in facilitating change. Sometimes the most ambiguous, obscure metaphors can have the greatest effect.

> The last time I went to see Milton Erickson, he said something to me. And as I was sitting there in front of him, it didn't make sense. Most of his covert metaphors have made . . . eons of sense to me. But he said something to me which would have taken me awhile to figure out. Milton said to me "You don't consider yourself a therapist, but you are a therapist." And I said "Well, not really." He said "Well, let's pretend . . . that you're a therapist who works with people. The most important thing . . . when you're pretending this . . . is to understand . . . that you are *really* not . . . you are just pretending . . . and if you pretend really well, the people that you work with will pretend to make changes. And they will forget that they are pretending . . . for the rest of their lives. But don't you be fooled by it." (Bandler & Grinder, 1979, p. 136)

The Sufi Master, a spiritual and religious group leader of the East, relies almost exclusively on the use of parables to bring enlightenment to group members. According to Einhorn (1979), the instrumental functions of such therapeutic tales include promoting psychological shocks to group members by exposing their unconscious motives, invalidated feelings, and spiritual inertia. The Sufi stories contain themes that are purported to connect with the "essence" of the group. These "internal dimensions" help promote self-awareness and insight on hidden levels. They stimulate discussion of significant themes and help group members confront their foolish behavior:

> Nasrudin is sitting in his living room when an eagle alights on his windowsill. Having only seen pigeons before, he regards the bird as a misshapen pigeon. "What an unfortunate bird!" he exclaims, "Someone has neglected you!" Fetching his scissors, he trims its magnificent beak and talons. "There," he says with satisfaction, "Now you look more like a bird." (Williams, 1971)

The Chinese proverb that one picture is worth a thousand words is also true of metaphors, which are verbal pictures—concise, purposeful images that convey vivid messages. But metaphorical pictures are abstract, left open for many possible interpretations. They are powerful communicative devices for promoting insight, motivating action, or initiating group interaction precisely because they can be personally applicable to each individual.

The best stories have always been those with many different symbolic meanings. They not only transmit cultural information but have morals as do Aesop's *Fables*, themes as do Grimms's fairy tales, or lessons as do Homer's parables. In our technological world, film has replaced the campfire as the most common storytelling medium. People leave theaters with tears or smiles. Through the process of identification, they conquer armies, slay dragons, and win lovers, all the while munching popcorn in an airconditioned room.

All stories, whether in the form of metaphor, parable, epic poem, fable, song, novel, or tale, have a protagonist who must resolve a conflict by overcoming obstacles (Gordon, 1978). For the audience, confronted by equivalent personal struggles, dramatic metaphors provide an illuminated path through the dark unknown. They offer hope, stimulate action, and sometimes even offer specific solutions that can be adapted for personal use.

Waldren, McElmurry, Bowens, and Israel (1980) note that the reading of children's stories to college-age students reduces their level of tension, facilitates discussion of sensitive issues, cements peer relationships, and helps them relive the magic of being read bedtime stories. In the dormitories, students gather together in their pajamas with cuddly stuffed animals while a guest group leader reads from a favorite children's book such as *The Cat in the Hat*, *The Little Prince*, *The Wind in the Willows*, *The Gnome from Nome*, or *The Giving Tree*. Hidden within the pictures and prose of childen's stories are often found wonderfully powerful metaphors for grown-ups. *The Velveteen Rabbit* tells how toys become real:

> "What is REAL?" asked the Rabbit one day, when they were lying side by side near the nursery fender, before Nana came to tidy the room. "Does it mean having things that buzz inside you and a stick-out handle?"
> "Real isn't how you are made," said the Skin Horse. "It's a thing that happens to you. When a child loves you for a long, long time, not just to play with, but REALLY loves you, then you become Real."
> "Does it hurt?" asked the Rabbit.

"Sometimes," said the Skin Horse, for he was always truthful. "When you are Real you don't mind being hurt."

"Does it happen all at once, like being wound up," he asked, "or bit by bit?"

"It doesn't happen all at once," said the Skin Horse. "You become. It takes a long time. That's why it doesn't often happen to people who break easily, or have sharp edges, or have to be carefully kept. Generally, by the time you are real, most of your hair has been loved off, and your eyes drop out and you get loose in the joints and very shabby. But these things don't matter at all, because once you are real you can't be ugly, except to people who don't understand." (Williams, 1975, pp. 16–17)*

The astute group leader can do a lot with the metaphoric messages in the previous passage. In a group of college sophomores, the discussion revolved among several intense issues.

> **Ellen**: My boyfriend treats me like a shabby old toy, but I don't think it's exactly because he loves me.
>
> **David**: That brought back such vivid memories of the freedom I had as a kid. It was so much fun to stay locked in my room and occupy myself all day long, talking to my toys as if they were my best friends. Now my life is so damn complicated I don't even have the time to talk to myself.
>
> **Julio**: Sometimes I just don't know what is real anymore. Are all of you real or just figments of my imagination? You sure don't act real with all the games that are played in this group. Or, maybe I'm just like the rabbit who wants to be real. I'm just a wind-up toy with a busted spring.
>
> **Lia**: If you've got to be hurt to be real, I don't want any part of that nonsense. I've been dropped on my head so many times I can't feel my brain any longer. Oh, I've tried to be real with people before; but every time I act up-front and honest, I end up vulnerable and rejected. I think it's better to stay away from reality; fantasy is a lot more fun.
>
> **Dan**: That was one heavy-duty little story. If I understand what it's all about, I think it's saying that to be real you have to take risks, you have to love without fear. There are those of us in this group who act fragile or have sharp edges, and until we stop being afraid of getting broken we will never learn to love ourselves, much less anyone else.

Techniques for Using Metaphors

Milton Erickson, the consummate storyteller who used metaphors as a primary therapeutic device, found almost unlimited uses for various types of anecdotes. These uses included expressing various points in a language

*Excerpt from *The Velveteen Rabbit* by Margery Williams. Reprinted by permission of Doubleday & Company, Inc.

that clients were more willing to attend to, suggesting solutions to problems indirectly, inspiring or motivating action, seeding ideas that could be used later, and circumventing conscious resistance to access more receptive unconscious processes (Zeig, 1986). To this list, Barker (1985) adds a number of other uses for metaphors, all of which are summarized with examples in Table 11-1.

Team Building

In addition to the uses of metaphors described in Table 11-1, there are also adaptations of the process that are particularly well suited to groups. It has even been said that the whole context for therapeutic groups is a metaphor, in that whereas the leader must tune into the life of each individual at the same time, each disclosure also has relevance for the group as a whole (Cox & Theilgaard, 1987). "In the early group, the *circle* serves as the congealing image of commonality and unity that brings and holds disparate individuals together in purposeful community. As the group begins to formulate norms and catalytically questions its aims and operations, the container must become a flexible and malleable *crucible* allowing and restraining the diverse and bubbly energies within. In the working phase of group, the container must be a *mortar* in which grinds the pestle of change. In the final stages of group, the container can no longer greedily hold the mead of the group mix, but rather as a *pitcher*, must pour energies and substance back into the diversity of life's various holds" (Ettin, 1987, p. 424).

Table 11-1 Therapeutic uses of metaphors

Type of Metaphor	Example
Suggest indirectly	Telling a story in which the protagonist acts as the client could in a parallel situation
Inspire motivation	Relating an anecdote in which a character has overcome similar problems
Seed ideas	Introducing a nugget of an idea that can be referred to later
Access unconscious	Using strongly symbolic themes that are not immediately obvious
Decrease resistance	Gradually and ambiguously describing an idea that is too complex to be rejected capriciously
Reframe problems	Using a story to redefine the way in which issues are understood or handled
Model effectiveness	Describing characters with qualities similar to client but with added dimensions
Desensitize fears	Telling anecdotes in which fears are gradually brought under control

In order to build a spirit of team cooperation, cohesion, and shared intimacy, participants develop their own language system, complete with an invented jargon that helps define their unique identity. Metaphors become a significant part of this group vocabulary; they symbolize the past that has been shared and represent a shortcut to bringing specific themes to collective attention.

Shared Language

Attending to the metaphors embedded in client speech and in the larger language of the group creates a distinct culture. A culture, after all, is organized around its language system; the metaphors, similes, and descriptors contained therein provide evidence of what people think of themselves and of their group identity.

Gladding (1984) distinguishes between two kinds of metaphors that emerge in group settings. The first are *borrowed* metaphors, in which a group member introduces an image from another context: "That reminds me of a line from. . . ". The second are *original* metaphors, those that are constructed spontaneously from interpersonal action: "We are struts for one another, structural links that each support us as a whole. When a single link loses its flexibility or strength, the whole structure of our group sways in the wind."

Metaphors such as the latter become the unique language of a group culture. They create a pool of shared knowledge, a form of coded communication that expresses the common experience of participants. Once a metaphor is adopted into group lore, it is revisited again and again as a source of inspiration and understanding; it becomes a model to explain the unique ways in which members function in relation to one another. In the following interchange, a group member responds to another who is discussing his floundering marriage.

> **First member**: It's like my wife's nagging is wearing me down to the point that I can't hold up my end of this group. That's why I'm so irritable. My wife is the rain, or even a torrential hurricane, and I am that single strut bending, rusting, losing its grip as bolts snap loose in the wind.
>
> **Second member**: Yes, that may be the way it feels to you—as if you are alone, blowing in the wind. The reality, however, is that you are connected to each one of us. As you waver, we just hold on tighter until you can once again retain your balance.

This metaphoric language of the group continues to evolve as each person contributes a part. It is a frame of reference that influences how members view themselves in relation to each other. This metaphor remains in the mind of each participant long after the group has ended. It is the lasting souvenir of the journey that they took together.

Utilizing Cultural Worldviews

In an article on the use of cultural metaphors, or *dichos*, with Spanish-speaking clientele, Zuniga (1991) found that these proverbs package wisdom in ways that reflect the values of a people: "El miedo no anda en burro" ("fear does not ride on a burro"). We are not expected to be fluent in the metaphors of each client's culture; rather, we must consult with group members to help them mine the dichos from their own past, especially those that offer fortified strength in the face of stressful situations.

One of the most marvelous side effects of participation in a group is not only that members work on their own individual issues and grow as a result of vicarious learning by observing others at work, but also that they have the opportunity to become more culturally educated about people from diverse backgrounds. If groups are to offer assistance to any member there should be a requirement that everyone become functionally literate in the language, customs, and even dichos of each participant. Thus, during the final session of a group of middle-school children, in which each partici-pant was disclosing what he or she learned as a result of the group ex-perience, one child who had been fairly quiet during most of the sessions disclosed: "I know I didn't say much but I sure learned a lot." He was then pressed by the others who seemed skeptical: "Like what?" He proceeded to recite some of the favorite cultural expressions he had memorized from this culturally diverse group of children, including sayings from Yiddish, from African-American street language, from Mexican-American and Cuban Spanish, and even from the group leader who was of Irish descent.

Reciprocal Positioning

Metaphors are also ideal structures for communication in groups because of the opportunities that arise in groups to interpret interactional patterns. Metaphors can thus be reciprocally constructed to reflect the complemen-tary positions of two or more people in a relationship. In a therapeutic pro-cess designed to represent relational choreography as a metaphor, Papp (1982) asks couples to visualize one another in symbolic form, each identi-fying a form in relation to the other. Afterward, the partners may be asked to imagine a dance or to enact a fantasy in the group that represents their characteristic interactions. They are then helped to reflect on the central themes that emerged, the reciprocal positions of each person in relation to the other, and how their relative positions are maintained. Papp advocates this metaphoric method not only as a diagnostic tool to identify interactive patterns but also as a way to measure change over time.

Imagine, for example, a couple who originally viewed their pattern of interaction as that between a cat and a mouse; the couple later changed this image to a more egalitarian relationship, such as that of the land and the sea. Groups are especially fertile ground for creating and acting out these reciprocal metaphors.

Illustration and Reinforcement

Certain themes predictably recur in groups. The question "Whom can I trust?" always arises, as does the fear that any progress made will be short-lived. It is not uncommon, and perhaps not unrealistic, for clients to believe that they will eventually slip back to self-defeating behavior patterns in spite of the momentum that has been created. Again, some group members will inevitably express a concern related to approval seeking or psychological dependence. And does there exist a single group in which at least one person is not having difficulty cutting an overprotective parent's apron strings?

The issues of parental dominance and destructive dependence can be approached in several ways. We can give a mini-lecture on the subject or lead eventually into an opportunity for rehearsal confrontation in the group. Whichever strategy is preferred, therapists are always hungry for verbal images to illustrate major themes dramatically.

So much have we been talked to in our lives, so many lectures and so much advice given, that we remember very little of it all. While geometric proofs and algebraic formulas come and go in our memories, the image of our math teacher doing something strange remains indelible. To ensure that group members will forever remember crucial therapeutic messages, particular tales can be collected to illustrate themes. Dyer (1976) is fond of stimulating psychological independence by relating an anecdote that demonstrates the masterful behavior he is discussing.

> Walt Disney produced a superb film some years ago entitled *Bear Country*. It traced a mother bear and her two babies through the first few months of the cubs' lives. Mama-bear taught the cubs how to hunt, fish, and climb trees. She taught them how to protect themselves when they confronted danger. Then one day, Mama-bear, for her own instinctive reasons, decided that it was time to leave. She forced them to scamper up a tree, and without even looking back, she left. Forever! In her own bear mind, she had completed her parental responsibilities. She didn't try to manipulate them into visiting her on alternate Sundays. She did not accuse them of being ungrateful, or threaten to have a nervous breakdown if they disappointed her. She simply let them go. (p. 191)

Promoting Insight

Much of what is called client resistance is in fact the awkward attempt of a therapist to effect change. Insight and self-awareness often hurt; it is painful to confront discrepancies between what we have always believed to be truth and what we now learn is delusion. This revelation often forces a domino effect: altering one part of a system changes the whole system.

When a group member declares that he has for years been stifling his wife by trying to make her fit into his mold, he also suggests that this is a condition he will have to change. If this man is to discover the destructive pattern of his behavior, he must do so in a way that will be palatable to him. Metaphorical anecdotes offer a way of diplomatically confronting clients with their foibles so that they will be more willing to listen with both ears. The man might not respond to being directly confronted with the destructive interdependence of his marriage, but he may be willing to listen to a story with a similar theme.

Dominance always creates victims. Threats and aggression provoke open or smoldering hostility. One human being who seeks to dominate and control another will eventually encounter rebellion. A point comes when a person will no longer accept being ordered about; a child, a spouse, a prisoner will eventually realize there is nothing left to lose. Alexander Solzhenitsyn skillfully relates the determined resistance of a person without power, freedom, or independence. The interrogator dominates by the threat of consequences until the prisoner refuses to play the game any longer.

> "Listen, don't go too far just because I choose to be polite to you. . . ."
>
> "If you were rude to me I wouldn't talk to you at all. You can shout at your colonels and your generals as much as you like because they've got plenty to lose."
>
> "We can deal with your sort too if we have to."
>
> "No you can't." Bobykin's piercing eyes flashed with hatred. "I've got nothing, see? Nothing! You can't touch my wife and child—they were killed by a bomb. My parents are dead. I own nothing in the world except a handkerchief. These denims and this underwear—which hasn't even got any buttons"—he bared his chest to show what he meant—"is government issue. You took my freedom away a long time ago and you can't give it back to me because you haven't got it yourself. I'm forty-two years old. You gave me twenty-five years. I've done hard labor, I know what it is to have a number instead of a name, to be handcuffed, to be guarded by dogs, to work in a punitive brigade—what more can you do to me? Take me off this special project? You'd be the loser. I need a smoke." (Solzhenitsyn, 1968, p. 106)*

Listening Landscape

Another kind of metaphor is one that is inadvertently supplied by group members themselves. In classical psychodynamic fashion, a client's choice of words creates a profound image, but it is unlike the Freudian connection that starts on the surface and moves to deeper levels. As poet Gaston Bachelard wrote, "the image has touched the depths before it stirs the surface" (Quoted in Cox & Theilgaard, 1987, p. xiii).

In their communications about their predicaments, group members will often describe behaviors that unwittingly create metaphors for themes in their lives; it's up to the leader to recognize the pattern. For example, an adolescent who has been caught stealing a number of times relates that the only thing he takes are people's personal objects, their most intimate possessions—photographs, charms, underwear, a piece of worthless jewelry. The boy is without friends or much experience with intimacy. His actions, as is true in so many instances, are a metaphor for what he is searching for. As he tells his story, other group members are quick to help him understand the underlying meaning of his behavior. This could only occur, however, in a group in which the leader has educated the members to be sensitive to and recognize metaphoric communication in themselves and in others. A "listening landscape" is created in which perception is attuned to the symbols and subtleties contained in speech.

Evoking Interest

From Aristotle and Greek mythology to the Bible, metaphoric communication has been the most interesting way to get points across. Well-constructed narratives can be inspirational in encouraging people to think about or do things they would not have considered before. In addition to this point, Barker (1985) has also listed a number of time-honored reasons that metaphors are such an important part of therapeutic endeavors: for one, they are perceived as less threatening than direct communications, since their messages are ambiguous; for another, using metaphors requires the client's more active participation, supplying meaning when a number of options are possible.

> **Group leader**: This group has become a kind of sanctuary for the wounded.
> **Member 1**: (Angrily) What do you mean by that?
> **Group leader**: What does that mean to *you*?
> **Member 1**: That you are calling me wounded.
> **Group leader**: That is one possible interpretation. What does my observation say to the rest of you?
> **Member 2**: That it feels safe here, a place for us to lick our wounds.
> **Member 3**: I was thinking more along the lines that we—I mean I— act like a victim here, complaining about what the world has done to me.
> **Member 4**: Yeah, and we treat each other like walking wounded, afraid to confront one another; (to group leader) is that what you meant?
> **Group leader**: Perhaps.

The meaning of metaphors is created by the listeners as they fill in missing details and interpret the stimulus from a personal perspective. This process can even take place unconsciously, in which a message that is too threatening to hear in more simple communication may be conveyed indirectly (Gordon, 1978). Thus parables, anecdotes, and fairy tales help clients construct their own solutions by reflecting on what the story means to them personally (Bettelheim, 1977).

Group Discussion on a Focused Issue

In quick succession, several group members disclose their dependency problems in various relationships, a theme of several recent sessions. Some members complain about how little say they have in their lives; others wish that their spouses or lovers would take a more active role. One woman feels helpless because she must wait for her husband to initiate sex. A meek gentleman whispers that he wishes he could spend more time alone without his wife ordering him about. Others describe how they are so melded to their spouses that they have lost their sense of personal identity. Everything is togetherness at the exclusion of separateness. Everything is "we," "if you want to, dear," and "O.K., I'll be right with you."

The group leader can initiate a theme-oriented group session related to dependent love relationships by introducing a metaphor borrowed from biology.

> The self-marking of invertebrate animals in the sea, who must have perfected the business long before evolution got around to us, was set up in order to permit creatures of one kind to locate others, not for predation but to set up symbiotic households. The anemones who live on the shells of crabs are precisely finicky; so are the crabs. Only a single species of anemone will find its way to only a single species of crab. They sense each other exquisitely, and live together as though made for each other.
>
> Sometimes there is such a mix-up about selfness that two creatures, each attracted by the molecular configuration of the other, incorporate the two selves to make a single organism. . . . And, more surprising, they cannot live in any other way; they depend for their survival on each other. They are not really selves; they are specific *others*. (Thomas, 1979, pp. 4–5)

This account of collaboration between the nudibranch sea slug and the medusa jellyfish in the Bay of Naples is a wonderful metaphor for explaining interdependent relationships in marriages. If one partner becomes destructively parasitic, the collaboration abruptly ends, to the dissatisfaction of both species. Yet by completely pooling their resources, they also lose their sense of identity. Similarly, when two human beings live together, each with separate bodies and individual needs, they too must reach a state of mutual compromise allowing both to flourish.

The tone is then set to pursue the interdependency topic further. Participants can collectively brainstorm about the causes of the conflicts, how they may be handled, and which strategies may prove most successful in resolving the issues.

Countering Self-Defeating Thinking

Many people demand that the world conform to their needs and expectations. They engage in chronically irrational thought patterns, deluding themselves that they occupy the center of the universe. Like spoiled 2-year-olds, they believe that Mommy, Daddy, Humpty Dumpty, and all the King's Men were put on Earth to cater to their every whim. They surrender their intellect in the delusional pursuit of some abstraction known as Truth or Justice, at least for themselves. (This, of course, is but one of many possible thought distortions common in client behavior.)

But truth, according to Nietzsche (1864/1972), is a worn-out illusion that no longer has the power to affect the senses. All language, all thought, is metaphorical. We translate a sense perception into an image, then metaphorically name this thing, even give it a masculine or feminine gender. In the chaos around us we attempt to make order to justify our existence, as if it needs an excuse. To the client who exaggerates self-importance and thus feels a need to inflate the significance of every act, Nietzsche offers a metaphorical challenge. Although certainty of knowledge would be nice and absolute prediction would be convenient, the reality of daily life provides only ambiguity and frustration. And ambiguity is, after all, what metaphors are all about.

> In some remote corner of the universe, effused into innumerable solar-systems, there was once a star upon which clever animals invented cognition. It was the haughtiest, most mendacious moment in the history of this world, but yet only a moment. After Nature had taken breath awhile the star congealed and the clever animals had to die.—Someone might write a fable after this style, and yet he would not have illustrated sufficiently, how wretched, shadow-like, transitory, purposeless and fanciful the human intellect appears in Nature. . . . Nothing in Nature is so bad or so insignificant that it will not, at the smallest puff of that force cognition, immediately swell up like a ballon, and just as a mere porter wants to have his admirer, so the very proudest man, the philosopher, imagines he sees from all sides the eyes of the universe telescopically directed upon his actions and thoughts. (Nietzsche, 1864/1972, p. 1)

Because metaphors are literary devices, their frequent use can excite clients to continue their renaissance education by exploring literature. Whereas there are specific instances when metaphors can be optimally beneficial, such as to englighten or entertain, verbal images can also provoke change if they are carefully constructed.

The Structure of Metaphors

Metaphors began to take on a therapeutic value under Freud and his fellow psychoanalysts, who realized that the world's great literary classics offered symbolic allusions to the major themes of human conflict. During the decade following Freud's death, Milton Erickson began systematic clinical investigations of the role that metaphors could play in therapeutic communication. He devised hypnotic routines by which to promote unconscious changes in subjects, noting that the structure of language in metaphors, the precise choice of words and vocal intonation, were as important to the cure as was the metaphor's theme. Thus, sharing an anecdote reached dizzying levels of complexity in the Erickson technique.

> The words, by their arrangement into phrases, clauses, and sentences, and even their introductory, transitional, and repetitive uses, could be made to serve special purposes: building up emphasis or cutting it short, establishing contrasts, similarities, parallelisms, identifications, and equations of one idea to another, all of which would effect a building up of a series of associations and emotional responses stimulated, but not aroused directly, one idea to another, sequential relationships of various ideas, and objects, shifts of responsibility and action from one character to another; the use of words that threatened, challenged, distracted, or served only to delay the development of the narrative were all employed to formulate a story possessing a significance beyond its formal content. (Erickson, 1944, p. 312)

Erickson might pronounce the word *you* to involve the client in the story gently; he might later use the command *you will* as part of the narrative when he is really offering the client a therapeutic suggestion. Enunciating the single word *you* in the metaphor takes on the significance of a double entendre, a directive, an invitation for identification, a distraction, and a reinforcer. Erickson used anecdotes and metaphors as a subtle way to promote change at preconscious levels. He planted cued images in clients' brains that would later help to make previously unacceptable ideas more palatable.

The construction of metaphors in therapy has become even more complicated and so much more than just telling a little story to highlight a point. Gordon (1978) provides a blueprint for clinicians interested in weaving metaphors in their work that includes attention to syntactic patterns, referential indexes, imbedded markings, nominalizations, unspecified verbs, contextual cues, recalibration of recursive situations, isomorphism, transderivational searches, synthesia, and intradimensional shifts. In an even more challenging system (if you thought that were possible), Cox and Theilgaard (1987) introduce concepts such as the Aeolian Mode, poiesis, aesthetic imperatives, points of urgency, paronomasia, deictic stress, and cryptophors that can be included in metaphoric narratives.

Given all the other stimuli to which group leaders must direct their attention, creating elaborately constructed metaphorical tales is probably not as likely (or even appropriate) as would be true in individual sessions. If these narratives have as much power to promote change as the practitioners claim, and if they must be so specifically designed to the needs and situation of a specific client, it is clearly not likely that a group setting is the place for this type of intervention. Although a story may be directed to one particular member, a much larger audience is listening. Such use would be similar to a physician gathering together the dozen patients waiting for appointments, examining the first who has a strep infection, and then prescribing antibiotics for everyone in the room.

A good rule of thumb to consider is that any metaphor that we use for a single client in the group also has to have some utility for the other members as well.

Characteristics of Effective Metaphors

Metaphoric language provides clues about the stage of group development that is currently in operation, as well as information about individual members' internal states. Metaphors provide a retreat from emotionally charged situations, allow for much more complex communication, consolidate ideas into images, and sometimes even suggest solutions to group problems (McClure, 1989a). They provide easier access to inner processes and enhance the range and power of therapeutic interventions (Ettin, 1987). They are less threatening ways to explore threatening material from a safe distance (Boyd, 1990; Rossel, 1981b).

Group leaders have choices regarding how to facilitate members' awareness that metaphoric communication is occurring. Leaders can: (1) label what is taking place, interpreting possible meanings ("This could mean . . ."); (2) involve members in the process of illuminating ("I wonder what this means?"); or (3) match the figurative language that is being used ("So this *thunderstorm* that stopped you from venturing outside. . ."). In stating his preference for employing this third option whenever possible, McClure (1987) argues that resistance is more often circumvented and the complexity of the full communication preserved if leaders stay with the members' own metaphoric language.

Before we do anything with a metaphor, it is important to acknowledge the inherent risks of this kind of intervention (McClure, 1989b). Because metaphoric communication is often employed to deal with risky material, bringing things out in the open can be perceived as threatening. Also, there are problems inherent in taking a complex visual phenomenon and trying to reduce it to a single verbal interpretation. Obviously, given the limitations of language, much can be lost in the translation. Last, as with all insight-oriented strategies, we must consider whether the need for explicit understanding comes from member needs or from the leader's own preference to make sense of what is going on.

The best metaphors have three features: they present unconscious fantasies, they combine abstract and concrete elements that progress from what is known to what is unknown, and they elicit some degree of affective insight

(Siegelman, 1990). Metaphors are also more helpful if clients can see a visceral connection to a body sensation, a vital connection between prose and passion (Shengold, 1981).

Metaphors convey abstract ideas as visual images, usually as new ways of seeing something in a different light. In order for this transformation to take place, for affective insight to occur, the images must be vivid in their descriptions. But more than have the poetic and powerful primacy of the description, a metaphor must carry a compelling therapeutic message.

Metaphors are most likely to be influential if they are deliberately vague in their use of nominalizations, unspecified verbs, and referential indexes. Group members can personalize the themes to fit their unique situations if they are allowed to fill in the details. Gordon recommends that if the details of a description are insignificant to the major themes of the story, the description should be left ambiguous so that clients have the freedom to visualize the scene according to their perceptual preferences.

Effective metaphors are concise and efficient, using the fewest possible words to convey the most powerful images. They are an economical form of communciation insofar as they say more than ordinary language but in a more memorable way. In *The Executioner's Song* (1979), for example, Norman Mailer succinctly describes the reactions of two friends listening to a story Gary Gilmore tells about his antics in prison: "Brenda and Johnny's smiles had become as congealed as the grease on a cold steak" (p. 68).

Good metaphors are both appropriate to the situation and tailored to the audience. They are designed to heighten certain aspects of a message in a manner that will be best received by the listeners. Goldberg (1990) has cataloged a whole collection of such metaphors that could be useful to group leaders in their efforts to stimulate client insight and change. Some of his more interesting entries include: "the Achilles syndrome," the tendency of a group member to deny weak spots and thereby repeat the same mistakes; or the "Nimby reaction" (as in Not In My Back Yard), in which members of a group are all placing blame on one another for the collective garbage that has accumulated.

Ettin (1987) especially likes the way that metaphoric language can be used by group leaders to depict client experiences more graphically without triggering defensive reactions. In dealing with one client who was reticent to reveal herself in the group, Ettin attempted to draw her in by highlighting her consistent posture within the group: "Judy was told that she appeared as a vase, a shiny container (capable of holding many things, e-vasive, bright, and commanding attention), with a lacquered finish (a thick and hard veneer used for protection), placed on a high dresser (projections of superiority and removal from the normal traffic of living, isolated, protected from being smashed or looked into)" (Ettin, 1987, p. 411).

Ettin points out how this image helped the leader express feedback in a capsulized form. He reports that this intervention then became a turning point for Judy, in which she described her lifelong feelings of vulnerability.

Even more interesting, she maintained parallel metaphoric language in which she expressed her fears of having her fears "smashed."

With the advent of even more refinements in metaphor construction, including such techniques as intradimensional shifts, recalibration, Satir categories, synesthesia, submodality crossovers, anchors, triggers, and reality-stackings, the simple art of storytelling seems startingly complex. Whatever happened to lullabies and bedtime stories? In spite of technological breakthroughs and scientific methodologies, the creation of metaphors will forever be an artistic enterprise, a showpiece of human communication and therapeutic action.

CHAPTER 12

The Uses of Humor in Groups

Counseling and therapy are notoriously serious businesses, involving tears, anguish, guilt, conflict, deceit, suicide, violence, helplessness, and turmoil. Therapists add little comic relief to lighten the aura of despair. The traditional stereotypes of pipes, tweed jackets, white lab coats, omnipotent nods, framed diplomas, book-lined walls, and the cliniclike odors aren't exactly conducive to a good time. But clients aren't paying to have a good time. They want to suffer and do penance, and we are to keep them in line.

There are medications for the balance of mood alterations, straitjackets and wet sheets for discipline, shock treatments for control, and verbal spankings for suppression of individual initiative. Mental institutions are particularly instructive examples of how the mental health profession frowns on laughter. Rachel, who passed her adolescence in a mental hospital, reports that humor was strictly forbidden. Although humor became an underground form of rebellion on the wards, inmates were repeatedly warned: "This is no laughing matter. You know where you are, don't you?" Yet humor was the only way to maintain sanity in an insane place. By making fun of her predicament, ridiculing the staff, and laughing at herself, Rachel was able to exercise minimal control over her life, to pretend she had freedom in a completely powerless situation.

Ironically, although patients are not allowed to laugh at themselves or at us, it is socially acceptable for the public to laugh at them. We appear to find emotionally disturbed people amusing and entertaining. A partial list of insensitive terms that have been invented for referring to clients is absolutely staggering—crazy, demented, bonzo, parboiled, out-to-lunch, space cadet, been visited upstairs, few pickles shy of a barrel, spacey, playing without a full deck, whacko, veged out, goggle-eyed, freaked out, and punchy, to name but a few.

We are allowed to laugh at them, but they aren't allowed to laugh at us, their keepers? ''Exactly,'' Rachel replies. ''You see, on the wards, the only time we were given official permission to laugh was in our therapy group—when the shrink told a joke. If we slipped up at any other time we were tied in wet sheets or punished in some other devious ways for 'resisting treatment.' ''

When humor is mentioned at all, some of the literature of psychotherapy claims that it impedes therapeutic progress. Unless carefully monitored and kept in control, humor can ''mask hostility behind a false facade,'' block the client's stream of feeling, confuse a client who is unable to determine when the therapist is serious, interfere with free association, ''restrict the range of the patient's responses,'' be used as a defense for handling anxiety, diminish the importance of a client's illness, bottle up repressed anger, and encourage the therapist to be self-indulgent, exhibitionistic, and hostile (Kubie, 1971). Might it also cause cancer?

True, there may be some danger in abusing humor within groups because it makes ridicule easier and may waste valuable time if things stay silly for too long. There are also a few leaders who use their groups as a stage for themselves to win appreciative applause. In his scathing criticism of humor in therapy, Kubie (1971) reluctantly admits that most abuses occur among beginning practitioners. Among more experienced therapists, humor can be an effective tool. The group leader who is aware of the many potential abuses of humor may use it judiciously to accomplish various therapeutic functions.

Uses and Abuses of Humor

Bloch, Browning, and McGrath (1983) note ten different ways that humor can be used in groups: some related to the leader, some to the member, and some to the group as a whole. Similarly, Bloch and his associates also identify the ways that these same categories of humor can be misused (see Table 12-1).

Leader-related uses and abuses of humor are illustrated in the case of a therapist who inserts self-deprecating comic relief during periods of undue criticism on the part of the members. This same transparency can also become a narcissistic self-display if the intent is to keep the focus on oneself and the effect is to sabotage group progress.

Member-related exhibitions of humor are evident when certain clients have lost their sense of perspective, exaggerating the significance of an event in their lives. In coming to the rescue, another member may attempt to lighten the grimness on the one hand or engage in distracting clownish behavior on the other. Another common occurrence is that one member is repeatedly ridiculed.

Table 12-1 The uses and misuses of humor in groups

Uses	Misuses
Leader-Related	
Modeling—demonstrating spontaneity, lightheartedness, and attitudes conducive to good humor	*Defense*—against one's own discomfort and anxiety
Transparency—revealing humanness and warmth through discreet and thoughtful self-revelations	*Aggression*—hostile or punitive behavior, such as sarcasm or belittling
Interpretation—introducing an incongruent image to stimulate alternative views	*Self-display*—meeting one's own needs to be liked or to have attention
	Confusion—distracting focus through digressive humor
Member-Related	
Sense of proportion—lightening a client's despair and exaggerated perspective	*Clowning*—member's attempt to win approval and attention at expense of others
Overearnestness—diluting a client's rigidity and gravity through playfulness	*Scapegoating*—making one member the butt of jokes
Social skills—improving clients' capacity for appreciation of the sublime and the absurd	*Self-mockery*—avoiding painful issues by mocking oneself
Self-disclosure—indirect and disguised sharing of self in less threatening communication	
Group-Related	
Cohesiveness—shared experience of laughter to promote acceptance and belongingness	*Frivolousness*—silly, carefree behavior that avoids important work and issues
Group dynamics—making themes and processes more explicit through humor	*Irrelevance*—wastes time by focusing on irrelevant aspects of subject
Tension reduction—reduced discomfort and anxiety associated with taboo subjects	

Source: Adapted from "Humor in Group Psychotherapy" by S. Bloch, S. Browning, and G. McGrath. In the *British Journal of Medical Psychology*, 56, pp. 89–97. Copyright © 1983 by the British Psychological Association.

Group-related humor, at its best, becomes the glue that can bind people together through "in-jokes" and shared laughter. At its worst, humor can become frivolous and prevent the group from conducting its work-related tasks. As the Martian discovers in Heinlein's classic novel, *Stranger in a Strange Land*, the most perplexing aspect of human culture is humor: What makes humans laugh? Finally, while at the zoo observing a chimpanzee beat another unmercifully, the Martian breaks out in raucous laughter, much to the consternation of his guide. He has finally understood that humor is usually made at someone else's expense.

Indeed, many jokes are barely disguised racial, ethnic, or gender slurs in which others are ridiculed. These are usually expressions of hostility or derision (Rossel, 1981a). Bad humor can also lead to silliness, wasted time, distractions, digressions, competitiveness, resentment, and retribution (Napier & Gershenfeld, 1989). For these reasons, the safest kind of humor in groups is that which is directed toward oneself (Machan, 1987) and avoids ridicule (Duncan, 1985). Foster (1980) has created a continuum of therapeutic humor in groups that summarizes the range of possible applications from destructive abuse (Level 1) to constructive use (Level 5). This diversity of possible applications is described in Table 12-2.

In a systematic effort to study what types of humor are beneficial in groups, Peterson and Pollio (1982) rated occurrences of members' laughter and smiling by reviewing videotaped sessions. They discovered, among other things, that incidences of humor occurred about once every two minutes and that 75% of humorous remarks had a specific target, the majority of which were negative in tone and appeared to inhibit therapeutic effectiveness. They concluded their study by suggesting the following paradigm for understanding the various functions of humor in different contexts:

When humor is targeted toward another group member. . .   it signifies a request for redirection in group focus or level of intensity.

When humor is directed toward someone outside the group. . .   the result is greater cohesion and bonding among members.

When humor is targeted at oneself. . .   it can mean several possible things.

The latter form of humor may imply a request for redirection away from or toward the person initiating the joke; or it may be used to facilitate or inhibit therapeutic work, depending on motive, style, and effect. The fact that humor definitely can be used to enhance or nullify group goals seems clearer in the other two varieties of humor. The implications of this study are that group leaders need to monitor closely the kinds of humor that are in evidence, the frequency of their occurrence, the parity with which humor is distributed among members, and most important, the impact humor has on accomplishing therapeutic goals. We need to be especially vigilant about discouraging humor that may be distracting or self-indulgent, whether it is associated with the leader, the members, or the group process as a whole.

Table 12-2 A continuum of therapeutic humor in groups

Destructive Humor			Constructive Humor	
Level 1	Level 2	Level 3	Level 4	Level 5
Humor is hostile, tasteless, or derisive; puts a group member down or ridicules an ethnic, sex, or minority group; causes withdrawal and emotional damage	Detracts from client concerns; is irrelevant and ill-timed; wastes valuable group time; is self-indulgent; results in "polite," false laughter; masks true feelings	Mild sense of group member appreciation; alleviates boredom; group members acknowledge humor	Humor deeply appreciated by group members; much spontaneous laughter; cohesion develops; more relaxed atmosphere; strengthened relationships; greater willingness to explore relationships	Humor transcends laughter; provides major insight and self-awareness to group members; significantly moves a client toward action

Source: Adapted from "Humor and Counseling: Close Encounters of Another Kind" by J. A. Foster. In *Personnel and Guidance Journal,* September 1978, pp. 46–49.

Therapeutic Effects of Humor

What is this strange behavioral display that involves, in Desmond Morris's (1977) observation, howling, hooting, barking, wrinkled nostrils, weeping, crinkled lips, closed eyes, and a stamping foot? Koestler (1964) adds to the description "the co-ordinated contraction of fifteen facial muscles in a stereotyped pattern and accompanied by altered breathing" (p. 29). Bierce (1911/1940) further defines it as "An interior convulsion, producing a distortion of the features and accompanied by inarticulate noises. It is infectious and, though intermittent, incurable" (p. 75).

Laughter is a discharge of energy that results from sustained tension. It eases strains and shock. It is a means of handling the incongruous, unexpected, awkward, disorderly, and nonsensical. As reviewed by Hertzler (1970), laughter also serves many useful social purposes. It is among the most expressive forms of communication. It may convey quiet appreciation or self-assurance. It may indicate shame or embarrassment, delight or exhilaration. It may signify shock, surprise, exuberance, incredulity, or nervousness. In group situations, laughter may communicate warmth and friendliness, collective amusement and exuberance. Laughter can send messages of approval and applause, insult and defiance, bitterness and sarcasm, rejection and ridicule. There are few expressive forms that can say so many varied things, and there are few communicative devices that can serve so many therapeutic uses.

Humor and Group Cohesion

Inoffensive, esteeming humor has been found consistently to increase the solidarity of group members (Martineau, 1972). It acts as a social lubricant, easing group cohesion into a unified experience (McGhee, 1979). Humor draws people closer together by relating to a common focus—the shared response to a single stimulus. In fact, the first signs of genuine laughter can sometimes be used as a yardstick to measure the progress of affiliative relationships. The creation of in-jokes that can be understood only by members of the group offers evidence that true cohesion has developed. And every group seems to create its own special jesting style, usually focusing on characteristics of individual participants or of the leader.

The therapist can take an active role in modeling the importance of humor by introducing concepts of self-parody. Ordinarily, the "them-against-me" attitude that is part of a group's beginning can be quickly dissipated by revealing the attitude in a humorous fashion. Even a self-conscious group leader finds subtle ways to draw people closer together by getting them to laugh at their predicaments, suggesting "We're all in this together." A social equalizer, humor cuts across status lines. It emphasizes commonality and invites intimacy. Group members feel closer to one another, more trusting and cohesive, when they can laugh together.

Humor and Therapeutic Parody

An experienced group leader can use humor to cut through layers of client inertia. Napier and Gershenfeld (1981) suggest that group leaders should deliberately make use of humor by taking advantage of spontaneous occurrences, absurd situations, discrepancies, inconsistencies, paradoxes, and irony. They believe that group members become more sensitive, less fearful of taking risks, and more open when they feel comfortable laughing at their mistakes and failures.

Group members prone to pathological self-pity are so skilled at feeling sorry for themselves, at making themselves miserable, that it takes a dramatic exaggeration to help them confront their concerns directly. Although sarcasm and parody may be interpreted as ridicule, they can also be used constructively: "If you're going to suffer, why do a half-baked job of it? Why not become an expert at self-torture?" Dan Greenberg (1966) offers advice on such important life skills as creating a first-class anxiety, the power of negative thinking, selecting a three-dimensional worry, optimum brooding conditions, basic worries about noises in the night, how to lose friends and alienate people, and—the most important misery-making ploy for a group session—how to get people to reject you.

He suggests adopting a "reject-me" image ("be apologetic, boring, critical, complaining, impatient, irritable, jealous, nervous, suspicious, and wishy-washy"), developing a whiny, nasal, reject-me tone of voice, and a reject-me posture ("Learn to enter a room as though you expected at any moment to be struck in the face") (Greenberg, 1966). The innovative group leader can even structure a rejection exercise along the Greenberg scheme in which participants practice rejecting one another in the most brutal ways possible.

> **Maria**: Could I get some feedback from the rest of you as to how I come across as a person?
>
> **Sharon**: I think you're OK.
>
> **Leader**: Come on, you can do better than that.
>
> **Tran**: Well, sometimes you do act a little snobby.
>
> **Maria**: I act snobby? Thank you for being honest.
>
> **Leader**: No, no, Maria. If you really want to get rejected, defend yourself, be argumentative and obnoxious. Act hurt so the rejector will know that he or she is on target.
>
> **Maria**: I see. Gee, I didn't realize I was such a loser. I guess that means nobody in here would possibly want to be my friend. I mean, since I think I'm too good for you and everything, and because I'm—

Leader: Excellent, Maria. Let your shoulders sag a bit and pout your lips. That's right. Now go in for the kill.

Maria: I'm having a party tonight after the group, and my boyfriend thinks it would be real fun to invite the neurotic dingbats over from my group. I told him you probably had better things to do, and besides you wouldn't know how to handle yourselves in my house. But he insisted I go through the motions of asking you anyway. Would you like to come?

Humor and Boredom

Nothing is more conducive to retarded learning than boredom. Ask any overactive kid or class clown. It is unrealistic to expect anyone to pay attention to a group happening, however brilliant its message, if its delivery is without vigor. People are allergic to boredom; it makes existence intolerable. In *Catch 22*, Joseph Heller created a character who was so terrified of dying that he attempted to stretch every second to its peak by deliberately boring himself. He noticed that if he lay on his back staring at the ceiling for hours, time would seem to last much longer, thereby prolonging his subjective life. But group members are usually more interested in making time fly. Ambivalent about joining a group in the first place, they will seize any excuse to drop out. Boredom may be more responsible for creating dropouts (in schools or groups) than any other single variable.

The growing pains associated with group experiences are quite enough without the prolonged misery of drawn-out time. Just because therapy is serious does not mean that it can't be enjoyable for participants, filled with laughter as well as tears. Frankl (1978), Klein (1974), Greenwald (1975), and Ellis (1977b) all enthusiastically endorse the use of humor to enliven sessions and make them more interesting for clients. Ellis (1977b) even suggests that

> emotional disturbance largely consists of taking life too seriously; of exaggerating the significance of things; of what I have called, with humor aforethought, catastrophizing, awfulizing, or horriblizing—like the reading of papers at scientific meetings, for example, an obvious disturbance in its own right. (p. 262)

As we recall our significant educational experiences, all the boring lectures, predictable discussions, and routine structures merge into one big meaningless blob. We probably don't know the 14 symbolic themes of a Shakespearean play, but we can certainly recite verbatim a joke the teacher told. Significant learning is synonymous with dramatic, interesting introductions to an issue. Humor, parody, fun, and laughter are prime ways to make group experiences more palatable.

Humor and Humanness

Viktor Frankl's method of "paradoxical intention" relies on exaggerating symptoms to create a more conscious awareness of a client's self-defeating behaviors. We can conquer our fears by distorting them to logical extremes. For a hysterical woman with chronic trembling, for example, Frankl (1978) prescribes a massive dose of humor to obliterate the undesired behavior.

> **Therapist**: How would you like to compete with me in shaking, Mrs. N.?
>
> **Patient**: (Shocked) What?
>
> **Therapist**: Let us see who can shake and tremble faster and for how long?
>
> **Patient**: Are you suffering from these shakes, too?
>
> **Therapist**: No, I am not suffering from them, but I can tremble if I want to. (*I began to shake.*)
>
> **Patient**: Gee. You are doing it faster. (*Trying to speed up and smiling.*)
>
> **Therapist**: Faster. Come on, Mrs. N., faster.
>
> **Patient**: I can't. (*She was becoming tired.*) Quit it. I can't do it any more. (*She got up, went in the day room, and brought herself a cup of coffee. She drank the whole cup without spilling it once.*) (p. 121)

Lantz (1978a) and Lamb (1980) also describe the systematic adoption of humorous exaggeration to help clients separate themselves from their neurotic symptoms. Laughter is substituted for anxiety in the process of spontaneously stripping oneself of negative defense mechanisms.

To isolate and even change problems, group members can exaggerate the unique humanness of clients. This strategy is often used in role-played situations, using mimicry to highlight blind spots in clients' perceptions of themselves. In a technique that Dyer and Vriend (1977) term "role shifting," group members randomly select the name of a fellow participant and enact that person throughout the duration of the session. There is no more entertaining method for confronting one's characteristic flaws and foibles than to observe someone else sitting, talking, and gesturing in imitation. The humor implicit in dramatic license allows people to see how others perceive them.

Humor and the Taboo

Most jokes are either sexual, prejudicial, or aggressive in character. They usually deal with taboo subjects that are not ordinarily allowed entry into conversation. They ridicule minority groups, express forbidden thoughts, poke fun at someone else's expense, nonthreateningly confront people with their disapproved behavior, and give people an excuse to act cruelly. In short, much of humor deals with the taboo and is the only acceptable social outlet for discussing sensitive topics.

In therapeutic groups, humor can be used safely and supportively to provide a bridge between client reluctance and client motivation to change. Initial attempts to explore sensitive issues often take a jesting form to test the water before the plunge. For example, one gentleman, who had been withholding a dark secret since childhood, spent the better part of an hour building up to his disclosure by joking about brother/sister jealousies. Like a court jester, he interrupted the group proceedings to interject humorous comments about how kids can inadvertently hurt one another when they are only fooling around. Instead of ignoring or extinguishing the inappropriate comments, the group leader chose to respond in kind.

When she was a child, she said, she had once short-sheeted her little brother's bed to revenge some earlier mischief, and he had sprained his ankle from the force of thrusting his legs into the sabotaged bedding. The joking gentleman laughed heartily, then abruptly began to sob. When he was 5 years old he had accidentally killed his little sister in her crib while playing Cowboys and Indians with a loaded pistol. The guilt had been locked within him for four decades until the dam had burst through the hole punched in his wall of defense. Humor had set things in motion.

The celebrated humorists of our time make their living by sharing stories. They perform a necessary service for their audiences by making them laugh at subjects they would in other circumstances never think about. Lenny Bruce's infatuation with taboo language and Woody Allen's preoccupation with the taboo topic of death are typical:

> Once again I tried committing suicide—this time by wetting my nose and inserting it into the light socket. Unfortunately, there was a short in the wiring and I merely caromed off the icebox. Still obsessed by thoughts of death, I brood constantly. I keep wondering if there is an afterlife, and if there is will they be able to break a twenty? (Allen, 1976, p. 8).

Erma Bombeck's innocent portrayal of the sexual taboo provides still another example of how humor allows us to laugh at our inhibitions.

> My son was five years old when his teacher sent home a note informing me he was sexually immature.
> I confronted her the next day after school and said, "What is this supposed to mean, Mrs. Kravitz?"
> "It means we had a little quiz the other day on reproductive organs and he defined every one of them as Askyourfather. You are sending a child into the world, Mrs. Bombeck, who thinks Masters and Johnson is a golf tournament and fertilization is something you do in the fall to make the lawns green!" (Bombeck, 1972, p. 60)

Finally, in J. P. Donleavy's *The Unexpurgated Code* (1975) he advises prospective social climbers on appropriate manners for handling sensitive problems. Once again the taboo subject of death is handled with humorous irreverence, poking fun at the subject voted as most devastating to talk about: "Upon Being Told the Fatal News That You Have Only So Long to Live and That It Is Not Long."

> Of course this news may enrage you so much that you start throwing things, blaming and accusing everyone and generally behaving in a hostile manner. Of course this kind of antic only shows you should have been dead long ago.
>
> If you are the nice kind of average person, moisture in the eyes is permissible but do not burst into floods of tears. This alarms others into acute apprehension concerning the moment when their turn comes. Unless death has whispered I am here, make a reasonable effort to keep going. This is often a bleak period unless you have large assets and people around you who will benefit thereby and which prospect keeps them cheerful beyond belief. However, take strong objection to any dancing joy at your sinking. Your final will and a pen handy, plus a couple of witnesses hostile to your heirs, should make the merry take heed. (Donleavy, 1975, p. 51)

Humor and Ambiguity

As much as group members would like to have their conflicts wrapped in neat little bundles containing clear and definitive answers, they are instead confronted by the ambiguous. Words and phrases like *probably, perhaps, maybe, how about, try this,* and *I don't know* preface most leader statements because there are no certainties in therapy, only probabilities. Group members are helped to think realistically when they are requested to try a new behavior or to wrestle with a novel thought and "see if it works for you."

Most adult humans seem cognitively retarded when it comes to Piaget's stages of development: although we have the ability to think abstractly after age 12, we still prefer to think concretely. We like tidy solutions to our problems, and, most of all, in the face of the eternal mysteries, we like some semblance of order and predictability. This strong aversion to dealing with ambiguity can sometimes deter progress in therapeutic groups as reasoning and exploration powers become severely restricted.

Humor can be useful for encouraging group members to confront ambiguous issues in subtle ways. After all, jokes and jests rely on basic incongruity for their appeal, as Kant and Schopenhaur first observed (Keith-Spiegel, 1972). Humor simultaneously forces people to think on different planes, to resolve the paradox satisfactorily, to reason abstractly, to discover meanings, to create possible interpretations. And the best humor, like the best art and music, may be legitimately interpreted in a number of different ways according to one's perceptions and powers of observation.

Humor and Existential Angst

At the root of anxiety is *angst*, an old German word that describes the free-floating human condition in which the meaning of life becomes muddled and frighteningly elusive. This "existential disease" of spiritual emptiness occurs during periods of adjustment and stress, when a person is confronted by questions of death, isolation, alienation, responsibility, freedom, will, and other issues that Jean-Paul Sartre, Martin Heidegger, and Paul Tillich have explored. Although it has no exact English equivalent, *angst* is a first cousin to *anguish* but may also be more accurately related to *dread*, a more powerful affective state (May, 1958). Angst is anguish of the soul and a mummified psyche, usually a temporary state that all persons experience at different levels of intensity when considering the meanings of life.

Angst can be as trying for the therapeutic practitioner to work with as it is for group members to handle. Essentially, life is taken too seriously. Every action is given inflated importance; every decision is seen as a crucial struggle. Listlessness and boredom alternate with manic efforts to reduce dissonance, to take some action, *any* action. And until some constructive plan is discovered for moving forward, angst holds on. It sinks in deeper and keeps people going around in a depressive cycle.

When attempts are made to tackle angst with the same serious intensity in which it thrives, the negative feelings are sometimes validated. Whereas individual sessions are well suited to the necessary dialogues for giving life meaning, group atmospheres can be counterproductive. Angst is contagious. Some clients who are feeling fine allow themselves to be pulled down by the depressing stuff of others, and content of the group takes on a somber, monkish tone.

One way to combat angst is by following rules different from its own. When group members persist in wallowing in existential grief, humor can make a dramatic contrast between pain and pleasure. At worst, humor only temporarily distracts the client from self-torture. At best, however, its potential for therapeutic good is boundless.

Humor and Hostility

Peterson (1975) studied the management of humor in therapy groups by plotting the patterns of laughter that occurred throughout sessions. It was noted that a typical 90-minute group contains about 20 separate attempts at humor, usually initiated by three principal members. Pollio and Edgerly (1976) comment on the prevalence of laughter in groups: "It is as if everyone knows humor is important in group (and individual) psychotherapy; no one seems to know exactly how to teach would-be therapists what to do with it" (p. 222).

In their systematic analysis of comic style, they discovered hostility to be a universal theme. Both in Peterson's study of therapy groups—in which

75% of the jokes tended to be self-directed or other-directed aggression—and in professional comedians who rely on "butts" for their jokes, the hostility denominator accounted for most of the variance among eight different style factors. Don Rickles, Richard Pryor, and Andrew Dice Clay exhibit obvious aggression in their humor, but almost every other comedian demonstrates the characteristic in more subtle form. Thus, Johnny Carson and Dick Cavett were reasonably polite with their condescending witticisms; Woody Allen, Phyllis Diller, Tommy Smothers, the Three Stooges, and Laurel and Hardy were all self-deprecating.

The problem for the group therapist is to manage humor to minimize aggressive and hostile effects. Clients must be taught to discriminate between the kinds of jokes that are used for smoke screens or to belittle people and those that celebrate life and display self-enhancing creativity.

Humor as a Creative Enterprise

Freud (1960) regarded the practice of humor as one of the most creative activities in which a human being can engage. It is the highest expression of the pleasure principle, the most sophisticated of defense mechanisms, and a never-ending challenge to expand one's sense of play. Singer (1973), in fact, proposes that the earliest signs of human creativity are found in the 2-year-old's game of make-believe and fantasy, behaviors that are associated with creativity in later adulthood (Helson, 1965). In a review of the relationship between humor and creativity, McGhee (1979) also concludes that creative children tend to be those who better appreciate, initiate, and understand humor. They use fantasy as a playground for experimenting with novel ideas and creating the most stimulating and chuckling internal environment possible.

In perhaps the most ambitious treatise exploring humor and creativity, Arthur Koestler drew parallels between a sense of humor and other creative activities in literature, science, and the arts. According to Koestler (1964), the riddle, pun, satire, witticism, joke, or comic simile all share common elements with the works of a poet, composer, or artist.

> Humor depends primarily on its surprise effect: the bisociative shock. To cause surprise the humorist must have a modicum of originality—the ability to break away from the stereotyped routines of thought. Caricaturist, satirist, the writer of nonsense-humor, and even the expert tickler, each operates on more than one plane. Whether his purpose is to convey a special message, or merely to entertain, he must provide mental jolts caused by the collision of incompatible matrices. (pp. 91–92)

Humor is a spontaneous expression of joy and—the culmination of human cognitive evolution—the power to improvise in abstractions and create multilevel messages. Certainly, there ought to be reservations regarding its use in groups such as those cited by Kubie (1971). As with any intervention, however, the therapist's skill, motive, and rationale will determine whether it will be helpful or harmful.

Cole and Sarnoff (1980) call for a closer marriage between creativity and counseling, emphasizing that psychological helpers should more often rely on techniques that encourage spontaneous, playful expression.

Timing is everything to the receptivity of humor, whether by a comedian or a group leader. This involves: (1) carefully reading cues from the audience, noting their moods and what they are responding to; (2) monitoring the anticipatory buildup of expectations as the narrative begins; (3) maintaining participants' interest in a way that they are left hanging . . . just long enough; (4) knowing when to milk the antic for more laughter and when to let go and move on to something else; and, most important, (5) continuously incorporating feedback from the audience to make timing even more on target in the future (Mosak, 1987).

Malamud (1980) invented "The Laughing Game" as a group exercise for increasing client self-responsibility. He uses structured experiences conducive to giggles that motivate passive group members by encouraging them to make one another laugh. Clients learn that they need not feel victimized by external conditions beyond their control. Dyer (1976) sees humor as the antidote for most emotional suffering because it is very difficult to feel depressed or anxious while laughing. Admittedly, laughter is a very temporary cure, but its beneficial effects far exceed the few pleasurable moments it creates. With the social interaction advantages of therapeutic groups, humor affords the leader intervention choices not possible in other circumstances. Laughter, like yawning, is a contagious phenomenon, infecting all persons within hearing.

Comparing Renaissance comedic theater and contemporary therapeutic practice Klein (1974) concludes "that the miniature world of the theatre and the phenomenological universe of the client both emerge from an arbitrary verbal syntax which circumscribes the number and nature of the possible alternative explanations of reality" (p. 233). The jester, the fool, the Falstaffian character speak truth behind their antics. Kings accept their candor only because the delivery appears so innocent. As the play unfolds, assumptions are clarified, distortions and inaccuracies are corrected, gaps of knowledge are filled in. Finally, the protagonist's self-ignorance is revealed. The audience laughs; our hero exits, stage left, enlightened—*with* the lover.

CHAPTER 13

Expanding the Range of Leader Behaviors

Most group leaders can reliably demonstrate a core of basic interventions. One such skill, *multiple attending*, requires the leader to maintain continuous surveillance on all the subtleties of human communication within the group—facial expressions, bodily movements, vocal intonations, message content (Allan, 1982). Gill and Barry (1982) have integrated several existing classification schemes into a definitive catalog of group-focused counseling skills that practitioners frequently use.

The range of common leader behaviors would include many of the following: accurately labeling various cognitive, affective, and behavioral data as they are manifested within and among group members; task refocusing to maintain theme-related coordinated behavior; eliciting observations, reactions, and feedback in response to group events; implicit norming of characteristic group behavior; consensus seeking to reach agreement on a course of action; diverting inappropriate participant involvements, and other skills identified by Dyer and Vriend (1973a), Yalom (1985), Jacobs, Harvill, and Masson (1988), Corey (1990), Johnson and Johnson (1991), and Nelson-Jones (1992).

Expanding this base of fundamental helping skills is necessary for survival in the field. The unique demands of group work require that practitioners continually augment their range of leadership behaviors in a given conflict situation. To hold clients' attention over the long haul, to encourage creative solution seeking, to facilitate spontaneous, productive interaction, and to help clients take risks, the group leader must have the widest range of tools available.

To expand their knowledge base as well as their skill competencies, group leaders should become at least minimally familiar with related fields that intersect our profession. Philosophy was mentioned earlier as desirable study for practitioners. A smattering of medicine would also be helpful so that group leaders can understand basic mind/body interactions—the effects of physical disease on psychological behavior and the effects of emotions on physical functioning. Moreover, therapists should know the potential uses and abuses of psychopharmacological agents that group members may be taking in conjunction with their treatment. It would be useful to know that constipation, lethargy, weight gain, and other side effects are common with tricyclic antidepressants or that diet restrictions limiting the intake of cheese, Chianti, and pickled herring are necessary with monamine oxidase inhibitors.

With all possible personal resources mobilized for immediate action, including a broad range of skills and knowledge, there is a greater likelihood that the most appropriate intervention strategy will be chosen for the greatest good of group members.

The Role of Techniques for Advanced Leaders

There are essentially four functions that leaders serve in groups: (1) to provide a supportive climate, (2) to process what takes place, (3) to stimulate interaction, and (4) to direct the norms, roles, and goals. Of these leader behaviors, Anderson (1985) notes that the first two—providing and processing—have a direct, linear relationship to positive outcomes; the more support and constructive processing that is built into the group experience, the more likely a successful group results. The second two functions, stimulating and directing, have a curvilinear relationship to outcomes; if too few or too many of these ingredients occur, the group will either become lethargic and predictable or chaotic and overemotionally charged.

Each of these four functions is carried out by the group leader through the use of techniques—that is; any explicit or direct procedure designed to provide direction, invite exploration, stimulate insight, facilitate goal completion, or otherwise accomplish therapeutic tasks (Corey, Corey, Callanan, and Russell, 1992). The choice of which technique to select at any given moment in group time is based on a number of factors including:

1. the leader's theoretical framework
2. the individual client's needs
3. the current group atmosphere
4. the past history of what has worked previously
   a. in similar groups
   b. in similar situations
   c. with this individual client
   d. with this particular group
5. the leader's intuition, logical reasoning, and perception of what is going on, what needs to be done next, and what is the best way to accomplish the identified objectives.

Note, for example, how this process works in the mind of one advanced group leader selecting particular interventions and techniques: ''Things seem to be bogging down. Probably the result of the members' apprehensions regarding their own fears of death *[leader's theoretical framework]*. As Tim talks about his impending surgery he seems to be asking for guarantees that his cancer will stay in remission *[the individual client's needs]*. Yet others seem so introspective; they have retreated deep inside themselves and don't appear to be listening to Tim any more *[the group atmosphere]*. I recall a marked reluctance on the part of these folks to share honestly reactions and feelings that are unpleasant *[history of the group]*. But I think that this is fairly typical of people when issues of death come up *[history of previous groups]*. Besides, Tim does not seem ready yet to be confronted with how frightening his plight is to others *[history of individual client]*. I think it is time *[logical reasoning]* to draw people out of their cocoons and help them reconnect with one another. I sense *[intuition]* an undercurrent of interest, even fascination, with exploring this issue further. Then again, maybe it is *my* interest in this subject? *[leader's mood]*. What I need to do, then, is to bring them back to the present, but to do so in a way that is neither going to frighten them too much nor to ignore Tim's craving for honest feedback. I think that I will try . . ."

And so goes the internal dialogue of selecting a technique, a process that is always changing, whether the decision is made to use an individual intervention to reflect a client's feelings, an interactive technique to bridge connections between members, or to introduce a structured exercise.

There are a number of reasons that a structured technique might be initiated in a group.

To help focus discussion on a particular issue: "Since a number of you seem to be struggling with a fear of death, let's try an imagery exercise."

To invigorate the lethargic, passive mood: "O.K., everyone stand up for a minute and face out from the group."

To increase comfort levels with an ambiguous situation: "Perhaps it would be helpful if each of you wrote down on a sheet of paper what your impressions are."

To create some fun: "Pick somebody else in the group to imitate for a few minutes."

To deepen the level of interaction: "It would be helpful if you formed three different subgroups so each of you has more time to explore your reactions to what took place."

To move the focus from one mode of experience to another: "Rather than talking about this issue with your families, let's sculpt a typical interaction."

To lessen tension or anxiety associated with intense affect: "Perhaps each one of you could take a step back and describe what you observed."

To ensure there is greater participation among all members: "Before we move on to something else, I would like everyone to have a chance to respond to what was said."

To make group decisions or reach consensus: "You have ten minutes to reach unanimous agreement on what to do next."

To encourage more creativity: "I would like everyone to draw a picture representing how you feel about this group."

Although the examples that accompany these opportunities for stuctured techniques appear to be spontaneous ideas on the part of the leader, in fact, there is a quite deliberate decision-making process going on; one in which the advanced practitioner might reason as follows:

1. "Something isn't working. Something is different. What is it?"
2. "People are attentive. They don't appear to be bored or restless. Avoidant maybe?"
3. "What is unusual? Nobody is looking at anyone else, or at me. What are they avoiding?"
4. "Structure might help to make it easier for them to explore this issue. It will focus all of us more concretely."
5. "What activity can I invent or adapt that will accomplish what will fit best right now? Something in which each person is required to talk. Something that will get their energy flowing again. One that will be reflective, yet interactive. I know, how about . . ."

These inner dialogues are familiar to most of us because they illustrate how, even though the inclusion of a structured technique may appear impulsive ("It might be fun to try this"), the advanced leader is actually quite systematic in defining goals and designing the means to reach them.

Equally important to selecting and implementing the right technique is how it is processed afterward. This usually takes the form of a series of silent queries: "What did I observe? Why did I do that? What are some other ways that I could have done the same thing? What might I do next time in a similar situation?"

Flexibility in the Use of Techniques

In the preceding internal dialogues of advanced group leaders, one readily apparent characteristic was the tremendous flexibility in the leaders' willingness to move in a number of different directions, depending on what was required. Feilbert-Willis, Kibel, and Wikstrom (1986) attempted the rather daunting task of running a group for severely disturbed, low-functioning, hospitalized patients who, on top of their mood swings and regressed behavior, were also quite unmotivated and resistant to change. For example, most participants appeared angry and sounded angry but categorically denied feeling any anger. Many others were withholding, mistrustful, and acted out constantly. In short, this group was composed of candidates least likely to respond to treatment.

The authors evolved a style that was specifically designed to address the needs and challenges of this particular group. Applying one dictum of strategic therapy—if something doesn't work, don't do it anymore—they began to catalog all the interventions they tried that did not have much effect: when they identified self-defeating behavior, the members felt persecuted and subsequently became depressed or agitated; when they tried to remain more neutral in pointing out dysfunctional behavior, the members still reacted defensively and felt chastised; when the leaders then tried emphasizing the positive features of the progress that was being made, without mentioning crucial elements as well, the members did not believe anything that was said and mistrusted the leaders' sincerity.

By reviewing the history of ineffective interventions, the leaders were able to put together a style that supported the positive and acknowledged the negative and that finally produced desirable results. This process of systematic analysis helped the group leaders identify the dynamic forces in the group that were preventing change. The leaders were then able to invent techniques that broke the resistant cycle. Such a flexible operating style would not have been possible without certain other characteristics common to advanced group leaders.

Personal and Physical Considerations

Personal Control

First and foremost, advanced group leaders are maximally in charge of their own bodies and minds. As an athlete rigorously exercises to improve muscle tone, strength, agility, and endurance, the group leader, too, must be in superb physical shape. The mind is similarly finely tuned and trained; vocal tonality is extremely well developed, providing a range rivaling that of an operatic soprano. Facial expressions are constantly monitored, sometimes a poker face is shown to hide inadvertent value judgments; other times, the face is openly expressive for the purpose of providing clear feedback or reinforcement. To demonstrate support or authority, the body, too, conveys subtle nonverbal messages on demand.

In short, group leaders are meticulously in charge of their personal space so that the fullest range of messages may be sent at will and communications will not be misinterpreted. Hence, the more therapeutic skills and choices that leaders add to their repertoires, the more effectively they can accurately read and convey verbal messages.

Territoriality

The next consideration, after personal control, is that of understanding and readily employing therapeutic variables in the physical environment. In a sense, the group leader becomes a spatial engineer who can manipulate physical space with the assurance of a chiropractor rearranging spinal alignments.

The concept of *territorial privacy*, for instance, has important implications for therapists in their expanded knowledge and application of group dynamics and outcomes. In Robert Ardrey's (1966) careful observation of the Ugandan kob's arena behavior, he notes that these creatures respect territorial space and rights over their mating instincts. Once a male kob has secured a stamping ground, it may not be invaded except through rigid rules of challenge and combat. The strongest and most virile antelopes thus command the choicest real estate in the center, with invisible but nevertheless impenetrable boundaries warning all but the sexiest females to stay away.

The invisible boundaries that insulate a kob against invasion, the nervous compulsion of a dog to sprinkle every tree with the scent of its urine, and the human passion for building fences around our backyards or our bodies, all attest to the significance of territoriality in group behavior. The group leader must fully understand this behavior, both to interpret it and to facilitate other behaviors, such as cooperation or respect. Among nations or individuals, war occurs when one party feels that its legitimate territorial space (physical or psychological) has been invaded. All animals have a need for privacy:

> antelopes, golden and gleaming, spread across a swelling African veld; spaced cattle in an English field; birds resting on a telephone line that we pass in our cars, each separated from his neighbor by a distance so invariable that they resemble beads on a string or markers on a giant ruler. (Ardrey, 1966, p. 159)

Human behavior in groups is not much different. Group members are very reluctant to give up their seats once they have claimed them; ownership is determined by squatters' rights. Invisible boundaries pervade group behavior. Characteristic interaction distances become established depending on factors such as age, gender, race, social status, or cultural differences (Shaw, 1981). In addition, many other physical factors affect group behavior, including lighting intensity (Carr & Dabbs, 1974), noise (Glass, Singer, & Friedman, 1969), and physical proximity (Sommer, 1969)—all variables that the group leader can manipulate with a wide range of intervention strategies.

That we group leaders are addicted to the use of circles, that we deliberately seat ourselves next to antagonistic clients or across from passive ones, typifies the attention we pay to physical interventions. Even an elementary school teacher attempts to break up destructive coalitions by rearranging seats as the first disciplinary strategy. We could, of course, carry this a step further in our work by creatively enlarging on the physical dynamics of groups. For example, we may attempt to centralize communication patterns by spreading the more garrulous clients around the group or hope to stifle approval seeking by deliberately seating ourselves outside the group for a time.

Spatial Interventions

When the marital therapist arranges chairs about the room so that each of the three participants—husband, wife, and therapist—sits equidistant from one another, the physical environment acts in a therapeutic capacity. Husband and wife must face each other when they speak. Neither feels the therapist to be aligned more with one partner than with the other. Each participant has an equal contribution to make. In contrast, the therapist who sits enthroned behind a desk, expecting clients to pay homage when in the sanctuary, will get quite a different set of responses.

> It is important to remember that the client *is not your equal*, he has come to you for help and thus he should indicate this symbolically by some action, such as giving you a rose or three of his paychecks or groveling a bit. Some practitioners have settled for the expedient of letting the client sit in the less comfortable chair and being addressed by an old Greek title pronounced "doctor" and spelled G-O-D. (Tyler & Thurston, 1977, p. 102)

Participants choose their seats with deliberation. Dominant individuals choose central positions; passive people attempt to hide under the leader's wings. People jockey for position next to those for whom they feel an affinity or attraction. The leader, too, will play musical chairs each week, hoping to encourage participants to break social barriers. The leader may sit across from someone who needs drawing out or between two distracting participants.

My policy is to suggest that members make it a point to sit in a different seat, next to different people, each week. This strategy encourages people to take their security with them rather than feeling that it is mystically vested in their favorite chair. It also dramatically alters group interaction patterns as people have more opportunities to get to know more people as a function of geographic proximity. Also, when the leader changes location each week, members don't get in the bad habit of looking in one direction every time they speak.

Milton Erickson was particularly sensitive to the impact of spatial positions in groups. Erickson, who would go so far as to match his breathing rate to that of his clients, imitate their speech patterns to win greater rapport, or use his body to accentuate hypnotic suggestions, also strongly advocated using whatever physical manipulations were possible. When working with hostile family members, he was likely to use spatial compartmentalization techniques to prevent other group members from barging into the conversation. He might also control a session by frequently requesting clients to switch chairs, leaving their resistance behind in their previous place. Haley (1968) reports a typical Ericksonian intervention capitalizing on the potential of spatial manipulations.

> If I send someone out of the room—for example, the mother and the child—I carefully move father from his chair and put him into mother's chair. . . . Or if I send the child out, I might put mother in the child's chair, at least temporarily. Sometimes I comment on this by saying, "As you sit where your son was sitting, you can think more clearly about him." (p. 33)

Nonverbal and Physiological Variables

Certain Indian medicine men have so sensitized themselves to the most minute color changes in the flush of a person's cheek that they can distinguish a dozen different emotional states. The martial arts student of Shin-Shin-Toitsu Akido is trained to monitor the most infinitesimal shifting of weight in a sparring partner in order to mirror the movement with perfect grace. Stage magicians can appear to have telepathic powers by their ability to see things invisible to the untrained eye. During his apprenticeship to Don Juan, Carlos Castaneda taught himself to transcend looking into seeing to perceive the essence of things in the world.

Magician, wizard, and therapist all require an extraordinarily finely tuned perceptual system to see a heightened reality that is invisible to the uninitiated. As group leaders we command respect because of the training, experience, and hard work that has made us exquisite instruments for interpreting human behavior. We appear to read minds. We understand things that are incomprehensible to others. We can predict that certain behaviors will produce certain outcomes. All the same, we have a lot farther to go. We still tune into only a limited number of possible actions; we attend to perhaps a few hundred different variables; we collect data that is relevant only to our immediate concerns. Yet the number of possible data to monitor and add to our conceptual vocabulary is infinite.

Few nonmedically trained professionals, for instance, pay attention to psychophysiological and autonomic responses in group members. Shallow breathing, pupil dilation, pallor, rashes, and other physical symptoms don't exist for those who are not trained to notice them. Similarly, blinking, tremors, and other nonverbal movements have meaning only when acuity notes their existence. We have, in short, an impossible mission: to notice everything in a client's behavior that might have meaning.

Subgrouping

Though we are fond of dyads and triads, many other combinations are possible depending on desired outcomes. For instance, after two group members have used group time to confront each other about long-standing conflicts, they may each be asked to take half the group to receive structured, private feedback before they re-encounter each other. In one subgroup, all six colleagues may agree that a client has overstepped her bounds by ignoring the other person's rights or that she should stop responding so defensively to every attempt at being helpful. In the other subgroup, the client may be cautioned that he is playing it too safe, being dishonest with himself, and trying to placate everyone's wishes. After the feedback, the group may be reunited to help the clients reach some resolution.

In another structure, triads can be used to reduce initial hesitance and mistrust in a risk-taking exercise. If one client was exploring his fear of having homosexual impulses and other members shared similar fears but were reluctant to disclose details, the leader might decide to subdivide the group for the purpose of their sharing feelings, values, and fears about being sexually attracted to the same sex.

In a subgrouping structure that is a common introduction to sexual attitude reassessment groups (SARs), participants are asked to explore their body images. First, group members are paired off to interview each other regarding their attitudes and feelings toward male and female bodies, as well as their dislikes and joys about their own bodies. Questions may be asked about shame, inhibition, favorite body parts, or whatever is interesting. Next, the group members meet to introduce their partner's body, share insights, and discuss less threateningly sensitive issues related to sexuality.

Finally, group members may also be paired in fishbowl structures. Two members who rarely listen to each other may be asked to move their chairs to the middle of the group, tune out the audience, and practice listening and responding skills. The others will remember the same principles in their future encounters. As witnesses to the exercise, they can also help process what happened and offer valuable suggestions for improving communication.

Thinking on One's Seat

I was once running a group in which a member was working on her compulsive need for winning the approval of significant people in her life. She spent a disproportionate amount of energy figuring out what her sister-in-law, husband, and college professors wanted to hear and would then do her best to satisfy their expectations. I found it appropriate to solicit the reactions of other group members to her approval-seeking behaviors within the group itself. Did she defer to any specific people? Would she stifle her true feelings in favor of those that would be universally accepted? Did her bodily movements, posture, eye contact, vocal tones signal placating gestures? Was she deliberately engaging in bootlicking behaviors within the group?

One or two initial comments made it clear that the other clients were focusing on how incredibly, disgustingly nice this woman acted. She was always coming to people's rescue, defending them against injustices by confrontive co-leaders. She always had something wonderfully sweet to say about everything. Meanwhile, this sweet little old lady (as she liked to project herself) batted her eyes, smiled indulgently, and promptly thanked each member for his or her kind thoughts. Things were going nowhere. In fact, her approval-seeking behaviors were inadvertently being reinforced by polite peers who didn't wish to sully her self-image of a "proper" lady who always knew the "right thing to say."

It was time to abandon the agenda. The true sign of advanced group leaders is their willingness to try something new when they are confronted by inertia. Flexibility and creative improvisation are the keys to successful quarterbacking, to great jazz, and to effective group leadership as well. Plans are made to be altered, and no therapeutic strategy is going to be optimally beneficial unless it can be molded to fit the ever-changing circumstances within a group.

This constructive feedback strategy, which had always worked for me before, is supposed to help clients assess the impact of their self-defeating actions realistically. It's not supposed to make things worse. But here this woman was rattling off the fantastic psychological benefits she was getting from approval seeking: avoidance of conflict and of risk taking, making other people happy, not having to think for herself, and a score of other payoffs.

Then it occurred to me that her physical presence made stark honesty impossible. No one could be so heartless as to tell this gentle cocker spaniel with the big brown eyes that she was a lazy coward afraid of taking risks. It seemed that she had either to leave the room or become invisible for group inhibitions to be reduced. But by turning her chair so that her back would face the group, we could talk about her more openly. The effect was immediate and fantastic. (Only later did I learn that others had used this technique before.)

Once her back was turned, group members described her as a coward, an invisibility indistinguishable from the wallpaper, a well-meaning but meek person who enjoyed being stepped on, and a woman who acted as if she were to be thrashed at any moment. Her downcast eyes, stiff posture, nervous hand movements, and apologetic voice were all noted. Finally, group members described the ways in which they felt offended and cheated because they could never distinguish the woman's true feelings from those she worked so hard to manufacture.

In the hush that followed as group members awaited her reactions, the little old lady, wearing a grandmotherly smile, slowly turned her chair around and proceeded to articulate all the reactions that she'd stored up for each person during the past months. Gone was the self-deprecating manner. With both candor *and* diplomacy, she expressed her thoughts on every imaginable subject, responded to each person on an intense level, even deliberately said some controversial things to note how they were received. To her surprise, spontaneous applause broke out. Not only was no one offended by her reaction, but group members respected her all the more for her honesty.

And so a vicious approval-seeking cycle ended because the group leader was willing (1) to determine the specific outcomes he wished to reach; (2) to formulate a strategy and rationale for accomplishing that goal; and, most important, (3) to alter his agenda to design spontaneously a new, improved version better suited to the therapeutic situation. In this case, the leader was able to reason through the dynamics that appeared to be restricting maximum effectiveness and then systematically remove the obstructions that prevented change.

Using Time

Time is not only an absolute that is measured by a clock. No two seconds are perceived to weigh the same. Time seems to expand during boredom and contract during involvement. The experience of time is affected by a number of factors that radically influence the behavior of different people. A younger person experiences a single minute as lasting much longer than does an older person. People of different cultures and ethnic backgrounds also relate differently to time. For example, an American businessman who equates time with money will act differently from an Indian who believes in reincarnation and that life therefore is timeless.

In this sense, we are not dealing with a standardized unit called a *second*, which is actually "1,192,731,700 cycles of the frequency associated with the transition between the two energy levels of isotope cesium 133" (Austin, 1968). In therapeutic groups, the concept of time becomes most significant in the *relative* value it has for clients. People who escape from the present by living in the past through nostalgia, guilt, or reminiscence; people who live in the future through fantasy, anticipation, and worry; people who use drugs or sleep to hide from their troubles obviously don't value their time very greatly.

Group leaders must think in terms of cost-effectiveness and be guardians of time to make certain that it is neither wasted nor abused. Rambling and small talk are rarely tolerated; on a prorated basis, minutes may cost up to $3 apiece (if 12 members are paying $25/session for a 100-minute group). In these terms, a long-winded story could cost $30! When the leader is extremely time conscious and group members are extremely time wasteful, either because they don't realize the value of each minute or because they are sabotaging time utility as a form of resistance, it creates a difficult situation.

Perhaps a primary motive of group leaders is to use the concept of time as an overriding factor: "Do we want to be using *our* time in this way?" "How have you maximized *your* time in the last three minutes of silence?" "In what ways are you not appreciating *your* time as much as you could?" Time is also important in the pacing of certain interventions. As does the trial lawyer, stand-up comic, or playwright, the group leader must time comments to coincide with the readiness of group members to hear them (McClure, 1978).

Bridging

Advanced practitioners who are used to staying on top of things may be doing the other group members a disservice by intervening too quickly when a group member acts out (Corey, Corey, Callanan, & Russell, 1992). Although leaders certainly have a responsibility to muzzle members who act inappropriately or disrupt others' work, the more that leaders do, the fewer opportunities other members have to learn to be more assertive.

It takes tremendous restraint on our part to exert the patience to wait far longer than we would prefer until other group members reach their frustration tolerance and gather the courage to do something decisive to cut off the distracting member. We, of course, can move this process along by cuing members who we sense are on the verge of enforcing group norms; at the same time, we forge closer connections between members.

> **Leader**: Mycah, I notice that every time Arthur speaks, you roll your eyes toward the ceiling and seem to withdraw. Why don't you tell him what you are experiencing?

This craft of *bridging* involves making more and more connections between group members in an effort to build more open communication and greater cohesion. Ormont (1990) describes several ways that advanced group leaders can expand their repertoire of bridging techniques by adapting the following time-honored interventions.

> *Open-ended questioning:* "What do you sense she is feeling when she folds her arms like that?"
> *Directed questioning:* "Are you aware that he started to withdraw right after you pointed at him?"
> *Questioning about interactions:* "What are they doing right now?"

In each case, the group leader is indirectly guiding the group's movement while bridging connections between members in such a way that members become more active. That is the hallmark of the advanced practitioner; one who can lead by encouraging others to do the work.

Using the Drama of Change

When the Austrian hypnotist Franz Mesmer set up his "animal magnetism" baths that were purported to produce startling behavioral changes among group participants, he gave great attention to the dramatic elements of the therapeutic milieu. Lighting, music, and his own dress and demeanor all heightened the suggestive effect of his treatment and procedures. Today, we still play on clients' favorable expectations to change. The traditional diplomas on the wall, book-lined shelves, plush furniture, suits or white lab coats certainly lend an aura of authority to the setting.

We group therapists are also fantastically accomplished dramatists. We write scripts that rival the plays of Tennessee Williams in their realism and passion. We participate as players in dramatic productions so absurd as to make Eugene Ionesco or Edward Albee's plays look predictable. We are versatile in our performances—sometimes harsh, brittle, cynical; other times, soft, sincere, and responsive. We play heroes and heavies, character parts and supporting roles. Sometimes we produce, direct, or write the musical scores for the productions. In any case, we spend a good part of our time participating in the drama of change.

The tasks of a group therapist have expanded considerably since the days of Victorian Vienna when the leader was expected to play the part of a nononsense nursemaid to control the antics of participants. Yet, at about the same time that Freud was experimenting with his "talking cure," J. L. Moreno was playing with kids in a park, helping them to act out their fantasies. Moreno had hit upon great subects for his "dramatic therapy" because children are spontaneous, uninhibited, creative, and enthusiastic about pretending. Moreno learned from the children as much as they learned from him; indeed, all group therapists could profit by expanding their repertoire of child skills.

From these attempts to act out real-life experiences for catharsis, for insight, and to resolve conflicts, psychodrama was born. Although psychodramatic structures and role playing have now become standard operating procedures for most group leaders, the underlying principles of these techniques have not. The drama of group interaction is often relegated only to appropriate instances: "Now it is time to do a role play." The visible variables clearly indicate this procedure: a confrontation is necessary; the subjects are willing; tension and inhibition are high. Structured practice and rehearsal are indicated.

Yet the role of drama in group leadership can be considerably expanded by the advanced leader. Drama *is* a unity of themes with heightened interest. The function of dramatic literature is first to entertain and, once audience attention has been secured, then to instruct. Dramatic movements are exaggerated. They alleviate boredom and capture interest. They spread enthusiasm and excitement contagiously.

A drama student trains the vocal cords, musculature, and facial expressions to convey even the subtlest gestures. Similarly, group leaders have trained themselves as mimes when they parody client actions; as improvisationists when they forcefully create dramatic metaphors; as comedians when they attempt to relieve tension; as poets when they construct memorable verbal images; as playwrights, directors, producers, and, above all, as actors in everything they do. Rather than merely walking through a role, however, they exhibit genuineness and sincerity in their performances.

Whether the therapeutic situation calls for an affectionate friend or Merlin the Magician, the therapist must deliver an award-level performance. With little time for rehearsal, the group leader is *always* before a critical audience. Frowns are misinterpreted as rejection. A vacant stare may be read as boredom. It is difficult to scratch an itch without the gesture being noticed, interpreted, and personalized by attentive participants.

Once the seats are occupied, the curtain rises, lights dim, and an air of expectancy settles around the circle: "What surprises are in store for us today? I hope it's a good show. The critics liked it last week. But you know how inconsistent these temperamental shrinks are." And during the next two hours, usually without intermission, the group leader will run through a complicated series of dramatic performances.

- Karen reports that she forgot to complete her self-imposed assignments in risk taking and then searches the group leader's eyes for a glint of disapproval. The group leader feigns casual indifference.
- Samuel hedges his bet by demonstrating reluctance to make a decision. While he claims contentment as a spectator, the group leader leaps out of a chair and assumes a scarecrow pose, humorously illustrating the consequences of total inertia.
- Jalaine expresses a strong desire to confront her nagging, insensitive boss. The group leader spontaneously assumes the boss' role, imitating his habits and the chronically irritating whine that she finds so offensive.
- Bernard speaks in a soft, melodic whisper. His words, however insightful, are seldom heard. Yet his face is constantly lighted with feeling. The group leader delivers a sensitive monologue on what Bernard's face is expressing while his voice is silent.
- Following an initial surge of progress, group sessions begin to lose intensity after the fifth week. The group leader recites a carefully worded, impassioned soliloquy to encourage further involvement.

These examples fail to mention the subtle changes in voice modulation, body expression, and facial communication that are part of *every* leader intervention. The group therapist is a veteran of first-run dramatic performances that make soap operas pale in comparison.

Utilizing Imagery

Previous chapters have discussed the expanded roles of metaphoric language in group leadership. Therapeutic imagery is only one example that has been selected as a technological outgrowth of the attention directed toward linguistic/cognitive leadership strategies for promoting change. Advanced group leaders have the awesome task of keeping up with the latest innovative techniques so that they may be altered to fit the unique requirements of group situations.

Clients use imagery to overcome fears, phobias, or anxieties by imagining pleasant scenes when confronted by stressful situations. Panic responses can be blocked by using enjoyable fantasies as distractions to overcome problems such as school phobias (Lazarus & Abramovitz, 1962) or the pains of childbirth. Since therapeutic groups are usually highly stressful situations during the early stages, scenes of positive imagery can be constructed to help anxious and shy group members relax sufficiently to be able to verbalize their concerns.

One particularly high-strung group of clients, whose collection of symptoms included high blood pressure, ulcers, stuttering, hand tremors, and other physical signs of destructive stress, was given a dose of positive imagery as part of their orientation to group proceedings. They were instructed that on noticing the telltale signs of tension that make them feel reluctant to speak up, they should instead visualize themselves sitting around an open campfire with trusted good friends.

The open sky would be dotted with stars. In the background they could hear the steady drone of the ocean (the air-conditioner hum). They could smell the fire and feel its soothing warmth. Everyone would be preoccupied with his/her own thoughts, paying little attention to the others: "And all of a sudden you begin to feel safe and comfortable, completely relaxed. You find that you really want to speak up. You know that no one else is judging you; they are focused on their own concerns. And the more you feel the warmth of the fire, the great expanse of the sky, the vigilance of the stars, and the camaraderie of the people you trust, the more you want to open up to them."

Creating Homogeneous Groups

The latest movement in group practice seems to be to specialize in very specific client populations. For example, in three consecutive issues of the *Journal for Specialists in Group Work* (1991–1992) there were articles describing programs for the elderly, the very old, widowers, Alzheimer's patients, women, high school students, displaced homemakers, adult offenders, divorcees, and college-age children of alcoholics. In journals such as the *International Journal of Group Psychotherapy* or *Psychodrama*, every issue is similarly full of programs for rape victims, the homeless, borderline disorders, substance abusers, and the like.

There are a number of distinct advantages to organizing homogeneous groups, the most important of which is that it allows us to tailor make our structures and interventions to the specific needs of the population. Certainly, children suffering sexual abuse have different needs and are likely to respond better to certain kinds of group structures than would college students who have study-skill deficits, or adults who are undergoing divorce, or individuals who have psychotic conditions.

Let's take the population of sexually abused children as an example. The leader must be experienced enough to design the experience in a way that is consistent with the research on the subject. Groups should be smaller in size, limited to five or six children (Levine, 1979; Sugar 1974), and shorter in duration because children have shorter attention spans (Rose & Edelson, 1987). A greater range of developmental functioning must be addressed in terms of emotional maturity, physical competence, and moral and intellectual development (Lewis, 1985). Because of vast differences in children's cognition, reality testing, and impulse control, leaders must be more active in keeping the process on task (Siepker, Lewis, & Kandaras, 1985). There is greater need to focus on developmental tasks and action-oriented activities than on promoting insight alone (Schamess, 1986). There is an obvious need to include parents in the treatment planning and implementation, both because parents may be part of the problem and because they certainly are in the best position to support what is taking place in group (Gaines, 1986). There is a greater emphasis on play rather than on work, with more attention to making things fun and engaging (Schiffer, 1969).

It is clear that the advanced group leader must attend to a myriad of variables unique to this or any specific population. Homogeneous groups require more specialized expertise. Leaders must have knowledge not only about the intricacies of the specific disorders or client populations but also about the greater burden placed on leaders to deal with problems that will inevitably arise: members protecting and enabling one another, ganging up against the leader, presenting deficits similar to each other). These greater demands placed on the professional require leaders to be fluid enough in their craft that they can adapt their methods to the specific needs of each unique population.

Using Psychodramatic Structures

No other group technique has been adopted by so many divergent leadership approaches as has psychodrama. Even though J. L. Moreno originally practiced as a psychoanalytically trained psychiatrist, no less than half a dozen other theorists integrated his methods into their work. Behavioral group leaders may call it a form of social modeling or behavioral rehearsal. Gestalt practitioners routinely employ "double chairing." Cognitive therapists act out elaborate role-played scenarios in which group members confront their irrational beliefs. Existential, psychodynamic, and Adlerian groups liberally make use of psychodramatic structures to facilitate insight and work through conflicts.

What makes psychodrama such a spontaneous, powerful, and creative enterprise is that it simultaneously makes use of behavioral principles (modeling, giving feedback, reinforcing healthy behavior), phenomenological ideas (dramatic experiences), psychoanalytic concepts (catharsis, transference, unconscious motives), existential premises (authenticity), client-centered values (empathy, encounter), object relations theory (role reversal), and even spiritual components (Blatner, 1988a; Blatner, 1988b).

Moreno first "invented" psychodrama at age 4 when he played the role of God and directed his playmates to be angels. As a religious individual, the whole philosophy underlying his dramatic enactments was composed of moral and spiritual themes (Moreno, 1946). One of the major goals of Moreno's approach was to regenerate human spontaneity and creativity, as much for the group leader as for the members.

In the 1940s, when Kurt Lewin and his cohorts were operating out of the National Training Laboratory (NTL), the idea of groups for growth was based on the premise that they provide realistic opportunities for participants to experiment with new ways of being and acting. Groups were thus seen as laboratory settings in which members could run their own behavioral experiments.

Of all the group modalities that have evolved since the movement's beginnings, psychodrama (which actually predated NTL in its conception) has remained truest to its original mission: to provide a safe environment, one in which members can engage in a form of practical and creative science (Blatner, 1988a; Blatner, 1988b).

Interestingly, psychodrama represents an almost perfect blending of pure science and art. It offers the advanced group leader the challenge of helping members access their playful, creative, spontaneous, artistic expressiveness, and yet it is done in a scientific context. Group members literally conduct "laboratory experiments" with their own behavior in which they practice new ways of relating to others (and to themselves). They receive feedback from peers on the relative effectiveness of their efforts, and then they incorporate changes into their style. Art and science come together in the leader's attempt to encourage free expression and yet do so in an intentional and constructive way, one in which the experiments are tested and the implications of the results are drawn out.

Advanced group leaders have already mastered (or at least are familiar with) the basic psychodramatic process in which a protagonist (the client-in-focus) first describes the presenting concern and then is directed to act out a scenario as if it were really taking place. The action is stopped at various points so feedback can be offered by other group members; auxiliary roles can be included; certain behaviors can be redirected, exaggerated, or expanded; or the leader can help process what has occurred.

Several specialists on the subject of psychodrama (Blatner, 1988a; Cabral, 1987; Goldman & Morrison, 1984; Grainger, 1990; Kipper, 1986; Leveton, 1977; Moreno, 1946; Sacks, 1973; Treadwell, 1990; Wilshire, 1982) have described a number of therapeutic structures that seem particularly well suited for advanced practitioners. A few representative samples are described here.

Childhood Regression.   Because of the potential for decompensation and extreme affective expression, only the most experienced group leaders would attempt to take a client back into childhood to relive traumatic experiences. This is especially the case with those who we may suspect were victims of sexual or physical abuse but who are repressing the episodes.

Even with the potential dangers of a client losing control, childhood re-creations can be among the most potent of therapeutic structures. One illustration that stands out is a case in which a member of a counseling group for therapists felt blocked in her work with her own clients. She was feeling less and less satisfaction doing therapeutic work and sensed that the origins of her struggle lay in the past. Because of the high degree of trust she felt in the group and the respect she had for her peers and the leader, she consented to re-create a scene from childhood that seemed particularly significant.

The psychodramatic enactment that followed was indeed powerful. The woman did not *play* being a little girl, she *became* herself as a little girl. With the help of several group members who took on the roles of her parents, siblings, and auxiliary egos (including the persona of her present-day denial) she was able to identify the original introjections from her parents that were still blocking her from experiencing life and work more fully.

As is so often the case with creative group structures, what eventually evolved over time bore little resemblance to the originally constructed role play. By making continual adjustments according to the client's reactions and the group members' individual and collective responses, the group leader helped a spontaneous process develop rather than staying with a prescribed sequence of stages.

Sculpting.   As much a part of family counseling lore as group work, sculpting is the act of allowing or guiding participants to shape themselves into a symbolic representation of the ways they interact with one another (Satir & Baldwin, 1983). What makes this creative structure so challenging is the demands it makes on the group leader to help members process their experiences and identify their scapegoating, placating, and other defensive roles (Satir, 1972).

There are basically two versions of this methodology used in groups. In one, an individual client sculpts his or her own family using other group members as "fodder," such as in a family reconstruction process (Satir, Bitter, & Krestensen, 1988). The second, and somewhat more interesting, version for groups that have worked together for a while is to create a collective sculpture depicting everyone's role in the group. In its most ingenious form, coalitions become clearly evident, as do codependent and conflicted relationships.

Fishbowl.   One other example of a psychodramatic structure that offers multiple creative opportunities for the experienced group leader is one in which two subgroups are formed to monitor each other's behavior.

Unlike more structured techniques such as double chairing (Perls, 1969), guided fantasy (Samuels & Samuels, 1975), soliloquy (Moreno, 1959), role switching (Dyer & Vriend, 1977), behavioral rehearsal (Rose, 1989), or dramatic ritual (Grainger, 1990), fishbowl exercises have innumerable permutations.

In its generic form, the group is divided in two, with about half a dozen members huddled in the center. Each participant is assigned a partner on the outside circle who may be asked to do a number of things: to observe that individual during the process to provide feedback later; to engage that person in a personal exchange; to serve as an auxiliary or silent ego to the partner during the exercise; and so on—the possibilities are endless.

The intent of fishbowls is to heighten participants' awareness of group processes. With members subdivided into cohesive units, it is also likely that overly strong coalitions can be diluted in favor of other interpersonal connections. The most difficult part of running these activities is controlling the "chaos" to the extent that people remain task oriented during their spontaneous experiences.

Many of the advanced techniques just described seem very inviting and stimulating—at least when read in the pages of a book. A few words of warning, however: these ideas are presented more to stimulate your own creativity and imagination than they are to give you intact strategies to incorporate immediately into group settings. The hallmark of advanced versus beginning group leaders is their ability to be flexible and adaptable in their implementation of group interventions. I mention this obvious point primarily because of the potential for any innovative strategy to do as much harm as good.

One further point that I wish to mention is the reluctance on the part of some veterans to be more creative in their work because of a fear of failure.

Combating Fear of Failure

All group leaders learn *about* psychodrama and role playing in graduate school. We read about and are informed that it is a truly wonderful thing, a way to enliven groups and help members practice things that they are merely talking about. In classes, it is generally part of our training to observe, participate, and later direct with supervision various dramatic structures. The problem often comes after we counselors and therapists leave school and begin running groups in the real world. We quickly realize that our clientele are not quite as sophisticated or cooperative in getting into our structured activities as we experienced with our mentors, instructors, supervisors, and demonstration films.

Previously (Kottler & Blau, 1989), a colleague and I wrote extensively about our own experiences in feeling that we were professional failures. This was true not just with respect to psychodrama but in all our therapeutic training. We were exposed mostly to successes and rarely heard about instances of things going awry. Then, when we attempted to try out what we had learned from school or workshops and it didn't work with clients, we automatically assumed that, since the technique had been proved successful, we were incompetent or flawed.

There was a time when the more experienced I became as a group leader, the fewer risks I took in using creative structures. Certainly, in many ways I became more skilled, more confident, and more expert in leading groups, but some of that was true because I stayed in safe areas of competence. I had seen demonstrated in class a number of times a situation in which a group member was asked to imagine his or her antagonist sitting in the room and then was invited to tell that person all the pent-up things that he or she had always wanted to say. Of course, this demonstration always went fabulously; The "client" cooperated, really got into the experience, and we watched in amazement.

I will never forget the first time I tried this structure with a client and the lesson I subsequently learned. Sidney had been struggling with his prolonged grief toward his father, using up more than his fair share of time. The other members were becoming restless and bored. This was a perfect time to pull out that fail-safe technique that creates so much magic when things get dull.

> **Me**: Sidney, you obviously have a lot of unresolved feelings toward your father that have not diminished over time, nor do you seem to be doing any better after talking about him in group. (*A particularly smooth summary, I thought to myself.*) Perhaps it would help if you would say some of the things directly to your father, or at least to the image of him sitting in this chair. (*Seems to me to be clear and concise instructions.*)
>
> **Sidney**: Why would I want to do that?
>
> **Me**: Excuse me?
>
> **Sidney**: I said, why would I want to talk to my father? He's dead.
>
> **Me**: (*I know that.*) Yes, of course he is dead, but he is still very much alive in your mind. (*I was struggling and starting to lose the threads; then I remembered I could ask for help from other group members.*) Could anyone else explain to Sidney why this might be helpful to him? (*A good attempt to spread the responsibility.*)

Silence. The others have puzzled expressions on their faces.

> **Me**: (*What's going on? They are supposed to follow my lead and get into this. This isn't that complicated.*) Sidney, let's try again. Pick out somebody in the group who most reminds you of your father and then you can talk to that person as if he were your father. You can tell him all the things you wished you had said to him before he died. (*Good, that was better.*)
>
> **Sidney**: But why would I want to do that? My father can't really hear me.

That was the last time I tried psychodrama for quite a while. I could not figure out where I had gone wrong, and I assumed it had to be my error because the technique had always worked when others had tried it.

Now, as I look back on this episode, what I conclude from that experience seems comical. But the fact remains that the fear of making a mistake, of being proved incompetent, and of feeling like a failure stifled my creativity for quite some time. There are some advanced group leaders who never recover from their confrontations with their imperfections; they spend their professional life playing it safe and doing only what feels comfortable.

Thus the subject of risk taking, as mentioned in Chapter 10 with respect to clients, applies to advanced group leaders as well. The only way that we can ever hope to expand the range of our leadership skills is by becoming more creative and innovative in the methods we use. This rule applies not only to the things that we do during group sessions, but also to the adjunct structures that work to supplement therapeutic efforts when the therapist is not around.

CHAPTER 14

Adjunct Structures

The goal of therapeutic adjuncts is to intensify any work done within the more traditional latitudes of group work practice. Since the average client spends more than 100 waking hours each week outside the therapeutic encounter, the time logged in the group represents less than 2% of the thoughts and feelings clients experience. A client may enter the hallowed chamber each session, itching to get started on 2 intensive hours of hard work—introspection, confrontation, integration. But then the group disbands until next week, and the client re-enters the real world, perhaps acting just as ineffectively as before.

Within the safety of the group, the client is a superstar at risk taking because the atmosphere is conducive to trust, respect, acceptance, and human kindness. The client's comrades praise every intelligent comment; confronting a conflict head-on wins enthusiastic support. The client is continually reinforced for growing, at least until the following week. Once outside, however, smiles fade and the client may regress to prior behavior for a week. Tempers are lost. Self-pity returns. All is forgotten, or temporarily suspended, until the next group meeting.

This doesn't happen all the time, perhaps not even frequently; but group members report often enough that the glowing effects of the group experience don't even outlast the weekend. Unless members are given opportunities to think about their insights every hour—while they eat or drift off to sleep, when they are anxious and depressed, during television commercials or rides in the car—the memories quickly fade. If people do not practice new skills regularly, the skills will never become part of natural functioning.

It is to set the cure permanently that we group leaders invent adjunct structures for maintaining therapeutic changes. Unlike our colleagues in medicine who have the use of high-technology tools for assistance, we *create* tools to remind our clients to continue working on themselves between sessions. We use all the help we can get to ensure that changes are individually personalized by each client and that these desired changes are perpetuated long after the last group session.

"Booster" sessions are favored by some practitioners as a way to encourage maintenance of changes that were made (Rose, 1989). Other advanced leaders choose to include art therapy activities that build cohesion at the same time that participants create a joint project (Vogt & Vogt, 1983). And, of course, dolls, toys, and other play therapy tools are also favorite adjuncts in groups for both children and adults (Kraft, 1986).

In this chapter, we review some of the most functional adjuncts currently in use by group leaders who seek innovative ways to supplement their "talking cures." By combining the technology from pharmacology, electronics, cultural geography, the biological and social sciences, as well as the artistic contributions from literature and the humanities, we can more powerfully promote long-term client changes.

We now have access to various hardware from the communication field, such as audio and video recording equipment, computer systems, and absentee-cueing systems. From such writers as Anaïs Nin and Albert Camus we have inherited the literary legacy of journal keeping. Many novelists as well have provided psychologically sophisticated literature for self-reflective study, spawning the field of bibliotherapy. We can use behavioral technology, such as environmental programming, contingency reinforcements, psychological homework, and people monitoring. Field excursions are ways of augmenting group experiences creatively, and psychodramatic structures provide clients with systematic behavioral practice and insight. The medical profession has taught us to use psychopharmacology, regimented exercise programs, and even vitamin supplements to help group members to stabilize emotional reactions. In each case, sister disciplines have contributed valuable tools that innovative group leaders may incorporate into their repertoires.

Journal Keeping

Anaïs Nin's 150,000 pages of diary entries constitute one of the outstanding literary-autobiographical works of this century. Apart from acknowledging the journal's other uses to an aspiring writer, Nin and her colleagues saw the intensive journal primarily as a tool for self-exploration.

> We taught the diary as an exercise in creative will; as an exercise in synthesis; as a means to create a world according to our wishes, not those of others; as a means of creating the self, of giving birth to ourselves. We taught diary writing as a way of reintegrating ourselves when experience shatters us, to help us out of the desperate loneliness of silence and the anxieties of alienation. (Nin, 1978)

Progoff (1975) describes journal keeping as a "transpsychological" approach to growth because it capitalizes on techniques active within an

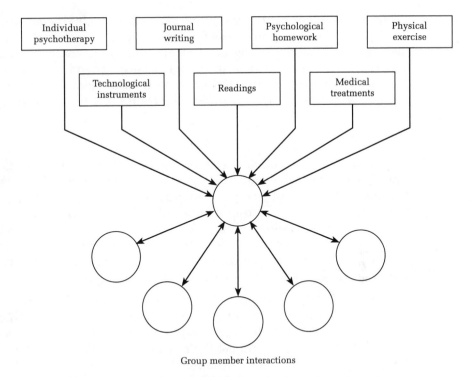

Figure 14-1   Intensified Therapeutic Influence through Adjunct Structures

individual that are not available to group sessions. It counterbalances the weness of groups or the helper's role in individual counseling by encouraging the creative and spiritual enrichment of one's inner life.

Although inclined toward mysticism, Zen, and spiritual enlightenment processes, Progoff nevertheless offers sound counsel to scientifically trained professionals. In his view, the journal teaches self-reliance; it provides an inner sanctum in which a person may practically and safely experience greater personal mastery. He suggests that it is possible to see the "Tao of growth" by guiding his group members in their personal journeys through the Period Log, Time-Stretching, Inner Wisdom, Steppingstones, Twilight Imagery, Internal Dialogues, Dream Enlargements, and other journal techniques that plan for self-exploration combined with group interaction and feedback.

> The *Intensive Journal* workbook is specifically designed to provide an instrument and techniques by which persons can discover within themselves the resources they did not know they possessed. It is to enable them to draw the power of deep contact out of the actual experiences of their lives so that they can recognize their own identity and harmonize it with the larger identity of the universe as they experience it (Progoff, 1975, p. 10).

The intensive journal is perhaps the single most useful therapeutic adjunct available to group members for deepening work accomplished during sessions. Journal keeping has become standard operating procedure among group leaders of various theoretical persuasions and for many sound reasons. The following potential uses are from the journals of a group member who wrote diligently during the course of a year-long group.

Catharsis

First and foremost, a journal is a convenient repository for all thoughts and feelings swelling inside and bursting to express themselves. Since Freud had originally intended therapy to be a vehicle for releasing stored psychic energy, the journal is a more appropriate place for self-expression than the group sessions themselves. All too often clients waste valuable group time complaining about their lives beyond the point where complaint is helpful; but the journal offers an eternally vigilant ear, always ready to accept unconditionally any and all cathartic entries.

> **(Journal entry)**: I despise this sonofabitching place. I'm so damn tired of all these idiots telling me what to do with my life, how I should think, what I should wear, how I should speak. It would be different (maybe) if they could get their own acts together first before they try to direct *my* life. I hate nothing worse than a bunch of loud-mouthed hypocrites who get off on the power of making other people feel miserable. I would so much like to stand up to these assholes and tell them what I really think—that they are self-centered, rigid-thinking, insensitive, irresponsible peasants who delude themselves into believing they are royalty.

Introspection

There are human needs both for completing unfinished business and for finding meaning in one's actions. The principal shortcoming of group experiences, where there is so much to do and so little time, is the lack of opportunity to draw closure on each participant's processing of whatever is going on. Writing in a journal, Pennebaker (1990) enthusiastically explains, provides the group participant with a structure for completing the "teasers" that may have begun in the group.

The journal is a place to talk to ourselves, to reflect on significant events both in the group and in the real world. Systematic writing trains us to think more analytically and introspectively about our actions, to ponder inconsistencies and underlying motives, to reconcile others' perceptions with our self-image.

> **(Journal entry)**: The feedback from the other group members as to their first impressions of me is very incongruent with how I think

I come across. I appeared shy and studious, which is certainly a new image for someone like me, who pretends so much to be a "man of action."

Self-Intimacy

Whereas group sessions usually focus on people as social beings, journal writing complementarily concentrates on the private self. By exploring their own intimate thoughts in conjunction with the interactive group work, clients are better ensured of making independent decisions as well as of preserving personal identity. A particular group meeting can often act as an impetus for clients to turn inward, explore the implications of an issue for themselves, and then further explore the most relevant dimensions in their journals.

> (Journal entry): I left the group with a boring, wasted feeling in the pit of my stomach, like I hadn't grown any. And I wasted my time watching one of my cohorts getting thoroughly grilled. It wasn't until now, after becoming more aware of my own dependencies on people I love, that I realize I had, in fact, been pounded on the head. I, too, feel guilt—obligation toward my grandparents who love me so devotedly and live their lives through mine. Must I repay this debt?

Processing Insights

Even an exceptional human mind cannot keep pace with the kaleidoscope of new ideas presented in a typical group meeting. Concepts are often introduced on an abstract or general plane, requiring systematic personalization of the material. Each participant must continually ask questions: "What are they *really* saying?" "What does this mean?" "What has this to do with me?" "How might I apply this to my life?"

Each novel concept, every lesson worthy of recall, must be fully understood, interpreted, generalized, applied, coded, and stored in memory for retrieval on demand. To accomplish these tasks, it is not only desirable but necessary for clients to process insights gleaned from group sessions into bite-size pieces that can be swallowed without indigestion.

> (Journal entry): One of the main points of last session is that a person is ultimately responsible only to himself. Problems that arise as the result of another person's actions must be seen only within the context of how I allow it to affect me. The implications of this are awesome: I need never feel helpless again.

Dialogue with Group Leader

One of the principal disadvantages of therapeutic groups is the premium placed on leader accessibility. The therapist is simply not readily available to clients in this time-shared structure in which each participant may command only one-sixth or even one-fifteenth share. When many people vie simultaneously for leader attention, some will inevitably be short-changed. Moreover, even a socially skilled and assertive client who is able to maximize leader expertise during sessions will be left in the cold between meetings. Questions and comments that come to mind during the week must often be shrugged off.

A possible solution to this problem lies in using the journal as a place in which clients can create dialogues with the leader. The leader's ear is thus always on call, at any time of the week, whenever the client has need for a confidential conference. If clients later decide to share their journals with the therapist, any responses, reactions, and feedback can be inserted throughout the pages.

> (Journal entry): I don't much like the idea of not being in control of what goes on in this group. These leaders act like they know it all, but I don't really trust them. Or I should say you, since you're both reading this journal. That's another thing I resent. How the hell am I supposed to privately explore my thoughts when I know that you two will be giving this the once-over?

Self-Discipline

People experimenting with journal writing often complain that it is hard work. Sometimes you're too busy or feel that you have nothing to say; other times it's too painful to get into personal matters. In either case, it takes resolve and effort to carry through with the task. Like the change efforts attempted in therapy, journal keeping requires considerable self-discipline.

> (Journal entry): I find myself, day by day, growing stronger. The reinforcement mechanisms for change are operating at an extremely effective level. I can't even put my finger on how I've changed; I just think differently. I'm much more positively critical, demanding of myself. Just by nature of the fact that it is 8:00 A.M. on a Saturday and I'm sitting here writing instead of sleeping is indicative of my new self.

Creative Expression

The unique communication style of group work lends itself to an emphasis on scientific inquiry, inquisitive exploration, and a playful experimentation with novel ideas. It is hoped that these qualities will become part of the content of the journal, making it a forum for creative expression.

> (Journal entry): Organization is the hardest part of writing, deciding what to put where. With the greatest fluidity I can sit down almost anywhere and write acceptable, if not interesting, prose. But my

writing style does not include a sequential flow of pages from beginning to end. Like the free association of a slot machine, a spark clicks, triggered by a memory, a sight, a sound. From there, the idea writes itself from the nucleus outward. A string of jumbled beads is thus left around my neck, in need of sorting. And *that* is the most confusing, challenging task of all. I get frightened by the power of a writer to alter pieces, no—first to create them from nothing, then to put them *anywhere*.

In addition to journal writing, members can use other forms of self-expression. These can involve helping children (Mazza, Mazza, & Scaturo, 1987) or adults (Gladding, 1992) write expressive poetry or compose personal logos or epigrams that represent each member's self-perception (Wenz & McWhirter, 1990). Following are some examples of self-expression.

• *Goal setting:* "I notice that I keep trying to win my father's approval for the things that I do. Alternative: to keep my own counsel and quit running to him each time I accomplish some task. Goal: to stifle the urge for others' approval. In the group I must restrain myself from saying things that I don't necessarily believe in—just to win approval and strokes."

• *Structured self-counseling:* "I have a desperate, neurotic need for recognition by an impartial audience. I am not at all concerned about the approval of my parents or friends or anyone else close to me. That is the confusing part: I don't feel I have to prove my wonderfulness to anyone I know; it is the people I don't know whom I make so important. I must make extraordinary efforts to remind myself that (1) I don't become a more worthy human being just because I convince strangers that I am important; (2) it is a losing proposition anyway since I cannot convince *everyone*; and (3) I must tell myself that I am important to myself and those who love me— what difference do other opinions make?"

• *Systematic practice of new thinking:* "What an interesting idea we learned today—that other people can't reject me unless I permit them. So often I let myself be put in vulnerable positions where other people can control my life. This evening I tried something new. I walked up to a girl, as usual; but *this* time when she didn't respond to me, instead of feeling dejected I told myself: 'Big deal. So she didn't like you. That doesn't mean you are ugly or stupid. Maybe next time things will work out differently. And if they don't . . . I can live with *that* too.'"

• *Dream analysis:* "Only since my baby was born have I had these incredibly vivid dreams. Naturally, I am being pursued by some suitably grotesque creature, who instead goes after the baby. I struggle. I fight. Just as the baby is devoured I wake up screaming, in tears. Never have I felt so damn vulnerable. It is bad enough to have to protect myself, much less this little one who cannot fend for himself."

• *Remembrances, memory:* "In this book I've been reading by John Nichols a little boy asks his mother if raindrops are alive. His mother nonchalantly replies: 'I think so, isn't everything alive and infused with the spirit of God?' The boy, not to be put off, asks again: "Then does the rain have dreams, too, like us?' While his mother stammers, searching her memory for the correct response, the boy inwardly smiles, points toward the sunlit mountains in the distance, and answers his own question: 'Rainbows are the rain's dreams.' If rain dreams, can it also cry?''

   • *Progress and growth*: ''Last night I stumbled into an opportunity to use the confrontation skills that I have unknowingly acquired in the past few weeks from this group experience. I found myself using phrases that I heard in the group. To be quite honest, I thought that last week wasn't that useful. Apparently I learned more than I thought.''

   • *A celebration of life*: "Today I have fulfilled my greatest dreams. Perched atop an overhanging cliff at 10,000 feet (higher than eagles dare fly) overlooking the valley below, my skis swinging in a rhythmic pattern to the wind and snow, I lived. It was then that I realized that I had been thinking about absolutely nothing—my mind a complete blank. How precious are these moments devoid of thought and feeling. I never once thought to myself 'This is beautiful.' My unconscious had already accepted this fact; felt no inclination to bother the rest of me with a lapse in concentration.''

Some Dangers of Journal Writing

Journals are sometimes structured as group logs, in which each participant is expected to document after each session what was accomplished, which personal goals were attained, observations of what transpired, what in particular was learned, and what was the personal reaction, inlcuding what the session felt like (Valine, 1983). The logs are then collected regularly so that the leader may read and react to each member's comments, giving individual attention to issues that are not possible in group formats.

This prescribed assignment is not without its hazards, however. Members may resent that even their most private reflections are open to scrutiny. In addition, knowing that the leader will read what has been written can foster greater approval seeking or even lead to manipulative games: "There is something I have been wanting to say to you that I have been unwilling to say in the group. . . ." Because opportunities are available for some members to disclose things in the log or journal, they may avoid doing so in the group. For the same reason, many family therapists are reluctant to communicate privately with any participant for fear they will become triangulated into family secrets.

Although there are many uses for or benefits of journal writing as an adjunct to group work, Pennebaker (1990) warns that overreliance on this structure can also create some problems; many of which are quite evident to those of us who have been reading member journals for many years.

   • *Journal writing can be a substitute for action.* In the same way that talking about a subject can prevent someone from *doing* something to take care of business, writing about one's plight can take the edge off the need to act.

   • *A journal can become a vehicle for complaining.* Depending on how it is used, some group participants have a tendency to write mostly about what they are upset about. They focus on what is going wrong rather than on what is right, become almost obsessively critical of themselves and others. Rather than serving as a means to apply the best lessons of what was learned in group, the journal becomes an endless stream of complaints.

   • *Self-dialogue can become intellectual game playing rather than truly self-reflective.* In a similar vein to the complaints just described, group members may act out their worst behaviors in their writing. Left unchecked and unsupervised, the journal deteriorates into an exercise of pompous self-absorption.

   The key is to remember that any group activity or therapeutic adjunct can be useful, benign, or harmful depending on how it is introduced and applied. It is not enough simply to suggest that writing might be helpful and to leave it at that; these entries must be treated as an extension of the group process itself.

Homework

Many writers, such as Shelton and Levy (1981), consider outside-group homework assignments to be the most important therapeutic process that takes place. Homework assignments give clients opportunities to practice new behaviors in real-life situations and to make any modifications necesssary before continuing to experiment in the group. They help clients generalize what they learned in group to other aspects of life. Finally, such structures provide ways for group members to function autonomously so they do not remain dependent on the group setting for approval.

   Rose and Edleson (1987) describe some of the more common examples of these adjunct structures.

   • *Interactive tasks* are those in which the group member agrees to do or say something to someone else: "Ok, so what I will try to do, I mean what I *will* do, is approach Kevin and introduce myself. I will talk to him for at least two minutes."
   • *Simulated tasks* are role-played interactive opportunities that take place outside of group: (group leader): "Since you and Tim are both in the same health class, perhaps you could find the time to practice cuing one another."
   • *Cognitive tasks* help the client rehearse new ways of thinking in response to an event that may take place: "When my mother yells at me for not cleaning my room the way she believes I should, I will tell myself, 'She's not being mean but only doing what she thinks is best.'"

- *Individual tasks* involve any assignment that helps a group member meet personally stated goals: These could include anything from meditative exercises and writing in a journal to completing a budget.

Questionnaires and Logs

There are ways that are more structured than journaling to systematically record reactions to group proceedings. As a way to access unexpressed affect and dissatisfaction of group members, Wright, Ingraham, Chemtob, and Perez-Arce (1985) use an adjunct structure in which opportunities were provided for reporting things held back during sessions. Members complete brief questionnaires at the end of each group in which they describe their degree of satisfaction with the proceedings as well as things they would have liked to have said or done.

The results of this study helped Wright and his associates better assess potential dropouts as well as encourage clients who were reticent and inhibited about expressing themselves more fully. Contrary to the therapists' initial concerns about using this structure, members did not use these after-group reports to confide things they would not say in group, nor did they create private contracts with their leader; in fact, these brief reviews helped them move more quickly into their areas of conflict.

Edelwich and Brodsky (1992) describe a postgroup log as a means to help participants focus their attention on specific areas after each session. They suggest that, between meetings, participants address some of the following questions: "What was the best part of the group for you?" "What changes have you made during this week?" "What things could you do differently?" "What unfinished business might you bring to the next session?" This type of writing assignment gives more structure and direction than does the more traditional open-ended journal.

Films and Videos

The use of videotape has been shown to be useful as a means of helping group members examine the impact of their own behavior. The camera does not lie. Clients are more likely to accept feedback, remain open to altering views about how they appear to others, and be more responsive to confrontation when they view themselves on video (Wachtel, 1983).

In spite of their research studies that have failed to demonstrate the effectiveness of videotaped feedback for improving group member self-esteem, Cooker and Nero (1987) still advocate the experimental use of this therapeutic adjunct. Observing oneself on video provides a kind of information about one's behavior and interaction patterns that is not available through any other process. It allows group members to observe both verbal and nonverbal aspects of the way they present themselves. They are able to relive poignant or significant moments that occurred and yet reflect *constructively* (rather than critically) about what took place and what they might do differently in the future.

In addition to videotaping clients, Duncan, Beck, and Granum (1986) advocate using popular films to initiate theme-centered discussions on particular topics. Adolescent groups, for example, might watch *Ordinary People* or *The Breakfast Club*; adult groups might view *Parenthood* or *Dad*. These dramatic visual stimuli serve to awaken the intensity of emotional responses to issues that are related to client concerns. With the shared experience of watching the film together, participants are able to use it as a platform from which to spring to their own individual concerns.

Recently, quite by coincidence, six of nine members of an ongoing adult counseling group had gone to see a movie that had been released the preceding week. They were thus able to speak about common experiences and their unique perceptions of what they observed, as well as how each one intended to apply the insights to his or her own life.

Bug-in-the-Ear

In training fighter pilots during World War II, it was discovered that students needed real-life experiences in the cockpit, with opportunities for independent judgment, while at the same time receiving immediate feedback on their performances from their flight instructors. An apparatus was thus constructed to allow trainees to receive continual, unobtrusive supervision during their mastering of new skills.

This electronic system, consisting of a headphone and a microphone, was later adapted by Korner and Brown (1952) into a "mechanical third ear." By converting a hearing aid into a private receiver or by using an inexpensive pocket radio with an earphone, an individual can receive unobtrusive feedback through a wireless microphone. This absentee cuing system has been used to teach projective testing to clinical psychology interns (Korner & Brown, 1952); to instruct student teachers (Herold, Ramirez, & Newkirk, 1971); to train group counselors (Cohn, 1973); and to provide immediate feedback supervision to therapy clients (Patterson, Jones, Whittier, & Wright, 1965; Stumphauzer, 1970).

According to Haney, Sewell, Edelstein, and Sartin (1975), a Bug-in-the-Ear can be created using a pocket-size transistor radio as a receiver by setting it on an open FM frequency and using an inexpensive wireless FM microphone as a transmitter. Requiring a capital investment of about $30, this instrument opens limitless therapeutic possibilities that may be integrated into group situations. Since the Bug-in-the-Ear provides instant support and feedback to the client *with no one else able to hear*, target behaviors may be reinforced, altered, or extinguished systematically and immediately at the same time that anxiety is reduced (Kottler, 1977).

Investigators who have experimented with this therapeutic instrument have noted several important points (Cohn, 1973; Kottler, 1977; McClure, 1978).

1. Client and therapist/coach should agree in advance on specific instances when intervention is indicated. Example: "Whenever you see me backing down from a confrontation, let me know."
2. Practice sessions with the instrument are necessary to familiarize the client with its operation and help him or her adjust to the difficulties in tuning into simultaneous conversations (the one going on in the group and the voice coming in from the "third ear").
3. Comments made on the device should be concise, clear, and abbreviated to minimize confusion. Example: Instead of the coach saying "You're kidding yourself when you believe that the client will do what you say," the comment could be more briefly worded "Follow through!"
4. Cues should be restricted, whenever possible, to timely pauses in discussion so that clients don't lose their place.
5. Clients prefer consulting rather than authoritarian roles on the part of the coach.
6. Dependency on the device can be minimized if cues are phrased to allow clients freedom on how to act.
7. Cues can be of different varieties:
   Reinforcement cues: "Well done!"
   Support cues: "You're doing fine."
   Cues on manner: "Slow down."
   Cues on timing: "Confront him now."
   Insight cues: "What are your payoffs from being silent?"
   Action cues: "Notice what you are doing with your hands."
   Content cues: "You completely ignored her feedback to you."
   Interpretation cues: "He's trying to test you."
8. The client, too, should create a signal system for communicating to the coach:
   Scratch eyebrow: "Repeat and explain, I don't understand."
   Touch ear: "Please be quiet. Not now. I want to hear what's going on."
   Look at coach: "Help me!"

Applications to Group Work

1. Clients can receive immediate feedback during the group sessions on their self-defeating or fully functioning behaviors. A group member may, for instance, request opportunities to become more assertive in the group, and the cuing system may be used to aid her with timing or phrasing. More

important, within seconds after an assertive attempt the coach can come in with a response: "Great effort! But you backed down at the end with your ingratiating smile."

2. Clients who act inappropriately or impulsively, as well as those who are attention seekers or poor reality testers, can be restrained without the embarrassment of public censure: "Now is not the time to speak about yourself. You're taking the focus off Marilyn."

3. Resistance and withdrawal in passive group members can be overcome by encouraging participation. The coach can supportively stay on the client's heels: "What are you afraid of? Tell them what *you* think."

4. Tension and anxiety can be reduced in group members afraid of taking risks: "Calm down a little. Just relax—take a few breaths—and *then* talk—that's it—you're doing just fine."

Printed Handouts

Fiction and nonfiction bibliotherapy has been relied on as a therapeutic adjunct for decades (Schrank & Engels, 1981). Short stories, novels, plays, even self-help books are routinely prescribed by group leaders to augment themes that arise in the course of treatment. A client experiencing career confusion may be directed to Studs Terkel's *Working*. An adolescent with difficulties may be guided to *The Diary of Anne Frank* or *Catcher in the Rye*. Creative practitioners may write original material.

Every group leader has a series of standard minilectures that are routinely delivered to groups or to specific group members when the need arises. They are sometimes introduced as teaching aids in skill training; more often they are selected from the leader's repertoire when required. A group member who exhibits confusion between appropriate and inappropriate emotional responses could profit from a minilecture on the anatomy of emotions —how they are caused and how they may be altered to fit a situation's natural requirements. A group member who repeatedly speaks of catastrophic failures when expectations are not fulfilled might be exposed to an educational module on the distinction between wants and needs. Many other frequently repeated subjects require the therapist to deliver sermons from time to time.

To save time, to minimize repetition, to avoid turning a therapeutic group into a classroom, and to ensure efficient quality control of crucial educational materials, the minilectures can be standardized as handouts for clients to read between sessions. Not only are group members gratified to leave each session with something tangible in their hands, but the handouts ensure that they will think in structured ways about new ideas to which they are exposed. Moreover, in many instances the written word carries more weight than the same message spoken aloud. Clients can digest written material at their own speed, mulling over stimulating areas, internalizing new ideas, rereading confusing or novel passages.

The handouts also help solve the recurring problem of educating loved ones about the nature of the group experience. Most group members feel some frustration in dealing with friends and lovers who have a vested interest in the changes being initiated. Some spouses feel threatened by the increased effectiveness their partners demonstrate as a result of the group. Others may show plain curiosity and interest in progress that can be readily observed. They don't want to be left behind; some may genuinely wish to upgrade the quality of their lives as well, once they see how masterful the client has become.

Handouts brought home can give everyone in the household a clear idea of what kinds of things the group covers. Loved ones can thus grow along with the group member as they are instructed in new learnings they find intriguing. A common language develops so that seeds planted in the group can begin to sprout within the interaction patterns at home. When the group member laughs at the "approval-seeking behavior" evident in a TV character, for example, family members will "understand where he is coming from."

The content of handouts can be tailored to fit the individual requirements of any group leader's philosophy and goals. Instead of always recommending readings from whoever your favorite theoreticians may be, personally created fare can be prescribed. Even those who regard writing as a chore will find that producing a series of handouts for captive audiences will not only improve their communication capacities but also raise their esteem among their clients. Although specific titles will be determined by individual preference and the unique demands of group members, I find the following to be particularly useful with most groups.

- "How You Make Yourself Miserable." An overview of the most common psychological self-torture techniques. Profiles such self-defeating behaviors as worry, guilt, and fear of failure, emphasizing that most internal suffering is self-inflicted.
- "How to Get the Most from Group Experiences." Detailed instructions for capitalizing on the learning opportunities available in therapeutic groups.
- "Developing Communication Skills to Help Others." A rationale for learning to be a more effective communicator. Specific guidelines help readers to improve their interpersonal skills.
- "Art of Confrontation." Applying knowledge of how groups function and of communication techniques to two very important situations: (1) a discussion of effective and ineffective confrontative styles shows the value of constructive feedback, and (2) readers are also shown how to assert themselves without threatening others and how to accept criticism without feeling attacked.
- "Take a Productive Risk." Motivates the reader to try new things enthusiastically, to experiment with creative behaviors, and to become more socially expressive.

- "How to Get Closer to People You Love." Motivates the reader to take risks in relationships by becoming more open and sincere. The reader is helped to initiate more intensity in existing love relationships as well as to find new relationships.
- "Are You Still Alive?" An explanation of how people "kill" their valuable present moments by avoiding living intensely. Sleep is viewed as an example of practicing for death. Suggestions are offered for sleeping less and living more.
- "What to Do When You Feel Depressed, Frustrated, Anxious, or Angry." Examines the most common negative emotions that upset internal tranquility—how these emotions arise, why they occur, how they can be controlled or virtually eliminated.

There is no limit to other titles that could be reserved for use as needed: "Becoming More Assertive," "Disciplining Children by Teaching Self-Discipline," "Why There Is More Than Your Symptoms," "Moving into Another Career," "A List of Books to Help You Grow," "Being More Creative," "How You Make Yourself Sick," and "What to Do After the Group Is Over."

Field Trips

Elementary school counselors and child therapists have long known that the most important work they do is outside their offices, on the playgrounds, in the sandboxes, on basketball courts, or on walks through the park.

Group leaders, too, are beginning to discover the practical advantages of taking field trips with their clients in order to help them apply newly learned skills to real-life situations. Under the therapist's supervision and support, group members can receive structured practice, constructive feedback, and encounter experiences similar to those they wish to master.

As a graduation exercise in a weight-loss group, all participants met for supper in an ice cream parlor. There they practiced self-restraint while ordering from the menu, slowed the pace of their eating, and still had a leisurely, delicious, healthful meal. The group leader was present to oversee the "therapeutic experience," reminding members of concepts they had learned and the weight-loss techniques they had internalized.

A group of young adults working on debilitating shyness was escorted to a dance by their group leader. As she waited behind the scenes, gently prodding her charges to take social risks, the adolescents began to feel a bit more comfortable and less conspicuous. One young lady, rejected by a potential suitor, was quickly surrounded by assigned partners who helped her talk through her feelings and encouraged her to try again. The group leader offered valuable suggestions regarding approach techniques.

Twenty senior citizens, growing increasingly dependent in their lives, consistently relied on others to do their bidding and complained of feeling increasingly useless. Group sessions focused on dependency issues, confidence building, and expanding their resources. Finally, they were sent unsupervised to the city's downtown area, each with only $3.50. Each senior had six hours for independent entertainment. But routes had to be interpreted and the money carefully budgeted so that they could find meals and keep themselves productively occupied.

In a large southwestern city, racial problems within the group had aligned blacks against Hispanics against whites. Group leaders assigned four persons from each minority group to a rubber raft that would ride the rapids of the Colorado River. Unless group members learned to cooperate, put aside their differences, and function as a team, they would find their outing very uncomfortable, dangerous, wet, and cold. Each night by the campfire the group leaders ran informal discussions to help participants respect and appreciate one another's cultural differences.

A nursery school had had an outbreak of gouges and scrapes as the result of fighting among 3-year-olds. The group leader spent a day in the playground demonstrating principles of sharing and asking permission for favors. When three children wrestled for the privilege of riding the one available tricycle, the group leader was on the scene to break things up and to initiate a session on taking turns.

There are many possibilities for field trips. A group of unemployed adults can be taken on a tour of various industries; people with drinking problems might be taken to a bar to practice self-restraint. In all these field trips, participants are offered opportunities to move realistically and to apply the insights they have gleaned from their group sessions.

Combined Individual and Group Treatment

It was first suggested by Wender (1940) that combining individual and group therapies offered a number of distinct advantages over either treatment alone. As a psychoanalyst, he was interested in the group as a vehicle for re-creating family issues that would arise during individual consultations. He also noted that psychodynamic theories played out in the group provided fertile material for later processing.

A number of other writers on the subject (Fried, 1954; Wong, 1983) have also found quite a number of advantages to concurrent individual and group sessions, although several contraindications for certain clients are also evident (see Table 14-1). Most notably, combined treatments seem to be ideal for those who most require opportunities for structured practice of new skills, reality testing, and confrontation for narcissistic tendencies. On the other hand, clients who tend toward exhibitionism, regressed behavior, and fragile ego structures or who have high needs for control are probably not good candidates (Scheidlinger & Porter, 1980; Wolf, 1974).

Table 14-1 Indications and contraindications for combined therapeutic modalities

Indications for Combined Individual and Group Sessions	Contraindications for Combined Treatments
Clients who need structured practice	Clients who exhibit regressed behavior
Clients who need feedback	Clients who are exhibitionistic
Clients who need to be confronted	Clients who feel too possessive
Clients who are isolated or fear contact	Clients who are controlling of leader
Clients who are not responding to in- dividual sessions alone	Clients who have complex, atypical transferences
Clients who are close to terminating individual sessions	Clients who have not yet worked through dependency
Clients who need multiple sessions per week but who have limited resources	Clients who need continuity and predict- able structures

Source: Adapted from ''Combined Individual and Group Psychotherapy'' by N. Wong. In *Comprehensive Group Psychotherapy* by H. I. Kaplan and B. J. Sadock (Eds.). Copyright © 1983 by Williams and Wilkins.

Other critics (Rosenbaum, 1952; Slavson, 1950) are concerned about the ways that both therapies can easily become ''polluted'' and each dilute the potency of the other, especially if the therapist communicates a preference for one over the other. Concurrent individual and group therapies can be particularly detrimental to one another when (1) they are led by two thera- pists who have incompatible approaches, (2) the client demands the same degree of narcissistic gratification in group as has occurred in individual sessions, or (3) too much affect is drained off during individual sessions to leave much for group encounters (Vinogradov & Yalom, 1989).

Note that the indications or contraindications for combined treatments are essentially the same as those for any group work in general, with the principal distinction that clients must be able to (1) adapt to the unique struc- tures of each, (2) be able to capitalize on the benefits of each, (3) be able to ''share'' therapists without feeling jealous or threatened, (4) feel suffi- cient trust in the therapist that confidences will not be revealed without permission, and (5) be able to integrate discrepant experiences from both settings into a unified perception of goals and issues.

Just as in Wender's (1940) original conception of a combination of the two modalities, the objectives of individual and group sessions are both different and complementary. Depending on a particular client's issues and needs, one of the therapeutic settings (usually, the individual sessions) can focus on generating insights and self-awareness, while the other (usually group work) can help the client translate these understandings into con- structive action. Sometimes, however, the reverse process can prove helpful, as was the case for one individual who was so emotionally constipated that he could hardly articulate any internal experiences during individual ses- sions. Instead, he would use the time to construct lists of things to do, decide how and when he would complete the tasks, and even rehearse the methods by which he would take progressive steps to accomplish his goals. Perhaps because of some male competition issues with his therapist, he could never quite get out of an action mode in which he would fearlessly do things but rarely reflect upon his behavior. Curiously, in the group he attended, while other members often used the time to practice acting in different ways, this man would internally make startling discoveries about himself that he would later bring to the individual sessions prepared to put into action.

Bugental (1990) also presents a beautifully interwoven narrative that highlights the stories of six clients (he includes himself among them, since he grew almost as much as they did as a result of the encounter) he saw in individual sessions who also attended group together. What becomes so evident in their stories is how powerful their group gathering became as an impetus for individual work. Each participant became a partner to every other in helping to clarify issues in need of further examination.

This coordination between individual and group treatments also helps prevent premature termination. In a review of 37 studies that examined why group members discontinue treatment, Bostwick (1987) concluded that one effective strategy for preventing dropouts is the early detection of disenfranchised members. These may be clients who are unsuitable for group treatment because they are unwilling to self-disclose or they manifest hostility. In other instances, they are individuals who do not know how to be "good" group members. They may lack psychological sophistication or have negative feelings they are unable to express. Bostwick concluded that individual sessions remain the single best way to help struggling group members deal with their ambivalence/avoidance and deter them from exiting in frustration.

Medical Interventions

The overlap between psychological and physiological mechanisms that account for client behaviors is often muddled. Anxiety, for example, as expressed in a group session, may take the form of tightness, tension, inhibition, jitters, or similar symptoms. Accompanying physical factors may include stomachaches, dizziness, diarrhea, sleep disorders, or increased heart rate. Further, group members who report that they are feeling anxious might also be experiencing symptoms of hyperthyroidism, hypoglycemia, tuberculosis, pheochromocytoma, or a head injury (Bockar, 1976). With depression also the causal relationships may be unclear. Does the depression result from a psychological problem, or might there be indications of Addison's disease or premenstrual tension?

When depression or anxiety is physically based, psychological treatments such as group work are likely to be ineffective and medical adjuncts more appropriate. For example, antianxiety psychotropic drugs such as Librium, Valium, Dalmane, and other benzodiazepines can be used to chemically alter a client's limbic system and subsequent behavior (Hare & Levis, 1981). Recently, vitamin therapy diet supplements are used to help clients stabilize certain mood states.

Although we have no way of knowing at this time whether vitamin therapy or diet alterations will make any significant difference in clients' lives, group leaders are turning more toward regular exercise programs as therapeutic adjuncts. In addition to the aerobic benefits of increasing circulation, reducing cholesterol levels, and with it reducing the risk of arteriosclerosis, exercises such as running are believed to provide a soothing balm for the soul. Group members often report a heightened sense of well-being, greater self-confidence, and increased vigor. They claim they feel better about themselves when their bodies are in shape. They sleep better and feel more relaxed during the working day. Group leaders are therefore likely to continue prescribing exercise routines and healthful eating habits as a way of life.

One obvious adjunctive treatment that is used with group therapy— especially in inpatient settings, but also with those clients experiencing severe depression, anxiety, and organic difficulties—is the use of medications and dietary supplements. For those of us who are not medically trained, these supplemental treatments are usually prescribed by other colleagues, a situation that presents some challenging complications.

Because in groups we have the opportunity to observe clients in normal interactions, we are better positioned than are the medical specialists to assess the effects of their adjunctive treatments. These effects could include mood alterations; agitation during stressful moments; or speech, cognitive, affective, or physical patterns that appear atypical. Similarly, whereas some clients may not be inclined to disclose all side effects to their physicians for fear of disappointing them, group leaders may hear members casually complain about urinary, vision, sexual, appetite, sleeping, or constipation problems.

Thus, we must have some working knowledge of the *Physician's Desk Reference*, the various classes of antidepressant, antipsychotic, antianxiety, and hypnotic agents. This would also include familiarity with concepts such as a drug's half-life, its side effects, and usual courses of action. We may be called upon to help monitor compliance to the treatment plan and especially to observe carefully how medications may precipitate negative client reactions. The intent of this adjunctive treatment is, after all, to reduce symptom-engendered interference that is blocking group and life functioning (Sussman, 1983). Obviously, clients will not do themselves or anyone else much good if they are not sleeping properly or cannot eliminate suicidal ideation or obsessive ruminations.

The problem for the group leader, then, is how to capitalize on the uses of medications without compromising or even sabotaging the benefits of therapeutic groups. In one group that had been exploring themes of external control and self-responsibility, for example, one member proudly announced that he had secured a prescription for the latest wonder drug purported to restore mood stability to those who have not responded to other anti-depressants. As a forest fire spreads out of control, other members then abandoned their quest for self-control and instead believed that pills could offer a shortcut to the group's painful process. This was especially tragic because no more than two of the other members were actually clinically depressed. An advanced group leader would help the group process this dynamic, explore its ramifications fully, and find ways to integrate the wonders of modern medicine into the rich fabric of therapeutic groups.

CHAPTER 15

Common
Unethical Behaviors*

It is common for a book of this sort to close with a chapter on ethics. Practitioners are usually admonished to watch their p's and q's, stay out of trouble, and follow the described guidelines (for examples, see Corey, Corey, & Callanan, 1993; Pope & Vasquez, 1991; Van Hoose & Kottler, 1985) as well as the ethical codes of the Association for Specialists in Group Work and the American Group Psychotherapy Association.

Clinicians are urged to study their discipline's ethical codes, familiarize themselves with relevant law, debate issues with colleagues, and closely monitor their behavior as well as the actions of peers, since ethics are virtually unenforceable from external sources. After all the furor and threats are over, professional organizations, licensing boards, and courts can do very little to scrutinize what goes on within the privacy of a therapist's office—unless, of course, a complaint is filed. Even then, it may be quite difficult to do anything to halt the destructive behavior.

The advanced group leader is, on the basis of greater experience, expected to demonstrate a far more acute sense of ethics than are those with less experience. No longer can we claim to be acting responsibly just because we aren't breaking any laws or professional codes. Ethics are not all-or-none phenomena, no matter what the judges and the Moral Majority would like us to believe. Most of the field, and most of the attention, is directed toward the grosser forms of misconduct—sexual impropriety, breach of confidentiality, incompetence, negligence, and malpractice.

Professionals are indignant when a colleague is caught acting inappropriately. An attitude prevails that ethics apply to "them," not "us." Yet we *all* act unethically at times. All of us in the field of group leadership are human beings prone to biases and weaknesses, vulnerable to deception and

---

*This chapter is an expanded version from *Journal for Specialists in Groupwork*, Vol. 7, No. 3. Reprinted by permission of the American Counseling Association.

deceit on a small scale. Occasionally we make mistakes. To bring ethics into greater focus for advanced group leaders, this chapter closes the book with a discussion of common unethical behaviors that often go unchecked. There is little reason to review major ethical issues as they affect group leaders and members, since the reader is already familiar with the many excellent discussions presented in introductory group texts (see Corey & Corey, 1992; Gazda, 1991; Gladding, 1991).

Ethics are of particular importance to group leaders because of the special problems that group work presents. As noted throughout the book, these problems make the practitioner vulnerable to error.

1. Verbal abuse and subsequent casualties are more likely to occur in groups than in individual treatment.
2. The therapist has less control over proceedings and client behavior. Potentially more things can go wrong before the leader can intervene.
3. The therapist has more control in influencing capabilities, a power that can be used for better or for worse.
4. Confidentiality can neither be guaranteed nor enforced because other group members don't necessarily live by the same moral code that we do.
5. Many group leaders practice without benefit of training, education, or supervision. There are no standardized criteria for acceptable qualifications. In the same city, a psychiatrist, psychologist, astrologer, palm reader, and prostitute can all label their professional activities as "group therapy."
6. Because groups are such intense environments, the risks for each member are greater. Change *and* damage are accelerated.
7. The screening of clients is frequently haphazard. Clients are often required to participate in the experience involuntarily.
8. Group work presents special re-entry problems for participants when the sessions have ended.
9. Dependency effects are more pronounced in groups.
10. There is no licensure, certification, or regulation that can effectively enforce the practice of responsible group leadership.

One Issue in Depth

One ethical issue that has disturbed social philosophers for centuries has great relevance for contemporary group leaders—the innate conflict between the coercive force of groups and the individual autonomy of each member. Once people decide to pool their resources and work toward a common purpose, individual needs are necessarily shelved in favor of what is good for the majority. This compromise ensures that none of us gets exactly what we want, although most people get a little bit of what they are willing to accept. Our children are taught early in their education the values of co-operation, compromise, and sharing. Independent spirit, personal freedom, and individual identity are diminished for the sake of serving the common good. Indeed, we would have chaos and anarchy without subjugating selfish interests for the benefit of human welfare.

Unfortunately, the indoctrination of The One by The Many has been only too successful. Human beings now live almost totally in a world of groups. Marriages are often interpreted as a melding of lives. The family unit, the PTA, the bowling team, the nation, neighborhood, country club, professional organization, school, employer, religion—all provide a group identity, a "we" that we can believe in.

The structure of the universe easily diminishes egocentricity. To look up at the stars is to confront our insignificance. Even on this tiny planet, biologists, zoologists, and ethnologists tell us of the ultimate irrelevance of a single life. We are like ants, part of a total human society that makes us expendable at the whim of a crushing footstep.

> Ants are so much like human beings as to be an embarrassment. They farm fungi, raise aphids as livestock, launch armies into wars, use chemical sprays to alarm and confuse enemies, capture slaves. The families of weaver ants engage in child labor, holding their larvae like shuttles to spin out the thread that sews the leaves together for their fungus gardens. They exchange information ceaselessly. They do everything but watch television. (Thomas, 1979, p. 12)

Lecturing to philosophy students at Columbia University, William James noted that *unity* has always been considered more important than *variety*. Mathematicians are constantly looking for common denominators, scientists for parsimonious principles, physicists for the reduction of matter into unifying laws, and philosophers for a vision of the world's unity. This preoccupation with oneness to the exclusion of manyness pervades all circles of intellectual achievement. Yet, as James asked, even though we pretend there is unity to the world, a cherished camaraderie of abstractions, "What is the practical value of the oneness for us?" (James, 1907, p. 29).

Always the empiricist, the pragmatist concerned with logical consequences, James investigated the meaning of unity. Does it really exist? Is it possible? Is it desirable? If there is a Oneness, it would have the following characteristics.

1. Nothing is omitted. Everyone and everything is included, with no exception.
2. There is a total union of parts. Everything is connected, hung together, continuous.
3. The lines of influence among parts of the whole can be identified. The conductors form an unbreakable chain.

4. There is a single, absolute causal unity responsible for the actions of many.

5. There is unity of purpose and a set of common goals.

In sum, if unity were possible, the history of the world could be told as one story. But such is obviously not the case; no two objects, much less persons, are identical. Monozygotic twins and precision die-cut instruments may appear alike but actually have minute individual differences. Such concepts as the *average* and *differences* describe general behavior rather than the actions of any single person. There is *similarity* of purpose, even cooperation, among living human beings with regard to collective intentions, yet individual goals are perpetually at war with one another.

There is no group of people, no matter how homogeneous in values, religious beliefs, background, or presenting problems, that satisfies the monistic conditions enumerated earlier. The ethical issue for group leaders, then, is to capitalize on the therapeutic advantages of group settings while simultaneously protecting individual rights and values, a difficult proposition for even the most clear-headed philosopher/scientist.

Slightly Unethical Behaviors

Sheldon Kopp solicited testimony from a number of prominent therapists concerning their most embarrassing mistakes. The contributions collectively portrayed the clinician as a fallible being, a wise fool, a person who acts "just plain silly from time to time" (Kopp, 1972, p. 222). The ethical transgressions (admittedly minor) they reported included developing inappropriate social relationships with clients, deliberately lying to save face (and getting caught), acting seductively, and accepting clients who cannot really be helped.

Other examples described by Kottler and Blau (1989) include blaming the client when things go wrong, persisting in a course of action that is more convenient for us rather than preferable for the group members, being punitive in the ways we respond to clients who get underneath our skin, and becoming excessively self-disclosing and self-indulgent. Several of these, and other slightly unethical behaviors commonly engaged in, are described here.

Little White Lies

"No Pressure Will Be Put on You to Participate Unless You Want To."   Like "the check is in the mail," this is one of the great lies of our time. Although I never begin a group without making that claim, I must later admit honestly that no matter how earnestly I attempt to protect each member's rights, incredible pressure—subtle, unconscious, sneaky, and overt—will be imposed on those reluctant to get involved. Occasionally we will jump on the band-wagon, temporarily ignoring our previous promise, and use all our skills to manipulate reluctant clients to join in, even against their will. Are we excused from such transgressions? Certainly; we're only human. But cop-ping a plea doesn't diminish the nature of an essentially unethical act.

There are constant tugs on every member to conform, to contribute, to be a "regular guy or gal," and there are good reasons that we underplay these forces, attempting to reassure clients that their privacy will be re-spected. Realistically, we couldn't even begin a group without convincing participants that their freedom of choice will be encouraged. Nevertheless, is lying for the clients' own good strictly a moral act?

"This Is a Safe Place."   Group work is a unique professional activity in which other clients, who have not received training and are not bound by confidentiality or any formal ethical codes, essentially function as co-leaders. They probe, confront, participate in role plays, and do many of the same things that therapists and counselors do. That is one of the principal benefits of group work—participants learn to be skilled helpers at the same time that they work on their own issues. This situation, however, presents quite an ethical dilemma.

When we promise participants that their group is a safe place in which to disclose personal secrets, explore sensitive areas, and take risks, can we really guarantee that other members will not: (1) act insensitively, manipula-tively, even abusively; (2) violate confidentiality by telling others what was revealed; or (3) pollute the therapeutic experience by being obnoxious, obstructive, or excessively self-centered?

The reality of group practice is that confidentiality cannot be enforced; individual privacy is diluted; participants feel coercion and pressure to con-form; verbal abuse is likely; and the leader has less control over proceedings, and clients receive less attention and close monitoring than is true in in-dividual treatment (Roback, Ochoa, Bloch, & Purdon, 1992; Van Hoose & Kottler, 1985).

"I Neither Like nor Dislike You; You're a Client."   Inevitably, some group members will ask directly how we feel about them. Recognizing the dangers of saying what we really think (whether positive or negative), we pretend that we don't feel at all. And most of the time, during sessions, we do guard against allowing our personal feelings to get in the way of therapeutic ac-tions. Again, however, the therapeutic options are limited.

First, if we respond honestly, we risk either being seductive if the feel-ings are positive or being perceived as hostile if the feelings are negative. Second, we could employ therapeutic maneuvers: "How would that be helpful for me to tell you?", "What difference would it make to you?", or "I'm sorry. I didn't hear you. Does anyone else have something to say?"

Third, we could share our problem: "I feel uncomfortable telling you my feelings because then I compromise my neutrality." But members might wonder why they should be honest when their leader is so evasive. Each of these responses creates potential problems we would prefer to leave alone. So, instead, we resort to little white lies—"but it's for their own good"— though not altogether certain that the excuse is valid.

"I Bet Your Mother Was a Meticulous Housekeeper."   How often we make interpretations, not to help the client, but to check out the accuracy of our predictions at the expense of wasting valuable group time. We formulate a hunch about why people act as they do, and although this hypothesis may be completely unrelated to what the group members are currently working through, we broadcast the interpretation and smugly await confirmation. We feel good because our investigative skills have once again proved accurate, but the whole episode is merely an exercise in self-indulgence.

"I Remember a Time When . . ."   Inappropriate self-disclosure is another way in which group leaders focus on themselves at the cost of valuable time. Unless a therapist has a specific, defensible rationale, sharing personal stories is likely to be digressive. Each time a group leader engages in a long-winded anecdote that is not specifically intended to deliver an important message or to help a group member work through the presenting concern, the action is unethical in that it negates the clients' importance and wastes time (Van Hoose & Kottler, 1985).

Facilitative self-disclosure that is well timed and appropriately implemented satisfies certain criteria mentioned by Corey, Corey, and Callanan, (1993): How crucial is it that group members perceive you as being human? What specific intentions do you have for revealing your personal life? How might clients' progress be hindered as the result of your self-disclosure? Only after these questions are addressed may the group leader be reasonably certain that self-disclosing interventions are indicated.

"I Know I Can Help You."   In an effort to implant favorable expectations for success, we sometimes exaggerate what we can deliver. Although uncertain that we can keep our promises, we believe that such claims are necessary to keep up morale. Group members enjoy hearing this little lie. They desperately want optimistic assessments. In the same way that a physician prescribes a placebo, saying "I believe this will make you feel better," we justify our own little deceits.

"I Wonder What Would Happen if I Tried . . ."   Another ethical conflict centers on using clients as guinea pigs to practice an experimental treatment procedure. Are we justified in trying out new technologies before we are sure they are safe and before we've had sufficient supervision in their execution? After returning from a workshop or course or following the end of a book such as this, many new therapeutic ideas float in our heads, itching to be applied. After all, we cannot determine what an idea is worth until we try it out for ourselves. But where do we experiment? Can we counsel a group of white rats and then observe their behavior before trying out a procedure on human subjects? Do we wear warning stickers on our foreheads reading "Caution. The surgeon general has determined that these procedures may be hazardous to your health"?

The only viable alternative to stagnation is to experiment with new group strategies cautiously and critically, fully aware that they may not work out as intended. "Group work is a risky business anyway," we reason. "If the technique doesn't do the job, we won't use it again in similar circumstances. Let's just hope that no one is hurt too badly."

"What I Think Does Not Matter."   To reveal or not to reveal our values, that is the question—if indeed it is a question at all. Even if we decide that withholding our beliefs regarding what is good or bad or what is right or wrong is desirable (and this is by no means a universal value in itself), is this physically possible? In spite of our best efforts to remain perfectly neutral, to restrain or disguise all personal preferences, it is utterly impossible to do so completely.

Suppose a group member discloses that he is about to leave his wife for his 19-year-old secretary; although we may show our neutral-accepting-unconditional regard mask, we may find our lips curling against our will. Indeed, we have strong opinions about almost everything that clients do or decide. Most of these value judgments we are able to restrain successfully (on the outside anyway); a few slip through our guard; still more we deliberately reveal.

We thus make no apology for espousing a number of values that we believe all members should adopt. A sampling of these universal truths that we not so subtly impose include the following.

- Being open, revealing, disclosing, taking constructive risks in group is a good thing.
- It is better to have more choices in life than fewer (except when you already have too many, in which case the opposite is true).
- It is not all right to settle for mediocrity; one should strive for excellence in order to be happy and satisfied.

In a study of ethical judgments among group leaders, there is remarkable agreement (about 95%) about what constitutes appropriate versus inappropriate conduct. Gumaer and Scott (1986) presented both experienced and beginning practitioners with a variety of ethical dilemmas dealing with issues related to screening, coercion, conjoint individual and group treatments, and imposing leader values. It was only the last ethical conflict that elicited the most uncertainty as to whether it is acceptable for group leaders to express their own values to clients.

"If You Work Hard Enough, You Can Be Like Me When You Grow Up."   Are we justified in creating miniature disciples, surrogate selves? So much of what constitutes group work involves great potential for clients to become dependent on the leader or on the group process. Many "groupies" do become addicted to group work, unable to function without a support system. Alcoholics Anonymous, for instance, operates on just that premise—that members must become as addicted to AA meetings as they used to be to their liquor.

If we are honest, we admit that some of us deliberately create dependencies in clients by sending out clear messages: "You *need* me to function. You can't get along without this group. This will take years of intensive treatment. By the way, do you have Blue Cross Insurance?" On a smaller scale, most of us sometimes see clients longer than is absolutely necessary, particularly professionals whose livelihood depends on client fees. It may be rationalized that *anyone* can profit from a group experience, no matter how long he or she attends the sessions. But there is usually a point of diminishing returns when a group member's cash investment results in nothing but greater dependency on the leader.

"Everybody in This Group Will Be Treated Equally."   The U.S. constitution guarantees that all people, regardless of age, sex, race, religion, appearance, and hair style, will have equal status. In reality, however, human beings have definite preferences as to the sort of people they would like to be around, and group leaders are no different. We like group members who are attractive, who think as we do, and who come from similar backgrounds. In spite of our restraint, we may give more attention to those who smile and laugh more often at our jokes. Although we attempt to hide our biases, there are some in the group to whom we give less of our time and patience. In short, it is no more possible to treat all clients alike than it is for parents to love all their children equally.

Inevitably, we all act unethically because we are all imperfect beings, inconsistent and hypocritical. We muddle in the dark doing our best to be genuinely helpful but knowing that we can't possibly please everyone all the time. This confession can only be admitted by group leaders who need no longer prove their competence.

> How does a doctor recognize the point in time when he is finally a "surgeon"? As my years as chief resident drew to a close I asked myself the question on more than one occasion.
>
> The answer, I concluded, was self-confidence. When you can say to yourself, "There is no surgical patient I cannot treat competently, treat just as well or better than any other surgeon"—then, and not until then, you are indeed a surgeon. (Nolan, 1968, p. 278)

The experienced group leader understands that naked confidence, a well-integrated ego, a few primitive helping skills, and a strong sense of ethical conviction are about all that is necessary to practice this craft. Legislating more stringent laws to enforce competence, more specific ethical codes to regulate behavior, peer monitoring, review boards, licensing exams, and other external watchdogs—such efforts are sometimes used as a smoke screen to convince the public that we are trying to police our own ranks rather than actually deterring unethical behavior.

Ethical codes and laws are all very fine for publishing in professional journals, hanging on walls, or presenting to graduate students. There is understandably great confusion about to whom the group leader is primarily responsible when there are conflicting demands. Professional codes, institutional policies, legislative mandates, state and federal laws, peer practices, societal expectations, institutional policies, client needs and parents' wishes all have legitimate claims.

Nowhere to Pass the Buck

The predicament of being caught between conflicting loyalties is the ultimate challenge for us as advanced group leaders, and it is sometimes even more stressful for us than it is for beginners. We are the ones whom others consult when they need help. We are the more experienced practitioners who are expected to know what to do when the ethical codes do not offer enough guidance.

In a group I am leading for other experienced group leaders, one member brought up the case of a client who disclosed that once, several years ago, he had been drinking and touched his stepdaughter inappropriately while she was sleeping. He had confessed the act many months earlier to his family therapist, worked with his whole family to process the issues, and had been attending Alcoholics Anonymous regularly since the incident without a single lapse or recurrent episode.

Now, here was the dilemma the group leader presented: should she report the incident to Protective Services? She looked at me expectantly. As would any skilled leader I, of course, stalled for time, hoping to sidestep the responsibility: "Gee, that's a great question. What do you all think?"

I was quite pleased with my deflection, reasoning that this was a great group issue. After wrestling with the dilemma for some time, some members argued that she was obligated to report the incident even though it appeared to be resolved. Others felt that such an action was only self-protective, since getting an agency involved might do more harm to the client than good. The decision came back to rest in my lap again.

I hemmed and hawed for a while, summarizing the conflict and the choices, and then sheepishly shrugged: "I don't have an answer for that question. I can tell you what the law says, what the ethical codes say, even what I think that I might do, but the awesome responsibility of group leadership is that, ultimately, practitioners must answer to themselves for their actions." There is nowhere to pass the buck.

References

ADAMS, H. B. (1964). "Mental illness" or interpersonal behavior? *American Psychologist, 19,* 191–197.

ADAMS, H. E., DOSTER, J. A., & CALHOUN, D. S. (1977). A psychologically based system of response classification. In A. R. Ciminero, K. S. Calhoun, & H. E. Adams (Eds.), *Handbook of behavioral assessment,* New York: Wiley.

ALEXANDER, F. G., & SELESNICK, S. T. (1966). *The history of psychiatry.* New York: Mentor.

ALFRED, A. R. (1992). Members' perceptions of co-leaders influence and effectiveness in group psychotherapy. *Journal for Specialists in Group Work, 17,* 42–53.

ALLAN, E. E. (1982, January). Multiple attending in therapy groups. *Personnel and Guidance Journal,* 318–320.

ALLEN, W. (1976). *Without feathers.* New York: Warner Books.

AMERICAN PSYCHIATRIC ASSOCIATION. (1993). *Diagnostic and statistical manual of mental disorders* (4th ed.). Washington, DC: American Psychiatric Association.

ANDERSON, J. D. (1985). Working with groups: Little-known facts that challenge well-known myths. *Small Group Behavior, 15,* 267–283.

ANDOLFI, M. (1980). Prescribing the families' own dysfunctional rules as a therapeutic strategy. *Journal of Marital and Family Therapy, 6*(1), 29–36.

ANTHONY, C. P., & THIBODEAU, G. A. (1979). *Textbook of anatomy and physiology* (10th ed.). St. Louis: C. V. Mosby.

ARDREY, R. (1966). *The territorial imperative.* New York: Delta.

ARGYRIS, C. (1976). Theories of action that inhibit individual learning. *American Psychologist,* 638–654.

ARGYRIS, C., & SCHON, D. (1974). *Theory in practice: Increasing professional effectiveness.* San Francisco: Jossey-Bass.

ASCH, S. E. (1951). Effects of group pressure upon the modification and distortion of judgments. In H. Guetzkow (Ed.), *Groups, leadership, and men.* Pittsburgh: Carnegie Press.

ASSOCIATION FOR SPECIALISTS IN GROUP WORK. (1990). Ethical guidelines for group counselors. *Journal for Specialists in Group Work, 15,* 119–126.

AUSTIN, A. V. (1968, March). Standards of measurement. *Scientific American,* 50–63.

AYER, A. J. (1952). *Language, truth, and logic.* New York: Dover.

AZIMA, F. J. (1983). Group psychotherapy with personality disorders. In H. I. Kaplan & B. J. Sadock (Eds.), *Comprehensive group psychotherapy,* Baltimore: Williams & Wilkins.

AZIMA, F. J. (1986). Counter transference: In and beyond child group psychotherapy. In A. E. Riester & I. A. Kraft (Eds.), *Child group psychotherapy.* New York: International Universities Press.

BACH, G. R. (1954). *Intensive group therapy.* New York: Ronald Press.

BACK, K. W. (1972). *Beyond words: The story of sensitivity training and the encounter movement.* New York: Russell Sage Foundation.

BAKKER, C. B. (1975). Why people don't change. *Psychotherapy: Theory, Research, and Practice, 12*(2), 164–172.

BALES, R. (1970). *Personality and interpersonal behavior.* New York: Holt, Rinehart & Winston.

BALGOPAL, P. R., & HULL, R. F. (1970). Keeping secrets: Group resistance for patients and therapists. *Psychotherapy: Theory, Research, and Practice, 11*(4), 559–606.

BANDLER, R., & GRINDER, J. (1975). *The structure of magic* (Vol. 1). Palo Alto, CA: Science & Behavior Books.

BANDLER, R., & GRINDER, J. (1979). *Frogs into princes.* Moab, UT: Real People Press.

BANDURA, A. (1969). *Principles of behavior modification.* New York: Holt, Rinehart & Winston.

BANDURA, A. (1971). Psychotherapy based upon modeling principles. In A. Bergin & S. Garfield (Eds.), *Handbook of psychotherapy and behavior change.* New York: Wiley.

BANDURA, A. (1977). *Social learning theory.* Englewood Cliffs, NJ: Prentice-Hall.

BANDURA, A., JEFFREY, R. W., & GAJDOS, E. (1975). Generalizing change through participant modeling with self-directed mastery. *Behavior Research and Therapy, 13,* 141–152.

BARGE, J. K. (1989). Toward a communication competency model of group leadership. *Small Group Behavior, 20,* 167–189.

BARKER, P. (1985). *Using metaphors in psychotherapy.* New York: Brunner/Mazel.

BARON, R. S., MOORE, D., & SANDERS, G. S. (1978). Distraction as a source of drive in social facilitation research. *Journal of Personality and Social Psychology, 36,* 816–824.

BAR-TAL, D. (1990). *Group beliefs: A conception for analyzing group structure, processes, and behavior.* New York: Springer-Verlag.

BASESCU, S. (1990). Tools of the trade: The use of self in psychotherapy. *Group, 14,* 157–165.

BATESON, G. (1977). *Mind and nature.* New York: Bantam Books.

BATESON, G., & JACKSON, D. D. (1968). Some varieties of pathogenic organization. In D. D. Jackson (Ed.), *Communication, family and marriage.* Palo Alto, CA: Science & Behavior Books.

BATESON, G., JACKSON, D. D., HALEY, J., & WEAKLAND, J. (1956). Toward a theory of schizophrenia. *Behavioral Science, 1*(4), 251–264.

BAYLESS, O. L. (1967). An alternative pattern for problem-solving discussion. *Journal of Communication, 17,* 188–197.

BECK, A. P., DUGO, J. M., ENG, A. M., LEWIS, C. M., & PETERS, L. N. (1983). The participation of leaders in the structural development of therapy groups. In R. R. Dies & K. R. MacKenzie (Eds.), *Advances in group psychotherapy: Integrating research and practice.* New York: International Universities Press.

BECK, A. T. (1976). *Cognitive therapy and the emotional disorders*. New York: Intentional Universities Press.

BEDNAR, R. L., COREY, G., EVANS, N., GAZDA, G. M., PISTOLE, M. C., STOCKTON, R., & ROBISON, F. F. (1987). Overcoming obstacles to the future development of research of group work. *Journal for Specialists in Group Work, 12*, 98–111.

BEDNAR, R. L., & LAWLIS, G. F. (1971). Empirical research in group psychotherapy. In S. L. Garfield & A. Bergin (Eds.), *Handbook of psychotherapy and behavior change*. New York: Wiley.

BEDNAR, R. L., MELNICK, J., & KAUL, T. J. (1974). Risk, responsibility, and structure: A conceptual framework for initiating group counseling and psychotherapy. *Journal of Counseling Psychology, 21*(1), 31–37.

BEGELMAN, D. A. (1976). Behavioral classification. In M. Herson & A. E. Bellack (Eds.), *Behavioral assessment: A practical handbook*. New York: Pergamon Press.

BEM, D. J., WALLACH, M. A., & KOGAN, N. (1965). Group decision making under risk of adversive consequences. *Journal of Personality and Social Psychology, 1*, 453–460.

BENJAMIN, A. (1978). *Behavior in small groups*. Boston: Houghton Mifflin.

BENNE, K. D. (1968). From polarization to paradox. In Bennis, Schein, Steele, & Berlew (Eds.), *Interpersonal dynamics*. Homewood, IL: Dorsey.

BENNIS, W., & NANUS, B. (1985). *Leaders: The strategy of taking charge*. New York: Harper & Row.

BENNIS, W., & SHEPARD, H. (1974). A theory of group development. In Gibbard, Hartman, & Mann (Eds.), *Analysis of groups*. San Francisco: Jossey-Bass.

BENSHOFF, D. L. (1978, November). A lesson "Psycholese" or how to "get a feel for" where your "helper" is "coming from." *Personnel and Guidance Journal*, 164–166.

BERG, D. N., & SMITH, K. K. (1990). Paradox and groups. In J. Gillette & M. McCollom (Eds.), *Groups in context: A new perspective on group dynamics*. Reading, MA: Addison-Wesley.

BERG, R. C., & LANDRETH, G. L. (1990). *Group counseling: Concepts and procedures* (2nd ed.). Muncie, IN: Accelerated Development.

BERN, D. J. (1971). The concept of risk in the study of human behavior. In R. E. Carney (Ed.), *Risk-taking behavior*. Springfield, IL: Charles C Thomas.

BERNARD, H. S., BABINEAU, R., & SCHWARTZ, A. J. (1980). Supervisor-trainee co-therapy as a method for individual psychotherapy training. *Psychiatry, 15*, 138–145.

BERNE, E. (1966). *Principles of group treatment*. New York: Oxford University Press.

BERTCHER, H. (1987). Effective group membership. *Social Work with Groups, 10*, 57–67.

BETTELHEIM, B. (1960). *The informed heart*. New York: Avon Books.

BETTELHEIM, B. (1977). *The uses of enchantment*. New York: Vintage Books.

BETZ, R. L., WILBUR, M. P., & ROBERTS-WILBUR, J. (1981, September). A structural blueprint for group facilitators: Three group modalities. *Personnel and Guidance Journal*, 31–37.

BEUTLER, L. E. (1983). *Eclectic psychotherapy: A systematic approach*. New York: Pergamon Press.

BEUTLER, L. E., & CLARKIN, J. (1990). *Systematic treatment selection: Toward targeted therapeutic interventions*. New York: Brunner/Mazel.

BIERCE, A. (1940). *The devil's dictionary*. New York: Dover. (Originally published 1911)

BLAKE, R. R., & MOUTON, J. S. (1970). The fifth achievement. *Journal of Applied Behavioral Science, 6,* 413–426.

BLATNER, A. (1988a). *Acting-in: Practical applications of psychodramatic methods* (2nd ed.). New York: Springer.

BLATNER, A. (1988b). *Foundations of psychodrama: History, theory and practice* (3rd ed.). New York: Springer.

BLOCH, S. (1986). Therapeutic factors in group psychotherapy. In A. J. Frances and R. E. Hales (Eds.), *Annual Review* (Vol. 5), Washington, D.C.: American Psychiatric Press.

BLOCH, S., BROWNING, S., & MCGRATH, G. (1983). Humour in group psychotherapy. *British Journal of Medical Psychology, 56,* 89–97.

BOCKAR, J. A. (1976). *Primer for the nonmedical psychotherapist.* New York: Spectrum.

BOLAN, R. S. (1980). The practitioner as theorist: The phenomenology of the professional episode. *Journal of the American Planning Association, 46*(3), 261–274.

BOMBECK, E. (1972). *The grass is always greener over the septic tank.* Greenwich, CT: Fawcett.

BOND, G. R. (1983). Norm regulation in therapy groups. In R. R. Dies & K. R. MacKenzie (Eds.), *Advances in group psychotherapy: Integrating research and practice.* New York: International Universities Press.

BORGERS, S. B., & KOENIG, R. W. (1983). Uses and effects of modeling by the therapist in group therapy. *Journal for Specialists in Group Work, 8,* 133–138.

BOSTWICK, G. J. (1987). "Where's Mary?" A review of the group treatment dropout literature. *Social Work with Groups, 10*(3), 117–132.

BOUCHARD, M. C., & GUERETTE, L. (1991). Psychotherapy as a hermeneutical experience. *Psychotherapy, 28,* 385–394.

BOULANGER, G. (1988). Working with the entitled patient. *Journal of Contemporary Psychotherapy, 18,* 124–144.

BOYD, R. D. (1990). An approach to facilitating personal transformations in small groups. *Small Group Research, 21,* 522–537.

BROWN, R. (1965). *Social psychology.* New York: Free Press.

BROWN, R. (1974). Further comment on the risky shift. *American Psychologist, 29,* 468–470.

BROWN, R. W. (1978). Choosing and evaluating group techniques: A systematic framework. *Journal for Specialists in Group Work, 3*(3), 146–153.

BRUNER, J. S. (1963). *The process of education.* New York: Vintage Books.

BUGENTAL, J. F. T. (1990). *Intimate Journeys: Stories from life-changing therapy.* San Francisco: Jossey-Bass.

BYRD, R. E. (1974). *A guide to personal risk taking.* New York: AMACOM.

CABRAL, R. J. (1987). Role playing as a group intervention. *Small Group Behavior, 18,* 470–482.

CANTELA, J. R. (1976). The present status of covert modeling. *Journal of Behavior Therapy and Experimental Psychiatry, 6,* 323–326.

CAPUTO, P. (1980). *Horn of Africa.* New York: Dell.

CARKHUFF, R. R., & BERENSON, B. G. (1977). *Beyond counseling and psychotherapy.* New York: Holt, Rinehart & Winston.

CARR, S. J., & DABBS, J. R., JR. (1974). The effects of lighting, distance, and intimacy of topic on verbal and visual behavior. *Sociometry, 37,* 592–600.

CARTLEDGE, G., & MILBURN, J. R. (1981). *Teaching social skills to children.* Elmsford, NY: Pergamon Press.

CARTWRIGHT, D. (1951). Achieving change in people: Some applications of group dynamics theory. *Human Relations, 4*, 381–392.

CARTWRIGHT, D. (1968). The nature of group cohesiveness. In D. Cartwright & A. Zander (Eds.), *Group dynamics: Research and theory*. London: Tavistock.

CARTWRIGHT, D., & ZANDER, A. (1968). *Group dynamics: Research and theory*. New York: Harper & Row.

CATTELL, R. B. (1948). Concepts and methods in the measurement of group syntality. *Psychological Review, 55*, 48–63.

CATTELL, R. B. (1966). Psychological theory and scientific method. In R. B. Cattell (Ed.), *Handbook of multivariate experimental psychology*. Chicago: Rand McNally.

CHARNEY, I. W. (1980). Why are so many (if not really all) people and families disturbed? *Journal of Marital and Family Therapy, 6*(1), 37–48.

CHESSICK, R. D. (1977). *Great ideas in psychotherapy*. New York: Jason Aronson.

CHILDERS, J. H., & COUCH, R. D. (1989). Myths about group counseling: Identifying and challenging misconceptions. *Journal for Specialists in Group Work, 14*, 105–111.

CLARK, C. H. (1958). *Brainstorming*. New York: Doubleday.

CLARK, R. D., III., (1971). Group-induced shift toward risk: A critical appraisal. *Psychological Bulletin, 76*, 251–270.

COCHE, J., & COCHE, E. (1990). *Couples group psychotherapy: A clinical practice*. New York: Brunner/Mazel.

COHEN, A. M., & SMITH, R. D. (1976). *The critical incident in growth groups: Theory and technique*. La Jolla, CA: University Associates.

COHN, B. (1973). Absentee-cueing. A technical innovation in the training of group counselors. *Educational Technology, 13*(2), 61–62.

COLE, H. P., & SARNOFF, D. (1980, November). Creativity and counseling. *Personnel and Guidance Journal*, 140–146.

COLEMAN, S. (1985). *Failures in family therapy*. New York: Guilford.

COLSON, D., LEWIS, L., & HORWITZ, L. (1985). Negative outcomes in psychotherapy and psychoanalysis. In D. T. Mays & C. M. Franks (Eds.), *Negative outcome in psychotherapy and what to do about it*. New York: Springer.

CONYNE, R. (1983). Sounds good, but does it work? *Journal for Specialists in Group Work, 8*, 58.

CONYNE, R. (1985). *The group workers' handbook: Varieties of group experience*. Springfield, IL: Charles C Thomas.

COOKE, T. P., & APOLLONI, T. (1976). Developing positive social-emotional behaviors: A study of training and generalization effects. *Journal of Applied Behavior Analysis, 9*, 65–78.

COOKER, P. G., & NERO, R. S. (1987). Effects of videotaped feedback on self-concept of patients in group psychotherapy. *Journal for Specialists in Group Work, 12*, 112–117.

COOPER, C. L., & MANGHAM, I. L. (Eds.). (1971). *T-groups: A survey of research*. London: Wiley-Interscience.

COOPER, I. S. (1981). *The Vital Probe*. New York: Norton.

COREY, G. (1982). *I never knew I had a choice* (4th ed.). Pacific Grove, CA: Brooks/Cole.

COREY, G. (1990). *Theory and practice of group counseling* (3rd ed.). Pacific Grove, CA: Brooks/Cole.

COREY, G., COREY, M. S., & CALLANAN, P. (1993) *Issues and ethics in the helping professions*. Pacific Grove, CA: Brooks/Cole.

COREY, G., COREY, M. S., CALLANAN, P., & RUSSELL, J. M. (1992). *Group techniques* (2nd ed.). Pacific Grove, CA: Brooks/Cole.

COREY, M. S., & COREY, G. (1992). *Groups: Process and practice.* (4th ed.). Pacific Grove, CA: Brooks/Cole.

CORMIER, W. H., & CORMIER, L. S. (1991). *Interviewing strategies for helpers.* (3rd ed.). Pacific Grove, CA: Brooks/Cole.

CORSINI, R. (1957). *Methods of group psychotherapy.* New York: McGraw-Hill.

CORSINI, R., & ROSENBERG, B. (1955). Mechanisms of group psychotherapy: Processes and practices. *Journal of Abnormal and Social Psychology, 51,* 406–411.

COUCH, R. D., & CHILDERS, J. H. (1987). Leadership strategies for instilling and maintaining hope in group counseling. *Journal for Specialists in Group Work, 12,* 138–143.

COURVILLE, T. J., & Keeper, C. S. (1984). The issue of sexuality in group psychotherapy. *Group, 8,* 35–42.

COX, M., & THEILGAARD, A. (1987). *Mutative metaphors in psychotherapy.* London: Tavistock.

COZBY, P. C. (1973). Self-disclosure: A literature review. *Psychological Bulletin, 79,* 73–91.

CREER, T. L., & MIKLICH, D. R. (1970). The application of a self-modeling procedure to modify inappropriate behavior: A preliminary report. *Behavior Research and Therapy, 8,* 91–92.

CSIKSZENTMIHALYI, M. (1975). *Beyond boredom and anxiety.* San Francisco: Jossey-Bass.

DAVIS, F., & LOHR, N. (1971). Special problems with the use of co-therapists in group psychotherapy. *International Journal of Group Psychotherapy, 2,* 143–157.

DAVIS, K. L., & MEARA, D. M. (1982). So you think it's a secret. *Journal for Specialists in Group Work, 1,* 3.

DECHENNE, T. K. (1988). Boredom as a clinical issue. *Psychotherapy, 25,* 71–81.

DECKER, R. J. (1988). *Effective psychotherapy: The silent dialogue.* New York: Hemisphere.

DELLA CORTE, M. (1980). Psycho babble: Why we do it. *Psychotherapy: Theory, Research, and Practice, 17*(3), 281–284.

DEWEY, J. (1909, January). The bearings of pragmatism on education. *Progressive Journal of Education,* 5–8.

DEWEY, J. (1983). *Logic: The theory of inquiry.* New York: Holt, Rinehart & Winston.

DIEDRICH, R. C., & DYE, H. A. (Eds.). (1972). *Group procedures: Purposes, processes, and outcomes.* Boston: Houghton Mifflin.

DIES, R. R. (1983). Bridging the gap between research and practice in group psychotherapy. In R. R. Dies & K. R. MacKenzie (Eds.), *Advances in group psychotherapy: Integrating research and practice.* New York: International Universities Press.

DIES, R. R. (1985). Research foundations for the future of group work. *Journal for Specialists in Group Work, 10,* 68–73.

DIES, R. R. (1992). The future of group therapy. *Psychotherapy, 29,* 58–64.

DIES, R. R. (1992). Models of group psychotherapy: Sifting through confusion. *International Journal of Group Psychotherapy, 42,* 1–17.

DILORETO, A. O. (1971). *Comparative psychotherapy.* Chicago: Aldine-Atherton.

DIMOND, R. E., HAVENS, R. A., & JONES, A. C. (1978). A conceptual framework for the practice of prescriptive eclecticism in psychotherapy. *American Psychologist, 33*(3), 239–248.

DONLEAVY, J. P. (1975). *The unexpurgated code*. New York: Delta.

DOSTOYEVSKY, F. (1960). *Notes from the underground*. Garden City, NY: Anchor Books. (Originally published 1864)

DOWD, E. T., & SEIBEL, C. A. (1990). A cognitive theory of resistance and reactance: Implications for treatment. *Journal of Mental Health Counseling, 12,* 458–469.

DREIKURS, R. (1960). *Group psychotherapy and group approaches: The collected papers of Rudolf Dreikurs*. Chicago: Alfred Adler Institute.

DUGO, J. M., & BECK, A. P. (1991). Phases of co-therapy team development. In B. Roller & V. Nelson (Eds.), *The art of co-therapy: How therapists work together.* London: Guilford Press.

DUMONT, F. (1991). Expertise in psychotherapy: Inherent liabilities of becoming experienced. *Psychotherapy, 28,* 422–428.

DUNCAN, K., BECK, D., & GRANUM, R. (1986). Ordinary people: Using a popular film in group therapy. *Journal of Counseling and Development, 65,* 50–51.

DUNCAN, W. J. (1985). The superiority theory of humor at work: Joking relationships as indicators of formal and informal status patterns in small, task-oriented groups. *Small Group Behavior, 16,* 556–564.

DUNN, MARIAN E., & DICKES, R. (1977). Erotic issues in co-therapy. *Journal of Sex and Marital Therapy, 3*(3), 205–211.

DURKIN, H. E. (1964). *The group in depth*. New York: International Universities Press.

DYER, W. W. (1976). *Your erroneous zones*. New York: Funk & Wagnalls.

DYER, W. W., & VRIEND, J. (1973a). Effective group counseling process interventions. *Educational Technology, 13*(1), 61–67.

DYER, W. W., & VRIEND, J. (1973b). Role-working in group counseling. *Educational Technology, 13*(2), 32–36.

DYER, W. W., & VRIEND, J. (1975). *Counseling techniques that work*. Alexandria, VA: American Counseling Association.

DYER, W. W., & VRIEND, J. (1980). *Group counseling for personal mastery*. New York: Sovereign Books.

EDELWICH, J., & BRODSKY, A. (1992). *Group counseling for the resistant client*. New York: Lexington Books.

EDLESON, J. L. (1979). *Group social skills training for children: An evaluative study*. Unpublished doctoral dissertation, University of Wisconsin.

EDLESON, J. L., & ROSE, S. D. (1981). Investigations into the efficacy of short-term group social skills training for socially isolated children. *Child Behavior Therapy, 3,* 1–16.

EDWARDS, W. (1954). The theory of decision making. *Psychological Bulletin, 51,* 380–417.

EGAN, G. (1976). *Interpersonal living: A skills/contract approach to human-relations training in groups*. Pacific Grove, CA: Brooks/Cole.

EINHORN, J. (1979). On sufism, sufi group study, and group leadership, *Journal for Specialists in Group Work, 4*(3), 140–147.

ELDER, I. R. (1990). *Conducting group therapy with addicts: A guidebook for professionals*. Bradenton, FL: Human Services Institute.

ELLERBROEK, W. C. (1978, Spring). Language, thought, and disease. *Co-Evolution Quarterly,* 30–38.

ELLIS, A. (1974). *Humanistic psychotherapy: The rational-emotive approach*. New York: McGraw-Hill.

ELLIS, A. (1977a). The basic clinical theory of rational-emotive therapy. In A. Ellis & R. Grieger (Eds.), *Handbook of rational-emotive therapy*. New York: Springer.

ELLIS, A. (1977b). Fun as psychotherapy. In A. Ellis & R. Grieger (Eds.), *Handbook of rational-emotive therapy*. New York: Springer.

ELLIS, A., & HARPER, R. (1975). *A new guide to rational living*. Englewood Cliffs, NJ: Prentice-Hall.

EPSTEIN, N., JAYNE-LAZARUS, C., & DE GIOVANNI, I. S. (1979). Co-trainers as models of relationships: Effects of the outcome of couples therapy. *Journal of Marital and Family Therapy*, 53–60.

ERIKSON, E. (1963). *Childhood and society* (2nd ed.). New York: Norton.

ERICKSON, M. H. (1967a). Further techniques of hypnosis: Utilization techniques. In Jay Haley (Ed.), *Advanced techniques of hypnosis and therapy*. New York: Grune & Stratton.

ERICKSON, M. H. (1967b). The method employed to formulate a complex story for the induction of the experimental neurosis. In J. Haley (Ed.), *Advanced techniques of hypnosis and therapy*. New York: Grune & Stratton.

ERICKSON, M. H. (1982, February). Spellbinders: Entrancing tales of a master hypnotist. *Psychology Today*, 39–45.

ERICKSON, R. (1984). *Inpatient small group psychotherapy*. Springfield, IL: Charles C Thomas.

ETTIN, M. F. (1987). Within the group's view: Clarifying dynamics through metaphoric and symbolic imagery. *Small Group Behavior*, 17, 407–426.

ETTIN, M. F. (1992). *Foundations and applications of group psychotherapy*. Boston: Allyn & Bacon.

EYSENCK, H. J. (1952). The effects of psychotherapy: An evaluation. *Journal of Consulting Psychology*, 16, 319–324.

EYSENCK, H. J. (1965). The effects psychotherapy. *Journal of Psychology*, 1, 97–118.

EYSENCK, H. J. (1967). The logical basis of factor analysis. In D. N. Jackson & S. Messick (Eds.), *Problems in human assessment*. New York: McGraw-Hill.

FARB, P. (1974). *Word play: What happens when people talk*. New York: Knopf.

FASHIMPAR, G. A., & HARRIS, L. T. (1987). Social work at 30 mph: Mini-bike rehabilitation groups for juvenile delinquents. *Social Work with Groups*, 10(1), 33–49.

FEDER, B., & RONALL, R. (Eds.). (1980). *Beyond the hot seat: Gestalt approaches to group work*. New York: Brunner/Mazel.

FEILBERT-WILLIS, R., KIBEL, H. D., & WIKSTROM, T. (1986). Techniques for handling resistances in group psychotherapy with severely disturbed patients. *Group*, 10, 228–238.

FENCHEL, G. H., & FLAPAN, D. (1985). Resistance in group psychotherapy. *Group*, 9, 35–47.

FENCHEL, G. H., & FLAPAN, D. (1987). Acting out in group psychotherapy. *Group*, 11, 94–107.

FESTINGER, L., PEPITONE, A., & NEWCOMB, T. (1952). Some consequences of de-individualization in a group. *Journal of Abnormal and Social Psychology*, 47, 382–389.

FIEVE, R. R. (1975). *Mood swing: The third revolution in psychiatry*. New York: Bantam Books.

FISH, J. (1973). *Placebo therapy*. San Francisco: Jossey-Bass.

FLANAGAN, J. C. (1954). The critical incident technique. *Psychological Bulletin*, 51(4), 327–358.

FLAPAN, D., & FENCHEL, G. H. (1984). Countertransference in group psychotherapy. *Group, 8,* 17–29.

FLOWERS, J. V., BOORAEM, C. D., & HARTMAN, K. A. (1981). Client improvement on higher and lower intensity problems as a function of group cohesiveness. *Psychotherapy: Theory, Research, and Practice, 18*(2), 246–258.

FOLEY, W. J., & BONNEY, W. C. (1966). A developmental model for counseling groups. *Personnel and Guidance Journal.* 576–580.

FOOT, H. C., & CHAPMAN, A. J. (1976). The social responsiveness of young children in humorous situations. In A. J. Chapman & H. C. Foot (Eds.), *Humor and laughter: Theory, research, and applications.* London: Wiley.

FORD, D. H., & URBAN, H. B. (1976). *Systems of psychotherapy.* New York: Wiley.

FORER, B. R. (1970). Therapeutic relationships in groups. In A. Burton (Ed.), *Encounter.* San Francisco: Jossey-Bass.

FOSTER, J. A. (1980, September). Humor and counseling: Close encounters of another kind. *Personnel and Guidance Journal,* 46–49.

FOULKES, S. H., & ANTHONY, E. J. (1965). *Group psychotherapy: The psychoanalytic approach* (2nd ed.). Baltimore: Penguin Books.

FRANCES, A., CLARKIN, J., & PERRY, S. (1984). *Differential therapeutics in psychiatry.* New York: Brunner/Mazel.

FRANK, J. D. (1973). *Persuasion and healing.* Baltimore: Johns Hopkins University Press.

FRANKL, V. (1978). *The unheard cry for meaning.* New York: Simon & Schuster.

FREEDMAN, S., & HURLEY, J. (1980). Perceptions of helpfulness and behavior in groups. *Group, 4,* 51–58.

FREMONT, S. K., & ANDERSON, W. (1986). What client behaviors make counselors angry? An exploratory study. *Journal of Counseling and Development, 65,* 67–70.

FREMONT, S. K., & ANDERSON, W. (1988). Investigation of factors involved in therapists' annoyance with clients. *Professional Psychology, 19,* 330–335.

FREUD, S. (1926). Inhibitions, symptoms, and anxiety. *Standard Edition, 20,* 77–175. London: Hogarth Press.

FREUD, S. (1959) *Group psychology and the analysis of the ego.* New York: Liveright.

FREUD, S. (1960). *Jokes and their relation to the unconscious.* New York: Norton.

FREY, D. H. (1972). Conceptualizing counseling theories: A content analysis of process and goal statements. *Counseling Education and Supervision, 11,* 143–150.

FREY, D. H. (1978). Science and the single case in counseling research. *Personnel and Guidance Journal,* 263–268.

FREY, D. H. (1979). Understanding and managing conflict. In S. Eisenberg & L. E. Patterson (Eds.), *Helping clients with special concerns.* Chicago: Rand McNally.

FRIED, E. (1954). The effect of combined therapy on the productivity of patients. *International Journal of Group Psychotherapy, 4,* 42.

FRIED, E. (1985). The processes of change in group psychotherapy. *Group, 9,* 3–13.

FRIEDMAN, W. H. (1989). *Practical group therapy.* San Francisco: Jossey-Bass.

FUHRIMAN, A., & BURLINGAME, G. M. (1990). Consistency of matter: A comparative analysis of individual and group process variables. *The Counseling Psychologist, 18,* 6–63.

GAINES, T. (1986). Application of child group psychotherapy. In A. E. Riester & I. A. Kraft (Eds.), *Child group psychotherapy.* New York: International Universities Press.

GALLOGHY, V., & LEVINE, B. (1979). Co-therapy. In B. Levine (Ed.), *Group psychotherapy: Practice and development.* Englewood Cliffs, NJ: Prentice-Hall.

GANS, R. (1957). The use of group co-therapists in the teaching of psychotherapy. *American Journal of Psychotherapy, 11,* 618–625.

GANS, R. (1962). Group co-therapists and the therapeutic situation: A critical evaluation. *International Journal of Group Psychotherapy, 12,* 82–88.

GARFIELD, S. L. (1980). *Psychotherapy: An eclectic approach.* New York: Wiley.

GARFIELD, S. L., & KURTZ, R. (1976). Clinical psychologists in the 1970s. *American Psychologist, 31,* 1–9.

GARFIELD, S. L., & KURTZ, R. (1977). A study of eclectic views. *Journal of Consulting and Clinical Psychology, 45,* 78–83.

GAZDA, G. M. (Ed.). (1975). *Basic approaches to group psychotherapy and counseling* (2nd ed.). Springfield, IL: Charles C Thomas.

GAZDA, G. M. (1989). *Group counseling: A developmental approach* (4th ed.). Boston: Allyn & Bacon.

GEIS, H. J. (1973). Effectively leading a group in the present moment: A highly artistic, probabilistic, and professional task if one would by-pass traditional myths about group work. *Educational Technology, 13*(2), 10–20.

GEMMILL, G. (1986). The mythology of the leader role in small groups. *Small Group Behavior, 17,* 41–50.

GETTY, C., & SHANNON, A. M. (1960). Co-therapy as an egalitarian relationship. *American Journal of Nursing, 69*(4), 767–771.

GIEDT, F. H. (1961). Predicting suitability for group psychotherapy. *American Journal of Psychotherapy, 16,* 582–591.

GILL, S. J., & BARRY, R. A. (1982, January). Group-focused counseling: Classifying the essential skills. *Personnel and Guidance Journal,* 302–305.

GILLETTE, J. (1990). Intimacy in work groups: Looking from the inside out. In J. Gillette & M. McCollom (Eds.), *Groups in contact: A new perspective on group dynamics.* Reading, MA: Addison-Wesley.

GLADDING, S. T. (1984). The metaphor as a counseling tool in group work. *Journal for Specialists in Group Work, 9,* 151–156.

GLADDING, S. T. (1991). *Group work: A counseling specialty.* New York: Merrill.

GLADDING, S. T. (1992). *Counseling as an art: The creative arts in counseling.* Alexandria, VA: American Counseling Association.

GLANTZ, K., & PEARCE, J. K. (1989). *Exiles from Eden: Psychotherapy from an evolutionary perspective.* New York: Norton.

GLASER, R., & CHI, M. H. (1989). Overview. In M. H. Chi, R. Glaser, & M. J. Farr (Eds.), *The nature of expertise.* Hillsdale, NJ: Erlbaum.

GLASS, D. C., SINGER, J. E., & FRIEDMAN, L. N. (1969). Psychic cost of adaptation to an environmental stressor. *Journal of Personality and Social Psychology, 12,* 200–210.

GLASSER, W., & IVERSON, N. (1966). *Reality therapy in large group counseling.* Los Angeles: Reality Press.

GLASSMAN, S. M. (1983). In, with, and of the group: A perspective on group psychotherapy. *Small Group Behavior, 14,* 96–106.

GLOSSOP, R. J. (1974). *Philosophy: An introduction to its problems and vocabulary.* New York: Dell.

GOERTZEL, V., & GOERTZEL, M. G. (1962) *Cradles of eminence.* Boston: Little, Brown.

GOERTZEL, M. G., GOERTZEL, V., & GOERTZEL, T. G. (1978). *300 eminent personalities*. San Francisco: Jossey-Bass.

GOLDBERG, C., & GOLDBERG, M. C. (1973). *The human circle: An existential approach to the new group therapies*. Chicago: Nelson-Hall.

GOLDBERG, C. (1983). The function of the therapist's affect in therapeutic conflict in groups. *Groups, 7*, 3–18.

GOLDBERG, M. L., PASSOW, A. H., & JUSTMAN, J. (1966). *The effects of ability grouping*. New York: Teachers College Press.

GOLDBERG, P. (1990). *The Babinski reflex*. Los Angeles: Tarcher.

GOLDFRIED, M. R. (1980). Toward the delineation of therapeutic change principles. *American Psychologist, 35*(11), 991–999.

GOLDFRIED, M. R., & GOLDFRIED, A. P. (1980). Cognitive change methods. In F. H. Kanfer & A. P. Goldstein (Eds.), *Helping people change*. New York: Pergamon Press.

GOLDMAN, E. E., & MORRISON, D. S. (1984). *Psychodrama: Experience and process*. Phoenix: Eldemar.

GOLDMAN, M. (1965). A comparison of individual group performance for varying combinations of initial ability. *Journal of Personality and Social Psychology, 1*, 210–216.

GOLDSTEIN, A. P., HELLER, K., & SECHREST, L. B. (1966). *Psychotherapy and the psychology of behavior change*. New York: Wiley.

GOODCHILDS, J. D. (1972). On being witty: Causes, correlates, and consequences. In J. H. Goldstein and P. E. McGhee (Eds.), *The psychology of humor*. New York: Academic Press.

GOODMAN, J. (1985). Grin and share it. *Laughing Matters, 3*, 29.

GOODMAN, M. (1992). Education and training in group psychotherapy. *The Psychotherapy Bulletin, 27*, 25–26.

GORDON, D. (1978). *Therapeutic metaphor*. Cupertino, CA: Meta Publications.

GORSUCH, R. L. (1974). *Factor analysis*. Philadelphia: Saunders.

GOTTMAN, J., & LEIBLUM, S. (1974). *How to do psychotherapy and how to evaluate it*. New York: Holt, Rinehart & Winston.

GOTTSCHALK, L. A. (1966). Psychoanalytic notes on T-groups at the Human Relations Laboratory, Bethel, Maine. *Comprehensive Psychiatry, 7*, 472–487.

GOULDING, R. L., & GOULDING, M. M. (1991). An intimate model for co-therapy. In B. Roller & V. Nelson (Eds.), *The art of co-therapy: How therapists work together*. London: Guilford Press.

GRAINGER, R. (1990). *Drama and healing: The roots of drama therapy*. London: Jessica Kingsley Publishers.

GREENBERG, D. (1966). *How to make yourself miserable*. New York: Random House.

GREENBERG-EDELSTEIN, R. R. (1986). *The nurturance phenomenon: Roots of group psychotherapy*. Norwalk, CT: Appleton-Century-Crofts.

GREENWALD, H. (1973). *Direct decision therapy*. San Diego: Edits.

GREENWALD, H. (1975). Humor in psychotherapy. *Journal of Contemporary Psychotherapy, 7*(2), 113–116.

GRIEGER, R., & BOYD, J. (1977). Psychotherapeutic responses to some critical incidents in RET. In A. Ellis & R. Grieger (Eds.), *Handbook of rational-emotive therapy*. New York: Springer.

GROTJAHN, M. (1983). The qualities of the group psychotherapist. In H. I. Kaplan & B. J. Sadock (Eds.), *Comprehensive group psychotherapy*. Baltimore: Williams & Wilkins.

GUMAER, J., & MARTIN, D. (1990). Group ethics: A multimodal model for training knowledge and skill competencies. *Journal for Specialists in Group Work, 15,* 94–103.

GUMAER, J., & SCOTT, L. (1986). Group workers' perceptions of ethical and unethical behavior of group leaders. *Journal for Specialists in Group Work, 11,* 139–150.

GUMMAN, A. S., & KNISKEM, D. P. (1978). Research on marital and family therapy. In S. L. Garfield & A. E. Bergin (Eds.), *Handbook of psychotherapy and behavior change.* New York: Wiley.

GUTTMACHER, J. A., & BIRK, L. (1971). Group therapy: What specific advantages? *Comprehensive Psychiatry, 12,* 546–556.

HADDEN, S. B. (1947). The utilization of a therapy group in teaching psychotherapy. *American Journal of Psychiatry, 103,* 644–648.

HALEY, J. (1968). *Uncommon therapy.* New York: Grune & Stratton.

HALEY, J. (1976). *Problem-solving therapy.* San Francisco: Jossey-Bass.

HALEY, J. (1980). How to be a marriage therapist without knowing practically anything. *Journal of Marital and Family Therapy, 6*(4), 385–392.

HALPEM, T. O. (1977). Degree of client disclosure as a function of past disclosure, counselor disclosure, and counselor facilitativeness. *Journal of Counseling Psychology, 24,* 41–47.

HAMILTON, J. D., DECKER, N., & RUMBAUT, R. D. (1986). The manipulative patient. *American Journal of Psychotherapy, 60,*189–200.

HANEY, J. N., SEWELL, W. R., EDELSTEIN, B. A., & SARTIN, H. H. (1975). A portable inexpensive walkie-talkie-type "Bug-in-the-ear." *Behavior Research Methods and Instrumentation, 7*(1), 19–20.

HANNA, F. J., & PUHAKKA, K. (1991). Where psychotherapy works. *Psychotherapy, 28.*

HANSEN, J. C. (Ed.). (1978). *Counseling process and procedures.* New York: Macmillan.

HANSEN, J. C., WARNER, R. W., & SMITH, E. J. (1980). *Group counseling: Theory and process* (2nd ed.). Chicago: Rand McNally.

HARDY, R. (Ed.). (1973). *Group counseling and therapy techniques in special settings.* Springfield, IL: Charles C Thomas.

HARE, N., & LEVIS, D. J. (1981). Pervasive anxiety: A search for a cause and treatment approach. In S. M. Turner, K. S. Calhoun, & H. E. Adams (Eds.), *Handbook of clinical behavior therapy.* New York: Wiley.

HARMON, H. (1967). *Modern factor analysis.* Chicago: University of Chicago Press.

HARTLEY, D., ROBACK, H. B., & ABRAMOWITZ, S. I. (1976). Deterioration effects in encounter groups. *American Psychologist,* 247–255.

HAVIGHURST, R. J. (1972). *Developmental tasks and education.* New York: David McKay.

HAYAKAWA, S. I. (1964). *Language in thought and action* (2nd ed.). New York: Harcourt, Brace & World.

HAZEL, J. S., SCHUMAKER, J. B., SHERMAN, J. A., & SHELDON-WILDON, J. (1981). *Asset: A social skills program for adolescents.* Champaign, IL: Research Press.

HECKEL, R. V., & SALZBERG, H. C. (1976). *Group psychotherapy: A behavioral approach.* Columbia: University of South Carolina Press.

HELLER, J. (1955). *Catch 22.* New York: Dell.

HELLWIG, K., & MEMMOTT, R. J. (1974). Co-therapy: The balancing act. *Small Group Behavior, 5*(2), 175–181.

HELSON, R. (1965). Childhood interest clusters related to creativity in women. *Journal of Consulting Psychology, 29,* 353–361.

HEROLD, P. L., RAMIREZ, J., & NEWKIRK, J. (1971). A portable radio communications system for teacher education. *Educational Technology.*

HERTZLER, J. O. (1970). *Laughter: A socio-scientific analysis.* New York: Exposition Press.

HESLIN, R. (1964). Predicting group task effectiveness from member characteristics. *Psychological Bulletin, 62,* 248–256.

HESSE, H. (1951). *Siddhartha.* New York: New Directions.

HIGBEE, K. L. (1973). Group influence on self-disclosure. *Psychological Reports, 32,* 903–909.

HILKEY, J. H., WILHELM, C. L., & HORNE, A. M. (1982). Comparative effectiveness of videotape pre-training versus no pre-training on selected process and outcome variables in group therapy. *Psychological Reports, 50,* 1151–1159.

HILL, C. E. (1990). Is individual therapy process really different from group therapy process? *The Counseling Psychologist, 18,* 126–130.

HILL, W. (1971). The Hill interaction matrix. *Personnel and Guidance Journal,* 619–622.

HILL, W. F. (1975). Further considerations of therapeutic mechanisms in group therapy. *Small Group Behavior,* 421–429.

HINES, M. (1988). Similarities and differences in group and family therapy. *Journal for Specialists in Group Work, 13,* 173–179.

HIPPLE, J. (1982). Group treatment of suicidal clients. *Journal for Specialists in Group Work, 7,* 245–250.

HOCH, P. (1950). Bisocial aspects of anxiety. In P. Hoch & J. Zubin (Eds.), *Anxiety.* New York: Grune & Stratton.

HOLLANDER, C. E. (1978). *A process for psychodrama training: The Hollander psychodrama curve.* Denver: Snow Lion Press.

HOPPER, G. (1978). Resistance in counseling groups. *Journal for Specialists in Group Work, 3*(1), 37–48.

HORAN, J. J. (1979). *Counseling for effective decision making.* Belmont, CA: Wadsworth.

HORNEY, K. (1945). *Our inner conflicts.* New York: Norton.

HORWITZ, L. (1980). Group psychotherapy for borderline and narcissistic patients. *Bulletin of the Menninger Clinic, 44,* 188–200.

HORWITZ, L. (1987). Indications for group psychotherapy with borderline and narcissistic patients. *Bulletin of the Menninger Clinic, 51,* 248–260.

HOSFORD, R., & DE VISSER, L. (1974). *Behavioral approaches to counseling: An introduction.* Washington, DC: American Personnel & Guidance Association Press.

HOWARD, G. S., NANCE, D. W., & MYERS, P. (1986). Adaptive counseling and therapy: An integrative, eclectic model. *The Counseling Psychologist, 14,* 363–442.

HUPPE, B. F., & KAMINSKY, J. (1962). *Logic and language.* New York: Knopf.

HURLEY, D. J. (1984). Resistance and work with groups. *Social Work with Groups, 7,* 71–81.

IVEY, A. E. (1991). *Developmental strategies for helpers.* Pacific Grove, CA: Brooks/Cole.

JACOBS, A. (1974). The use of feedback in groups. In A. Jacobs & W. W. Sprandlin (Eds.), *Group as agent of change.* New York: Behavioral Publications.

JACOBS, A., JACOBS, M., FELDMAN, G., & CAVIOR, N. (1973). Feedback 11—the credibility gap: Delivery of positive and negative emotional and behavioral feedback in groups. *Journal of Consulting and Clinical Psychology, 41,* 215–223.

JACOBS, E. E., HARVILL, R. L., & MASSON, R. L. (1988). *Group counseling: Strategies and skills.* Pacific Grove, CA: Brooks/Cole.

JAMES, W. (1902). Varieties of religious experience. New York: Random House.

JAMES, W. (1907). *Pragmatism.* New York: New American Library.

JAMES, W. (1950). *Principles of psychology* (Vol. 2). New York: Dover. (Originally published 1908)

JANIS, I. L. (1972). *Victims of groupthink.* Boston: Houghton Mifflin.

JANIS, I. L., & MANN, L. (1977). *Decision making: A psychological analysis of conflict, choice, and commitment.* New York: Free Press.

JANOV, A. (1970). *The primal scream.* New York:

JEFFERSON, L. (1964). These are my sisters. In B. Kaplan (Ed.), *The inner world of mental illness.* New York: Harper & Row.

JEFFRIES, D. (1973). Should we continue to deradicalize children through the use of counseling groups? *Educational Technology, 13*(1), 45–49.

JENSEN, J. P., BERGIN, A. E., & GREAVES, D. W. (1990). The meaning of eclecticism. *Professional Psychology, 21,* 124–130.

JOHNSON, D. W., & JOHNSON, F. P. (1991). *Joining together: Group theory and skills* (4th ed.). Boston: Allyn & Bacon.

JOHNSON, E. J. (1988). Expertise and decision under uncertainty: Performance and process. In M. H. Chi, R. Glaser, & M. J. Farr (Eds.), *The nature of expertise.* Hillsdale, NJ: Erlbaum.

JOHNSON, N. (1980, September). Must the rational-emotive therapist be like Albert Ellis? *Personnel and Guidance Journal,* 49–51.

JOURARD, S. M., & JAFFEE, P. E. (1970). Influence of an interviewer's disclosure on the self-disclosing behavior of interviewees. *Journal of Counseling Psychology, 17,* 252–257.

KAFKA, F. (1948). *The penal colony: Stories and short pieces.* New York: Schocken Books.

KAGAN, N. (1973). Can technology help us toward reliability in influencing human interaction? In J. Vriend & W. W. Dyer (Eds.), *Counseling effectively in groups.* Englewood Cliffs, NJ: Educational Technology Publications.

KAISER, R. B. (1981, March). The way of the Journal. *Psychology Today,* 64–76.

KANE, T. R., SULS, J., & TEDESCHI, J. T. (1977). Humour as a tool of social interaction. In A. J. Chapman & H. C. Foot (Eds.), *It's a funny thing, humour.* Oxford, England: Pergamon Press.

KANFER, F. H., & PHILLIPS, J. S. (1970). *Learning foundations of behavior therapy.* New York: Wiley.

KAPLAN, H. S., KOHL, R. N., POMEROY, W. B., OFFIT, A. K., & HOGAN, R. (1978). Group treatment of premature ejaculation. In J. Lo Piccolo & L. Lo Piccolo (Eds.), *Handbook of sex therapy.* New York: Plenum.

KAPLAN, K. L. (1988). *Directive group therapy.* Thorofare, NJ: Slack.

KAUL, T. J., & BEDNAR, R. L. (1978). Conceptualizing group research: A preliminary analysis. *Small Group Behavior, 9,* 173–191.

KAZDIN, A. E. (1974). Covert modeling, model similarity, and reduction of avoidance behavior. *Behavior Therapy, 5,* 325–340.

KEES, N. L., & JACOBS, E. (1990). Conducting more effective groups: How to select and process group exercises. *Journal for Specialists in Group Work, 15,* 21–29.

KEITH-SPIEGEL, P. (1972). Early conceptions of humor: Varieties and issues. In J. H. Goldstein & P. E. McGhee (Eds.), *The psychology of humor: Theoretical perspectives and empirical issues*. New York: Academic Press.

KELLERMAN, H. (1979). *Group psychotherapy and personality: Intersecting structures*. New York: Grune & Stratton.

KELLERMAN, P. F. (1987). Psychodrama participants' perception of therapeutic factors. *Small Group Behavior, 18,* 408–419.

KELLY, E. L., GOLDBERG, L. R., FISKE, D. W., & KILKOWSKI, J. M. (1978). Twenty-five years later: A follow-up study of the graduate students in clinical psychology assessed in the V.A. Selection Research Project. *American Psychologist, 33,* 746–755.

KIPPER, D. A. (1986). *Psychotherapy through clinical role playing*. New York: Brunner/Mazel.

KIVLIGHAN, D. M. (1985). Feedback in group psychotherapy: Review and implications. *Small Group Behavior, 16,* 373–385.

KLEIN, J. P. (1974). On the use of humor in counseling. *Canadian Counselor, 8,* 233–237.

KLINE, W. B. (1986). Working through the risks: A structured experience to facilitate self-disclosure. *Journal for Specialists in Group Work, 11,* 209–212.

KLINE, W. B. (1990). Responding to "problem" members. *Journal for Specialists in Group Work, 15,* 195–200.

KOESTLER, A. (1964). *The act of creation*. New York: Dell.

KOGAN, L. S. (1959). Validity, reliability, and the related considerations. In A. W. Shyne (Ed.), *Use of judgment as data in social work research*. New York: American Association of Social Work.

KOGAN, N., & WALLACH, M. A. (1967). Risk taking as a function of the situation, the person, and the group. In *New directions in psychology* (Vol. 111). New York: Holt, Rinehart & Winston.

KOPP, S. (1972). *The naked therapist*. San Diego: Edits.

KOPP, S. (1985). *Even a stone can be a teacher*. Los Angeles: Tarcher.

KOPTA, S. M., NEWMAN, F. L., MCGOVERN, M. P., & ANGLE, R. S. (1989). Relation between years of psychotherapeutic experience and conceptualizations and treatment plan costs. *Professional Psychology: Research and Practice, 20,* 59–61.

KORMANSKI, C. (1982). Leadership strategies for managing conflict. *Journal for Specialists in Group Work, 7,* 112–118.

KORNER, I. M., & BROWN, W. H. (1952). The mechanical third ear. *Journal of Counseling Psychology,* 81–84.

KOTTLER, J. A. (1977). *The effects of immediate feedback supervision on counselor anxiety and performance in a laboratory practicum*. Unpublished doctoral dissertation, University of Virginia.

KOTTLER, J. A. (1978a). How the effective group counselor functions. *Journal for Specialists in Group Work, 3*(3), 113–121.

KOTTLER, J. A. (1978b). A question of ethics. *Journal for Specialists in Group Work, 3*(1), 21–24.

KOTTLER, J. A. (1978c, November). The use of a journal in counseling. *Guidance Clinic,* 6–7.

KOTTLER, J. A. (1979). Promoting self-understanding in counseling: A compromise between the insight and action-oriented approaches. *Journal of Psychiatric Nursing and Mental Health Services, 17*(12), 18–23.

KOTTLER, J. A. (1981a). The development of guidelines for training group leaders: A synergistic model. *Journal for Specialists in Group Work, 6*(3), 125–129.

KOTTLER, J. A. (1981b). *Mouthing off: A study of oral behavior, its causes and treatments.* New York: Libra.

KOTTLER, J. A. (1982). Ethical issues in group work (Special Issue). *Journal for Specialists in Group Work, 7,* 138–214.

KOTTLER, J. A. (1983). *Pragmatic group leadership.* Pacific Grove, CA: Brooks/Cole.

KOTTLER, J. A. (1991). *The compleat therapist.* San Francisco: Jossey-Bass.

KOTTLER, J. A. (1992). *Compassionate therapy: Working with difficult clients.* San Francisco: Jossey-Bass.

KOTTLER, J. A. (1993). *On being a therapist.* (Rev. Ed.) San Francisco: Jossey-Bass.

KOTTLER, J. A., & BLAU, D. S. (1989). *The imperfect therapist: Learning from failure in therapeutic practice.* San Francisco: Jossey-Bass.

KOTTLER, J. A., & BROWN, R. W. (1992). *Introduction to therapeutic counseling* (2nd ed.). Pacific Grove, CA: Brooks/Cole.

KOTTLER, J. A., DYER, W. W., & VRIEND, J. (1975). Group counseling scale for the self-analysis of fully functioning and self-defeating behavior. In W. W. Dyer & J. Vriend (Eds.), *Counseling techniques that work.* Washington, DC: American Personnel and Guidance Association Press.

KOTTLER, J. A., VRIEND, J., & DYER, W. W. (1974). An evaluation scale for client use in individual and group counseling. *Michigan Personnel and Guidance Journal, 6*(1), 6–19.

KRAFT, I. A. (1986). Innovative and creative approaches in child group psychotherapy. In A. E. Riester & I. A. Kraft (Eds.), *Child group psychotherapy.* New York: International Universities Press.

KROHE, J. (1987). Take my boss—please. *Across the Board, 24*(2), 31–35.

KROLL, J. (1988). *The challenge of the borderline patient.* New York: Norton.

KRUMBOLTZ, J. D., & POTTER, B. (1973). Behavioral techniques for developing trust, cohesiveness, and goal accomplishment. *Educational Technology, 13*(1), 26–30.

KUBIE, L. S. (1971). The destructive potential of humor in psychotherapy. *American Journal of Psychiatry, 127*(7), 37–42.

LACAN, J. (1968). *Ecrits.* New York: Norton.

LAFARGE, V. V. S. (1990). Termination in groups. In J. Gillette & M. McCollom (Eds.), *Groups in context: A new perspective on group dynamics.* Reading, MA: Addison-Wesley.

LAFFAL, J. (1988). Concept analysis of language in psychotherapy. In R. Russell (Eds.), *Language in psychotherapy.* New York: Plenum.

LAING, R. D. (1965). *The divided self.* Baltimore: Penguin.

LAMB, C. S. (1980, December). The use of paradoxical intention: Self-management through laughter. *Personnel and Guidance Journal,* 217–219.

LANCASTER, A. (1981). Personal communication.

LANG, E., & HALPERIN, D. A. (1989). Co-leadership in groups: Marriage a la mode? In D. A. Halperin (Eds.), *Group psychodynamics: New paradigms and new perspectives.* Chicago: Year Book Medical Publishers.

LANKTON, C. H., & LANKTON, S. R. (1989). *Tales of enchantment: Goal-oriented metaphors for adults and children in therapy.* New York: Brunner/Mazel.

LANTZ, J. E. (1978a). *Family and marital therapy: A transactional approach.* New York: Appleton-Century-Crofts.

LANTZ, J. E. (1978b). Co-therapy approach in family therapy. *Social Work, 23*(2), 156–158.

LARKE, J. (1985). Compulsory treatment: Some practical methods of treating the mandated client. *Psychotherapy, 22,* 262–268.

LARRY, T. (1957). *Interpersonal diagnosis of personality: A functional theory and methodology for personality evaluation.* New York: Ronald Press.

LAUGHLIN, P. R., BRANCH, L. G., & JOHNSON, H. H. (1969). Individual versus triadic performance on a uni-dimensional complementary task as a function of initial ability level. *Journal of Personality and Social Psychology, 12,* 144–150.

LAZARUS, A. A. (1967). In support of technical eclecticism. *Psychological Reports, 21,* 415–416.

LAZARUS, A. A. (1973). Multimodal behavior therapy: Treating the "basic id." *Journal of Nervous and Mental Disease, 156,* 404–411.

LAZARUS, A. A. (1981). *The Practice of Multi-Model Therapy.* New York: McGraw-Hill.

LAZARUS, A. A. (1986). The need for technical eclecticism. In J. K. Zeig (Eds.), *The evolution of psychotherapy.* New York: Brunner/Mazel.

LAZARUS, A. A., & ABRAMOVITZ, A. (1962). The use of "emotive imagery" in the treatment of children's phobias. *Journal of Mental Science, 108,* 191–195.

LAZARUS, A. A., BEUTLER, L. E., & NORCROSS, J. C. (1992). The future of technical eclecticism. *Psychotherapy, 29,* 11–20.

LEE, J. L., & PULVINO, C. S. (Eds.). (1973). *Group counseling: Theory, research, and practice.* Washington, DC: American Personnel and Guidance Association Press.

LESGOLD, A., RUBINSON, H., FELTOVICH, P., GLASER, R., KLOPHER, D., & WANG, Y. (1988). Expertise in a complex skill: Diagnosing X-ray pictures. In M. H. Chi, R. Glaser, & M. J. Farr (Eds.), *The nature of expertise.* Hillsdale, NJ: Erlbaum.

LESZCZ, M. (1989). Group psychotherapy with the characterologically difficult client. *International Journal of Group Psychotherapy, 39,* 311–334.

LEVETON, E. (1977). *Psychodrama for the timid clinician.* New York: Springer.

LEVIN, J. (1977). *Learning differences: Diagnosis and prescription.* New York: Holt, Rinehart & Winston.

LEVINE, B. (1979). *Group psychotherapy practice and development.* Englewood Cliffs, NJ: Prentice-Hall.

LEVINSON, D. J. (1978). *The seasons of a man's life.* New York: Ballantine.

LEWIS, L. H. (1985). Stage III: Anxiety. In B. B. Siepker & A. M. Kandaras (Eds.), *Group therapy with children and adolescents: A treatment manual.* New York: Human Sciences Press.

LICHTENBERG, J. W., & KNOX, P. L. (1991). Order out of chaos: A structural analysis of group therapy. *Journal of Counseling Psychology, 38,* 279–288.

LIEBERMAN, M. A. (1983). Comparative analyses of change mechanisms in groups. In R. R. Dies & K. R. MacKenzie (Eds.), *Advances in group psychotherapy: Integrating research and practice.* New York: International Universities Press.

LIEBERMAN, M. A., YALOM, I. D., & MILES, M. (1973). *Encounter groups: First facts.* New York: Basic Books.

LOCKE, N. (1961). *Group psychoanalysis: Theory and technique.* New York: New York University Press.

LONG, L., & COPE, C. (1980). Curative factors in a male felony offender group. *Small Group Behavior, 11,* 389–398.

LONG, S. (1988). The six group therapies compared. In S. Long (Eds.), *Six group therapies.* New York: Plenum Press.

LORENZ, K. (1966). On aggression. New York: Bantam Books.

LUBELL, D. J. (1983). Art therapy in groups. In H. I. Kaplan & B. J. Sadock (Eds.), Comprehensive group psychotherapy. Baltimore: Williams & Wilkins.

MACASKILL, N. D. (1982). Therapeutic factors in group therapy with borderline patients. International Journal of Group Psychotherapy, 32, 61–73.

MACHAN, D. (1987). What's black and blue and floats in the Monongahela River? Forbes, 14(1), 216–220.

MACKENZIE, K. R. (1987). Therapeutic factors in group psychotherapy: A contemporary view. Group, 11, 26–34.

MACKENZIE, K. R., & LIVESLEY, W. J. (1983). A developmental model for brief group therapy. In R. R. Dies & K. R. MacKenzie (Eds.), Advances in group psychotherapy: Integrating research and practice. New York: International Universities Press.

MACLENNAN, B. W. (1965). Co-therapy. International Journal of Group Psychotherapy, 15(2), 154–166.

MAHLOR, C. A. (1969). Group counseling in the schools. Boston: Houghton Mifflin.

MAILER, N. (1979). The executioner's song. Boston: Little, Brown.

MALAMUD, D. I. (1980). The laughing game: An exercise for sharpening awareness of self responsibility. Psychotherapy: Theory, Research, and Practice, 17(1), 69–73.

MALLINCKRODT, B. (1989). Social support and the effectiveness of group therapy. Journal of Counseling Psychology, 36, 170–175.

MANN, B., & MURPHY, K. C. (1975). Timing of self-disclosure, reciprocity of self-disclosure, and reaction to an initial interview. Journal of Counseling Psychology, 22, 304–308.

MARCUSE, H. (1962). Eros and civilization. New York: Vintage Books.

MARKOWITZ, L. M. (1992, Mar./Apr.). Families of the poor. Family Therapy Networker, 12–13.

MARKUS, H. (1978). The effect of mere presence on social facilitation: An unobtrusive test. Journal of Experimental Social Psychology, 14, 389–397.

MARMOR, J., & WOODS, S. M. (1980). The interface between the psychodynamic and behavioral therapies. New York: Plenum.

MARTINEAU, W. H. (1972). A model of the social functions of humor. In J. H. Goldstein & P. E. McGhee (Eds.), The psychology of humor. New York: Academic Press.

MASLOW, A. (1954). Motivation and personality. New York: Harper & Row.

MASTERS, W. H., & JOHNSON, V. E. (1970). Human sexual inadequacy. Boston: Little, Brown.

MAY, R. (1958). Contributions of existential psychotherapy. In R. May, E. Angel, & H. F. Ellenberger (Eds.), Existence. New York: Simon & Schuster.

MAY, R. (1969). Love and will. New York: Norton.

MAZZA, N., MAZZA, J., & SCATURO, S. (1987). Poetry therapy with abused children. Arts in psychotherapy, 14, 85–92.

MCCLURE, B. A. (1987). Metaphoric illumination in groups. Small Group Behavior, 18, 179–187.

MCCLURE, B. A. (1989a). More metaphor concerns and considerations in groups. Small Group Behavior, 449–458.

MCCLURE, B. A. (1989b). What's a group meta-phor? Journal for Specialists in Group Work, 14, 239–242.

MCCLURE, W. J. (1978). Increasing group counseling effectiveness through appropriate pacing skills. Journal for Specialists in Group Work, 3(3), 139–145.

MCCOLLOM, M. (1990). Reevaluating group development: A critique of the familiar models. In J. Gillette & M. McCollom (Eds.), *Groups in context: A new perspective on group dynamics.* Reading, MA: Addison-Wesley.

MCGHEE, P. E. (1979). *Humor: Its origin and development.* San Francisco: W. H. Freeman.

MCGRATH, J. C., & ALTMAN, I. (1966). *Small group research.* New York: Holt, Rinehart & Winston.

MCGRATH, J. E. (1984). *Groups: Interaction and performance.* Englewood Cliffs, NJ: Prentice-Hall.

MCLEMORE, C. W., & BENJAMIN, L. S. (1979). Whatever happened to interpersonal diagnosis? *American Psychologist, 34*(1), 17–34.

MEDDIN, B. (1986). Unanticipated and unintended consequences of the group process: Enhancing successful group functioning. *Social Work with Groups, 9*(2), 83–92.

MEICHENBAUM, D. H. (1971). Examination of model characteristics in reducing avoidance behavior. *Journal of Personality and Social Psychology, 17,* 298–307.

MEICHENBAUM, D., & GOODMAN, J. (1971). Training impulsive children to talk to themselves: A means of developing self-control. *Journal of Abnormal Psychology, 77,* 115–126.

MELLAN, O. (1992, Mar./Apr.). The last taboo. *Family Therapy Networker,* 40–47.

MILES, M. B. (1957). Human relations training: How a group grows. *Teachers College Record, 55,* 90–96.

MILGRAM, S. (1965). Liberating effects of group pressure. *Journal of Personality and Social Psychology, 1,* 127–134.

MILLER, J. G., & MILLER, J. L. (1983). General living systems: Theory and small groups. In H. I. Kaplan & B. J. Sadock (Eds.), *Comprehensive group psychotherapy.* Baltimore: Williams & Wilkins.

MILLER, M. J., & WILLIAMS, J. M. (1989). Using an assistant coach to foster the learning of group counseling skills. *Journal for Specialists in Group Work, 14,* 170–172.

MILLON, T. (1988). Personologic psychotherapy: Ten commandments for posteclectic approach to integrative treatment. *Psychotherapy, 25,* 209–219.

MINTZ, E. E. (1963). Transference in co-therapy groups. *Journal of Consulting Psychology, 27*(1), 34–39.

MITCHELL, R. C., & MITCHELL, R. R. (1984). Constructive management of conflict in groups. *Journal for Specialists in Group Work, 9,* 137–144.

MORENO, J. L. (1946). *Psychodrama.* Beacon, NY: Beacon House.

MORENO, J. L. (1957). *The first book on group psychotherapy.* New York: Beacon House.

MORENO, J. L. (1964). *Psychodrama* (Rev. ed.). Beacon, NY: Beacon House.

MORENO, J. L., & ELEFTHERY, D. G. (1975). An introduction to group psychodrama. In G. Gazda (Ed.), *Basic approaches to group psychotherapy and group counseling* (2nd ed.). Springfield, IL: Charles C Thomas.

MORENO, Z. (1959). A survey of psychodramatic techniques. *Group Psychotherapy, 12,* 5–14.

MORENO, Z. T. (1983). Psychodrama. In H. I. Kaplan & B. J. Sadock (Eds.), *Comprehensive group psychotherapy.* Baltimore: Williams & Wilkins.

MORENO, Z. T. (1990). Note on some forms of resistance to psychodrama. *Journal of Group Psychotherapy, Psychodrama, and Sociometry, 43,* 44.

MORRAN, D. K., ROBINSON, F. F., & STOCKTON, R. (1985). Feedback exchange in counseling groups: An analysis of message content and receiver acceptance as a function of leader versus member delivery, session, and valence. *Journal of Counseling Psychology, 32*, 57–67.

MORRIS, D. (1977). *Man watching: A field guide to human behavior.* New York: Harry Abrams.

MOSAK, H. H. (1987). Ha ha and aha: The role of humor in psychotherapy. Muncie, IN: Accelerated Development.

MULLEN, H. (1978). Art therapy and the psychoanalytic group. In H. Mullen & M. Rosenbaum (Eds.), *Group psychotherapy: Theory and practice* (2nd ed.). New York: Free Press.

MURO, J. J., & FREEMAN, S. L. (Eds.). (1968). *Readings in group counseling.* Scranton, PA: International Textbook.

MYERS, G. E., & MYERS, M. T. (1973). *The dynamics of human communication.* New York: McGraw-Hill.

NAPIER, A., & WHITAKER, C. (1972). A conversation about co-therapy. In A. Ferber, M. Mendelsohn, and A. Napier (Eds.), *The book of family therapy.* Boston: Houghton Mifflin.

NAPIER, A. Y., & WHITAKER, C. A. (1988). *The family crucible.* New York: Harper & Row.

NAPIER, R. W., & GERSHENFELD, M. K. (1981). *Groups: Theory and experience* (2nd ed.). Boston: Houghton Mifflin.

NAPIER, R. W., & GERSHENFELD, M. K. (1989). *Groups: Theory and practice.* (4th ed.). Boston: Houghton Mifflin.

NELSON-JONES, R. (1992). *Group leadership: A training approach.* Pacific Grove, CA: Brooks/Cole.

NICHOLAS, M. W. (1983). The narcissistic personality in group psychotherapy. *Group, 7,* 27–32.

NIETZSCHE, F. (1972). On truth and falsity in their extramoral sense. In W. Shibles (Ed.), *Essays on metaphor.* Whitewater, WI: Language Press. (Originally published 1864)

NILES, J., & DE VOE, M. (1978, October). Counseling, risk taking, and the learning process. *Personnel and Guidance Journal,* 99–102.

NIN, A. (1978). Preface. In T. Rainer (Ed.), *The new diary.* Los Angeles: J. P. Tarcher.

NOBLER, H. (1986). When group doesn't work: An examination of the types and causes of individual, group, and leader failures. *Group, 10,* 103–110.

NOLAN, E. J. (1978). Leadership interventions for promoting personal mastery. *Journal for Specialists in Group Work, 3,* 132–138.

NOLAN, W. A. (1968). *The making of a surgeon.* New York: Dell.

NORCROSS, J. C., & GLENCAVAGE, L. M. (1989). Eclecticism and integration in counseling and psychotherapy: Major themes and obstacles. *British Journal of Guidance and Counseling, 17,* 227–247.

NORCROSS, J. C., & NAPOLITANO, G. (1986). Defining our journal and ourselves. *International Journal of Eclectic Psychotherapy, 25,* 209–219.

O'CONNOR, G. G. (1980). Small groups: A general systems model. *Small Group Behavior, 11,* 145–173.

OHLSEN, M. (1977). *Group counseling* (2nd ed.). New York: Holt, Rinehart & Winston.

OHLSEN, M. M., & PEARSON, R. E. (1965). A method for the classification of group interaction and its use to explore the influence on individual role factors in group counseling. *Journal of Clinical Psychology, 21,* 436–441.

OKUN, B. F., & RAPPAPORT, L. J. (1989). *Working with families: An introduction to family therapy.* Pacific Grove, CA: Brooks/Cole.

OMER, H., & LONDON, P. (1988). Metamorphis in psychotherapy: End of the systems era. *Psychotherapy, 25,* 171–180.

ORMONT, L. (1990). The craft of bridging. *International Journal of Group Psychotherapy, 40,* 3–17.

OSBORN, A. F. (1963). *Applied imagination: Principles and procedures of creative problem solving.* New York: Scribner's.

PAIN, M. D., & SHARPLEY, C. F. (1989). Varying the order in which positive and negative information is presented: Effects on counselors' judgments of clients' mental health. *Journal of Counseling Psychology, 36,* 3–7.

PALAZZOLI, M. S., BOSCOLO, L., CECCHIN, G., & PRATA, G. (1980). The problem of the referring person. *Journal of Marital and Family Therapy, 6*(1), 3–10.

PALMER, J. O. (1980). *A primer of eclectic psychotherapy.* Pacific Grove, CA: Brooks/Cole.

PALOMARES, U. (1975). *A curriculum on conflict management.* La Mesa, CA: Human Development Training Institute.

PAPP, P. (1982). Staging reciprocal metaphors in a couples group. *Family Process, 21,* 453–467.

PARNES, S. J. (1967). *Creative behavior guidebook.* New York: Scribner's.

PATTERSON, G. T., JONES, R., WHITTIER, J., & WRIGHT, M. A. (1965). The hyperactive child. *Behavior, Research, and Therapy, 2,* 217–226.

PAYNE, R., and COOPER, C. L. (1982). *Groups at work.* New York: Wiley.

PENNEBAKER, J. W. (1990). *Opening up: The healing power of confiding in others.* New York: Morrow.

PERLS, F. (1969). *Gestalt therapy verbatim.* Lafayette, CA: Real People Press.

PETERSON, J. P., & POLLIO, H. R. (1982). Therapeutic effectiveness of differentially targeted humorous remarks in group psychotherapy. *Group,* 39–50.

PETERSON, P. (1975). *Laughter in a therapy group.* Unpublished doctoral dissertation, University of Tennessee.

PIAGET, J. (1956). *The origins of intelligence.* New York: International Universities Press.

PILKONIS, P., IMBER, S., LEWIS, P., & RUBINSKY, P. (1984). A comparative outcome study of individual, group, and conjoint psychotherapy. *Archives of General Psychiatry, 41,* 431–437.

POLLIO, H. R., & EDGERLY, J. W. (1976). Comedians and comic style. In A. J. Chapman & H. C. Foot (Eds.), *Humor and laughter: Theory, research, and applications.* London: Wiley.

PONZO, Z. (1991). Critical factors in group work: Clients' perceptions. *Journal for Specialists in Group Work, 16,* 16–23.

POPE, K. S., & VASQUEZ, R. J. (1991). *Ethics in psychotherapy and counseling.* San Francisco: Jossey-Bass.

POSTHUMA, B. W. (1989). *Small groups in therapy settings: Process and leadership.* Boston: Little, Brown.

POWDERMAKER, F. B., & FRANK, J. D. (1953). *Group psychotherapy.* Cambridge, MA: Harvard University Press.

POWLES, W. E. (1990). Problems in diagnosis and group treatment design with borderline personalities: Can focal conflict theory help? In B. E. Roth, W. N. Stone, & H. D. Kibel (Eds.), *The difficult patient in group.* Madison, CT: International Universities Press.

PROGOFF, I. (1975). *At a journal workshop.* New York: Dialogue House.

PRUITT, D. G. (Ed.). (1971). Special issue on the risky shift. *Journal of Personality and Social Psychology, 20,* 339–510.

RAINER, T. (1978). *The new diary.* Los Angeles: J. P. Tarcher.

REDL, F. (1966). *When we deal with children.* New York: Free Press.

REEDER, C., & KUNCE, J. (1976). Modeling technique, drug abstinence behavior, and heroin addicts: A pilot study. *Journal of Counseling Psychology, 23,* 560–562.

RHODE, R. I., & STOCKTON, R. (1992, Winter). The effect of structured feedback on goal attainment, attraction to the group, and satisfaction with the group in small group counseling. *Journal of Group Psychotherapy, Psychodrama, and Sociometry,* 172–179.

RICE, D. G., FEY, W. F., & KEPECS, J. G. (1972). Therapist experience and ''style'' as factors in co-therapy. *Family Process, 11,* 227–241.

RICE, J. K., & RICE, D. G. (1975). Status and sex role issues in co-therapy. In *Couples in conflict: New directions in marital therapy.* New York: Aronson.

RICKEY, G. L., & DUSTIN, D. (1988). *Group counseling: Theory and practice.* Englewood Cliffs, NJ: Prentice-Hall.

RITTER, B. (1968). The group treatment of children's snake phobias using vicarious and contact desensitization procedures. *Behavior Research and Therapy, 6,* 1–6.

ROARK, A. E., & RADL, M. C. (1984). Group process: A systematic analysis. *Journal for Specialists in Group Work, 9,* 192–203.

ROBACK, H. B., OCHOA, E., BLOCH, F., & PURDON, S. (1992). Guarding confidentiality in clinical groups: The therapist's dilemma. *International Journal of Group Psychotherapy, 42,* 81–103.

ROBACK, H. B., PURDON, S. E., OCHOA, E., & BLOCH, F. (1992). Confidentiality dilemmas in group psychotherapy: Management strategies and utility of guidelines. *Small Group Research, 23,* 169–184.

ROBBINS, T. (1976). *Even cowgirls get the blues.* New York: Bantam Books.

ROBERTIELLO, R. C., & SCHOENWOLF, G. (1987). *One hundred one common therapeutic blunders.* Northvale, NJ: Aronson.

ROBINSON, F. P. (1965). Counseling orientation and labels. *Journal of Counseling Psychology, 12,* 338.

ROBINSON, F. P. (1978). Modern approaches to counseling diagnosis. In J. C. Hansen (Ed.), *Counseling process and procedures.* (p. 313–322). New York: Macmillan.

ROBISON, F. F., MORRAN, D. K., & HULSE-KILLACKY, D. (1989). Single-subject research designs for group counselors studying their own groups. *Journal for Specialists in Group Work, 14,* 93–97.

ROGERS, C. (1970). *Carl Rogers on encounter groups.* New York: Harper & Row.

ROLLER, B. (1984). The group therapist: Stages of professional and personal development. *Small Group Behavior, 15,* 265–269.

ROLLER, B., & NELSON, V. (1991). *The art of co-therapy: How therapists work together.* London: Guilford Press.

ROMAN, M., & MELTZER, B. (1977). Co-therapy: A review of current literature (with special reference to therapeutic outcome). *Journal of Sex and Marital Therapy, 3*(1), 63–77.

ROSE, S. D. (1977). *Group therapy: A behavioral approach.* Englewood Cliffs, NJ: Prentice-Hall.

ROSE, S. D. (1989). *Working with adults in groups.* San Francisco: Jossey-Bass.

ROSE, S. D., & EDELSON, J. L. (1987). *Working with children and adolescents in groups.* San Francisco: Jossey-Bass.

ROSEN, R. D. (1977). *Psychobabble.* New York: Avon Books.

ROSENBAUM, M. (1952). The challenge of group psychoanalysis. *Psychoanalysis, 42.*

ROSENBAUM, M. (1971). Co-therapy. In H. I. Kaplan & B. J. Sadock (Eds.), *Comprehensive group psychotherapy.* Baltimore: Williams & Wilkins.

ROSENBAUM, M. (1983). Co-therapy. In H. I. Kaplan & B. J. Sadock (Eds.), *Comprehensive group psychotherapy.* Baltimore: Williams and Wilkins.

ROSENBAUM, M., & BERGER, M. (Eds.) (1963). *Group psychotherapy and group function.* New York: Basic Books.

ROSENHAN, D. L. (1973). On being sane in insane places. *Science, 179,* 250–258.

ROSENTHAL, L. (1992). The new member: "Infanticide" in group psychotherapy. *International Journal of Group Psychotherapy, 42,* 277–286.

ROSSEL, R. D. (1981a). Chaos and control: Attempts to regulate the use of humor in self-analytic and therapy groups. *Small Group Behavior, 12,* 195–219. *

ROSSEL, R. D. (1981b). Word play, metaphor, and humor in the small group. *Small Group Behavior, 12,* 116–136.

ROTHKE, S. (1986). The role of interpersonal feedback in group psychotherapy. *International Journal of Group Psychotherapy, 36,* 225–240.

ROWE, W., & WINBORN, B. B. (1973). What people fear about group work: An analysis of 36 selected critical articles. *Educational Technology, 13*(1), 53–57.

ROYCE, J. R. (1958). The development of factor analysis. *Journal of General Psychology, 58,* 139.

ROYCE, J. R. (1967). Factors as theoretical constructs. In D. N. Jackson & S. Messick (Eds.), *Problems in human assessment.* New York: McGraw-Hill.

ROYCE, J. R. (1975). Psychology is multi-: Methodological, variate, epistemic, world view, systemic, paradigmatic, theoretic, and disciplinary. *Nebraska Symposium on Motivation* (pp. 1–63). Lincoln: University of Nebraska Press.

RUDESTAM, K. E. (1978). Semantics and psychotherapy. *Psychotherapy: Theory, Research, and Practice, 15*(2), 190–192.

RUNYAN, D. L. (1974). The group risky-shift effect as a function of emotional bonds, actual consequences, and extent of responsibility. *Journal of Personality and Social Psychology, 29,* 670–676.

RUSSELL, A., & RUSSELL, L. (1979). The uses and abuses of co-therapy. *Journal of Marital and Family Therapy,* 39–46.

RUSSELL, B. (1961). In R. E. Egner & L. E. Denown (Eds.), *The basic writings of Bertrand Russell.* New York: Simon & Schuster.

RYAN, T. (1973). A goal setting in group counseling. In J. Vriend & W. W. Dyer (Eds.), *Counseling effectively in groups.* Englewood Cliffs, NJ: Educational Technology.

SACKS, J. M. (1973). Psychodrama: An underdeveloped group resource. *Educational Technology, 13*(2), 37–39.

SAGAN, C. (1977). *The dragons of Eden.* New York: Ballantine.

SALTMARSH, R. E., JENKINS, S. J., & FISHER, G. L. (1986). The TRAC model: A practical map for group process and management. *Journal for Specialists in Group Work, 11,* 30–36.

SALVENDY, J. T. (1991). Group psychotherapy in the late twentieth century: An international perspective. *Group, 15,* 3–13.

SAMUELS, M., & SAMUELS, N. (1975). *Seeing with the mind's eye: The history, techniques, and uses of visualization.* New York: Random House.

SARASON, I. G., & GANZER, V. J. (1969). Developing appropriate social behaviors of juvenile delinquents. In J. D. Krumboltz & C. E. Thoreson (Eds.), *Behavioral counseling: Cases and techniques.* New York: Holt, Rinehart & Winston.

SARETSKY, T. (1977). *Active techniques and group psychotherapy.* New York: Aronson.

SARTRE, J. P. (1957). *Existentialism and human emotions.* New York: Wisdom Library.

SATIR, V. (1964). *Conjoint family therapy.* Palo Alto, CA: Science & Behavior Books.

SATIR, V. (1972). *Peoplemaking.* Palo Alto, CA: Science & Behavior Books.

SATIR, V., & BALDWIN, M. (1983). *Satir step by step: A guide to creating change in families.* Palo Alto, CA: Science & Behavior Books.

SATIR, V., BITTER, J. R., & KRESTENSEN, K. K. (1988). Family reconstruction: The family within—A group experience. *Journal for Specialists in Group Work, 13,* 200–208.

SAUNDERS, L. (1954). *Cultural differences and medical care.* New York: Russell Sage Foundation.

SCARF, M. (1980, September). Images that heal. *Psychology Today,* pp. 32–46.

SCHAMESS, G. (1986). Differential diagnosis and group structure in the outpatient treatment of latency age children. In A. E. Riester & I. A. Kraft (Eds.), *Child group psychotherapy.* New York: International Universities Press.

SCHANCK, R. L. (1932). A study of a community and its groups and institutions conceived of as behaviors of individuals. *Psychological Monographs, 43.*

SCHATTNER, G., & COURTENEY, R. (1981). *Drama in therapy.* Drama Book Specialists.

SCHEIDLINGER, S., & PORTER, K. (1980). Group therapy combined with individual therapy. In T. Karasu & L. Bellak (Eds.), *Specialized techniques in individual psychotherapy.* New York: Brunner/Mazel.

SCHIFF, J. L. (1969). Reparenting schizophrenics. *Transactional Analysis Bulletin, 8,* 47–63.

SCHIFFER, M. (1969). *Therapeutic play group.* New York: Grune & Stratton.

SCHNEIDMAN, B., & MCGUIRE, L. (1978). Group therapy for nonorgasmic women: Two age levels. In J. Lo Piccolo & L. Lo Piccolo (Eds.), *Handbook of sex therapy.* New York: Plenum.

SCHON, D. A. (1983). *The reflective practitioner.* New York: Basic Books.

SCHRANK, F. A., & ENGELS, A. W. (1981, November). Bibliotherapy as a counseling adjunct: Research findings: *Personnel and Guidance Journal,* 143–147.

SCHUERGER, J. M. (1979). Understanding and controlling anger. In S. Eisenberg & L. E. Patterson (Eds.), *Helping clients with special concerns.* Chicago: Rand McNally.

SCHUTZ, W. C. (1958). *FIRO: A three-dimensional theory of interpersonal behavior.* New York: Holt, Rinehart.

SCHWARTZ, B. D. (1992). Group psychotherapy and social isolation. *The Psychotherapy Bulletin, 27,* 22–25.

SELIGMAN, M. (1981). *Group psychotherapy and counseling with special populations.* Baltimore: University Park Press.

SHAFFER, J. B., & GALINSKY, M. D. (1974). *Models of group therapy & sensitivity training.* Englewood Cliffs, NJ: Prentice-Hall.

SHANDS, H. (1970). *Semiotic approaches to psychiatry.* The Hague: Mouton.

SHAPIRO, J. L. (1978). *Methods of group psychotherapy and encounter.* Itasca, IL: F. E. Peacock.

SHAW, M. E. (1981). *Group dynamics: The psychology of small group behavior* (3rd ed.). New York: McGraw-Hill.

SHELTON, J. L., & ACKERMAN, J. M. (1974). *Homework in counseling and psychotherapy.* Springfield, IL: Charles C Thomas.

SHELTON, J. L., & LEVY, R. L. (1981). *Behavioral assignments and treatment compliance: A handbook of clinical strategies.* Champaign, IL: Research Press.

SHENGOLD, L. (1981). Insight as metaphor. *Psychoanalytic Study of the Child, 36,* 289–306.

SHEPARD, M. (1972). *Inside a psychiatrist's head.* New York: Dell.

SHERTZER, B., & STONE, S. C. (1980). *Fundamentals of counseling* (3rd ed.). Boston: Houghton Mifflin.

SHIBLES, W. (Ed.). (1972). *Essays on metaphor.* Whitewater, WI: Language Press.

SIEGELMAN, E. Y. (1990). *Metaphor and meaning in psychotherapy.* New York: Guilford.

SIEPKER, B. B., LEWIS, L. H., & KANDARAS, C. S. (1985). Relationship-oriented group psychotherapy with children and adolescents. In B. B. Siepker & C. S. Kandaras (Eds.), *Group therapy with children and adolescents: A treatment manual.* New York: Human Sciences Press.

SIMONSON, N. (1976). The impact of therapist disclosure on patient disclosure. *Journal of Counseling Psychology, 23.*

SIMONTON, O. C., & SIMONTON, S. S. (1975). Belief systems and management of the emotional aspects of malignancy. *Journal of Transpersonal Psychology, 7,* 29–47.

SINGER, J. L. (1973). *The child's world of make-believe: Experimental studies of imaginative play.* New York: Academic Press.

SKLAR, H. (1988). The impact of the therapeutic environment. *Journal of Contemporary Psychotherapy, 18,* 107–123.

SLAVINSKA-HOLY, N. (1983). Combining individual and homogeneous group psychotherapies for borderline conditions. *International Journal of Group Psychotherapy, 33,* 297–312.

SLAVSON, S. L. (1969). The anatomy and clinical applications of group interaction. *International Journal of Group Psychotherapy, 19,* 3–15.

SLAVSON, S. R. (1950). *Analytic group psychotherapy.* New York: Columbia University Press.

SLAVSON, S. R. (1964). *A textbook in analytic group psychotherapy.* New York: International Universities Press.

SMALL, L. (1978). The uncommon importance of psychodiagnosis. In J. C. Hansen (Ed.), *Counseling process and procedures.* New York: Macmillan.

SMITH, D. (1975). *Integrative counseling and psychotherapy.* Boston: Houghton Mifflin.

SMITH, M. J., & GLASS, G. V. (1977). Meta-analysis of psychotherapy outcome studies. *American Psychologist, 3*(9). 752–760.

SMITH, R. J., & STEINDLER, E. M. (1983). The impact of difficult patients upon treaters. *Bulletin of the Menninger Clinic, 47,* 107–116.

SNYDER, M., & THOMSEN, C. J. (1988). Interactions between therapists and clients: Hypothesis testing and behavioral confirmation. In D. C. Turk & P. Salovey (Eds.), *Reasoning, inference, and judgment in clinical psychology.* New York: Free Press.

SOLOMON, M. (1990). *Working with difficult people.* Englewood Cliffs, NJ: Prentice-Hall.

SOLOWAY, E., ADELSON, B., & EHRLICH, K. (1988). Knowledge and processes in the comprehension of computer programs. In M. H. Chi, R. Glaser, & M. J. Farr (Eds.), *The nature of expertise.* Hillsdale, NJ: Erlbaum.

SOLZHENITSYN, A. (1968). *The first circle.* New York: Harper & Row.

SOMMER, R. (1969). *Personal space: The behavioral basis of design.* Englewood Cliffs, NJ: Prentice-Hall.

SONNE, J. S., & LINCOLN, G. (1966). Importance of heterosexual co-therapy relationship in the construction of a family image. In J. Cohen (Ed.), *Family structure dynamics and therapy*. American Psychiatric Association, 20, 196–205.

SPECTOR, P. E., COHEN, S. L., & PENNER, L. A. (1976). The effects of real versus hypothetical risk on group-choice shifts. *Personality and Social Psychology Bulletin*, 2, 290–293.

SPIER, L. (1941). *Language, culture, and personality: Essays in memory of Edward Sapir*. Menasha, WI: Sapir Memorial Publication Fund.

SPINAL, P. (1984). Group resistance and leader intervention: An interactional analysis. *Small Group Behavior*, 15, 417–424.

SPITZ, H., KASS, F., & CHARLES, E. (1980). Common mistakes made in group psychotherapy by beginning therapists. *American Journal of Psychiatry*, 1(37).

STARAK, Y. (1988). Confessions of a group leader. *Small Group Behavior*, 19, 103–108.

STEIN, M. J. (Ed.). (1961). *Contemporary psychotherapies*. New York: Free Press.

STERN, J. A., BREMER, D. A., & MCCLURE, J. (1974). Analysis of eye movements and blinks during reading: Effects of Valium. *Psychopharmacologia*, 40(2), 171–175.

STERN, P. J. (1964). *The abnormal person and his world*. Princeton, NJ: D. Van Nostrand.

STINCHFIELD, R. D., & BURLINGAME, G. M. (1991). Development and use of the directives rating system in group therapy. *Journal of Counseling Psychology*, 38, 251–257.

STOCKTON, R., & MORAN, D. K. (1980). The use of verbal feedback in counseling groups: Toward an effective system. *Journal for Specialists in Group Work*, 5(1), 10–14.

STOCKTON, R., & MORRAN, D. K. (1982). Review and perspective of critical dimensions on therapeutic small group research. In G. M. Gazda (Eds.), *Basic approaches to group psychotherapy and group counseling*. Springfield, IL: Charles C Thomas.

STOGDILL, R. M. (1974). *Handbook of leadership*. New York: Free Press.

STONE, W. N. (1992). The place of self-psychology in group psychotherapy: A status report. *International Journal of Group Psychotherapy*, 42, 335–350.

STONE, W. N., & GUSTAFSON, J. P. (1982). Technique in group psychotherapy of narcissistic and borderline patients. *International Journal of Group Psychotherapy*, 32, 29–47.

STONER, J. A. F. (1968). Risky and cautious shifts in group decisions: The influence of widely held values. *Journal of Experimental Social Psychology*, 4, 442–459.

STRUPP, H. H., & BLOXOM, A. L. (1973). Preparing lower-class patients for group psychotherapy. *Journal of Consulting and Clinical Psychology*, 41, 373–384.

STUART, R. B. (1970). *Trick or treatment: How and when psychotherapy fails*. Champaign, IL: Research Press.

STUMPHAUZER, J. S. (1970). Low-cost, Bug-in-the-ear sound system for the modification of therapist and patient behavior. *Behavior Therapy*, 8, 124–129.

SUGAR, M. (1974). Interpretive group psychotherapy with latency children. *Journal of the American Academy of Child Psychiatry*, 13, 648–666.

SULLIVAN, H. S. (1947). *Conceptions of modern psychiatry*. New York: Norton.

SUSSMAN, N. (1983). Psychopharmacology and group psychotherapy. In H. I. Kaplan & B. J. Sadock (Eds.), *Comprehensive Group Psychotherapy*. Baltimore: Williams & Wilkins.

TEMERLIN, R. K. (1975). Suggestion effects in psychiatric diagnosis. In T. J. Scheff (Ed.), *Labeling madness*. Englewood Cliffs, NJ: Prentice-Hall.

THASE, M., & PAGE, R. A. (1977). Modeling of self-disclosure in laboratory and non-laboratory interview settings. *Journal of Counseling Psychology, 24,* 35–40.

THOMAS, L. (1979). *The medusa and the snail*. New York: Viking Press.

THORNE, F. C. (1973). Eclectic psychotherapy. In R. Corsini (Ed.), *Current psychotherapies*. Itasca, IL: F. E. Peacock.

TOCH, H. (1965). *The social psychology of social movements*. Indianapolis: Bobbs-Merrill.

TOMKINS, S. S. (1971). A theory of risk-taking behavior. In R. E. Carney (Ed.), *Risk-taking behavior*. Springfield, IL: Charles C Thomas.

TREADWELL, T. W. (1990, Fall). A survey of psychodramatic action and closure techniques. *Journal of Group Psychotherapy, Psychodrama, and Sociometry,* 102–115.

TROTZER, J. P. (1977). *The counselor and the group: Integrating theory, training, and practice*. Pacific Grove, CA: Brooks/Cole.

TROTZER, J. P. (1989). *The counselor and the group* (2nd ed.). Muncie, IN: Accelerated Development.

TUCKMAN, B. W., & JENSEN, M. A. (1977). Stages of small group development revisited. *Group and Organizational Studies, 2,* 419–427.

TURGENEV, I. (1965). *Fathers and sons*. Baltimore: Penguin.

TUTTMAN, S. (1990). Principles of psychoanalytic group therapy applied to the treatment of borderline and narcissistic disorders. In B. E. Roth, W. N. Stone, & H. D. Kibel (Eds.), *The difficult patient in group*. Madison, CT: International Universities Press.

TYLER, A. J., & THURSTON, N. (1977). Platitudinal counseling. *Worm Runner's Digest, 19,* 102–103.

UNGER, R. (1989). Selection and composition criteria in group psychotherapy. *Journal for Specialists in Group Work, 14,* 151–157.

UNGER, R. (1990). Conflict management in group psychotherapy. *Small Group Research, 21,* 349–359.

VALINE, W. J. (1983). Intensifying the group member's experience using the group log. *Journal for Specialists in Group Work, 8,* 101–104.

VAN DE WTERING, J. (1974). *The empty mirror: Experiences in a Japanese monastery*. Boston: Houghton-Mifflin.

VAN HOOSE, W. H., & KOTTLER, J. A. (1985). *Ethical & legal issues in counseling and psychotherapy* (2nd ed.). San Francisco: Jossey-Bass.

VINOGRADOV, S., & YALOM, I. D. (1989). *Concise guide to group psychotherapy*. Washington, DC: American Psychiatric Press.

VISCOTT, D. S. (1972). *The making of a psychiatrist*. Greenwich, CT: Fawcett.

VOGT, J., & VOGT, G. (1983). Group art therapy: An eclectic approach. *American Journal of Art Therapy, 22,* 129–135.

VRIEND, J. (1981). *Variables I look for in any person I want to recruit in my world*. Unpublished manuscript.

VRIEND, J., & DYER, W. W. (1973a). Behavioral characteristics of personal mastery (Tape 2), *Counseling for personal mastery: A cassette tape series for building counselor competencies*. Washington, DC: American Personnel and Guidance Association Press.

VRIEND, J., & DYER, W. W. (1973b). A case for a technology of group counseling and a delineation of major group categories. *Educational Technology, 13*(1), 12–18.

VRIEND, J., & DYER, W. W. (Eds.). (1973c). *Counseling effectively in groups.* Englewood Cliffs, NJ: Educational Technology.

VRIEND, J., & DYER, W. W. (1973d). Counseling the reluctant client. *Journal of Counseling Psychology, 20*(3), 240–246.

WACHTEL, A. B. (1983). Videotape and group psychotherapy. In H. I. Kaplan & B. J. Sadock (Eds.), *Comprehensive group psychotherapy.* Baltimore: Williams & Wilkins.

WACHTEL, P. L. (1980). What should we say to our patients? On the wording of therapists' comments. *Psychotherapy: Theory, Research, and Practice, 17*(2), 183–188.

WACHTEL, P. L. (1981). *Resistance: Psychodynamic and behavioral approaches.* New York: Plenum.

WALDREN, T., MCELMURRY, T., BOWENS, L., & ISRAEL, D. (1980, October). The story of story hour. *Personnel and Guidance Journal,* 108–109.

WARNER, S. J. (1984). The defeating patient and reciprocal abrasion. In. E. M. Stern (Eds.), *Psychotherapy and the abusive patient.* New York: Haworth Press.

WATTS, A. (1966). *The book.* New York: Vintage Books.

WATZLAWICK, P. (1976). *How real is real?* New York: Vintage Books.

WATZLAWICK, P. (1978). *The language of change.* New York: Basic Books.

WATZLAWICK, P., WEAKLAND, J., & FISCH, R. (1974). *Change: Principles of problem formation and problem resolution.* New York: Norton.

WEIL, A. (1980). *The marriage of the sun and the moon.* Boston: Houghton Mifflin.

WEINER, M. F. (1977). Catharis: a review. *Group Process, 71,* 173–184.

WEINER, M. F. (1983). The assessment and resolution of impasses in group psychotherapy. *International Journal of Group Psychotherapy, 33,* 313–331.

WEINSTEIN, I. (1971). Guidelines of a choice of a co-therapist. *Psychotherapy: Theory, Research, and Practice, 8,* 301–303.

WEISS, J. C. (1988). The D-R model of coleadership of groups. *Small Group Behavior, 19,* 117–125.

WELLS, L. (1990). The group as a whole: A systemic socioanalytic perspective on interpersonal and group relations. In J. Gillette & McCollom (Eds.), *Groups in context: A new perspective on group dynamics.* Reading, MA: Addison-Wesley.

WELLS, M. C., GLICKAUF-HUGHES, & BUZZELL, V. (1990). Treating obsessive-compulsive personalities in psychodynamic/interpersonal group therapy. *Psychotherapy, 27,* 366–379.

WENDER, L. (1940). Group psychotherapy: A study of its applications. *Psychiatric Quarterly, 14,* 708.

WENDER, L., & STEIN, A. (1949). Group psychotherapy as an aid to outpatient treatment in a psychiatric clinic. *Psychiatric Quarterly, 23,* 415–424.

WENZ, K., & WCWHIRTER, J. J. (1990). Enhancing the group experience: Creative writing exercises. *Journal for Specialists in Group Work, 15,* 37–42.

WEST, M., & LIVESLEY, W. J. (1986). Therapist transparency and the frame for group psychotherapy. *International Journal of Group Psychotherapy, 36,* 5–19.

WHORF, B. (1956). Grammatical categories. In J. E. Carrol (Ed.), *Language, Thought, and Reality.* New York: Wiley.

WIENER, P. P. (1949). *Evolution and the founders of pragmatism.* Gloucester, MA: Peter Smith.

WILDER, T. (1958). *Our Town: Three plays by Thornton Wilder.* New York: Bantam Books.
WILLIAMS, M. (1975). *The velveteen rabbit.* New York: Doubleday.
WILLIAMS, R. J. (1971). *You are extraordinary.* New York: Pyramid Books.
WILSHIRE, B. (1982). *Role playing and identity.* Bloomington: Indiana University Press.
WINTER, S. K. (1976). Developmental stages in the roles and concerns of group co-leaders. *Small Group Behavior, 7*(3), 349–362.
WISE, P. S., & LOWERY, S. (1989). Applying family supervision models to counselors and supervisors of groups. *Journal for Specialists in Group Work, 14,* 53–60.
WODAK, R. (1986). *Language behavior in therapy groups.* Berkeley, CA: University of California Press.
WOLBERG, L. R. (1954). *The technique of psychotherapy.* New York: Grune & Stratton.
WOLD, C. N., & FAGUNDES, J. O. (1977). Resolution of co-therapist's conflicts mirrored in brief family therapy. *Family Therapy, 4*(1), 31–41.
WOLF, A. (1974). Psychoanalysis in groups. In S. De Schill (Eds.), *The challenge for group psychotherapy.* New York: International Universities Press.
WOLF, A. et al. (1970). *Beyond the couch: Dialogues in teaching and learning psychoanalysis in groups.* New York: Science House.
WOLF, A., & SCHWARTZ, E. K. (1962). *Psychoanalysis in groups.* New York: Grune & Stratton.
WOLFE, T. (1980). *The right stuff.* New York: Bantam Books.
WOLMAN, R. N. (1976). Women's issues in couples treatment: The view of the male therapist. *Psychiatric Opinion, 13*(1), 13–17.
WONG, N. (1983). Combined individual and group psychotherapy. In H. I. Kaplan & B. J. Sadock (Eds.), *Comprehensive group psychotherapy.* Baltimore: Williams & Wilkins.
WORTHY, M., GARY, A. L., & KAHN, G. M. (1969). Self-disclosure as an exchange process. *Journal of Personality and Social Psychology, 13,* 59–63.
WRIGHT, T. L., INGRAHAM, L. J., CHEMTOB, H. J., & PEREZ-ARCE, P. (1985). Satisfaction and things not said: Clinical tools for group therapists. *Small Group Behavior,* 565–572.
WUBBOLDING, R. E. (1988). *Using reality therapy.* New York: Harper & Row.
WYLIE, M. S., & MARKOWITZ, L. M. (1992, Sept./Oct.). Walking the wire. *Family Therapy Networker,* 19–30.
YALOM, I. D., (1975). *The theory and practice of group psychotherapy.* New York: Basic Books.
YALOM, I. D. (1980). *Existential psychotherapy.* New York: Basic Books.
YALOM, I. D. (1983). *Inpatient group psychotherapy.* New York: Basic Books.
YALOM, I. D. (1985). *The theory and practice of group psychotherapy* (3rd ed.). New York: Basic Books.
YOST, E. B., BEUTLER, L. E., CORBISHLEY, M. A., & ALLENDER, J. R. (1986). *Group cognitive therapy: A treatment approach for depressed older adults.* New York: Pergamon Press.
YOUNG, R. (1987). Collectivity vs. group: A framework for assessment. *Social Work with Groups, 10,* 33–43.
ZAYAS, L. H. (1986). Fantasy role-playing for mutual aid in children's groups: A case illustration. *Social Work with Groups, 9*(1), 53–67.

ZEIG, J. K. (1986). The evolution of psychotherapy—fundamental issues. In J. K. Zeig (Ed.), *The evolution of psychotherapy*. New York: Brunner/Mazel.

ZIGLER, E., & PHILLIPS, L. (1961). Psychiatric diagnosis: A critique. *Journal of Abnormal and Social Psychology, 63,* 607–618.

ZIGLER, E., & PHILLIPS, L. (1965). Psychiatric diagnosis and symptomatology. In O. Milton (Ed.), *Behavior disorders*. New York: Lippincott.

ZIMPFER, D. G. (1971). Multi-leader approaches to groups in counseling and therapy. In J. C. Hansen & S. H. Cramer (Eds.), *Group guidance and counseling in the schools: Selected readings*. New York: Appleton-Century Crofts.

ZIMPFER, D. G. (1992). Personal communication.

ZINGER, N. (1975). A working paper for group auxiliary egos. *Group Psychotherapy and Psychodrama, 28,* 152–156.

ZUBIN, J. (1967). Classification of the behavior disorders. In P. R. Famsworth (Ed.), *Annual review of psychology* (Vol. 18). Palo Alto, CA: Annual Reviews.

ZUKAV, G. (1979). *The dancing wu lu masters*. New York: Bantam Books.

ZUNIGA, M. E. (1991). ''Dichosl'' as metaphorical tools for resistant Latino clients. *Psychotherapy, 28,* 480–483.

Name Index

Subject Index

To the owner of this book:

I hope that you have enjoyed *Advanced Group Leadership* as much as I enjoyed writing it. I'd like to know as much about your experiences with the book as you care to offer. Only through your comments and the comments of others can I learn how to make this a better book for future readers.

School: _____

Address of school (city, state, and zip code): _____

_____

Your instructor's name: _____

1. What did you like *most* about *Advanced Group Leadership*? _____

_____

_____

2. What did you like *least* about the book? _____

_____

3. Were all of the chapters of the book assigned for you to read? _____

(If not, which ones weren't?) _____

4. What material do you think could be omitted in future editions? _____

_____

_____

_____

5. In the space below, or on a separate sheet of paper, please let me know what other comments about the book you'd like to make. (For example, were any chapters *or* concepts particularly difficult?) Please recommend specific changes you'd like to see in future editions. I'd be delighted to hear from you!

Optional:

Your name: _____ Date: _____

May Brooks/Cole quote you either in promotion for *Advanced Group Leadership* or in future publishing ventures?

Yes: _____ No: _____

Sincerely,

Jeffrey A. Kottler

Brooks/Cole is dedicated to publishing quality publications for education in the human services fields. If you are interested in learning more about our publications, please fill in your name and address and request our latest catalogue.

Name: _____

Street Address: _____

City, State, and Zip: _____

Clearinghouse interventions